Constraining Elites in Russia and Indonesia

This is a thought-provoking analysis on why democracy succeeds in some countries but not others, comparing the post-transition experiences of two cases of contemporary democratization: Russia and Indonesia. Following authoritarian regimes, democracy eroded in Russia but flourished in Indonesia – so confounding dominant theories of democratization that predicted the opposite outcomes based on their levels of socioeconomic development and histories of statehood.

Identifying key behaviours and patterns of political participation as a factor, Lussier interweaves ethnographic interview and quantitative public opinion data to expand our understanding on how mass political participation contributes to a democracy's survival. The integration of both micro- and macro-level data in a single study is one of this project's most significant contributions, and will enhance its appeal to both researchers and instructors.

Danielle N. Lussier is an assistant professor in political science at Grinnell College, Iowa. Her research focuses on democratization, public opinion and political participation, and religion and politics, with a particular emphasis on Eurasia and Indonesia. Her work has appeared in the *Journal of Democracy, Politics and Religion, Problems of Post-Communism, Post-Soviet Affairs,* and *Slavic Review.*

Constraining Elites in Russia and Indonesia

Political Participation and Regime Survival

DANIELLE N. LUSSIER
Grinnell College

CAMBRIDGE
UNIVERSITY PRESS

CAMBRIDGE
UNIVERSITY PRESS

University Printing House, Cambridge CB2 8BS, United Kingdom

One Liberty Plaza, 20th Floor, New York, NY 10006, USA

477 Williamstown Road, Port Melbourne, VIC 3207, Australia

314-321, 3rd Floor, Plot 3, Splendor Forum, Jasola District Centre, New Delhi - 110025, India

79 Anson Road, #06-04/06, Singapore 079906

Cambridge University Press is part of the University of Cambridge.

It furthers the University's mission by disseminating knowledge in the pursuit of education, learning and research at the highest international levels of excellence.

www.cambridge.org
Information on this title: www.cambridge.org/9781107446342

© Danielle N. Lussier 2016

First published 2016
First paperback edition 2018

A catalogue record for this publication is available from the British Library

Library of Congress Cataloging in Publication data
Names: Lussier, Danielle N., author.
Title: Constraining elites in Russia and Indonesia: political participation and regime survival / Danielle Lussier, Grinnell College.
Description: New York, NY: Cambridge University Press, 2016. |
Includes bibliographical references and index.
Identifiers: LCCN 2016023869 | ISBN 9781107084377 (hard back)
Subjects: LCSH: Political participation – Russia (Federation) | Political participation – Indonesia. | Democracy – Russia (Federation) | Democracy – Indonesia. | Elite (Social sciences) – Russia (Federation) – Political activity. | Elite (Social sciences) – Indonesia – Political activity.
Classification: LCC JF799.L87 2016 | DDC 323/.0420947–dc23
LC record available at https://lccn.loc.gov/2016023869

ISBN 978-1-107-08437-7 Hardback
ISBN 978-1-107-44634-2 Paperback

For John

Contents

List of Figures   *page* viii
List of Tables   ix
Acknowledgments   xi
Note about Referencing Interview Subjects   xv
Notes on Russian and Indonesian Language   xvii

1   Introduction: Activating Democracy   1
2   Extending Democratization Theory: The Cases of Russia
    and Indonesia   40
3   Elite-Constraining Participation and Democracy's Survival   78
4   Testing the Model: Predicting Nonvoting Political
    Participation   118
5   Tocqueville Revisited: Civic Skills and Social Networks   147
6   Political Efficacy and "Throwing the Rascals Out"   194
7   Political Trust and Regime Legitimacy   232
8   Conclusion: Political Participation and the Future
    of Democracy   264

List of Expert Interview Subjects   279
References   281
Index   295

Figures

1.1 Democracy's dimensions: Political rights and
     civil liberties, 2012.   *page* 9
1.2 Freedom House scores in Russia and Indonesia,
     1989–2012.   10
1.3 The causal chain of democracy's survival.   19
2.1 Political rights and civil liberties in Russia, 1986–2012.   58
2.2 Political rights and civil liberties in Indonesia, 1989–2012. 68
3.1 Percentage of survey respondents who contacted public
     officials, 1990–2004.   92

Tables

1.1 Values for Hypothesized Causes of Democracy in Russia
and Indonesia   *page* 4
3.1 Participation in Campaign Work in Russian
Election Study   90
3.2 Participation in Contentious Politics in Russia (WVS)   95
3.3 Nonvoting Political Participation in Indonesia (EAB 2006)   99
3.4 Indonesian Participation in Contentious Politics (WVS)   100
3.5 Comparisons of Russian and Indonesian Nonvoting
Participation   101
4.1 Summary of Logistic Regression Analyses of Nonvoting
Political Participation in RES and EAB   127
4.2 Predicted Probabilities for Engaging in Nonvoting Political
Participation, Holding Efficacy and Trust Constant   132
4.3 Predicted Probabilities for Engaging in Nonvoting
Political Participation Varying Efficacy and Associational
Membership   133
5.1 Organizational Membership in Russia and Indonesia
(WVS 2005–2008)   156
6.1 Could You Do Anything to Influence a Debate or Decision
Taken by the Central Government?   202
6.2 What Could You Do to Influence the Debate or Decision
Taken by the Central Government?   203
6.3 Political Efficacy Measures from RES (1995–1996) and
EAB (2006)   206
6.4 In General How Do You Regard Voting or Election
Campaigns?   217
6.5 Russian Attitudes about Elections as Constraint on Elites   219

7.1 Trust in Political Institutions (WVS)   246
7.2 Trust in Political Institutions in Indonesia (EAB)   248
7.3 Trust in Political Institutions in Russia 1990–2006
    (WVS and RES)   250

Appendix B to Chapter 1

Citizen Sample in Kazan, Tatarstan   35
Citizen Sample in Krasnoyarsk, Krasnoyarsk Krai   36
Citizen Sample in Surabaya, East Java   37
Citizen Sample in Medan, North Sumatra   38
Comparative Summary of Citizen Samples in
    Russia and Indonesia   39

Appendix to Chapter 4

Logistic Regression Models for Contacting in 1995–1996 RES   141
Logistic Regression Models for Contacting in EAB   142
Logistic Regression Models for Campaigning and Party Work
    in 1995–1996 RES   143
Logistic Regression Models for Campaigning and Party Work
    in EAB   144
Logistic Regression Models for Contentious Politics in
    1995–1996 RES   145
Logistic Regression Models for Contentious Politics in EAB   146

Acknowledgments

A project of this size cannot be completed without the guidance, assistance, and support of innumerable people on multiple continents. The dissertation that formed the first draft of this book would not have been possible without assistance from a Department of Education Jacob K. Javits Fellowship, which supported my field research, as well as from the University of California, Berkeley Dean's Normative Time Fellowship and the University of California Dissertation-Year Fellowship, which enabled the subsequent analysis and writing. A Kennan Institute Title VIII Research Scholarship provided me with both a dynamic community and a quiet workspace that facilitated the majority of my manuscript development.

Many individuals have mentored me throughout this process. My dissertation committee – M. Steven Fish, Henry Brady, Jack Citrin, and Jeffrey Hadler – made the most significant and lasting contributions. Steve provided tireless stewardship on all aspects of this project, from its conceptual origins to book proposal. Henry's work on measurement, political participation, and the study of public opinion was a source of inspiration for my research, and I valued his constant feedback throughout the process. The idea for this project originated in Jack's graduate seminar on mass politics, and I am grateful to Jack for helping me bridge the subdisciplines of political behavior and comparative politics. Jeff introduced me to the world of Southeast Asian studies, offered insightful critiques, and played a key role in filling the gaps in my knowledge of Indonesian politics and history.

I am grateful to the more than 240 Russians and Indonesians who gave of their time in interviews, and I am thankful to the many scholars and analysts in Russia and Indonesia who assisted me in the process of conducting fieldwork. Unfortunately, given the current political climate in Russia and the sensitivity of the material analyzed in this book, I believe it would be perilous to mention by name the many individuals who helped me over the course of my research in Moscow, Kazan, and Krasnoyarsk. This group includes several dedicated scholars, analysts, journalists, and contemporary and former political activists, including two exceptional scholars who took on the task of recruiting interview respondents for me in Kazan and Krasnoyarsk. I am also grateful to the many friends I made along the way, who opened their homes and families to me, ensuring that I was always in good company. The research on the pages before you would have been impossible without their selfless dedication to my work, and it saddens me to not be able to share their names in print.

For my fieldwork in Indonesia, I am particularly grateful to LP3ES, which served as my research sponsor. I am especially indebted to Muhammed Husain and Suhardi Suryadi, who arranged my visa invitation and access to the LP3ES library archives. In Surabaya, I was assisted by Wawan Kokotiasa, who recruited interview respondents, made introductions, and helped with tasks large and small. I am also grateful for the discussions and introductions shared by several members of the faculty at the University of Airlangga in Surabaya, especially Haryadi and Kacung. In Medan, I benefited from the help of Henry Sitorus and his excellent undergraduate assistants – Eko J. T. Lase and Ade Rahma Ayu Siregar – who recruited respondents and shuttled me off to the far corners of the city. Nina Karina Sitepu provided transcripts of Indonesian interviews with extraordinary speed. The Sunartos in Yogyakarta and the Nababans in Medan shared homes away from home and important insights into the Javanese and Batak cultures.

I also wish to thank the numerous other scholars whose knowledge, advice, and generosity in sharing resources strengthened the design and implementation of this project. David Collier and Diana Kapiszewski provided invaluable feedback on the research design and organization. Diana also offered substantial assistance as I thought through the process of turning my dissertation into a book. Timothy Colton and Henry Hale generously shared their survey data from the Russian Election Study. Michael Buehler, Don Emmerson, Bauni Hamid, Marc Morjé Howard, Eunsook Jung, Cynthia Kaplan, and Matthew Winters provided valuable fieldwork advice and facilitated important introductions.

The arguments in this book were sharpened by opportunities to present and discuss my work at the Woodrow Wilson International Center for Scholars and at the University of Wisconsin–Madison's Center for Russia, East Europe, and Central Asia. I am particularly grateful to William Pomeranz for organizing several presentations of my work in progress during my residency at the Kennan Institute and to the Wilson Center's library staff for connecting me to a wealth of valuable sources. I thank Yoshiko Herrera for encouraging my thinking on the concept of elite-enabling participation. Karina Ibrahim and Corina Varlan provided important research assistance for manuscript revisions. Celeste Arrington and Crystal Chang read multiple versions of most chapters and offered criticism that productively pushed my thinking and improved my writing. Jody LaPorte read many parts of the manuscript at various stages and was a constant sounding board for my ideas and questions from dissertation proposal to final book manuscript. Supportive and encouraging conversations with Margaret Boittin, Veronica Herrera, Amy Lerman, Robert Orttung, and Wendy Sinek helped me see through cloudy moments more clearly. Neil Abrams, George Breslauer, Yoshiko Herrera, Kelly McMann, Laura Stoker, and Ned Walker all read and commented on sections of the text. Bill Liddle read the penultimate manuscript draft in its entirety, saving me many errors. The feedback of all these individuals has strengthened this book, and any remaining flaws are my own.

I am also grateful to my colleagues in the Department of Political Science and the Russian, Central, and East European Studies Concentration at Grinnell College, who have been constant cheerleaders throughout the writing and revision process. The members of my Scholarly Women's Achievement Group at Grinnell inspire me with their productivity, humor, and valuable practical advice. I am particularly thankful to Gemma Sala and Ed Cohn for their encouragement and friendship in this process. My students at Grinnell constantly force me to revisit and strengthen my arguments, and this book is a better product due to my exchanges with them.

Last, my deepest thanks and gratitude belong to my family. My parents, Marcel and Pamela Lussier, show constant support. My parents-in-law, Tim and Celeste Grennan, gave regular refuge from fieldwork at their home in Sacramento. My sister and brother-in-law, Dawn and Rich Bird, housed my family and provided numerous hours of babysitting as I powered through to finish my manuscript revision before departing for Indonesia on my next project. Most significant, my husband, John Grennan, has been a partner through every step of the process – accompanying me on fieldwork to Indonesia, reading and editing the entire manuscript three times, selecting the cover image, compiling the index, and helping with dozens of other tasks in between. Few scholars have the great fortune to be married to a professional editor, and the book before you is much clearer and more interesting owing to his contributions. Our son, Abraham, has served as my constant inspiration and motivation for completing this project. This book would not have been possible without their unwavering love and encouragement.

Note about Referencing Interview Subjects

The forthcoming analysis is based largely on interviews I conducted with 100 citizens from Russia and Indonesia, as well as on about 140 expert interviews with scholars, journalists, and representatives of political parties, nongovernmental organizations, and civic associations in these two countries. The interviews with ordinary citizens were conducted anonymously. Throughout the text, I refer to these subjects based on relevant demographic characteristics and do not disclose the dates of the interviews. Summary tables of these interview subjects can be found in Appendix B to Chapter 1.

My expert interviews involved varying degrees of confidentiality. In most instances, respondents were comfortable with full-name attribution, while in other instances the degree of confidentiality they requested depended on the content discussed. Yet, due to the current lack of protection for free speech in Russia, as well as the political sensitivity of the subject matter, I have decided to reduce the vulnerability of my expert respondents by not referencing them by name. In order to ensure balance in the text, I am treating my Indonesian expert respondents with the same level of confidentiality. Each expert interview is indicated by a specific number that corresponds to a description of the interview subject provided in a reference list at the end of this book. The descriptions are specific enough to communicate the general source of the information being cited, yet do not provide sufficient detail to reveal the identity of the interview subject.

Notes on Russian and Indonesian Language

Transliteration

Throughout the text, I use a modified version of the Library of Congress's transliteration system for the Russian language. In instances when a proper noun is commonly rendered in English with an alternate transliteration, such as "Yeltsin" instead of "El'tsin" or "Chechnya" instead of "Chechnia," I employ the more common form. When referencing secondary sources, I maintain the transliteration used in the specific source.

Acronyms

Throughout the text, I use acronyms for political parties and other organizations based on their formulation in the original language, with two exceptions. Western scholarship has long referred to the Union of Soviet Socialist Republics and the Communist Party of the Soviet Union using their English-language acronyms, USSR and CPSU, which I use here.

Indonesian Names

The use of surnames is not widespread in Indonesia. Many Indonesians use only one name, while others might have two or three names, one of which is usually a dominant name. Throughout the text, when only one name is used in reference to an Indonesian, the reader should infer that this is the prominent name of the respective individual.

I

Introduction

Activating Democracy

With the collapse of communism at the end of the twentieth century, democracy supplanted authoritarianism as the most common political regime around the globe. Since the 1970s, more than sixty countries (almost one-third of the countries in the world) have made transitions to democracy (Papaioannou & Siourounis, 2008). At the turn of the twenty-first century, 60 percent of the world's countries were democratic (Diamond, 2008, p. 36). Democratic gains have occurred across all continents, and more people live in free societies today than ever before.

Yet, as examples from Russia to Nigeria to Thailand demonstrate, the collapse of authoritarian governments and the introduction of competitive elections do not ensure that stable, democratic regimes will persist. When Samuel Huntington described the global expansion of open politics in the last quarter of the twentieth century as the "third wave" of democratization, he noted that democratic breakdowns had followed each previous wave (1991). According to Freedom House's annual *Freedom in the World* survey, as of 2014, global freedom had declined for nine consecutive years – the longest continuous period of setbacks since the yearly surveys began in 1972 (Puddington, 2015). Some of the most dramatic declines have occurred in strategically important countries, such as Egypt, Russia, and Iraq. But in countries ranging from Mexico to Benin to Indonesia, democracy has endured. Fair and free elections persist and are accompanied by expansive protections for civil liberties.

What explains these trends? Why do some democracies survive beyond initial elections while others revert to more authoritarian regimes? What can the new range of cases where democracy failed tell us about the factors that facilitate or hinder open political regimes?

This study offers some answers to these questions through a comparative analysis of two deviant "third wave" cases of regime change: post-Soviet Russia and post-Suharto Indonesia. In both countries, democratizing systems replaced authoritarian regimes in the 1990s. Their subsequent regime trajectories, however, have diverged in surprising ways that depart from global trends. After almost a decade of reform, Russia turned back to authoritarianism. Indonesia, meanwhile, continues as a democracy more than a decade after its antiauthoritarian breakthrough. Yet most theories of democracy would predict the *opposite* outcomes: Russia's significantly higher level of socioeconomic development and long history of independent statehood should foster democracy, whereas Indonesia's low level of socioeconomic development and short postcolonial history should hinder democratization. Rather than examining these two countries in comparison with their regional neighbors, as often happens in political science, this project seeks to analyze these crucial cases from a broader, cross-regional perspective.

I argue that patterns of political participation in Russia and Indonesia explain their deviations from global democratization trends. By comparing two cases at opposite ends of theoretical expectations, this study demonstrates that patterns of political participation play a decisive role *after* a democratic transition occurs. While Russians retreated from political participation and remain wary of the institutions that characterize democracy, Indonesians quickly grew accustomed to pressuring elites and learned to use new democratic institutions to manage conflict and channel popular preferences for governance. Mass behavior made all the difference in the trajectories of regime change in these countries.

I find that patterns in mass political participation constitute the crucial link between a country's socioeconomic and historical factors and democracy's survival. When a society adopts *elite-constraining* forms of participation, it impedes leaders from abusing democratic norms and procedures between elections. Civil society engagement, political efficacy, and political trust drive these patterns of participation. Individuals who are civically engaged, who believe in their ability to influence political outcomes, and who trust political institutions are more likely to become involved in elite-constraining forms of participation, such as campaigning, building political parties, and protesting. When *elite-enabling* participation (such as contacting public officials and supporting incumbent party machines) predominates, democratic institutions become more vulnerable to elite manipulation and democracy's survival is at risk. Elite-enabling activities give power holders more latitude to manipulate elections, constrict rights and freedoms, and repress real and imagined opponents.

Democratization in Russia and Indonesia

The record of countries that have experienced political regime change since the mid-1970s suggests several factors that may be conducive to democracy, including higher levels of socioeconomic development, stronger parliaments, weaker presidents, and a longer history of independent statehood (Bunce, 2000; Fish, 2005; Fish & Wittenberg, 2009). Contravening factors include economic reliance on hydrocarbons, contested national borders, and low levels of socioeconomic development (Fish, 2005; Ross, 2001; Rustow, 1970). These factors, however, cannot account for the political experiences of Russia and Indonesia – two of the world's largest countries.

In the 1990s, both Russia and Indonesia completed democratic transitions during which governments came to power by fair and free elections. Russia's political liberalization followed seventy years of Communist Party rule in the Soviet Union, which dissolved in 1991. After several years of democratic reform, Russia gradually moved back toward authoritarianism in the second half of the 1990s.

Like Russia, Indonesia's political history was largely authoritarian. After a protracted struggle following the country's 1945 war for independence, Indonesia had a brief spell of open politics in the 1950s. But in 1957, President Sukarno introduced "guided democracy," which curtailed democratic institutions. After a failed coup attempt in 1965, General Suharto came to power and introduced the "New Order" regime, which imposed severe restrictions on civil liberties and conducted a bloody purge of suspected communists and sympathizers, killing at least half a million Indonesians by the end of 1966. This brutally repressive regime lasted for more than thirty years, until popular protests forced Suharto's resignation in 1998, leading to immediate political liberalization and free and fair elections in 1999.

Over the next decade, Indonesia undertook a wide range of democratic reforms. It held direct elections for the presidency in 2004, bolstered regional autonomy and decentralized administrative authority, and eliminated the military's role in the legislature. Indonesia's successful democratization is as puzzling as Russia's backsliding. After all, Indonesia is a lower middle-income country that remains largely rural and only weakly industrialized.[1] It also has a short history of independent statehood and a

---

[1] GDP per capita at purchasing power parity in 2007 was $3,712 for Indonesia and $14,690 for Russia (UN Development Program, 2009); the percentage of the student-age population enrolled in tertiary education in 2009 was 22 percent in Indonesia and 76 percent in Russia (World Bank); and the percentage of the population employed in agriculture in 2009 was 40 percent in Indonesia and 10 percent in Russia (World Bank).

TABLE I.I. *Values for Hypothesized Causes of Democracy in Russia and Indonesia*

Factors[a]	Russia	Indonesia
Modernization variables		
Socioeconomic development (+)	High	Medium
Urbanization (+)	High	Low
Educational attainment (+)	High	Low
Economic reliance on hydrocarbons (−)	High	Medium
Corruption (−)	High	High
Statehood variables		
History of independent statehood (+)	Long	Short
Former colony (−)	No	Yes
Contested national borders (−)	Yes	Yes
Sociocultural variables		
Ethnic heterogeneity (−)	Medium	High
Muslim majority population (−)	No	Yes

[a] (+)positive for democracy; (−) negative for democracy.

long shadow of colonial rule – structural conditions deemed unfavorable for democracy's survival (Fish & Wittenberg, 2009).

If the level of socioeconomic development and a history of independent statehood fully predicted the outcome of regime change, Russia, rather than Indonesia, would be a democracy today. Table 1.1 compares Russia and Indonesia along several factors believed to influence prospects for democracy. I have grouped these factors into three general categories: modernization, statehood, and sociocultural variables. If we look at the modernization variables, Russia has a clear advantage over Indonesia, demonstrating higher levels of socioeconomic development, urbanization, and educational attainment. Russia's only negative variables in this category are its high levels of corruption and economic dependence on hydrocarbons. As of 2010, fuel exports constituted 64 percent of Russian merchandise exports. Hydrocarbons and corruption play a considerable role in the Indonesian economy as well, with fuel exports constituting 30 percent of Indonesia's merchandise exports for the year 2010 (World Bank).

While Russia's natural resource endowment may have hindered its democratic development, this factor alone cannot explain the variation between Russia and Indonesia, which also has an economy that depends heavily on natural resources.[2] Moreover, if we consider the steps that link

[2] Much has been written about Indonesia's extensive natural resources that extend beyond oil and gas to include minerals and timber. According to an analysis by Budy P. Resosudarmo,

natural resources to democratic failure in Russia, the natural resource explanation is complemented by my argument. As M. Steven Fish asserts, natural resource wealth did not stymie modernization in Russia, but rather facilitated opportunities for repression and corruption (2005, pp. 118–138). In both Russia and Indonesia, natural resource endowments provided elites with resources to push back against democratization. Yet, while the Russian population did not resist elites' moves to hinder democratization, Indonesians fought back against elites' encroachments on democratic gains.

Another possible impediment to democratization is corruption. Corruption enhances political elites' interests in preserving the benefits of their rents and keeping the polity closed, thereby providing an obstacle to democratization. As Transparency International's Corruption Perceptions Index (CPI) (www.transparency.org/research/cpi/) demonstrates, both Russia and Indonesia have long-standing problems with corruption. The first CPI, issued in 1995, placed Indonesia last among the forty-one countries included. From 1998 until 2007, Indonesia fared worse than Russia on the CPI yet still managed to achieve greater democratization success.

When we consider the statehood variables, Russia again has better odds than Indonesia. While both countries confront secessionist struggles, Russia has a long history of independent statehood and has never been colonized. Indonesia, on the other hand, declared independence only in 1945, and parts of the country had been under colonial rule since the seventeenth century.

In terms of sociocultural variables, Russia also has a slight advantage. Both countries have large, ethnically diverse populations, a quality that scholars often cite as an impediment to democracy. Indeed, Indonesia has greater ethnolinguistic heterogeneity than Russia. Democratization scholars have also suggested that religious traditions emphasizing obedience to authority, such as Catholicism, Orthodox Christianity, Confucianism, and Islam, may foster belief systems antithetical to democracy (Bollen, 1979; Huntington, 1991, 1993; Lipset, 1960; Pye, 1968). Yet, as the third wave of democratization has shown, numerous countries with populations adhering to these religious beliefs have built open political regimes. At present, the democratic deficit among predominantly Muslim countries has focused particular attention on a possible relationship between Islam and authoritarianism (Donno & Russett, 2004; Fish, 2002, 2011;

in the 1990s, oil and gas constituted about 30 percent of Indonesia's total exports, minerals and related products accounted for 19 percent, and forest products accounted for 10 percent (2005, "Introduction," pp. 1–9, p. 3).

Midlarsky, 1998), suggesting that Indonesia's status as a Muslim-majority country might create an obstacle to democratization there.

In short, if we compare Russia and Indonesia on the factors generally believed to foster democracy, Russia has greater advantages for democratic survival. Yet scholars might cite Russia's communist heritage as a particular disadvantage. Does a communist history present a greater impediment to building democracy than a history of noncommunist authoritarianism? The all-encompassing ideology of communism promoted a thorough transformation of public and private life that is not generally seen in noncommunist authoritarian regimes (Linz, 2000; Linz & Stepan, 1996). In his well-known articulation of the perils of the "Leninist legacy," Ken Jowitt highlights the "fragmented, mutually suspicious, societies with little religio-cultural support for tolerant and individually self-reliant behavior" (1992, p. 304). Scholars have also bemoaned Russia's "authoritarian collectivism" (Meyer, 2003), "culture of impersonal measured action" (Jowitt, 1992, p. 291), and numerous other ills associated with the structures, institutions, and norms that took shape during the Communist period, all of which contribute to "an authoritarian, not a liberal democratic capitalist, way of life" (Jowitt, 1992, p. 293).

Yet this explanation for Russia's failure at democracy is overly simplistic. First, it fails to account for the substantial variation in the organization of communist regimes across Eurasia. Communism differed dramatically across regimes and within the Soviet Union's republics. Many formerly communist countries in the Balkans, such as Bulgaria and Romania, have built sustainable democracies after their repressive communist regimes, suggesting that the relationship between a communist history and a post-communist regime type is more complex than a simple legacy explanation permits. Second, the argument that Russia's communist heritage cast a weightier burden than Indonesia's New Order regime ignores the significant levels of repression that existed under Suharto.

Several Soviet regime features that are considered impediments to democracy in Russia have parallels in Indonesia's New Order. As Chapter 2 discusses, both regimes had ideological underpinnings, thoroughly penetrated society, relied on mobilized participation to ensure regime compliance, and built large, coercive apparatuses to control the population. Both the Soviet and New Order regimes were transformative and exhibited low levels of tolerance for views outside of official regime doctrine.

Nevertheless, they did exhibit one important difference. While both regimes engaged in political repression, the Soviet regime was more pervasive in its grip over social life, including prohibitions regarding religion and political party formation. As Chapter 5 details, the Soviet monopolization of civic life meant Russians endured an experience of social repression that differs from that of Indonesians, who enjoyed limited social pluralism under Suharto. This variation in levels of social control is perhaps the most profound difference between the Communist (Soviet) and the noncommunist authoritarian (New Order) regimes in this paired comparison. Yet Communist social control alone did not predetermine democracy's failure in Russia. While Russia was disadvantaged at the beginning of political liberalization, patterns of political participation that obtained *after* initial elections – not during the Soviet period – fostered authoritarian reversal.

If none of the factors just described is sufficient for explaining Russia's and Indonesia's outlier status, why did democracy survive in Indonesia and not in Russia?

Democratization and Democracy's Survival

To answer this question, I must clarify some concepts. I define democracy as the procedures that ensure competition for leadership positions through free, fair, and frequent elections, and the assurance of open debate about candidates and policies through freedoms of speech, media, and association. This definition encompasses all of the characteristics that Robert Dahl defines as the "procedural minimum" for polyarchy.[3] Dahl's characteristics can be roughly collapsed into two dimensions: (1) institutions that guarantee free elections determine access to political power and (2) civil liberties that ensure equal access to these institutions. This is a proceduralist definition of democracy that does not presume additional conditions, such as level of socioeconomic equality, which is frequently cited in definitions of democracy rooted in socialist and Marxist traditions (Barber, 1984; Marshall, 2000; Roemer, 1999). Yet, by including the dimension of civil liberties, this definition protects against the fallacy of equating the presence of elections with democracy (see Karl, 1986; Lindberg, 2006; Linz & Stepan, 1996; Schmitter & Karl, 1991).

---

[3] Dahl's characteristics are: 1) elected officials have control over key government policy decisions; 2) elected officials are chosen in free, fair, and frequent elections; 3) practically all adults have the right to vote; 4) practically all adults have the right to run for office; 5) there is a protected right to free expression; 6) there is a protected right to seek out alternative sources of information; and 7) there is a protected right to form parties, associations, and interest groups (1989, p. 233).

Most social scientists concur that democracy is a continuous variable that can be measured by degrees of political openness. A fully consolidated democracy constitutes one extreme, while a fully consolidated "monocracy," or rule by a single individual or unified collective actor, marks the other (Fish, 2005, pp. 19–20). Between these two extremes stand political systems that are either more or less democratic. This continuum includes meaningful thresholds that categorize countries along an ordered scale. Some countries meet Dahl's procedural minimum for a democracy; other countries meet some conditions; and others fail to meet any. This ordering leaves us with three groupings of countries: democracies, hybrid regimes, and authoritarian regimes.

What happens when a country democratizes? Huntington's (1991) articulation of the "third wave" described three stages of democratization: extrication from the authoritarian regime, transition to democratically elected government, and consolidation of democratic institutions. In this framework, a "transition" is complete after an initial round of fair and free elections. In most countries, however, initial democratic elections are not the endpoint that determines democracy's subsequent survival. Instead, they represent a new benchmark of political competition that must be repeated regularly for democracy to endure. To that end, institutions that ensure political competition and safeguard civil liberties – the two dimensions of democracy Dahl outlined – usually require further deepening and institutionalization after the first election.

If democracy exists along a continuum with clearly defined thresholds, then a country can make progress in strengthening and extending the institutions and practices of democracy to move further along this continuum. Ensuring democracy's survival involves institutionalizing democratic rules of political competition and access to political power and sanctioning those who violate these rules. When democratic rules and practices are institutionalized and become "the only game in town" (Linz & Stepan, 1996), democracy's chances of survival increase. Without the institutionalization and strengthening of democratic rules and practices, political elites can more easily roll back democratic gains, threatening democracy's survival. In short, a country that has introduced political liberalization might deepen or restrict democracy. Some scholars would call this process "democratic consolidation." I believe it is more accurate to call it "democratic survival."

How should we measure democratic survival? Numerous indices measure democracy, but only Freedom House provides annual rankings for political openness among the world's 193 countries. Freedom House

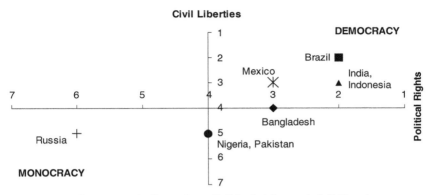

FIGURE 1.1. Democracy's dimensions: Political rights and civil liberties, 2012.

determines its yearly scores by averaging two separate ratings for political rights and civil liberties. The scores range from a high score of "1" for complete political openness to a low score of "7" for a completely closed system, and these scores are further divided into groups labeled as "free" (1–2.5), "partly free" (3–5), and "not free" (5.5–7).[4] Some regimes in the middle have democratic political institutions, but fail to protect civil liberties. Others do a better job at protecting civil rights, but lack competitive political institutions. The level of political openness can rise and fall on either or both dimensions, thereby affecting a regime's overall level of democracy. Additionally, along this continuum, clear and meaningful thresholds appear that constitute the empirical minimum for calling a regime a democracy, as well as the empirical minimum for calling a regime a hybrid – that is, more politically open than a monocracy, but not open enough to be a democracy.

Figure 1.1 depicts the two dimensions of political rights and civil liberties. For illustrative purposes, I have plotted all countries with a population of more than 100 million that have undergone some form of political liberalization since the 1970s. The values on the graph correspond to Freedom House's annual political rights and civil liberties scores in its *Freedom in the World* rankings for 2013. As Figure 1.1 demonstrates, countries in the upper right-hand quadrant meet the minimum qualifications of political rights *and* civil liberties to be considered democracies. Among the eight countries plotted in Figure 1.1, three earn this distinction: Brazil, India, and Indonesia, all of which Freedom House

---

[4] For more details on how Freedom House develops these scores, see the "Methodology" section of Freedom House, *Freedom in the World*, available at www.freedomhouse.org.

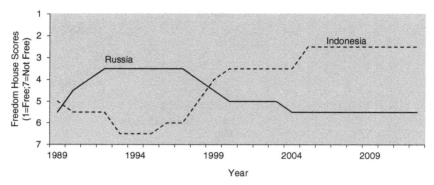

FIGURE 1.2. Freedom House scores in Russia and Indonesia, 1989–2012.

considers "free." Countries located in the lower left-hand quadrant do not meet standards of even partial freedom in political rights and civil liberties and are best thought of as authoritarian regimes. The only case that fits this category is Russia, which Freedom House ranks as "not free." Countries clustered around the intersection of the two axes are ones that Freedom House deems "partly free." Figure 1.1 displays four cases in this category: Bangladesh, Mexico, Nigeria, and Pakistan.

I consider a country as having engaged in substantial democratization if it achieved a combined score of "4" or better (the midway point for "partly free" countries) for at least five consecutive years after climbing from a score of "5" or below. I measure democracy's survival as having achieved a score of "2.5" or better for five consecutive years. A country can be said to have deviated from the path toward democratization if it dropped a full two points on the Freedom House scale and stayed in this position for at least five consecutive years.

As Figure 1.1 shows, Russia and Indonesia demonstrate opposite outcomes of democratic survival. Figure 1.2 plots each of their combined annual Freedom House scores from 1989 to 2012. Since beginning political liberalization in 1998, Indonesia has continued on the path of democratization. It entered Freedom House's "free" category in 2005, and its democracy has survived over four national election cycles. Russia's level of democracy, by contrast, peaked at the initial point of political liberalization in 1991. It stagnated and then gradually eroded over the next decade. Russia's nascent democracy did not survive, and Freedom House has designated it as "not free" since 2004.

As scholars have noted, the factors that facilitate a democratic transition are not necessarily the same as those that foster democracy's survival. In his seminal article, Dankwart Rustow makes precisely this point, suggesting that the multistage nature of democratization means that different causal mechanisms exert force at different stages of regime development (1970, pp. 345–346). A democratic transition where initial fair and free elections occur is a necessary, but not sufficient, condition for democratic survival.

In this book, I take democratic transition as my starting point, examining the trajectories of two countries following the introduction of reforms that dramatically liberalized political institutions, established meaningful civil liberties protections, and fostered political competition. Less than a decade into their respective post-transition eras, these countries were heading down divergent paths: Indonesia was strengthening democratic institutions and practices while Russia had begun rolling back early democratic reforms. In subsequent years, the variation in these trajectories continued – Indonesia has established one of the most robust democracies in the developing world, while Russia has reconstituted a stable authoritarian regime. Over the next several chapters I show that patterns of mass political attitudes and behaviors account for the variation in these countries' trajectories.

The Steps in Democracy's Causal Chain

Theories about democracy and democratization rely on numerous assumptions about the behavior of elites, masses, and the social groups that connect them. Simplifying assumptions are necessary for social inquiry; the social world is too complex to measure every possible interaction. In a valuable discussion on comparative historical analysis, Ira Katznelson writes, "Microbehavior, we must continue to remember, requires historical macrofoundations. Yet, equally, large-scale comparative analysis is underspecified and incomplete when its microfoundations are left implicit, ad hoc, or undertheorized" (2003, p. 272). This project analyzes two diverse countries that defy our conventional expectations about the macro-level relationships between structural variables and democratic survival by investigating democracy's microfoundations. In particular, I focus on the individual-level attitudes and behaviors that ultimately determine whether the mass public constrains elites from manipulating nascent democratic institutions.

One of the most common assumptions about democracy involves its relationship to socioeconomic development. Lipset (1960; 1994) argued that economic growth engenders a culture of democracy that in turn provides the foundations for democratic institutions. Prosperity reduces class conflict and promotes compromise, making democracy viable. Lipset was generally correct: socioeconomic development remains the foremost predictor of democratic survival, as evidenced by numerous studies of third wave democratization (Acemoglu & Robinson, 2006; Bollen, 1983; Bunce, 2000; Przeworski, 1991). The proposed relationship between socioeconomic development and democracy is indirect: economic development promotes the micro-level shift away from agrarian production toward an urban working class. These transformations in society also engender micro-level increases in literacy and education, thereby fostering the skills necessary to form viable trade unions, political parties, and civic associations, which may ultimately alter power relations between political elites and the people under their control.

In this story, the attitudes and behaviors of an emerging middle class are the mechanism that produces democracy. The middle class counterbalances the political and economic power concentrated among the wealthy and finances political opposition. Whether actors *other* than the middle class can create alternate power sources and finance political opposition remains an open question. Both Russia and Indonesia lack a category of individuals who fit traditional classification as a "middle class."

The hypothesized causal relationship between socioeconomic development and democracy includes numerous stages of action where a particular human response – by both the masses and the elites – is implied but not clearly articulated. The general logic can be summarized as follows. If individuals become empowered economically, they will then want to protect their economic gains from arbitrary seizure by the state or other individuals. This goal will engender attitudes that are supportive of transparency and the rule of law. This attitudinal preference will prompt the newly advantaged individuals to demand greater participation in the government. These individuals will demonstrate this demand by financing and participating in independent organizations that seek to influence the ruling political elite. Likewise, as education, literacy, and urbanization increase, knowledge of and support for the new independent organizations will spread to a larger portion of the masses. Finally, elites will view public demands for greater participation as credible threats to their power and will choose to liberalize the political system to maintain political authority.

The economic growth that promotes rising levels of urbanization and education, however, does not always derive from a market economy. State-led growth – like that experienced in the Soviet Union, in pre-reform China, and in economies with large state sectors throughout the developing world – can foster urbanization and advancement in human development without necessarily creating privately held capital and a middle class. Alternatively, as we have observed in China over the past three decades, it is possible to create a middle class that does not apply significant public pressure for democratization (Gallagher, 2002; Tsai, 2007). Distinguishing between economic growth that fosters independent entrepreneurship and that which does not is important. The former creates bases for alternate sources of power; the latter does not.

Post-Soviet Russia is a case where high levels of economic development facilitated urbanization and extremely high levels of education and skill development, but did not create a propertied middle class. Even though the Communist Party relinquished its hold on the productive assets of the economy, an entrepreneurial, propertied middle class did not emerge following Russia's transition to a market economy. Rather, marketization in Russia was accompanied by hyperinflation that wiped out most Russians' savings. A dramatically flawed privatization scheme created a small economic oligarchy that held much of the country's productive assets. While there was great potential to build a broad-based, propertied middle class in Russia, it never developed. Consequently, economic development did not foster the development of alternate sources of power in society. The only group who could demand protection of its assets and meaningfully present itself as a counterweight to the state's political power was the small, insider oligarchy.

Indonesia has a much lower level of economic development than Russia, with a GDP per capita that is approximately one-fourth the size of Russia's. While urbanization, literacy, and educational attainment expanded rapidly in Indonesia in the second half of the twentieth century, they still lag in cross-national comparisons. Even though Indonesia has always had a market economy, the state sector looms large and the government controls prices on several basic goods, including fuel, rice, and electricity (U.S. Department of State, 2010). These features have limited the development of an independent bourgeoisie in Indonesia.

As the examples of Russia and Indonesia suggest, the connection between socioeconomic development and democracy is determined by several intermediate, micro-level steps where deviation from the prescribed path is possible. For example, individuals might not seek to protect their assets by demanding greater participation in government, but rather by forming private militias. Evidence of this outcome emerges in both

Russia and Indonesia. In addition, independent associations can develop without middle-class financing, as we see in Indonesia. Individuals in societies that are becoming more educated, urban, and literate might be attracted to liberalism as an ideology and subsequently develop support for democratic values, which is what happened in Western Europe. But other possible outcomes include communism, fascism, and radical theocracy, which attracted millions of followers in the twentieth century. Clearly, the multistage process connecting economic prosperity to democratic survival offers numerous opportunities for the results to diverge from the predicted pattern.

In this book, I challenge several assumptions about how macro-level structures promote or hinder democracy's survival. I do so by focusing on the attitudes and behaviors a population exhibits toward a political system undergoing democratization. These factors, when aggregated, influence democratic survival in ways that may deviate from theoretic predictions. Most important, I argue that citizens' micro-level steps to constrain political elites are the key factor that determines democracy's survival.

An Alternate Approach: Citizen Participation as a Constraint on Elite Action

Most democratization scholars do not contend that socioeconomic development or a long history of independent statehood directly cause democracy. Rather, macro-structural theories make an implicit assumption that a history of open politics and independent statehood will increase both the popular demand for democratic institutions and practices, and elite incentives to provide them. Instead of assuming that citizens and elites respond in uniform and predictable ways to advances in socioeconomic development, I focus on the more proximate means by which structures and institutions can shape democracy's survival.

Working backward from the ultimate outcome of interest – whether a democracy survives several years after initial democratic elections – the decision to uphold or rescind democratic institutions (free and fair elections, checks and balances among different branches of power, protection of minority rights) is in the hands of the political elite. A population can want these institutions, but desire does not produce democracy if elites do not prioritize democratic institutions. Similarly, as many transitions have shown, democratic institutions can exist on paper but fail to translate into democracy in practice. This failure regularly results from an absence of behavioral norms and other ancillary support structures (free media, open civil society, human rights) that reduce the likelihood of elite manipulation of democratic institutions. Ultimately, decisions by political elites are the last step in a causal chain that determines whether democracy persists over time.

Political elites in both dictatorships and democracies make decisions under the influence of mass opinion. The decision-making environments of all governing elites are conditioned by the desires, demands, and behaviors of the mass public. While it is true that citizens have a more direct impact on elite decisions in established democracies, it would be incorrect to presume that public preferences are irrelevant to authoritarian leadership. For example, in Communist China, citizens are encouraged to visit local complaint bureaus, and the Communist Party sometimes uses information gathered in these bureaus to adjust its policymaking (Chen, 2008; O'Brien & Li, 1995; Thireau & Linshan, 2003). Although the mass public does not exercise its will directly in authoritarian systems, a dictator must mind the general public mood to maintain power.

Several studies demonstrate that political elites can be motivated by public opinion offering indications of how citizens *might* behave (Brady & Kaplan, 2008; Lee, 2002; Risse-Kappen, 1991). The credible threat of being unseated – often predicated by low levels of public support for a specific incumbent or his policies – may be sufficient for an incumbent to promote democratization. Similarly, elites who see little indication that the public would object to rollbacks of certain democratic institutions or freedoms are more likely to make these moves without fear of losing their positions. We see this dynamic in the numerous reforms adopted during Vladimir Putin's presidency in Russia: the government placed greater restrictions on political parties, canceled elections for regional executives, and increased state control over media – all without widespread popular objection. Putin responded as we would expect an unconstrained leader to behave – by expanding his power as far as he could without unsettling the public.

The decision to maintain or rescind democratic institutions rests with elites, yet the process of democratic survival involves a dynamic relationship between elites and the masses. Governing elites supply a certain degree of democracy through their decisions and practices. The public also demands a certain degree of democracy through its own behaviors – by voting for certain types of candidates and responding with outrage or acceptance to elite decisions to rollback or entrench democratic institutions. In extreme instances, the public might revolt to express its desire for more democracy.

While the elite–mass dynamic is not uniform across all polities, we can make a few, simplifying assumptions about the incentives that govern elite and citizen behaviors. It is relatively safe to assume that the population as a whole has an interest in maintaining peace and prosperity – and that government policies may play an important role in determining peace and prosperity. Likewise, we can assume that governing elites have an interest in maintaining political power, if not for themselves personally, then for their political allies. I assume that most governing elites – left unchecked – would choose a monopoly on political power. Not all leaders would use this monopoly to engage in violent repression or self-enrichment. Some would undoubtedly use the monopoly to reduce the number of veto players encountered in trying to enact policies that are in accordance with the popular will. Few political leaders, even in a democracy, would voluntarily choose to reduce the power that is at their disposal, if for no other reason than a concentration of power can lead to greater governing efficiency. It is for this reason that citizens in new democracies must engage in political participation: to constrain elite attempts to act on the impulse to hold and maintain a greater share of political power.

To prevent elites from acting exclusively in their own self-interests, citizens must expend resources to constrain them. Citizens generally work to limit elite excesses through political participation. In this project I employ Joan Nelson's definition of political participation as "action by private citizens intended to influence the actions or the composition of national or local governments" (1979, p. 8). At a minimum, political participation involves parting with the resource of one's free time. For most individuals living in long-standing democracies, the allocation of time for participation is not substantial: approximately the amount of time it takes to stand in line and vote in regular elections. Yet, for other individuals who become involved in nonvoting forms of political participation, the investment of time can be much greater. In countries where democratic institutions are new, even the simple act of voting can involve a considerable investment of both time and cognitive resources. Voters do not have the heuristic device of tried and true party labels to help simplify their decision-making calculus. They might need to invest more time simply to learn who is running for office and what the new offices entail. In more authoritarian regimes, constraining elites is even more costly. Participating in any activity that threatens the existing order could make individuals vulnerable to violence and repression.

Thus, citizens must pay a price for constraining elites, though the price varies with the polity's level of political openness. Once political liberalization has begun and the minimum procedural features of a democracy are in place, there are greater possibilities for citizens to hold elites accountable without threatening their own livelihoods. The most obvious mechanism is regular elections. Yet periods between elections offer numerous opportunities for newly elected elites to engage in actions that could undermine the procedures and freedoms meant to ensure subsequent elections will also be fair and free. In other words, until all stakeholders accept competitive elections (and the norms and institutions that support them) as "the only game in town," democracy is vulnerable to elite abuse, and authoritarian backsliding remains a constant threat. Under these circumstances, the process of political liberalization creates a functional need for ongoing citizen oversight between elections to hold elites accountable and constrain them from manipulating the process to suit their own interests. Throwing the rascals out during elections is not enough to keep democracy in place – the rascals need to be held in check at more regular intervals. While public demands for democracy can be met, ignored, or repressed, and elites can behave democratically or not regardless of public opinion, ongoing political participation by citizens provides an important constraint on elites. This constraint makes repression more costly and compels elite actions to uphold and extend democracy if they want to stay in power.

Political participation can facilitate democratic survival in several ways. At a basic level, mass actors might vote out elected officials who do not promote democratic reforms and practices and replace them with those who will. There is evidence of this outcome in Indonesia. Alternatively, the mass public might elect officeholders who do not adhere to democratic norms and institutions and instead roll back democratic gains. This result accurately describes Putin's Russia. Yet nonvoting political participation can also influence democracy's survival *between* elections.

Some forms of political participation serve to either constrain political elites from overstepping their constituted authority or hinder them from undertaking unpopular policy decisions. These types of acts can be thought of as *elite-constraining*. Other forms of political participation can empower elites to enhance their formal or informal political authority by building loyalty among select constituents, who may be willing to tolerate an expansion of elites' power in return for certain public or club goods. Such participation is *elite-enabling*.

Elite-constraining participation comprises activities that foster meaningful competition in electoral and policy domains. Examples include building opposition political parties (including donating labor or money, campaigning for candidates, or attending campaign rallies or events for opposition candidates) and acts of nonviolent contentious politics, such as peaceful protest and civil disobedience. These forms of participation send the signal to officeholders that continued public support for their incumbency is contingent. Such actions display alternatives to the ruling administration and its policies, thereby constraining the options available to officeholders if they hope to maintain power.

In contrast, elite-enabling participation increases either the informal or formal authority of incumbents, thereby giving them greater resources for monopolizing and wielding political power. Examples include contacting public officials for constituent appeals and lobbying requests, as well as party-building activities aimed at enhancing or expanding the existing party or ruler in power. These participatory acts allow officeholders to build constituent loyalty by providing benefits – sometimes selectively – that may have nothing to do with democratic rights and procedures. Such loyalty allows incumbents to slowly constrict nascent democratic institutions while maintaining sufficient public support to win electoral mandates.

If a democratic transition fails to spur an expansion of elite-constraining political participation, it is unlikely that a country will entrench democratic procedures and norms to such an extent that democracy can survive past the first several years. Elite-constraining participation abounds in Indonesia, contributing to democracy's survival there. In contrast, Russians have favored elite-enabling participation, which made it easier for political leaders to roll back the democratic gains of the 1990s.

Conceiving of democratization as a dynamic interaction between citizens and elites helps us to develop a more precise understanding of the process of democratic survival. By examining how macro-structural variables connect to the specific agents who ultimately make the decisions to democratize or rescind democracy, we may learn whether these structural variables are indeed necessary conditions for building democracy. Perhaps these perceived "causes" of democracy are themselves important only because they tend to foster a separate set of intermediary conditions – conditions that might obtain even in the absence of certain macro-level factors.

Factors Influencing Political Participation

Why did Russians adopt elite-enabling forms of participation, while Indonesians adopted elite-constraining forms? I find three causes for this variation: 1) the robustness of civil society engagement, 2) the

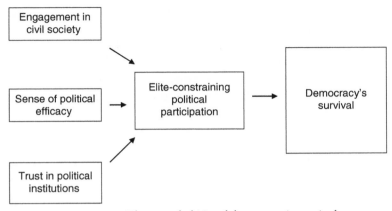

FIGURE 1.3. The causal chain of democracy's survival.

populations' feelings of political efficacy, and 3) the level and objects of political trust. High levels of civil society engagement, political efficacy in favor of elite-constraining activism, and trust in political institutions foster conditions that inspire an expansion of elite-constraining political participation among the mass public once political liberalization occurs. This participation is the primary mechanism by which citizens can prevent elites from encroaching upon nascent democratic institutions and practices. As such, political participation intervenes between the individual-level variables of civil society engagement, sense of efficacy, and political trust and the macro-level variable of regime type (see Figure 1.3).

Engagement in civil society, with civil society defined as the autonomous, intermediary stratum of society that exists between one's home and the state, leads to an expansion of elite-constraining political participation by providing individuals with the resources they need to engage effectively in political life. Moreover, individuals who participate in civil society at higher rates have broader, overlapping social networks through which they can be recruited to participate in new political opportunities, including political party development and acts of contentious politics. As Chapter 5 demonstrates, Russians have extremely low levels of engagement in civic and social life while Indonesians have unusually high rates. As a result, Russians never applied their civic skills to sustained demand for democratic institutions and practices over time. In contrast, Indonesians – in spite of low levels of educational attainment and economic resources – used their involvement in civil society to develop meaningful civic skills that they then deployed to establish and support effective opposition parties and to engage in ongoing acts of protest to constrain elite actions.

Political efficacy, defined as the beliefs about the impact an individual and others like himself can have on the political process (Campbell, Gurin, & Miller, 1954), influences individuals' decisions about how to participate. When individuals believe that a specific participatory act will yield meaningful results, they are more likely to take part. As Chapter 6 discusses, Russians and Indonesians who feel that their vote or activism might influence a political outcome participate relatively frequently. Yet Indonesians are more inclined to view elite-constraining participation as efficacious, while Russians find elite-enabling acts more effective. In addition, overall levels of efficacy are much higher in Indonesia than in Russia. This variation further contributes to these countries' differences in participation and democratic survival.

Last, political trust influences levels of participation and levels of support for the regime and for specific incumbents. When trust in political institutions is high, individuals are more likely to accept the decisions – the uncertain outcomes – these institutions generate, which helps the new regime develop legitimacy. When individuals trust political institutions – such as elections, the legislature, and political parties – they are more likely to participate in them. I observed this outcome in Indonesia, where the population exhibits levels of trust in political institutions that are generally higher than the global average. Russians' trust in institutions, meanwhile, is below the global average, and Russian engagement in political institutions is weak. Alternatively, when trust is placed in specific individuals rather than impersonal institutions, either democratic survival or retrenchment can result. If a leader takes steps to strengthen democratic institutions and practices, democracy survives. Again, we see evidence of this outcome in the policies of each of the presidents in post-Suharto Indonesia. Yet high levels of trust in a person who enacts policies that limit political openness and civil liberties – such as Russia's Vladimir Putin – hamper democracy's survival.

Figure 1.3 portrays a unidirectional relationship between civil society engagement, political efficacy, political trust, and political participation. This image is a simplified scheme of a more complex set of interactions. First, we might expect a reciprocal relationship between political participation and each of the independent variables described earlier. For example, political participation might make an individual more engaged overall and contribute to her becoming involved in civil society. As Chapter 6 explains, the act of participating can foster an individual's sense of efficacy. Similarly, we might expect individuals' experiences in political participation to shape their trust in political elites and institutions.

Second, it is logical to hypothesize that civil society engagement, political efficacy, and political trust are themselves interrelated. Civic engagement might contribute to one's sense of overall efficacy, including political efficacy, and strengthen one's trust in institutions. Alternatively, an individual who feels efficacious may choose to engage in civil society as a method for bringing about political, civic, or social change. Such an individual might have a higher sense of trust in political institutions as well. And perhaps more trusting individuals are more inclined to join civil society organizations, or feel more efficacious. Any of these interrelationships is plausible. Whether they obtain, however, is an empirical question that should be tested, not assumed. The reciprocal nature of the relationships between these variables is not alone sufficient evidence to refute the scheme proposed in Figure 1.3. As I show in the next several chapters, civil society engagement, political efficacy, and political trust do influence patterns in political participation, and higher scores on these variables in the early years following a democratic transition have consequences for democracy's subsequent survival.

As Chapter 3 discusses, the process of political liberalization creates a paradox for mass political participation. Political liberalization entails a broadening of the political opportunity structure for collective action (Tilly & Tarrow, 2007), as well as a need for the population to hold political elites accountable to newly democratized institutions. Yet, when a population has been socialized in an authoritarian political system, people are likely to approach political participation with caution and suspicion. Thus, just when collective action is needed most to ensure democracy's survival, it may be hardest to mobilize. Both Russia and Indonesia experienced an expansion of possible forms of political participation following liberalization, yet the countries diverged in the extent to which citizens took part in activities that effectively constrain elites and protect democracy's survival. Higher levels of civil society engagement, political efficacy, and trust translated into elite-constraining patterns of participation in Indonesia, facilitating democracy's survival. Low levels of civic engagement, political efficacy, and trust in institutions engendered a reliance on elite-enabling participation in Russia, which provided support to political leaders who derailed democracy.

Why Compare Russia and Indonesia?

This book focuses on how individual-level attitudes and behaviors found in a democratizing polity contribute to democracy's survival after a transition occurs. As such, it represents a fundamentally different approach than most scholarship of democratization has taken, requiring a particular research design. My research design offers several advantages for gaining inferential leverage. First, this project employs the deviant case method of analysis. Deviant-case selection involves the comparison of "outlier" cases – in this project, Russia and Indonesia – that perform much differently than a particular theory or model would predict. According to existing theories of democratization, Russia's advantages in modernization, statehood, and sociocultural variables would predict a much higher level of democracy than has occurred as of 2012. Indonesia, meanwhile, deviates from democratization theory on the other end of the spectrum. Indonesia is more democratic than its levels of modernization and statehood would predict. The goal of deviant case analysis is to uncover the factors that contribute to the particular cases' nonconformity with established models. Deviant case analysis is used to generate hypotheses that lead to new explanations of an outcome of interest – in this case, democracy's survival (Gerring, 2007, pp. 89, 105–107).

Russia and Indonesia are not only deviant cases of democratization, they are also crucial cases for study in their own right. Indonesia has the world's fourth largest population, and Russia has the eighth. Collectively, more than 5 percent of the world's population lives in these two countries. Russia is physically the biggest country in the world, has the world's largest volume of combined oil and natural gas reserves, and inherited the Soviet Union's nuclear arsenal. Indonesia is the largest Muslim-majority country in the world, making Indonesia also the largest Muslim democracy. More Muslims live in Indonesia, in fact, than in all of the Middle East. These countries are not outliers we should dismiss. If our theories fail to account for the regime outcomes in these two crucial cases, we should understand why.

Second, this paired comparison presents a fresh approach to comparative studies of democratization. Most of what we have learned about the causes of democracy comes from findings yielded by two standard research designs: cross-national statistical analysis and regionally focused case studies. Large, cross-national statistical analysis has focused primarily on hypothesis testing of possible macro-structural factors leading to democracy, using large sample sizes that often approximate the world's population of political regimes (Boix & Stokes, 2003; Fish & Wittenberg, 2009; Przeworski et al., 2000; Przeworski & Limongi, 1997). These studies rely on correlations between variables for inferential leverage. The relationship that has received the most scrutiny through such large-N statistical studies is that between economic development and democracy. While large-N statistical analysis has yielded interesting information about the role of modernization in democracy's survival, it is of limited utility in helping us understand outlier cases. Additionally, it tells us nothing about the steps in the causal chain that connect economic development to open politics, and whether these steps obtain in the cases under investigation.

The second standard research design looks at cases of democratization in single countries or in a smaller, purposive sample of countries from the same geographic region in order to engage in theory building through the identification of new variables or causal mechanisms (Collier & Collier, 1991; Compton, 2000; McLaren, 2008; McMann, 2006). Cross-country comparisons within the same region regularly rely on the "most similar systems" design (Przeworski & Teune, 1970). Because countries from the same region often share important structural similarities, including level of modernization, history of statehood, and ethnic or religious composition, numerous structural factors that may correlate with democratization are considered "constant" in the research design. One limitation of this approach, however, is that it removes potentially important independent variables from investigation by not allowing them to vary. Consequently, it leaves unexplored many theoretically interesting comparisons (Tarrow, 2010). As Valerie Bunce (2000) noted, several findings from studies of third wave democratizations are regionally bounded. That is, some explanations seem contained to specific regions. To test whether the potential causal variables that drive these explanations are part of a more generalizable theory, we need to look at cases from different regions.

This book's research design combines many of the positive attributes of the cross-national large-N analysis with the benefits of structured small-N analysis. Sidney Tarrow proposes that choosing cases with substantial differences can offer several benefits that elude similar case analysis. First, drawing attention to similar processes in a wide variety of cases can expand or limit the scope conditions of established research findings. When similar patterns are observed in dissimilar environments – such as countries in different regions with no shared history, like Russia and Indonesia – we become more persuaded that a particular phenomenon may indeed be generalizable. Alternatively, when a factor that is viewed as a dominant explanatory variable in one set of cases – such as the importance of a middle class for democracy's emergence in Western Europe – fails to adequately account for the emergence of democracy in another global region or time period, we become less convinced of its overall theoretical importance. Second, examining outliers within a large-N population of cases can help identify the variables responsible for general outcomes of interest in core cases when these are reversed in the case of the outlier (Tarrow, 2010, p. 235). As I argue, patterns of mass political participation may be such an overlooked variable in democracy's survival.

Expanding the set of cases from which we draw comparisons to countries from different regions allows us to test the implicit assumptions about the relationship between the slow-moving structures that are often viewed as fixed historical or regional causes and the agents viewed as responsible for the more proximate actions that set democratization in motion. Explanations that center on a country's or region's specific features frequently identify factors that might have been overlooked or underappreciated in other contexts. As this study seeks to demonstrate, Indonesia's success at building democracy has hinged on a robust associational and social life – a factor Alexis de Tocqueville identified almost 200 years ago as essential to the success of American democracy, yet it is rarely discussed in contemporary debates on democratization. Cross-case analysis offers an opportunity to generate a new hypothesis, validate it with a cross-test case, and uncover causal mechanisms (George & Bennett, 2005; Gerring, 2007).

Multilevel Research Design

In demonstrating how civil society engagement, political efficacy, and political trust have contributed to political participation patterns that subsequently influenced the survival of democracy in Russia and Indonesia, this study draws on several levels of comparison and multiple data sources. By framing democratization as a dynamic interaction between masses and elites, this project recasts the question "What causes an authoritarian regime to democratize" into the query: How do citizens constrain elite actions to ensure democracy's survival after initial elections?

In investigating this question, I engage four levels of analysis. The first and most macro-level is the cross-national comparison of two outlier cases, Russia and Indonesia. By comparing Russia and Indonesia at one particular point in time – more than a decade after political liberalization began in each country – I uncover several differences in indicators of mass political attitudes and behaviors between the two countries. Building on these cross-national findings, I employ a longitudinal study of variation within each country as a second level of analysis. By examining the same indicators used in the cross-national analysis over time, I identify patterns in political attitudes and behaviors that correlate with the trajectory of democracy in both Russia and Indonesia. The combination of longitudinal and cross-case analysis allows me to focus on several key variables that exhibit stability both across country cases and over time.

The third level of analysis involves subnational comparisons within each country. Both Russia and Indonesia are large, geographically expansive, multiethnic countries. Russia sits on the largest land mass in the world – more than 17 million square kilometers that straddle two continents. Indonesia's territory covers an area of more than 17,000 islands (6,000 inhabited) that reaches more than 5,000 kilometers from east to west and nearly 2,000 kilometers from north to south (Central Intelligence Agency, 2011). When we evaluate macro-level indicators for these countries – whether they measure socioeconomic development, political attitudes and behaviors, or the level of democracy – we must bear in mind that these indicators are actually aggregate summaries of outcomes that might vary considerably across the subnational units of each country. In order to account for the diversity of experiences one might expect to find in Russia and Indonesia, I selected two provincial capitals in each country for closer analysis: Kazan and Krasnoyarsk in Russia and Surabaya and Medan in Indonesia.[5]

The subnational level of analysis allows me to test hypotheses that relate to potentially meaningful ethnic, historical, and geographic factors while holding national-level factors constant. Subnational analysis also offers an opportunity to examine whether cross-national patterns hold across different regions within the same country. I do not claim that the results of my analysis of two provincial capitals in each country can be generalized to apply to all regions in Russia and Indonesia. Yet I believe that the purposive sampling of these four cities yields findings that provide a useful corrective to analyses that focus primarily on national capitals or national-level indicators.

My final and most micro level of analysis is the individual. Ultimately, my examination of how political participation influences democracy's survival relies on the aggregation of individual-level attitudes and behaviors. Using both large-N surveys and medium-N interview samples, I look at

---

[5] For information on subnational case selection, see Appendix 1.A.

how individual Indonesians and Russians have responded to democratic transition and the factors that motivate the behaviors and attitudes that have further shaped democratic survival in each country. By building my analysis up from the individual level, I am able to determine whether the variation between Russian and Indonesian attitudes and behaviors is the consequence of fundamentally different processes or a difference in the total sum of particular factors that one finds more of in one country than the other.

Data: Public Opinion Surveys, Open-Ended Interviews, and Event History

The findings of this study are based on multiple data sources, including analysis of key historical events, quantitative analysis of survey data, and qualitative analysis of interview records. The forthcoming chapters scrutinize indicators culled from several cross-national and national-level public opinion surveys in Russia and Indonesia, including the Survey of Soviet Values (1990), the World Values Survey (1991, 1995, 1999–2001, 2005–2008), the Keio University Research Survey of Political Society (2005, 2006), the Russian Election Study (1995–1996, 1999–2000, 2003–2004), and the Asian Barometer Indonesian Survey (2005).[6] In addition to using country-specific surveys to map within-country trends over time, the World Values Survey and the Keio University survey, which administered similar questionnaires in both countries, allow me to compare attitudes and behaviors across these two countries. With these data, I establish correlations between mass attitudes and behaviors at certain points of time and the political debates and reforms of those periods.

I validate survey data trends with original interview data I gathered in Russia and Indonesia from 2007 to 2009. The first population I examined was political and social experts and elites. In each country I conducted approximately seventy open-ended interviews in Russian and Indonesian with scholars, analysts, journalists, representatives of political parties, and representatives of mass voluntary organizations. I carried out elite interviews in Russia in 2008 in the cities of Moscow, Kazan,

---

[6] The data files and documentation for the Survey of Soviet Values and the 1995–1996 Russian National Election Study are both available from the Inter-University Consortium for Political and Social Research (www.icpsr.umich.edu/icpsrweb/ICPSR/). The data files and documentation for the World Values Survey are available at www.worldvaluessurvey .org. The Asian Barometer data were provided to me from the Asian Barometer Survey team upon request. Timothy Colton and Henry Hale generously shared the data files and documentation from the 1999–2000 and 2003–2004 Russian National Election Study.

and Krasnoyarsk, and interviewed Indonesian elites in 2007 and 2009 in the cities of Jakarta, Yogyakarta, Surabaya, and Medan. The purpose of these interviews was to help me evaluate the extent to which elites had strengthened or rescinded democracy, as well as to gauge the elites' sense of public support for democratic institutions and practices.

The second population I investigated was voting-age citizens. I interviewed a quota sample of individuals in each country who corresponded to specific predetermined demographic categories.[7] In 2008, I interviewed twenty-five citizens in both Kazan and Krasnoyarsk (fifty total) using a semi-structured questionnaire. I adapted the same semi-structured questionnaire to Indonesia and interviewed twenty-five individuals in both Surabaya and Medan in 2009 (fifty total). By asking extensive questions about individuals' opinions and activities and how these have evolved over time, I have created a unique data set that chronicles the attitudinal and behavioral patterns of Indonesian and Russian citizens since political liberalization. These data have helped me trace the mechanisms through which political participation contributes to democracy's survival.

This project's design and use of multiple types of data provide many opportunities for analytical leverage. First, historical data and longitudinal surveys facilitate analysis of both democratization and political participation over time in each country. Second, the use of subnational cases allows me to compare different hypotheses within a single-country context. Last, the cross-national analysis lets me consider which factors appear to apply to general theories of democratization versus those that may be nationally (or regionally) specific. The use of historical, survey, and qualitative interview data provides unique opportunities to triangulate information, thereby helping reveal causal mechanisms that explain how a society's response to democratization at a particular moment can influence further regime development.

Book Overview

The contribution this book makes to the study of democratization is to identify how the attitudes and behaviors of individual citizens

---

[7] While scholars of survey research view quota samples as inferior to random sampling for establishing a group representative of the population, in the case of small samples, quota sampling better ensures that a diverse cross-section of the population is represented. For a sample size of twenty-five, random sampling would not guarantee that respondents from key demographic groups are included. See the appendices to this chapter for more information about respondent recruitment and the demographic profiles of respondents.

intersect with the elites and political institutions we have traditionally viewed as driving democratization. My approach is agent-centric. It puts actors – elites, citizens, and organizations – at the center of the story. It focuses on the role of mechanisms – how the work of democratic survival is accomplished, who carries out that work, and which factors facilitate it.

The post-transition trajectories of Russia and Indonesia call for such an approach. These outliers defy expectations of the standard factors that account for regime type in most instances. Indonesia is an example of democratic survival amid scarcity, while Russia provides an illustration of democratic failure amid wealth. This book does not scrutinize the relative importance of socioeconomic development, a history of independent statehood (or colonialism or communism), the repressiveness of the antecedent regime, or other macro-structural variables hypothesized to be at the heart of democratization. These factors have not proven decisive in the trajectories Russia or Indonesia have taken, or in explaining how these two cases diverge from the rest of the world. It is for this reason that one must look elsewhere to explain Russia and Indonesia's deviation from the norm.

The analysis of my findings will unfold over the next seven chapters. Chapter 2 presents an overview of Russia and Indonesia's post-regime change political experiences, with particular emphasis on the ways that citizen participation influenced elite decisions. Chapter 3 analyzes nonvoting political participation as a mechanism that shapes democracy's chances of survival. Chapter 4 demonstrates my argument quantitatively with a series of statistical models that show consistent relationships between civil society engagement, political efficacy, political trust, and nonvoting political participation in Russia and Indonesia. Chapter 5 examines the relationship between civil society and democracy, particularly the role civic engagement can play in expanding elite-constraining political participation. In Chapter 6 I show that political efficacy influences participation in both electoral and non-electoral forms of political and civic life. I also find that the experience of effectively removing an incumbent through the ballot box or otherwise influencing an elite transfer of power serves to reinforce individuals' sense of efficacy in the early years of democratization, thus potentially shaping democracy's survival. Chapter 7 focuses on the influence of political trust on different forms of political participation and democracy's survival. The concluding chapter explores the future viability of democracy in Russia and Indonesia given current political circumstances.

Appendix A

Case Selection and Respondent Recruitment

I used four criteria to select provincial capitals[8] for this study: size, geographic diversity, ethnic composition, and historically important cleavages. In Russia, I picked one capital west and one east of the Ural Mountains. I also selected one city situated in a region with a sizeable non-Russian ethnic minority and one city with a predominantly Russian population. Kazan and Krasnoyarsk fit these criteria. Kazan is the capital of the ethnic republic Tatarstan, which is located on the Volga River in European Russia.[9] The population of Kazan is split almost evenly between ethnic Russians and ethnic Tatars. Tatars are a Turkic Muslim ethnic group and constitute the second largest ethnic group in Russia (3.8 percent, according to the 2002 census). The city of Krasnoyarsk is the capital of Krasnoyarsk Krai, located in central Siberia. Krasnoyarsk Krai is the second largest region in Russia (comprising more than 2.3 million square kilometers) and is the most populated region within the Siberian Federal District. The demographic profile of Krasnoyarsk is similar to Russia as a whole, and the region is known among political analysts as the "Russian New Hampshire" – for most of Russia's post-Soviet electoral history, the voting results in Krasnoyarsk have closely mirrored the national outcome.

In Indonesia, I sought one provincial capital on the culturally and politically dominant island of Java and one on a different island. Additionally, I wanted one city from a region with a predominantly Javanese population and one with more ethnic heterogeneity. Surabaya and Medan fit these criteria. Surabaya is the capital of East Java, the second most populated province in Indonesia and the region with the largest Javanese

---

[8] The level of urbanization is significantly higher in Russia than in Indonesia. According to the CIA World Factbook, as of 2008, 52 percent of the Indonesian population was urban, compared to 73 percent of the Russian population. Both countries, however, are organized into similarly structured provinces. In both cases, provincial capitals are usually the primary urban contact point for the countryside. Many residents in provincial capitals were raised in nearby rural areas and remain connected to them.

[9] Tatarstan has the second-largest population among all provinces in the Volga Federal District, registered at 3.8 million following the 2002 census. Only the population of Bashkortostan is higher.

population. With a population of more than 3 million, Surabaya is also the second largest city in Indonesia (after Jakarta), and is the closest major metropolis to the country's eastern islands. Medan is the capital of North Sumatra, the most populated province on an island other than Java.[10] The population of Medan is ethnically heterogeneous, including groups indigenous to the island of Sumatra and migrants from other regions. The two largest ethnic groups are the predominantly Christian Batak[11] and the predominantly Muslim Javanese. Medan is known among Indonesian social scientists as a microcosm of Indonesia – encompassing the full range of diversity one sees across the country.

In order to recruit respondents for interviews among the citizens of Russia and Indonesia, I first compiled a respondent frame using regional-level data from the most recent national census in each country, supplemented with relevant official statistics and information from local sociologists. The frame established categories for twenty-five respondents in each city who corresponded to specific groups based on gender, age, ethnicity, education level, and sphere of employment. In each city I worked with a local sociologist who conducted the recruiting to correspond with the respondent frame. In both Indonesian cities, we chose to stratify the sample to include a higher number of individuals with a university degree (three in each city), off-setting this by including a smaller number of individuals with only an elementary school education. We also aimed to include an accurate representation of the largest ethnic groups in the provinces of East Java and North Sumatra, while recognizing that in such a small sample it would be impossible to represent all ethnic groups.

In Kazan, Krasnoyarsk, and Surabaya, the local sociologists used established networks to recruit respondents across the full range of the city's regions. I found this to be the standard recruitment practice for most Russian sociologists and pollsters, who note that the refusal rate for random selection is prohibitively high. In Medan, the local sociologist first selected eight *kelurahan* (urban wards) and searched for three or four respondents corresponding to specific categories in the *kelurahan*.

Interview locations varied by city. In Kazan, Surabaya, and Medan, most interviews took place in respondents' homes or places of employment. Occasionally they took place at a convenient neutral location, such

---

[10] Sumatra is the second most populated island in Indonesia after Java.
[11] Following the Malay, the Batak are the second largest ethnic group in Indonesia that is not concentrated on the island of Java. It is the largest predominantly Christian ethnic group.

as a neighbor's home or a university office. The decision to interview primarily in respondents' homes stemmed from my local sociologists' recommendations. This approach brought several benefits. First, it generally provided a more comfortable atmosphere for respondents, with the interview taking on the tone of an informal and relaxed dialogue. Second, I was able to gather observational data about respondents' living situation that could serve as a useful supplement in measuring respondents' socioeconomic characteristics. In Indonesia in particular, it was very clear that few respondents would have agreed to an interview at an off-site location.[12]

A downside of interviewing in respondents' homes, however, was that I could not always ensure the privacy of our conversation or that other family members would not try to interfere in the interview, thereby influencing the content of respondents' answers. In Krasnoyarsk, the majority of interviews took place in a private classroom on a weekend when school was not in session. The decision to interview at this neutral location was made at the recommendation of my local sociologist, who noted that respondents were rarely comfortable receiving researchers in their homes. This format also ensured privacy and a lack of interruptions.

Overall, interviews ranged in time from about fifty minutes to three hours, generally averaging two hours. Interviews were conducted in Kazan in March 2008, in Krasnoyarsk in October–November 2008, in Surabaya in May–June 2009, and in Medan in July–August 2009. All Russian interviews were conducted after the country's March 2008 presidential election. In Indonesia, all interviews in Surabaya were conducted before the country's July 2009 presidential election, and all interviews in Medan were conducted after the election. Since my interview questions focused on long-term trends in attitudes and behaviors and not short-term attitudinal shifts, I do not believe the findings from the Medan sample are skewed as a result of the 2009 presidential election.

Interview dynamics varied between the two countries in ways that are consistent with cultural norms for privacy and receiving visitors. In Russia, most interviews took place one on one with limited

---

[12] This limitation was particularly true of women who did not work outside of the home and of lower-income individuals, who frequently worked in small trade and service sectors. Among this last group, I regularly conducted interviews in their food stands and cafes, pausing while they served customers.

interruption from other family members. Refreshments of tea and cook-ies were served during most interviews, even when the interview took place in an office or neutral location, which helped to create a relaxed environment.

In Indonesia, where most interviews occurred in respondents' homes, it was often difficult to establish conditions for a private conversation. Though my research assistants and I tried to communicate my preference that the interview take place in private, this preference was often difficult to implement given the limitations on space in many Indonesian homes and the expectation that family members would have the opportunity to greet their guest. In several instances other family members or neighbors were present during interviews, although they generally did not inter-fere in the conversation, and (barring a few exceptions) respondents did not seem daunted by their presence. It became clear over the course of my interviews that my respondents generally did not expect privacy for a conversation about their opinions and views.[13] Most interviews took place over cold beverages.

In all but a few instances,[14] respondents were recruited to participate in interviews without any promise of compensation. Respondents were asked to volunteer their time, but they usually were offered a small token of appreciation at the end of the interview. The process of offering com-pensation also varied between the two countries. In a few instances in Russia, I did not offer an honorarium as it was clear that the respon-dent would be greatly offended.[15] Many Russian respondents who were offered an honorarium refused it. In total, 64 percent of Russian respon-dents received an honorarium of 300 rubles ($12).

---

[13] The concept of anonymous is not well understood in Indonesia, especially among ordi-nary citizens. In order to convey to my interview subjects that our conversation would be anonymous and strictly confidential, I had to explain and show in great detail that I would not use their names and would not write or record their names in the inter-view. Privacy did not appear to be a paramount concern for most interview subjects in Indonesia.

[14] Russian sociologists differed in their opinions about whether to announce that an hono-rarium would be provided for interview participation. The local sociologist I worked with in Kazan found that it was occasionally useful to let possible respondents know about a material incentive when recruiting among lower-income respondents who have very limited free time due to working multiple jobs.

[15] For example, if I conducted the interview at someone's house and they refused to accept my offering of chocolate for tea (which is standard Russian hospitality if you are a guest in someone's house), I knew it would upset the respondent to offer payment.

In Indonesia, all respondents accepted the tokens of appreciation I offered. In Surabaya, respondents were offered an honorarium equal to 100,000 rupiah ($10). At the recommendation of my local assistant in Medan, respondents were given a gift equal in value to $10 rather than a cash honorarium.[16] At the end of each interview, I invited my respondents to ask me any questions they would like. Several respondents were interested in hearing my impressions of their country. Many of my Indonesian respondents, in particular, were interested in learning more about the structure of education and social services in the United States. A significant number of respondents in both countries were happy to be interviewed and appeared honored that a foreign scholar wanted them to participate in a research project.

The same basic interview guideline were used in each country, although adjustments were made over the course of the project to improve question wording, remove questions that were not eliciting useful responses, and add more precise questions. I first translated the questionnaire from English to Russian and Indonesian and had it professionally translated by native speakers of both languages. I then compared my translation and the official translation and worked with the translators to arrive at the most precise question wording. Questions focused on respondents' childhood memories and experiences, their reactions to specific historical events, their participation in political, social, and religious activities, their opinions about different state institutions, contacts they may have had with government officials, and their assessment of the existing political system. I also included a small number of closed-ended questions that measured satisfaction with the political and economic system and respondents' understanding of democracy.

In contrast to a closed-ended survey, semi-structured interviews offer greater opportunities for individuals to speak about their lives and opinions in their own terms. While a closed-form questionnaire is designed in such a way to only seek measures for specific concepts, open-ended interviews provide a different perspective – respondents can explain their own actions and opinions and how they have come to make certain decisions in their lives. They can also speak honestly about whether they have no opinion on a particular topic. Through this type of exchange, it is

---

[16] According to this sociologist, material gifts were the common form of appreciation scholars offered in North Sumatra. This scholar was concerned that if I offered a cash honorarium, this form of payment could set a negative precedent for future scholars wanting to conduct interview-based research in the region.

possible to learn not only about the attitudes and behaviors of ordinary citizens, but also about the scope of their interest in and understanding of political change. Another advantage of open-ended ethnographic interviews is the ability to gather context information about individuals and their families – their houses, neighborhoods, and patterns of speech – all of which can assist us in developing a more nuanced understanding of how particular communities and societies are affecting – and being affected by – democratization.

Appendix B

Summary of Citizen Samples in Russia and Indonesia

Russia

Kazan, Tatarstan

Age group*	Description of Respondent
17–29	1 female bank manager, Tatar (Muslim)
	1 male automobile mechanic, Tatar (Muslim)
	1 female hairdresser, Russian (Orthodox Christian)
	1 female homemaker, Russian (Orthodox Christian)
	1 female student, Tatar (Muslim)
	1 male student, Russian (Christian)
30–39	1 male working in private enterprise, Russian (Protestant Christian)
	1 male working in private enterprise, Russian (nonbeliever/atheist)
	1 male public opinion analyst, Tatar (Muslim)
	1 male chauffeur, Tatar (Muslim)
40–49	1 female public sector manager, Tatar Muslim
	1 male bank employee, Russian (Orthodox Christian)
	1 female retail employee, Tatar (Muslim)
	1 female municipal police employee, Russian (Orthodox Christian)
50–59	1 male security guard, Russian (Orthodox Christian)
	1 female factory worker, Tatar (nonbeliever/atheist)
	1 male public sector driver, Tatar (nondenominational/agnostic)
	1 female public sector lower clerical employee and cleaning woman, Tatar (Muslim)
	1 female janitor, Tatar (nonbeliever/atheist)
60–69	1 female retired engineer and social worker, Russian (Orthodox Christian)
	1 female retired engineer, Tatar (Muslim)
	1 male businessman, Tatar (nondenominational/agnostic)
	1 female retired retail worker, Russian (Orthodox Christian)
70+	1 male retired military officer, Tatar (Muslim)
	1 female retired worker, Russian (Orthodox Christian)

* Because years of birth and not exact birthdates were gathered, this table is arranged to ensure age as of December 31, 2008. In four instances, individuals were on the border of two age groups. Bordering ages, in part, explain the absence of some gender and nationality diversity in certain age groups.

Krasnoyarsk, Krasnoyarsk Krai

Age group*	Description of Respondent
17–29	1 male student working in IT, Ukrainian (nonbeliever/atheist)
	1 male student working in marketing, Russian (Orthodox Christian)
	1 female student, Russian (nonbeliever/atheist)
	1 female clerical worker, Russian (Orthodox Christian)
	1 male electrical technician, Russian (Orthodox Christian)
	1 female retail employee, Russian (Orthodox Christian)
30–39	1 male small business owner, Russian (nondenominational/agnostic)
	1 male laborer, Russian (Orthodox Christian)
	1 female midwife, Russian (Orthodox Christian)
	1 female sales clerk, Russian (Orthodox Christian)
	1 female bank employee, Ukrainian/Belorussian (Orthodox Christian)
	1 male factory worker, Russian (Orthodox Christian)
40–49	1 male construction worker, Russian (nonbeliever/atheist)
	1 male recently laid off from private sector management, Russian (Orthodox Christian)
	1 female university staff member, Russian (Orthodox Christian)
50–59	1 female homemaker, Russian (nondenominational/agnostic)
	1 female retail employee, Russian (nonbeliever/atheist)
	1 female retail employee, Russian (Orthodox Christian)
	1 male laborer in transportation sector, Russian/Ukrainian (Orthodox Christian)
	1 male laborer in wood processing, Russian (nondenominational/agnostic)
	1 retired male laborer, Russian (nondenominational/agnostic)
	1 female teacher/social worker, Russian (Orthodox Christian)
60–69	1 male artist, Russian (nondenominational/agnostic)
	1 female cleaning woman, Russian (nonbeliever/atheist)
70+	1 female pensioner, Tatar (Muslim)

* Because years of birth and not exact birthdates were gathered, this table is arranged to ensure age as of December 31, 2008.

Indonesia

Surabaya, East Java

Age group	Description of respondent
17–19	1 female university student, Javanese (Muslim)
	1 female commercial sex worker, Javanese (Muslim)
20–29	1 male university student, Javanese (Muslim)
	1 male civil servant, Javanese (Muslim)
	1 male unemployed, Javanese (Muslim)
	1 male laborer, Madurese (Muslim)
	1 female homemaker, Javanese (Muslim)
	1 female domestic worker, Javanese (Muslim)
30–39	1 male trader, Javanese/Madurese (Muslim)
	1 male janitor, Javanese (Muslim)
	1 male nonprofit employee, Nagekeo (Catholic)
	1 female working in informal sector, Javanese (Muslim)
	1 unemployed female, Javanese (Muslim)
	1 female cleaning woman, Javanese (Muslim)
40–49	1 female health clinic administrator, Madurese (Muslim)
	1 male trader, Javanese (Muslim)
	1 female university lecturer, Javanese (Muslim)
	1 male pedicab driver, Madurese (Muslim)
	1 female homemaker, Javanese (Muslim)
50–59	1 female homemaker, Javanese (Muslim)
	1 retired male, Javanese (Muslim)
	1 male working in informal sector, Javanese (Muslim)
60–69	1 retired male, Javanese (Muslim)
	1 female trader, Javanese (Muslim)
	1 female homemaker, Javanese (Muslim)

Medan, North Sumatra

Age group	Description of respondent
17–19	1 female recent high school graduate looking for work, Batak Toba[a] (Protestant Christian)
	1 male high school graduate about to enter college, Batak Toba (Protestant Christian)
	1 female vocational high school graduate about to enter college, Javanese-Batak Mandailing (Muslim)
20–29	1 male university student, Batak Pakpak (Protestant Christian)
	1 unemployed male, Javanese (Muslim)
	1 unemployed male, Malay (Muslim)
	1 female homemaker, Javanese (Muslim)
	1 female janitor, Javanese (Muslim)
30–39	1 male kiosk vendor, Nias (Catholic)
	1 male construction worker, Batak Simalungun (Protestant Christian)
	1 male construction worker, Batak Mandailing (Protestant Christian)
	1 male laborer, Tamil (Buddhist)
	1 unemployed male searching for work, Batak Karo (Catholic)
	1 female public sector employee, Javanese (Muslim)
	1 female service sector employee, Minang (Muslim)
40–49	1 female homemaker, Batak Toba (Protestant Christian)
	1 female corner café owner, Batak Karo (Catholic)
	1 female public sector employee, Javanese (Muslim)
	1 female public sector employee, Batak Mandailing (Muslim)
	1 male laborer, Malay (Muslim)
50–59	1 male businessman, Minahasan (Protestant Christian)
	1 female homemaker, Minang (Muslim)
60–69	1 male laborer, Batak Karo (Protestant Christian)
	1 female homemaker, Javanese (Muslim)
	1 female traditional healer, Chinese (Buddhist)

[a] Batak are comprised of five sub-ethnicities. Batak Toba, Karo, Simalungun, and Pakpak are primarily Christian. Batak Mandailing, who originate from the southern part of the province, are primarily Muslim.

Comparative Summary of Citizen Samples in Russia and Indonesia

	Russia		Indonesia	
	Kazan	*Krasnoyarsk*	*Surabaya*	*Medan*
Sex Education level	14 women; 11 men 1 incomplete secondary 3 secondary 8 specialized secondary 13 tertiary degree	13 women; 12 men 1 incomplete elementary 4 secondary 11 specialized secondary 9 tertiary degree	13 women; 12 men 11 elementary school or less 6 junior high school 5 senior high school 3 tertiary degree	13 women; 12 men 6 elementary school or less 6 junior high school 10 senior high school 3 tertiary degree
Religion	8 Orthodox Christian 9 Muslim 3 nonbelievers/atheists 3 agnostics 2 Protestant/other Christian	14 Orthodox Christian 5 nonbelievers/atheists 5 agnostics 1 Muslim	24 Muslims 1 Catholic	12 Muslims 8 Protestants 3 Catholics 2 Buddhists
Ethnicity	14 Tatar 11 Russian	21 Russian* 2 Russian/Ukrainian 1 Belarusian/Ukrainian 1 Tatar	20 Javanese 3 Madurese 1 Javanese/Madurese 1 Nagekeo	10 Batak 6 Javanese 1 Javanese/Batak Mandailing 2 Malay 2 Minang 1 Chinese 1 Tamil 1 Nias 1 Minahasan

* Includes individuals who self-identified as "*rossianin,*" "*rossiskii,*" "*slavyanin,*" and Russian-speaking in addition to those who identified as "*russkii.*"

2

Extending Democratization Theory

The Cases of Russia and Indonesia

Authoritarian regimes have ruled Russia and Indonesia for most of their histories. Russia was governed by dynastic monarchies for more than a millennium before revolutions ushered in a Communist regime that lasted more than seventy years. The territory comprising contemporary Indonesia has been governed by several kingdoms, Dutch colonial rulers, and modern authoritarian regimes. While both of these countries can point to specific experiences of democracy in small, village-level settings, their national-level encounters with democratic governance were sporadic before the 1990s. Yet both countries embarked on transitions to democracy, successfully liberalized political institutions, strengthened civil liberties, and held fair and free elections. Opportunities for continuing along a democratic path existed in both countries. Nevertheless, democracy survived in Indonesia while it failed in Russia.

This chapter examines the political trajectories Russia and Indonesia traveled after making a transition to democracy – that is, after they first elected governments in fair and free elections. I look at the specific policies, actions, and inactions that collectively determine the degree of democracy in each of these countries. In particular, I focus on whether the mass publics in these countries, through their attitudes or behaviors, operated as a constraint on elite action. While most studies of democratization look at the interplay among elites during moments of decision making, I aim to consider the dynamic interaction between masses and elites. It is not my goal to scrutinize every decision in the transition and post-transition period. Such a mammoth undertaking would be a separate study unto itself. Rather, my objective is to take the public's pulse at key democratization inflection points to understand if real or threatened mass participation strengthened or hindered elite attempts to embolden or weaken nascent democratic institutions.

I find that while mass attitudes and behaviors played a role in the collapse of both the Soviet and New Order regimes, these attitudes and behaviors provided different levels of elite constraint in Russia and Indonesia once democratic transitions took place. Indonesians continued to express strong support for democratic procedures and norms through large-scale, nonvoting political participation, including ongoing acts of contentious politics. Russians, in contrast, did not defend democratic institutions against elite manipulation. Within the first decade after transition, Russian leaders reversed the country's democratization gains without public interference.

This chapter has five parts. First, I discuss how mass political attitudes and behavior can constrain political leaders, particularly during periods of political transformation. In the second section, I provide an overview of the authoritarian political periods in Russia and Indonesia and the collapse of authoritarianism in these countries. The third section analyzes the transitions to democracy that took place in each country. In the final two sections, I examine the subsequent divergence in regime trajectories that led to a rollback of democracy in Russia and to its strengthening in Indonesia.

Mass Politics as a Constraint on Elites

The Parameters of Democracy

Democracy is a form of political regime. Democracy is not analogous with good governance, equality of outcomes, widespread socioeconomic prosperity, or social justice. Democracy also does not equate governing with public approval. As Philippe Schmitter and Terry Karl note, democracies are not necessarily more efficient; they are not likely to appear more orderly or stable than the autocracies that previously governed a country; and they do not necessarily have more open economies (1991). While popular conceptions of democracy in Indonesia, Russia, and other parts of the world might infuse political openness with the normative characteristics described earlier, the measure of democracy employed here does not.

It is especially important to distinguish between the presence of procedural democracy and good governance. The presence and survival of democracy in Indonesia is a separate issue from the quality of governance in the country (Aspinall, 2010; Lussier & Fish, 2012). In stating that Indonesia has achieved a democratic transition and that its democracy has survived, I make no claims about the quality of its governance or about how Indonesian leaders have performed under democracy. The same is true for Russia. Most observers would agree that the highpoint of political openness in post-Soviet Russia occurred in the early to mid-1990s, a period when the Russian state was at its weakest and quality of governance was low. The presence of democracy and the quality of governance are two separate issues. This project is concerned with the former, not the latter.

Additionally, procedural democracy can beget outcomes that are antithetical to core democratic principles. For example, Russian President Vladimir Putin's electoral mandate in 2000 and 2004 granted him the political capital to undertake reforms that undermined democracy, decisions that were popular with the public. In discussions about Putin's 2004 decision to cancel gubernatorial elections, several acquaintances have argued that the people were dissatisfied with their governors and wanted Putin to appoint regional executives – implying that if a decision was consistent with the will of the people, it was a democratic decision. Yet the cancellation of gubernatorial elections is a clear example of a *reduction* in the procedures that ensure competition for leadership positions through fair, free, and frequent elections. In other words, it operates *against* the definition of democracy employed in this study, even if the decision might have received public approval.

Constraining Elites

As Chapter 1 described, elite decisions mark the final step in a causal chain of events that liberalize or restrict political action. Elites who make these decisions find themselves in positions of political authority, which inherently provide them with resources for exercising leadership. Elites' resources include instruments of formal authority, allies within and outside the relevant political structure, and favorable public opinion. Constraints on political elites can be formal (deriving from an institutional configuration) or informal (originating from public expectations or the expectations of allies). Both formal and informal constraints can influence leadership in the context of democratization.

Comparative politics scholarship emphasizes how political institutions structure and limit the action of officeholders. The institutions of democracy are generally thought to constrain elites by limiting their power, thereby preventing despotism. Yet institutions serve a role in authoritarian regimes as well. Autocrats rarely rely exclusively on their own personal charisma for legitimacy; they derive some authority from constitutions and legal bases that facilitate authoritarianism. It is logical to expect all officeholders to maximize their potential power, and thus push existing institutional limits. Leaders under authoritarian regimes are often able to maximize power with little resistance from the public since the regime imposes severe penalties for opposition behavior. Yet democracy, which combines certainty in the rules for accessing power with uncertainty of outcomes, generally curbs elites' ability to manipulate institutions to suit their short-term interests. Indeed, the very structure of democracy, which derives its legitimacy from citizens' votes, takes egregious power grabs by individual incumbents off the table.

The formal constraints that institutions provide on elite behavior are relatively straightforward and clear. The informal constraints, which generally come from the mass public, are harder to foresee and can vary in meaningful ways. Nevertheless, no political leader makes a decision that is fully independent of mass opinion. Elites expect that their decisions will encounter public support, criticism, or indifference, and the anticipated reaction acts as an informal constraint. While many decisions a political leader makes are met with indifference, some high-stakes decisions may provoke meaningful support or criticism. As Ronald Heifetz points out, "Authority is a constraint because it is contingent on meeting the expectations of constituents. Deviating from those expectations is perilous" (1994, p. 88).

Elites' decisions involving political transformation can have a dramatic impact on the structure of politics and societies, and most political elites making decisions carefully consider how the mass public might react. In the context of democratization, both formal and informal constraints shape elites' behavior in office. Moreover, the same citizen attitudes and behavior that constrain sitting incumbents can also serve as a resource for the political opposition.

For democracy to survive over time, citizens must mount credible threats against leaders who do not adhere to democratic rules and practices. The public can communicate such threats to political leaders in several ways, including supporting opposition parties, engaging in acts of contentious politics, and demanding adherence to democratic rules and procedures. These forms of participation are elite-constraining because they communicate to incumbents and aspirants to office that deviating from citizens' expressed preferences may inhibit a leader's ability to govern effectively. Other forms of mass participation or nonparticipation are elite-enabling because they strengthen a leader's informal authority to implement changes irrespective of their consistency with democratic procedure. If the public responds with indifference or approval when a political leader uses his formal authority to engage in activities that threaten democracy, the response serves as a resource that enables the leader to take antidemocratic actions. As this chapter shows, Russian citizens have rarely attempted to constrain post-Soviet elites who reversed democratic gains. In contrast, Indonesians' mass behavior has constrained elites and thereby limited the scope of acceptable actions political elites can take without jeopardizing their careers.

From Authoritarianism to Political Liberalization

Russia: Communism and the Soviet Union (1917–1985)

Russia's inclusion in the Union of Soviet Socialist Republics (USSR) shaped its authoritarian experience in the twentieth century. In the Soviet system, political power was officially in the hands of local councils, or soviets. In practice, however, the soviets came under the control of the Communist Party of the Soviet Union (CPSU), which developed into a centralized bureaucracy that penetrated all aspects of life. Other organizations that developed following the 1917 Bolshevik Revolution, such as trade unions and cooperatives, were subordinated to party control. The CPSU was intolerant of institutions that existed before the revolution and of rival political parties, all of which the secret security forces eliminated. All independent spheres of economic activity were brought under state control. Atheism was part of official party doctrine, which led to the confiscation of church property and the persecution of religious leaders. By the 1930s, the CPSU controlled every aspect of Soviet life, including employment, education, and culture.

Like most authoritarian regimes, the Soviet Union was marked by a strong disjuncture between a broad set of political and civil rights guaranteed in theory, and their narrow implementation in practice. In theory, the 1,500-member Supreme Soviet was the highest governing body for most of Soviet history. Elections to the Supreme Soviet were held every four or five years. Yet only a single CPSU-approved candidate would run in each district, and the Supreme Soviet convened only twice per year. Therefore, these legislators lacked any real power, and were only called upon to ceremonially approve legislation. A similar structure was in place for regional and local soviets, where membership was determined by uncontested elections among CPSU-approved candidates.

Although the Supreme Soviet and local soviets constituted the official political structure, the CPSU was the only party legally allowed to participate in Soviet politics, meaning genuine political power was concentrated in internal CPSU organs. The party's top authority was the

Central Committee, which in turn voted for a Politburo, a Secretariat, and a general secretary. The general secretary of the Communist Party, in effect, held the highest political office in the USSR. Controlling the CPSU essentially meant controlling the state.

The Soviet regime relied heavily on coercion to ensure popular compliance. The CPSU, the army, and the secret security forces were the main instruments of this implicit threat of force. Their primacy inhibited the organization of any internal opposition in Russia. While repression decreased considerably after Stalin's death in 1953, it remained a constant aspect of Soviet life. Most intimidation, however, was subtle and related to individuals' access to scarce and coveted resources, such as housing, educational opportunities, and desirable jobs. People who participated in CPSU politics had a much better chance to access these benefits. Consequently, mass participation in the Communist Party increased throughout the Soviet period. Protests erupted in parts of the Soviet Union at various points, but were quieted with state-sanctioned violence. The Soviet regime regularly punished dissidents, often sentencing them to long prison terms, committing them to psychiatric hospitals, placing them under internal exile, or deporting them (Marples, 2011).

Russia: Glasnost', Perestroika, *and the* End of the USSR *(1986–1991)*

The rise of Mikhail Gorbachev and the Soviet liberalization policies of *glasnost'* (opening) and *perestroika* (reconstruction) have been analyzed extensively (Breslauer, 2002; Dallin & Lapidus, 1995; McAuley, 1992; Melville & Lapidus, 1990; Remington, 1989) and do not require thorough discussion here. The relevant point for this book is that *glasnost'* and *perestroika* constituted a significant step in political liberalization in the authoritarian Soviet Union, which ultimately paved the way for Russia's democratic transition. *Glasnost'* was introduced in 1986 in an effort to stimulate constructive policy debates about how to reform ailing aspects of the Soviet system. While the CPSU still controlled how much "openness" society would see in the media, the intelligentsia and organized elements of society enjoyed substantial freedom of speech. As a result, topics such as civil and political freedoms, the separation of powers, and discriminatory policies soon became part of genuine political debate.

Perestroika involved a restructuring of the Soviet economic and political systems, including a move toward democratization (*demokratisatsiya*). In January 1987, Gorbachev called for multi-candidate elections for posts within the CPSU and for local soviets, which began in parts of the country by that summer. In 1988, Gorbachev pushed for dramatic, union-wide democratization reforms that included a partially elected Congress of People's Deputies, which would elect the members of the Supreme Soviet from among its own members. The new Congress and Supreme Soviet were empowered with genuine political authority.

The Congress of People's Deputies elections were held in March 1989. One-third of all seats was reserved for candidates from "public organizations," such as trade unions, the CPSU, and the Communist Youth League, but elections for a majority of the remaining seats had two or more candidates. While not fully democratic, these elections offered voters genuine choice for the first time in Soviet history and the population seized on this opportunity to express its frustration with Soviet governance. Although CPSU members won about 88 percent of the seats in the Congress, the new legislators expressed dramatically different views from the party's seasoned deputies. For example, Boris Yeltsin – who had been removed as Moscow party chief in 1987 for being too critical of the Politburo – won a seat in Moscow with 90 percent of the vote. The Congress provided a new forum to articulate grievances and engage in genuine political debates. The initial session of the Congress was broadcast live for two weeks on television and radio, and a record 200 million viewers from across the Soviet Union tuned in to watch (Miller, n.d.).

The opening of public debate to competing viewpoints raised political elites' interest in public opinion. Political discourse in the Soviet Union changed in fundamental ways once people could contrast political elites' statements against the views expressed in surveys. Public opinion polls became "part of the pressure from below" that pushed Soviet leaders to undertake greater steps toward democratization (Brown, 2010, p. 141). In an analysis of available public opinion surveys over the course of Soviet history, Donna Bahry found that by the early 1980s, most people supported political liberalization (1993, p. 554).

Russians began to express these attitudes behaviorally as well. In 1988, a surge occurred of "informal" (*neformaly*) groups, whose activities were not limited to discussion, but also began to include street demonstrations. By 1989, these groups evolved into more serious political actors who supported non-CPSU candidates in the March 1989 elections (Fish, 1995). Workers also became more openly confrontational with the regime, and in summer 1989, nearly 500,000 coal miners went on strike in western Siberia, the far north, and eastern Ukraine (Marples, 2011, p. 283).

Popular unrest also took on more sophisticated organizational forms, as informal groups and reform factions in the Congress of People's

Deputies developed stronger links. As opposition to the CPSU began to coalesce, public disaffection was often channeled in the form of mass demonstrations. For example, hundreds of thousands of people demonstrated in Moscow in January and February 1990, which forced the CPSU Central Committee to yield to the opposition's demand that the Soviet Constitution be amended to end the CPSU's monopoly on political power (Reddaway, 2010, p. 170).

Throughout the Soviet Union, support for Gorbachev and his reform agenda declined while support for populist leaders like Yeltsin and their calls for sovereignty increased. An indirectly elected Soviet presidency was introduced, for which Gorbachev ran unopposed, but a sizeable minority of the Congress of People's Deputies voted against him and delegates from the Baltic republics boycotted the vote altogether.

Gorbachev responded to the increasing strength of pro-democracy and pro-sovereignty politics by tightening the reins of control. In January 1991, he received several special decree powers from the Congress of People's Deputies. Political reporting became more cautious, and several independent publications were shut down. Central government troops forcefully took control of the TV station in Vilnius, Lithuania. The public reacted negatively to these moves, and pro-democratic public demonstrations took place in many Russian cities.

In a forthcoming book, Henry Brady and Cynthia Kaplan demonstrate that Gorbachev enjoyed high support for *perestroika* early on, but as the country's economy deteriorated, public support for *perestroika* and for Gorbachev declined.[1] Meanwhile, liberal democratic reformers and conservative Russian nationalists tapped into public frustration with *perestroika* and rallied around Yeltsin, significantly increasing his popularity. Yeltsin used his broad-based and diverse popular support to push for the adoption of Russian sovereignty from the Soviet Union in June 1990, which emboldened other Soviet republics to follow suit. The Soviet Union officially dissolved on December 25, 1991.

Indonesia: Democracy, Guided Democracy, and the New Order (1945–1989)

Indonesia has existed as an independent state for just over seventy years. The islands that comprise Indonesia were home to a large number of kingdoms that gradually came under European colonization. The

---

[1] Earlier versions of Brady and Kaplan's analysis can be found in Brady and Kaplan (2007) and Brady and Kaplan (2008).

Dutch East Indies Company built a settlement in the region in 1619 to aid with its exploitation of spices, and in 1798 the Netherlands formed the Dutch East Indies colonies. Dutch colonial administration layered political control over existing forms of traditional authority on the archipelago, relying on local lords (*bupati*) as their political and administrative agents. After the nineteenth-century Java War, most members of the aristocracy became "docile clients of the Dutch" (Ricklefs, 2008, p. 143), losing any chance for independent control of their government. The outer islands of contemporary Indonesia came under colonial administration only in the nineteenth and early twentieth centuries, often after violent conflicts left local elites powerless (Ricklefs, 2008).

With the spread of basic education and literacy in the beginning of the twentieth century, educated individuals across the Dutch East Indies began to form social, economic, and educational organizations, which helped increase the strength of their ethnic and communal identities (Ricklefs, 2008, pp. 196–201). Following World War I, organizations became more political, and the idea of establishing an independent Indonesian state gained traction across the colonial archipelago (Ricklefs, 2008, p. 216). This anticolonial, nationalist movement was based on the principles expressed in the 1928 Youth Oath: one motherland, one nation, one language, which sought to transcend differences among ethnicities, regions, and languages in the shared goal of achieving independence from colonial powers.

Indonesia declared independence on August 17, 1945. The following day, the Central Indonesian National Committee proclaimed Sukarno, one of the main nationalist leaders, the country's first president. A four-year war ensued before the Dutch officially recognized Indonesia's independence. Indonesia introduced a parliamentary system of government in 1950, holding elections only in 1955. The pro-Sukarno Indonesian Nationalist Party (PNI) won the largest vote share (22 percent), followed by the Islamic Masyumi party (21 percent), the Islamic Nahdlatul Ulama (NU) (18 percent), and the Communist Party of Indonesia (PKI) (16 percent). The remainder of the vote went to twenty-four other smaller parties (Feith, 1957). This diffuse distribution of power resulted in weak governing coalitions and considerable political infighting.

Indonesia's brief experience with democracy was cut short in February 1957 when President Sukarno declared his policy of "guided democracy" (*demokrasi terpimpin*), where the president would direct the government through a blend of nationalism, religion, and communism, known popularly by its Indonesian acronym NasAKom. He declared martial law a month later, and in 1959 dissolved the parliament and set up an appointed legislature and advisory council. In implementing this authoritarian system, Sukarno relied on the PKI and its widespread grassroots support for some issues, and on the military and its coercive power for others (Ricklefs, 2008, pp. 294–296). By 1963, the military became increasingly concerned that Sukarno was leaning too heavily to the left, making the country vulnerable to a Communist takeover amid a deteriorating economy (Ricklefs, 2008, p. 313). On September 30, 1965, six senior army generals were assassinated in an apparent coup attempt. Hours later, General Suharto mobilized forces under his command and took control of Jakarta. Ultimately, Sukarno was forced to transfer most political and military powers to Suharto, who was named acting president in March 1967.

Suharto's regime, known as the New Order, blamed the PKI for the coup attempt. From 1965 to 1967, the government engaged in widespread repression of PKI members and alleged sympathizers, killing an estimated half a million people (Cribb, 2001, p. 233). Another 100,000 alleged Communists were imprisoned for more than a decade. Throughout the decades that followed these mass killings and incarcerations, Suharto's regime engaged in less violent forms of repression that prevented meaningful mass opposition from developing (Liddle, 1985). While the Soviet regime is well known as one of the most brutal regimes in the twentieth century, government repression in the New Order era had a greater impact on Indonesian society than most people outside the country realize. Mass killings in the 1960s, and a sustained military presence throughout Indonesian society during the New Order period, deterred political opposition and dissent (Ricklefs, 2008, p. 343).

After Suharto was formally elected to the presidency in an uncontested election in 1968, he consolidated control over the country and further curtailed political rights and civil liberties. In exercising political and coercive power, Suharto relied on the military and his new political vehicle – the "functional groups" of civil servants, laborers, and other constituents more commonly known by their Indonesian acronym, Golkar. Suharto stressed that Golkar was not a political party, and therefore not subject to the laws and regulations that dramatically restricted the activities of other parties (Antlov, 2004). In the heavily controlled legislative elections of 1971, Golkar took nearly 63 percent of the vote. In 1973, Suharto forced Indonesia's remaining political parties to merge into two large parties that represented nationalism and Islam, the primary ideological alignments that remained after the decimation of communism.

The Indonesian Democratic Party (PDI) was a fusion of three nationalist and two Christian parties. Four Islamic parties were forced together into the United Development Party (PPP).

Indonesia held highly controlled elections to the House of Representatives (DPR) every five years from 1971 to 1997, in which Golkar never won less than 62 percent of the vote (Liddle, 2007). After each election, the People's Consultative Assembly (MPR),[2] which was comprised of both elected DPR deputies and government and military appointees, would convene to elect the president and vice president. Suharto and his chosen deputy never faced opposition in MPR elections. Under the New Order, Golkar election campaigns had the outright support of all state agencies and the military. Most civil servants were required to sign an oath of loyalty to Golkar, preventing them from voting with a free conscience. Additionally, Golkar's status as "functional groups" allowed it to have a presence down to village and neighborhood levels, penetrating Indonesian life in a way that was impossible for the PDI or PPP.

A combination of threats, intimidation, and accommodation prevented the PDI and PPP from becoming credible threats to Golkar dominance. They acted, at best, as semi-opposition to the government, constrained by laws that restricted their mobilization (Antlov, 2004; Ricklefs, 2008). At worst, however, these parties were tokens meant to create a façade of democracy. Government intervention in intra-party affairs was constant. Parties depended on government funding, candidates at all levels were screened by the government, and military officials regularly monitored PDI and PPP actions by attending party functions (Aspinall, 2005, pp. 146–147). Moreover, Suharto's New Order perpetuated the idea endorsed by Sukarno that political opposition was conceptually foreign to Indonesians, who expected harmonious forms of consensus for decision making. In practice, however, Suharto interpreted that consensus.

Suharto's primary tool for coercion and repression was Indonesia's armed forces, which adopted a policy of *dwifungsi*, or "twin functions." The *dwifungsi* doctrine tasked the military with protecting Indonesians against both external threats and perceived domestic threats (Reeve, 1985), essentially enabling Suharto to create a variety of military institutions that acted as internal security forces (Liddle, 1985; Ricklefs, 2008,

---

[2] Indonesia's House of Representatives (DPR) is responsible for adopting legislation in accordance with the broad directives of the MPR. The MPR has the authority to amend the constitution, provide broad policy outlines, and issue decrees. Under the New Order, the MPR was comprised of the DPR together with appointed representatives of the regions and social groups.

p. 326). Together, Golkar and the military ensured Suharto's dominance over the New Order regime. In spite of the presence of multiple parties and the appearance of legislative and presidential elections, all political power was concentrated in Suharto's hands (Liddle, 1985). The public had no meaningful recourse to constrain Suharto or influence his decisions. Political parties and other mass organizations were banned, co-opted by the state, or kept under close surveillance. In many areas of apolitical social and civic life, the regime permitted only one association and forced this association to affiliate with Golkar, an attempt at regime control over social organization similar in style to the Soviet Union (Liddle, 2007). For example, only one labor union (Serikat Pekerja Seluruh Indonesia, SPSI) was permitted under the New Order. The press was monitored closely and regularly sanctioned, fostering a culture of self-censorship and regular government pressure to not publish certain stories. Individuals who defied the regime were violently suppressed. From the 1970s through the 1990s, it was not uncommon for students, Muslim activists, and other dissidents to be arrested and jailed for extensive periods of time (Bertrand, 1996; Liddle, 1985; Noorani, 1977).

Indonesia: The Rise of Popular Opposition and Suharto's Downfall (1989–May 1998)

In 1989, the outgoing U.S. ambassador to Indonesia, Paul Wolfowitz, called for greater openness, or *keterbukaan*, in Indonesian politics. Newspapers and academics likened *keterbukaan* directly to Soviet *glasnost'* (Emmerson, 1991; Pereira, 1998; Schwarz, 1997; Uhlin, 1997). Curiously, the military faction of the Indonesian legislature initiated debate about *keterbukaan* by discussing political reforms and encouraging the press to report on controversial topics.

Suharto's reaction to the military's call for openness was twofold. He made veiled threats against challengers while simultaneously endorsing debate in an attempt to control it. Press restrictions loosened, but Suharto's primary response was to try to strengthen his alliances within the Islamic community as a counterweight to relying on the military (Aspinall, 2005, pp. 37–42). In response to the modest liberalization that accompanied *keterbukaan*, societal groups – especially students, farmers, and underground dissidents – began to test the boundaries of the regime's tolerance. When the government did not violently suppress early protest attempts, citizens felt emboldened to engage in acts of contentious politics, which increased dramatically in the 1990s, further fanning elite conflicts within the regime.

The ascension of Megawati Sukarnoputri, the daughter of the late President Sukarno, to the leadership of PDI in 1993 marked the beginning of the New Order regime's unraveling. Megawati's election as PDI chair was an unprecedented, open act of defiance against Suharto, who had tried to block her selection (Ricklefs, 2008, p. 377). Grassroots support for Megawati, who had emerged as a symbol for pro-reform factions within the PDI in the late 1980s, and supporters' refusal to cave in to standard forms of intimidation created a fissure in the government's apparatus for control (Aspinall, 2005, pp. 155–162).

Immediately after Megawati's rise to the PDI leadership, Suharto loyalists began attacking her from all sides, preventing her from consolidating control over party structures and paralyzing the party. Recognizing that Megawati's election had exposed cracks in the New Order's foundation, the regime initiated new repressive measures, including a government ban on the country's three largest weekly publications.

The regime's repressive tactics, together with Megawati's personal popularity, galvanized opposition forces that had generally remained outside of the noncompetitive party system to coalesce around PDI as a possible pro-democracy vehicle. While everyone understood that a combination of pressure on voters, manipulation of results, and the large number of appointed members in the MPR would prevent Megawati from mounting a credible campaign to unseat Suharto in the 1998 presidential election, the possibility that Suharto might have to face an opponent threatened to undermine the regime's legitimacy. In response, Suharto resorted to crude tactics of suppression by forcing Megawati's removal at a contrived and restricted PDI congress in June 1996 (Aspinall, 2005).

Following this maneuver, it proved impossible to reconcile the two camps in PDI. Pro-Megawati supporters refused to leave PDI headquarters in Jakarta and gathered outside to make speeches criticizing the government. On July 27, 1996, several thousand police officers, soldiers, and thugs forcibly took control of the PDI headquarters. Rioting broke out across the city, spawning further unrest across Java. Amid this turmoil, Indonesia held its regular DPR elections in May 1997, and Golkar emerged with 75 percent of the vote. The campaign was arguably the most destructive in Indonesian history, with rallies devolving into riots between PPP supporters and Golkar, and between pro-Megawati PDI supporters and the official PDI camp (Bird, 1998).

During this period, Indonesia's economy teetered on the brink of collapse. By 1997, Indonesian companies had amassed $80 billion in foreign debt. The Asian Financial Crisis led to a dramatic weakening of the Indonesian rupiah, which experienced the largest devaluation in the world in 1997 (Bird, 1998). The Indonesian stock market plunged and inflation reached double digits. Consequently, factories closed, workers lost jobs, and food prices soared. In order to prevent a major private sector debt default, Suharto agreed to a $43 billion loan from the International Monetary Fund (IMF) in October 1997 in return for a variety of economic liberalization reforms, the brunt of which affected poor and working-class Indonesians (Pepinsky, 2009).

Transitions to Democracy

Russia: 1990–1993

Russia's transition to democracy began with the 1990 legislative elections in the Soviet republics as a major turning point. In the lead-up to the elections, mass demonstrations were held in Moscow and other large Russian cities, largely without incident. Yeltsin was elected to the Russian Congress and became speaker of the newly formed Russian Supreme Soviet. Under Yeltsin's leadership, the Russian parliament became increasingly assertive. In June 1990, it adopted a declaration of sovereignty that stated that Russian parliamentary decisions superseded those of the Soviet parliament. Related legislation placed natural resources, foreign trade, and budgetary control under Russian jurisdiction as well. While this legislation did not transfer the main levers of power of the USSR, it essentially elevated the status of the Russian republic over the Soviet Union, stripping the Soviet Union of significant political and economic authority.

After the republic elections, a Democratic Russia group arose in the legislature, with a Democratic Russia Movement (DRM) also emerging as an umbrella organization uniting various grassroots voting associations and other informal political organizations. At its inaugural conference, DRM estimated that the group comprised fewer than half a million members, a rather modest number for a country the size of Russia (Fish, 1995, p. 45).

In March 1991, the Soviet Union held a referendum regarding a new Union Treaty, to which Russia added a question about electing its own republic-level president. Seventy percent of Russian voters voiced their approval for a Russian presidency. Presidential elections were held in June 1991. CPSU authorities did not manipulate the vote, and the elections were considered largely fair and free. Yeltsin was the clear front-runner, and his primary opponent was former Soviet Prime Minister Nikolai Ryzhkov, a CPSU stalwart. Four other candidates also participated, representing a diverse set of constituencies, including Communists, nationalists, and the military. Yeltsin won with 57 percent of the vote, while Ryzhkov came in second with 17 percent. These elections constituted the first time that a national-level executive had been popularly elected on Russian territory. Yeltsin's election and the collapse of the Soviet Union later in 1991 are regularly viewed as the events culminating in Russia's democratic transition. Yet, as Fish (1995) pointed out, Russia lacked a "founding election" that included multiparty competition for the national legislature. This type of an election would not happen until 1993.

In August 1991, the Soviet republics were poised to sign a new Union Treaty – one creating a Union of Soviet Sovereign Republics – that would have essentially broken the CPSU's hegemony and reduced Moscow's power over the republics. In order to prevent the end of the party's hold over the USSR, a group of CPSU hardliners staged a coup on the night of August 19. By August 20, about 200,000 people had gathered by the Supreme Soviet building to oppose the coup, and Boris Yeltsin used his authority in Moscow to bring the army under his control and force the coup-plotters to surrender (Marples, 2011, pp. 297–298). The coup attempt and its resolution made clear that a reconstituted Soviet Union had little chance of survival, and the Union was officially dissolved in December 1991.

Russian opposition forces, including DRM, had organized themselves to fight *against* Communist Party rule, not necessarily *for* a different type of political organization. Once it accomplished the job of extricating Russia from Communism, the opposition movement struggled to establish a coherent program to advance the democratization agenda. While DRM succeeded in mobilizing mass demonstrations in 1990 and 1991, it lacked the cohesive organizational structure of the successful pro-democracy movements in Eastern Europe. Discord among the parties that comprised the Democratic Russia legislative group impaired efforts to expand membership.

Moreover, no other mass movement or organization arose to fill the void left by DRM. Russia, in contrast to many non-Russian Soviet republics and their Eastern European neighbors, lacked a large popular front or other movement organized around ethnic and national interests. Similarly, labor organizations did not succeed in establishing a nationwide independent union movement to represent workers' interests. Consequently, no non-Communist mass movement succeeded in establishing effective party institutions for representing societal interests in democratic institutions. Society had failed to organize a challenge that could dislodge the custodians of power in a way similar to that of Poland's Solidarity or the Czech Republic's Civic Forum.

In the aftermath of the Soviet Union's collapse, Russia had a freely elected president and legislature, but operated without a clear constitutional structure. The legislature polarized into pro-Yeltsin and anti-Yeltsin camps, and a coalition of Communists and nationalists in the Supreme Soviet blocked reform attempts (Remington et al., 1994). Yeltsin responded to this gridlock by ruling more and more by presidential decree, heightening tensions with his opponents. The Congress announced an April 1993 referendum that put four questions to the Russian population regarding its confidence in Yeltsin and his policies and its preference for early presidential and parliamentary elections. The majority of voters expressed confidence in Yeltsin and his policies and opposed early presidential elections, but favored early parliamentary elections.

Using the referendum to justify his actions, Yeltsin superseded his constitutional authority by dissolving the Congress on September 21 and calling for a new constitutional referendum and legislative elections for December (Marsh, 2002; White, 2011). Two days later the Congress declared Yeltsin's decree null and void, dismissed him from power, and appointed Vice President Aleksandr Rutskoi as acting president. Yeltsin responded by cutting off the electricity and phones in the parliamentary building as members barricaded themselves inside (Marsh, 2002, p. 56).

This crisis provoked popular reaction in Moscow. Several thousand demonstrators took to the streets in support of the parliament (McGowan, 1993). Pro-parliamentary forces occupied the mayor's office and attacked a television station, resulting in sixty-two deaths (Lally, 1993). On October 2, Yeltsin signed a decree announcing a state of emergency in the city. On October 4, army tanks shelled the barricaded parliament, killing more than 150 people (McGowan, 1993).

A nationwide public opinion poll on October 12 showed a broad range of reactions to these events (VTsIOM online data archive). Twenty-eight percent blamed Rutskoi and Congress Speaker Ruslan Khasbulatov, 23 percent blamed Yeltsin together with Rutskoi and Khasbulatov, 15 percent blamed Yeltsin, and 12 percent blamed the Supreme Soviet. In short, public opinion over the crisis did not side universally with either Yeltsin or the parliament.

On December 12, Russians approved a new constitution that gave the executive branch considerable powers, including the power to issue decrees that have the force of law, as long as these decrees do not contradict the constitution or existing laws. It also restructured the parliament into a bicameral Federal Assembly. The lower house, the State Duma, includes 450 deputies and the upper chamber, the Federation Council, includes two deputies from each of the subnational units of the Russian Federation.[3] The constitution eliminates the post of vice president, and requires Duma approval for appointing the prime minister. The president has the power to dismiss the Duma if it rejects his nominee for prime minister three times.

On the same day that Russians approved the new constitution, they also elected representatives to the new Federal Assembly. Having finally completed a fair and free legislative election to accompany the 1991 presidential election, Russia met the minimum standards for completing a democratic transition by the end of 1993.

Indonesia: 1998–1999
Against the background of economic chaos from the Asian Financial Crisis and widespread citizen unrest, the MPR elected Suharto to his seventh term as president in March 1998. In early May, the government announced a fuel subsidy reduction that amounted to a 70 percent increase in gasoline prices (Bird, 1999). Student demonstrations broke out, and subsequent stand-offs between Suharto and the people escalated, resulting in violence, rioting, and a convergence of student and non-student activists on the parliament building in Jakarta. The military stood down and did not try to suppress the protesters. Having lost the support of the military, Muslim leaders, and most of Golkar, Suharto resigned on May 21 and Vice President B. J. Habibie became president.

Habibie took several immediate steps to establish political legitimacy by meeting the public's demands for reform and restoring calm. He removed press restrictions, guaranteed political parties and other organizations the right to organize, and released some political prisoners (Bird,

---

[3] Until 2007, half of the members of the State Duma were elected from single-mandate districts, while the other half were elected from party lists. Since 2007, all deputies are elected via proportional representation. In 2014, Russian President Vladimir Putin signed a law restoring half of the State Duma to single-mandate districts. At the time of this writing, no elections had been held under the new law. Initially, Federation Council members were elected. From 1995 to 2000, the governor and speaker of the legislature of each federation subject automatically became their regions' Federation Council members. Since 2000, members are appointed.

1999). By the end of 1998, the MPR had agreed on reforms that would result in an empowered legislature and a weaker presidency, as well as an open, multiparty system. The parliament was also redesigned to give greater weight to territorial representation and reduce the influence of the military. These reforms constituted dramatic improvements for both political rights and civil liberties.

Indonesia completed its transition to democracy with DPR elections in June 1999 and the election of the president by the MPR in October 1999. Forty-eight parties competed in the parliamentary election, with twenty-one winning at least one seat. Elections were also held for the legislatures of the then twenty-six provinces[4] and more than 300 districts and municipalities. The 1999 elections constituted the first free elections in Indonesia since 1955, and no major group was barred from running candidates. Five parties collectively managed to win more than 90 percent of the seats in the DPR: Megawati's branch of the PDI – renamed the Indonesian Democratic Party of Struggle (PDI-P) – won a plurality of seats (153), followed by Golkar (120) and the PPP (58). Two new Islamic parties also won a large number of seats. The National Awakening Party (PKB), led by Abdurrahman Wahid, the longtime chairman of Nahdlatul Ulama (NU), won fifty-one seats. The National Mandate Party (PAN), headed by Amien Rais, the former chairman of Indonesia's second largest Islamic organization, Muhammadiyah, won thirty-four seats.

Throughout most of 1999, Habibie and Megawati were considered the two main rivals for the presidency. Megawati was the favored candidate among the opposition forces that pushed for Suharto's resignation. Habibie, however, represented the position of modernist Muslims, and his early steps toward political liberalization and democratization made him a credible agent of reform. Golkar was consumed by intra-party factionalism and its representatives in the MPR were unable to muster support for a single presidential candidate. A divided Golkar left the Muslim factions concerned about the possibility of Megawati coming to power and pursuing secular strategies that would sideline their interests. This concern opened the way for a third candidate: Aburrahman Wahid from the PKB, who garnered enough support from Golkar and the Muslim parties to win the presidency.

---

[4] East Timor, which passed a referendum in August 1999 declaring independence from Indonesia, did not elect a provincial legislature or representatives to the MPR.

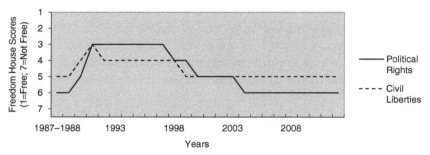

FIGURE 2.1. Political rights and civil liberties in Russia, 1986–2012. *Scores from 1986–1991 are for the USSR.*

Democracy's Trajectory in Russia

Gradual Retreat to Complete Authoritarian Reversal

Russia's political trajectory following the 1993 constitutional crisis and subsequent legislative election can be divided into roughly three periods. From 1994 to 1997, the country's level of democracy stayed constant. Civil liberties and political rights were widespread, providing great opportunity for Russians to extend and strengthen democracy. The second period started around 1998, when Yeltsin began to retreat gradually from democracy by restricting some political rights and civil liberties. This trend continued apace once Vladimir Putin came to office in 2000. The third period began with Putin's reelection in 2004. The deepening of authoritarianism after 2004 comprised further restrictions on political rights, which survived through the election of Putin's anointed successor, Dmitrii Medvedev, in 2008, and Putin's return to the presidency in 2012.

These three periods are visible in the country's Freedom House scores. Figure 2.1 provides Russia's political rights and civil liberties scores from the introduction of *glasnost'* in 1986 through 2012. As Figure 2.1 shows, Russia's highest scores for political rights and civil liberties occurred in 1991, during the year the Soviet Union was dissolved. For most of the 1990s, Russia's scores for civil rights and political liberties were constant, before both dropped in the late 1990s. By 1999, Russia's civil liberties score had fallen to the same level it was during 1988–1989. Political rights declined even further, dropping in 2004 to a score of 6, the same score the Soviet Union held before it liberalized elections.

The changes in political rights and civil liberties over the course of these three periods are discussed later. While political rights and civil liberties constitute two distinct components of democracy, civil liberties are supporting actors to political rights in many respects. Civil liberties are what guarantee that political rights can persist. Without meaningful civil liberties, political rights cannot be actualized. Yet the process of establishing civil liberties is less complicated than the process of building political institutions that operationalize political rights. For this reason, my analysis places greater emphasis on variation in political rights.

Democracy's Apex: 1994–1997

The first period – the highpoint of democracy in post-Soviet Russia – did not include major political liberalization efforts beyond the adoption of the 1993 Constitution. One further liberalization reform that occurred during this period was the introduction of gubernatorial elections in Russia's eighty-nine federal units. By the end of 1997, almost all regions had elected their executives. Local self-government and elections for local executives also became more widespread. Media began operating freely in the early 1990s and there were no meaningful constraints on political, civic, or social organization. Yet, even during this highpoint of political openness, there were no major societal efforts to build institutions aimed at supporting and strengthening democratization.

Even though elections became more widespread starting in 1993, party-building in Russia remained weak throughout the 1990s. Citizens who had marched in the streets demanding the end of Communism were less interested in the work of building new organizations to promote their political interests. The lack of party organization was apparent in the 1993 legislative election results. Independents and representatives from parties without a clear programmatic direction comprised the plurality of deputies, followed by reformers, left-leaning parties, and nationalists. The Duma did not provide Yeltsin with the legislative mandate he had wanted to enact reform. The economy continued to deteriorate and the ruble plummeted. Coal miners went on strike again, and Yeltsin's popularity dropped precipitously.

The results of Russia's second Duma elections in 1995 reflected people's frustration with the government's policies. The Communist Party of the Russian Federation (KPRF) emerged as the largest political party in the country and effectively controlled a legislative majority in the Duma. In early 1996, Yeltsin's popularity was in the single digits and it seemed inevitable that a KPRF candidate would win the June 1996 presidential elections. Powerful allies in the Russian media and business community, however, came to Yeltsin's aid, giving him an unfair advantage over other competitors. In the first round of voting, Yeltsin took 35 percent and KPRF candidate Gennady Zyuganov won 32 percent of the vote in a field of eleven candidates. Yeltsin emerged victorious in the second round, winning nearly 54 percent of the vote. Yeltsin's reelection was not a resounding call for greater democracy, but rather reflected a majority preference to not return to a Communist system (McFaul, 2001b). For many, a vote for Yeltsin was the lesser of two evils.

Nevertheless, politics operated more or less democratically in the early part of Yeltsin's second term. Even though the 1993 Constitution granted considerable power to the executive, Yeltsin did not have total control over the executive branch or the regions, in part because of divisions among elites. Moreover, the absence of a pro-president majority in the legislature meant that small factions in the Duma could band together and serve as a counterweight to the president. Throughout Yeltsin's presidency, the Duma and Federation Council used their limited powers to place checks on the president. While the policy outcomes of this period fell far below public expectations and did little to advance political rights or civil liberties, the political process was largely democratic.

In addition, mass political action declined in Russia following the 1993 constitutional crisis and subsequent elections. The pro-democracy forces that had helped bring down Communist rule did not evolve into political parties or mass movements that pushed to sustain democratization in Russia. As Chapter 5 discusses, associational life that provides the foundation of civil society remained very underdeveloped in Russia throughout the 1990s, with the exception of participation in closed-shop trade unions that carried over from the Soviet system. In contrast to developments in neighboring democratizing systems, independent trade unions, professional organizations, and charitable groups did not quickly emerge in Russia to fill the space opened by the collapse of the Communist Party's monopoly on associational life. For example, 1990s Russia stands in stark contrast to 1990s Poland, where the Solidarity movement fractured and split into several smaller political parties and associations that served to represent the different constituents that had come together under the pro-democracy umbrella. In Russia, the only form of visible political participation was voting in elections. Electoral competition, as discussed earlier, did not stimulate the development of robust political parties that could help structure citizen interests. The only formidable party was the KPRF. Elites – especially Yeltsin – were left relatively unconstrained during this period.

Democracy's Retreat: 1998–2003

Like Indonesia, Russia also experienced an economic crisis in 1998. The stock market crashed, world oil prices dropped, and foreign investment fled the country. In August, the government was forced to devalue the Russian ruble and default on its international loans. This financial catastrophe came after months of protracted disputes between the Duma and the president, who had made reshuffling his cabinet a regular activity. Following the financial crisis, Yeltsin dismissed his entire cabinet. The Duma refused to accept Yeltsin's new choice for prime minister, forcing him to select a candidate more acceptable to the legislature.

In May 1999, the Duma voted to impeach Yeltsin, but failed to secure enough votes. In August, Vladimir Putin was appointed prime minister, and on December 31, 1999, Yeltsin resigned, making Putin acting president and forcing early presidential elections. Putin handily won a majority of the vote in the first round in March 2000. After winning this mandate, Putin immediately embarked on a series of reforms aimed at recentralizing state authority. He spoke of the need for a "dictatorship of the law" through "guided democracy" (*upravlyaemaya demokratiya*). The use of the term "guided democracy" was no coincidence, and appears to have been appropriated directly from Sukarno's own combination of strong executive rule and weak representative institutions.[5]

Many of Putin's centralizing reforms reduced political rights and civil liberties. For example, a May 2000 presidential decree divided the country into seven federal districts, each headed by a direct presidential representative. This reform diluted the political power of popularly elected governors and granted greater authority to Putin-appointed officials. Two additional reforms further curtailed regional executives' political power. First, in 2000 Putin removed regional governors and speakers of regional legislatures from the Federation Council, replacing them with appointed representatives. While allegedly intended to minimize governors' lobbying abilities and strip them of the immunity from criminal prosecution held by Federation Council members, this reform also dampened political rights by replacing elected officials with Kremlin appointees. Since only individuals who are loyal to the president are selected, the president essentially controls the upper house of the Federal Assembly (Remington, 2010). Second, in 2001, the Duma passed amendments to federal law that granted the president the authority to disband regional legislatures

---

[5] See, for example, Pribylovskii (2005), SOVA Center website (www.sova-center.ru) and "Mir i Strana" (2007).

and to remove popularly elected regional governors from office when criminal activity is suspected. Collectively, these reforms reinstituted central authority over all matters relating to federation subjects and granted more power to nonelected officials.

In 2000 Putin also began a sustained attack on independent media. By the end of 2003, the state controlled all national television stations either directly or through stakes held by state-owned companies. The act garnering the most public attention occurred in April 2001, when the state-owned energy company Gazprom exercised its rights as a minority shareholder of the popular independent television station NTV to install a new board of directors. NTV journalists refused to accept the new management, barricaded themselves inside the TV station, and ultimately left to work for a different network.

These early rollbacks of democracy did not appear to stifle political participation. The public reacted to the takeover of NTV by staging protests in Moscow and St. Petersburg. Twenty thousand protestors turned out in Moscow – making these the largest pro-democracy demonstrations in Russia since 1991 – but the response outside of major cities was one of indifference (Baker & Glasser, 2001). Comparatively speaking, 20,000 is a relatively small number of protestors for a country with a population of more than 140 million. In 1996, when President Franjo Tudjman's government in Croatia (population 4.4 million) refused to renew the broadcasting license of the popular Radio 101, about 100,000 people protested in Zagreb (Ottoway, 1996; Woodard, 1996).

The lack of widespread public rancor about curtailed media freedoms was not a consequence of fear, but rather one of either indifference or even support for Putin's actions. Russian public opinion reveals that the majority of Russians did not view Putin's actions in the early 2000s as an attack on freedom of the press. A national public opinion poll of 1,600 respondents on April 15, 2001, asked respondents if they thought that the change in management at NTV, the closure of the newspaper *Segodnya*, and the firing of the staff at the magazine *Itogi* signified a mass attack on freedom of speech. The majority – 55 percent – said certainly or likely "no," while 45 percent said certainly or likely "yes" (VTsIOM online data archive). Yet the 45 percent of the population who viewed these events as an attack on the press did little to express displeasure.

In the 2003 State Duma elections, the pro-Putin United Russia party won 38 percent of the vote, while the Communists took 13 percent, and pro-democratic parties only won seven seats. Smaller parties and independents quickly joined the United Russia faction, giving it a legislative majority. As United Russia successfully became a hegemonic party, the Duma no longer posed the slightest constraint to the president.

Elite moves that rolled back democratic gains during this period were accomplished gradually and skillfully so that many citizens were not fully aware that their political rights were being eroded. As Ellen Carnaghan has argued, Russian "citizens do not perceive the same threats to democracy that some experts do" (2007, p. 61). Reforms to the electoral system and press freedoms that effectively stifled competition, replaced elected with appointed positions, and established United Russia's hegemony assumed the rhetoric of state centralization and reining in corruption. Citizen action was not circumscribed – low levels of elite-constraining participation permitted political leaders to chip away at democratic institutions and practices with impunity.

The Return of Authoritarianism: 2004–2012

In March 2004, Putin stood for reelection in a race that was boycotted by all other major political actors and won 71 percent of the vote. With legislative power and popular opinion firmly on his side, Putin passed further reforms that weakened Russia's remaining democratic institutions and the shift toward authoritarianism became more severe. Taking advantage of his enormous personal popularity and low levels of mass involvement in elite-constraining participation, Putin pushed through legislation that reduced both pluralism and accountability in democratic institutions. The move toward authoritarianism regularly preyed on citizens' fears about their physical security, especially after the Beslan school massacre in September 2004, which left more than 330 individuals dead.

After Beslan, Putin proposed several pieces of legislation further curbing political rights, which the Duma dutifully passed. The first ended the popular election of governors, replacing them with presidential appointees who are confirmed by regional legislatures. The second eliminated single-mandate district seats from the Duma, requiring that all 450 seats be allocated by proportional representation. This reform reduced the representation of local interests in the Duma, and weakened its ability to draw on local power bases to check presidential power (Remington, 2010).

Changes Putin introduced in 2005 to the Election Law and the Law on Political Parties further emasculated democratic institutions. Amendments to these laws raised the threshold for entrance to the Duma to 7 percent, prevented the formation of electoral blocs, removed the "against all" option from the ballot, and prohibited election monitoring except by parties participating in the election or through invitation from the state. The revisions also raised the requirements for registering political parties, demanding that a party have 50,000 members and branches with at least 500 members in at least half the country's regions.[6] Only registered parties were allowed to run candidates in elections.[7]

These provisions raised barriers to competition for smaller parties, and prohibited the governors' machines and oligarch-led financial industrial groups that had served as formidable electoral vehicles in the 1990s and early 2000s (Hale, 2006) from participating in elections. There was little reason to suspect that these reforms were introduced because Putin perceived a threat to his leadership. Rather, Putin took advantage of his popularity to create formidable obstacles that were impossible for his rivals to overcome. Because Russian party-building has been historically weak, legislative reforms have benefited large existing political parties – namely, Putin's United Russia. Regional political actors, who were severely hampered by these laws, were pressured to affiliate with United Russia. Stricter registration requirements have also given authorities more legal instruments to deny parties registration and access to political competition. These reforms brought about a dramatic decline in the number of registered political parties, effectively eliminating their ability to present a check on executive power. By 2008, only two parties mattered – United Russia and the Communist Party – and the strength of the Communists was only a fraction of what it was ten years earlier. United Russia had successfully become a hegemonic party, while the Communists were reduced to token opposition.

Several other techniques have ensured large electoral victories for United Russia and pro-Putin candidates. While any incumbent enjoys certain advantages when running for an election – visibility, perks of office, and considerable media coverage – Putin and United Russia candidates also rely on something Russians call "administrative resources." Administrative resources include unlimited access to state-sponsored media, unregulated use of official offices to campaign on behalf of United Russia candidates, and pressure on state employees and other voters who depend on budgetary resources, all of which have become fixtures

---

[6] Amendments adopted in 2009 gradually reduced these numbers, and in 2012 the membership requirement was lowered to 500 and there are no longer lower limits on the number of party members needed in regional branches.

[7] In 2012, the requirement that political parties gather signatures to run in legislative elections was eliminated and the number of signatures required to register a presidential candidate was reduced from 1 million to 100,000 for party candidates and from 2 million to 300,000 for independents.

in Russian electoral campaigns. Given the controlled environment Putin created, it is no surprise that United Russia won 64 percent of the votes in the December 2007 Duma elections and that Putin's anointed successor, Dmitrii Medvedev, sailed to a first-round victory in the March 2008 presidential elections with 71 percent of the vote. Neither the Duma nor presidential elections met international standards for fair and free balloting. Medvedev immediately appointed Putin as prime minister, and Putin was regarded as the primary decision maker in the Russian government throughout Medvedev's tenure. At the end of 2008, the Russian Constitution was amended to extend the presidential term from four to six years beginning with the 2012 elections.

Putin's authority was further confirmed when he announced in September 2011 that he – not Medvedev – would run for the presidency in 2012. He was aware that existing political conditions would prevent anyone from mounting a feasible opposition campaign, and the election was just a formality. The December 2011 Duma elections saw a drop in votes for United Russia to 49 percent, which was still enough for the party to maintain a slim legislative majority when votes were converted into seats. Allegations of electoral fraud led to a wave of protests throughout Russia in December. More than 100,000 individuals protested in Moscow on December 10 and December 24 – the largest protests Russia had witnessed since the collapse of the Soviet Union. Despite these protests, however, the Duma election results were confirmed and Putin was reelected to a third term in March 2012 with 63 percent of the vote. While the regime made some tactical gestures toward liberalizing the political system as a way of quieting protests – namely by introducing highly restrictive gubernatorial elections and allowing the registration of some new political parties – these moves were largely for show.

Further assaults on civil liberties – often couched in rhetoric about national security and measures to fight terrorism – continued during Putin's second term in office. A 2006 law placed onerous administrative burdens on NGOs, dramatically limiting their autonomy, especially in fundraising. In July 2008, Putin cancelled the tax-exempt status of most foreign foundations and NGOs, essentially denying any group critical of the government substantial financial resources, and in 2012, the Duma passed a law requiring any NGOs that receive foreign funds to register as "foreign agents" and submit to inspections. Shortly after Putin's inauguration in 2012, the Duma passed a law that dramatically increased fines for participating and organizing unsanctioned protests. Other actions taken in 2012 that curbed civil liberties included a bill that broadened the definition of a "spy," amendments to Russian law that partially recriminalized slander, and an Internet censorship law. In 2013, Putin signed a law that essentially prohibited the representation of homosexuality, effectively outlawing LGBT activism and legalizing discrimination against same-sex couples and their families. The Duma passed the law with only one abstaining vote.

Freedoms of speech, media, association, and religion have all declined in Russia in the past several years. The state does not protect citizens seeking to exercise these civil liberties. Violence against non-Russian minorities has increased, and perpetrators are rarely brought to justice. Assassinations of journalists and human rights activists have captured international headlines. At least nineteen journalists have been killed in Russia since Putin came to power (Freedom House, 2010).

With the rare exception of the protest movement that emerged at the end of 2011, the Russian public has met Russia's return to authoritarian practices with little resistance. Although the level of authoritarianism in Russia in the past several years has undoubtedly hindered Russians from engaging in elite-constraining participation, citizens had considerable opportunities to organize and challenge government practices and policies before 2006. Indeed, evidence of these opportunities was visible in early 2005, when protests against government reduction of pensioners and veterans' social benefits erupted across Russia (Bondarenko & Migalin, 2005; Nikitina et al., 2005). In this case, public pressure compelled federal and provincial governments to increase financing for pensions and to offer some new benefits to offset the cost of the ones that were revoked (Chandler, 2008). In this example, Russians succeeded in constraining elites. Russians have taken to the streets in other instances as well. In late 2008, for example, small-scale protests erupted across Russian cities in response to a government plan to raise tariffs on imported automobiles. While fear of suppression might keep some citizens from acts of contentious politics, significant numbers have shown that they are quite willing to speak out against government policies they dislike. Government policies that curb political freedoms and institutions, however, have generally not inspired such a reaction. The wave of protests that erupted from December 2011 until summer 2012, which I discuss in the concluding chapter, marks a brief aberration from the Russian norm of nonparticipation.

On the whole, Russians have failed to constrain political elites in the post-Soviet era. The dismantling of democratic institutions and practices under Putin is not the sole cause, but rather the primary effect, of such inaction. While the authoritarian nature of the contemporary Russian regime likely depresses political action that might occur in a more open environment, citizens could engage in nonvoting participation quite freely during the first fifteen years of the post-Soviet regime. Yet during this period the mass public chose not to expand elite-constraining participation. Russians further developed a preference for elite-enabling acts. Consequently, their lack of engagement in political party development enabled a popular president to pass legislation that substantially reduced political rights and civil liberties. Additionally, low levels of contentious political activity from 1993 through 2011 made it easy for political leaders to roll back democratic institutions.

Democracy's Trajectory in Indonesia

Building and Expanding Democratic Institutions: 1999–2004

Indonesia's political trajectory following its 1999 transition to democracy can be divided into two periods during which democracy was extended and strengthened. This section describes the reforms from late 1999 through 2004. These reforms focused primarily on amending the 1945 Indonesian Constitution to provide the legal architecture for guaranteeing political rights and civil liberties. The following section discusses the second period, from 2005 to 2012, when the emphasis shifted to implementing these constitutional amendments and strengthening their execution.

The demarcation of Indonesia's post-transition trajectory into two periods is reflected in the country's Freedom House scores since 1999. Figure 2.2 shows Freedom House's political rights and civil liberties scores for Indonesia since the beginning of the country's political liberalization under *keterbukaan* in the late 1980s through 2012. According to this graph, civil liberties were stronger than political rights during the late New Order period. The political repression of the early 1990s is reflected in lower scores for both dimensions. Following Indonesia's democratic transition in 1999, both scores improved dramatically and were raised again in 2004. Throughout the post-transition period, Indonesia's score for political rights has remained higher than its score for civil liberties, but both are higher than the scores Russia has earned at any point in its post-Soviet history.

The extensive changes to Indonesia's political framework from 1999 to 2001 took place during a period of intense political instability. From summer 2000 through summer 2001, the DPR became increasingly frustrated

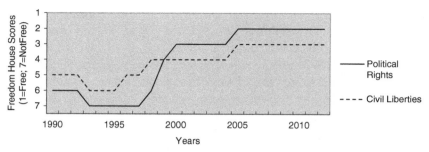

FIGURE 2.2. Political rights and civil liberties in Indonesia, 1989–2012.

with President Abdurrahman Wahid's approach to government. During the annual MPR session in August 2000, members raised concerns about several alleged financial improprieties involving the president. The members had decided in advance, however, not to push for the president's dismissal, as they believed that it would provoke a negative reaction from the public (Liddle, 2001). In this instance, public pressure constrained parliamentary elites from acting hastily, encouraging them to seek a resolution through due process instead.

In the following year, the DPR investigated two alleged cases of corruption against President Wahid and engaged in a lengthy official process tantamount to impeachment. As the MPR suspected, the public was not indifferent to the proceedings. Throughout the investigations and related hearings, the population took to the streets both to demand Wahid's resignation and to defend him. In November 2000, protestors stormed the parliament building and demanded the president's resignation. A *Tempo* magazine public opinion poll at the time found that 65 percent of Indonesians wanted the parliament to remove Wahid ("Parliament Stormed as Wahid Told to Resign," 2000). Protests gained momentum over the following months, and in January 2001, mass protests in opposition to Wahid took shape, in some cases clashing with police (Sims, 2001). The president's supporters staged their own demonstrations across Java, particularly in the president's stronghold in East Java, where they attacked Golkar offices and blockaded a major highway ("President Warns Military Not to Harm Protestors," 2001). Following these events, Wahid made a public appeal to his supporters, asking them to renounce violence and to trust in the democratic process.

As the DPR proceedings unfolded through spring 2001, anti-presidential protests and the counter-protests by Wahid's supporters continued across Indonesia, raising the specter of violence. Wahid warned security forces not to use "repressive actions" when dealing with protestors, and when his supporters' rhetoric became especially threatening, he appeared before some 20,000 followers in Jakarta, appealing that they "go home in peace" (Murdoch, 2001; "President Warns Military Not to Harm Protestors," 2001). At the end of May, the DPR voted to hold a special MPR session to consider impeachment. The military warned Wahid not to call a state of emergency before the MPR session (Aglionby, 2001). Yet, on July 23, as the MPR was about to start official impeachment proceedings, Wahid issued a presidential decree to dissolve the parliament and ordered the military to prevent the MPR from assembling. The army refused to implement the decree, and by evening the MPR had removed Wahid and appointed the vice president, Megawati, as president, in accordance with the constitution. The public mood had changed in favor of Wahid's removal, and protests and demonstrations served as a resource for both the MPR and military to follow democratic procedure. Indonesians had used political participation to help constrain Wahid from acting against democratic principles.

Megawati's presidency brought political stability to Indonesia for the first time since 1997. Yet, even as this drama over Wahid and Megawati commanded the national spotlight, the MPR was quietly embarking on a series of broad-reaching constitutional reforms. Four sets of constitutional amendments passed from 1999 to 2002 dramatically changed the 1945 Indonesian Constitution, which grew from thirty-seven to seventy-three articles.[8] Collectively, the amendments substantially reorganized political power in Indonesia and protected political rights and civil liberties. The reforms that ensured further democratization can be divided into five categories: 1) strengthening the balance of powers between the executive and legislative branches; 2) safeguarding popular rule through the expansion of elections and term limits; 3) articulating a broader list of guaranteed civil liberties; 4) strengthening judicial independence; and 5) reducing the *dwifungsi* power of the armed forces. I discuss each of these five areas next.

Regarding the executive-legislative balance of power, the constitutional amendments shifted considerable power from the president to the DPR, granting the DPR the power to make laws and reducing the president's power to only submitting bills (Indrayana, 2008). The amended constitution also stipulated that the president cannot suspend or dissolve the DPR – a direct response to Wahid's attempt to dismantle the DPR on

---

[8] The specifics of each of the amendments can be found in Indrayana (2008).

the eve of his impeachment. Further reforms changed the structure of the parliament to introduce a new Regional Representatives Council (Dewan Perwakilan Daerah, DPD) that would serve as an upper chamber in the MPR. The new MPR included the DPR and the DPD, thereby eliminating appointed members from the parliament altogether. The amendments also limited the president's judicial and diplomatic powers, giving the DPR more control in appointing ambassadors and consuls (Indrayana, 2008). Collectively, these changes reduced the strength of the executive and greatly empowered the legislature.

Amendments that expanded elections extended democracy further. Elections for the DPR, DPD, regional and local legislatures (Dewan Perwakilan Rakyat Daerah, DPRD), and president and vice president are now held every five years. Direct election was introduced for the offices of the president and vice president, a move the public widely supported. The president is limited to two terms in office, and amendments clarified the procedure for impeachment.

The constitutional amendments also incorporated new provisions to guarantee human rights, thereby strengthening Indonesian civil liberties. The specific provisions include freedom of religion, speech, information, and conscience. Civil liberties, in particular freedom of religion, were further enhanced by additional legislation. In 2000, President Wahid repealed a 1967 ban on the public expression of Chinese religion, beliefs, and traditions, making it possible for ethnic Chinese (about 3 percent of the Indonesian population) to engage openly in religious practices and traditions. In 2002, President Megawati announced Chinese New Year (*Imlek* in Indonesian) as a national holiday.

The constitutional amendments also strengthened the independence of the Indonesian judiciary. The power of the military court was reduced, and the armed forces became subject to the civil and criminal jurisdiction of the general court system. Perhaps most important, a new Constitutional Court with the right of judicial review of all legislation the DPR passes was established in addition to the preexisting Supreme Court. The Constitutional Court quickly developed a reputation for independence and adherence to legal principles. In 2004, for example, it restored political rights to people who were allegedly linked to the PKI, allowing them to vote in and contest elections for the first time in more than thirty years.

Several of these amendments have weakened the military's influence in political life. The movement to a fully elected DPR and DPD, for instance, eliminated military representation in the parliament. Changes to the jurisdiction of the military court were designed to make it easier to hold officers accountable for abuses of power. Amendments also altered the mechanism for appointing and dismissing the commander of the armed forces and the chief of police, requiring DPR approval of the appointments. Collectively, these changes dramatically reduced the military's ability to implement *dwifungsi* and act at the direct will of the president.

In addition to the constitutional amendments, the DPR passed two laws on decentralization in 1999 that transferred considerable administrative and fiscal authority from the central government to local governments at the district (*kabupaten*)[9] and municipality (*kota*) levels. Among the numerous powers transferred to local governments, the most important change for democracy was allowing popularly elected local legislatures to choose local executives rather than having the central government appoint them. The implementation of these laws has been described as the world's largest political decentralization project, as almost 2 million civil servants and more than 60 percent of the national development budget were transferred from central to local authorities (Smith, 2008).

The first stage of Indonesian democratic deepening is also noteworthy for proposed constitutional changes that were not accepted. In 2002, President Megawati proposed to revise the 1999 decentralization law, arguing that it threatened national unity. She met with sharp resistance from the district-level governments that were empowered by the law, as well as from national legislators (Malley, 2003). Recognizing that she would not have the legislative or popular support to amend the law, Megawati retreated. Of even greater importance was the MPR's rejection of a constitutional amendment requiring Muslim adherents to carry out *sharia* law. Both NU and Muhammadiyah, Indonesia's two largest Muslim organizations, spoke out against this proposal, providing important support to legislators of all religious and ideological backgrounds to oppose it (Malley, 2003).

Indonesians used their political freedoms to organize a broad range of political parties that quickly competed with the three parties whose existence was permitted under Suharto (Golkar, PPP, and PDI). The two Islamic parties – PKB and PAN – founded by members of NU and Muhammadiyah, respectively, quickly attracted a following. Other Islamic parties emerged, such as the Justice Party (PK) in 1998, which

---

9 A district is an administrative territory similar to a county in the United States. Below the province level, all Indonesian territories are organized into cities or districts.

grew out of the Islamist intellectual movement from university campuses, the Crescent Star Party (PBB), and other smaller parties emerging again from the NU and Muhammadiyah ranks. By 2004, a new centrist party, the Democratic Party (PD), had emerged as a solid challenger to Golkar and PDI-P dominance. While it is impossible to obtain accurate figures for membership levels during this period, the fact that twenty-four political parties met the rather heavy membership requirements for participating in the 2004 DPR elections suggests that political party-building proved more effective in Indonesia than Russia.[10] By 2006, according to the World Values Survey, more than 16 percent of Indonesians reported membership in political parties, compared to only 5 percent of Russians.

At the end of this first stage of democratic deepening, Indonesia held its second post-Suharto elections for the DPR and its first direct elections for the presidency in 2004. Eleven parties won seats in the DPR, and Megawati's PDI-P saw its vote share decline from 34 percent in 1999 to less than 19 percent in 2004. No candidate had secured 50 percent of the vote after the first round of presidential elections. Consequently, the top two vote winners – Susilo Bambang Yudhoyono (SBY) from the Democratic Party (PD), who won 34 percent of the vote, and incumbent President Megawati, who took 27 percent – advanced to a second round in September. SBY won the runoff with 61 percent of the vote. The turnover of power from Megawati to SBY, a former general who held positions in both Wahid's and Megawati's cabinets, was peaceful and uneventful. In a very significant development for democratization, Indonesians constrained elites by removing an incumbent from power through party-building and democratic elections. The electoral removal of an incumbent president has never taken place in Russia.

Strengthening Democratic Institutions: 2005–2012

The second phase of democratic deepening in Indonesia has emphasized stronger implementation of reforms introduced during the first period. Democracy has been strengthened in three general areas: 1) a further expansion of elections to provincial and local executives; 2) an enhancement of civil liberties that resulted from the settlement to the Aceh separatist conflict; and 3) an increase in judicial independence, as evidenced by the work of the Constitutional Court.

A new 2004 law on regional autonomy established direct election of local and regional executives, taking this power away from regional

---

[10] For a discussion of registration criteria, see Choi (2010).

legislatures, which had developed a reputation for engaging in predatory and rent-seeking activities. By carving out some institutional independence for executives, lawmakers hoped to increase the executives' accountability to the people (Hadiz, 2010). In 2005, approximately 180 governors, district heads, and mayors were elected directly, constituting the first nationwide election of local government executives in the country's history. According to Freedom House's 2007 report on Indonesia, 40 percent of incumbent executives had been voted out of office in popular elections, representing the kind of turnover that occurs in a healthy democratic system.

A lasting peace in Aceh also began in 2005, resolving a secessionist conflict with the central government dating back to the mid-1970s. Peace in Aceh was further strengthened by a 2006 law that introduced regional elections, provided greater regional autonomy, and permitted former rebels to reorganize into political parties.

While judicial independence remains weak in Indonesia, the Indonesian Constitutional Court has passed several decisions in recent years that demonstrate a commitment to procedure over outcome and that directly strengthen political rights and civil liberties. For example, in 2006 the Constitutional Court ruled against three articles in the criminal code that prohibited insulting the president and vice president. In 2007, it overturned two articles in the penal code that criminalized defamation, increasing protections of free speech. In 2010 the Court stripped the Attorney General's Office of its authority to ban controversial books ("Court Ruling Ends Government's Authority to Ban Books," 2010).

In addition to strengthening civil liberties, the Constitutional Court has also upheld political rights. For example, in 2007 it ruled to allow independent candidates to contest local elections ("Indonesian Government, House Agree to Revise Regional Administration Law," 2007). In 2008, the court overturned two articles in the 2008 Law on Legislative Elections to give priority in seat allocation to candidates who receive the largest number of votes on a party's list, regardless of their position on the list (Freedom House, 2009). This decision strengthens citizens' political rights by ensuring that their preferred candidates, rather than the party's, are seated in the legislature. The court has also rejected several appeals by defeated parties in regional, local, and national elections to overturn election results, upholding the integrity of elections and the authority of the Central Electoral Commission. Marcus Mietzner has argued that the Court's "judicial activism" has engendered such strong public support that it has become invulnerable to intervention attempts (2010).

Despite progress toward strengthening democracy, concerns about civil liberties persist. In particular, violence against religious minorities has increased in recent years, and the Indonesian government has done little to stem these attacks or to bring their perpetrators to justice. In April 2010, the Constitutional Court upheld a 1965 law that bans individuals from misrepresenting other religious faiths, but the law has generally been applied only to address perceived offenses to mainstream Islam by religious minority groups (Gelling, 2010). Politically motivated violence also continues in Papua, where security forces are regularly called to respond to a secessionist movement, yet are rarely held accountable for abuses of their power.

Throughout this second phase of democratic deepening, however, Indonesia proved remarkably stable, weathering the standard battles of governance without weakening the country's new democratic institutions. This period also saw a regularization of mass political action and elite responses, through the use of both electoral mechanisms and nonvoting participation between elections. Change in the composition of the national legislature and presidential turnover since 1999 also provides evidence that Indonesians are using their votes to punish and reward policymakers for their performance. For example, in April 2009, Indonesia held its third post-Suharto DPR elections, bringing nine parties into the legislature. SBY's Democratic Party won the largest vote share with 21 percent of the vote (148 seats), while both Golkar and PDI-P saw their vote shares decline to just more than 14 percent each. In July, SBY was elected to a second term in office, this time winning more than 60 percent of the vote in the first electoral round against well-known national figures former President Megawati (PDI-P) and Vice President Jusuf Kalla (Golkar).

In between elections, Indonesians do not shy away from expressing their views through acts of contentious politics. When the legislature introduces a controversial topic or the government takes an unpopular act, the public regularly responds with protests. For example, in 2006 a controversial anti-pornography law was introduced that would have outlawed acts such as baring shoulders and legs, kissing in public, and dancing in a "sensual" manner. The proposed legislation provoked a strong reaction from artists, women's rights groups, and the predominantly Hindu island of Bali, which argued that the new law would prohibit important components of Balinese cultural expressions and kill its tourism industry (Asmarani, 2006c; "Hundreds of Indonesian Activists Demonstrate against Pornography Bill," 2006). In response to these complaints, more than 100,000 demonstrators organized by numerous Islamic groups rallied in Jakarta *in support* of the measure ("Muslims Protest 'Porn,'" 2006; "Thousands of Indonesians Demonstrate in Demand of Anti-porn Law," 2006). As a result of the activism from both sides, an anti-pornography bill was eventually signed two years later, but in a significantly diluted form.

In 2006, proposed labor law changes that would have reduced workers' protections (with the goal of improving Indonesia's investment climate) triggered greater public unrest. Tens of thousands of protestors took to the streets in Jakarta, creating massive traffic jams, and substantial protests broke out in other cities across the archipelago ("Thousands of Indonesians Demonstrate against Labour Law Changes," 2006). Protestors and the labor leaders who organized them threatened a nationwide strike for May 1 if the government submitted the bill to the DPR (Asmarani, 2006b). The protests compelled SBY to withhold the bill until unions were included in discussions of the law's revisions (Asmarani, 2006a; Kagda, 2006).

Indonesians' willingness to protest shows no signs of abating, even as increased democracy has made their rights more secure. In the period between 2010 and 2012 alone, demonstrations were held in multiple cities to mark the first-year anniversary of SBY's inauguration for a second term in office, to protest U.S. President Barack Obama's visit to Indonesia, to express dismay at changes to government subsidies for fuel oil, and to criticize the government's record on curbing corruption. In this same time period, students engaged in protests over national and local issues, such as a government decree on places of worship, increases in the cost of electricity, sluggish land reform policies, the results of a local election in West Nusa Tenggara, the construction of a theme park on a historic site in Makassar, the unfinished regional budget in Bekasi, the development of a palm oil plantation in West Sumatra, and even the celebration of Valentine's Day.

In contrast to Russians, Indonesians have succeeded in organizing society to provide a credible check against political elites. Indonesians' success in this regard has not simply come from political parties mobilizing a mass of supporters to vote in elections. Rather, unions, religious organizations, cultural groups, student organizations, and other segments of society are sufficiently organized to mount collective political action between elections. In doing so, they have effectively used political participation to constrain political elites, not only by applying pressure regarding particular legislative decisions, but also by limiting the scope of the political agenda. In the post-Suharto era, Indonesian politicians have come to expect popular pushback. As a result, the range of possible actions a national leader considers taking is much more restricted. It is difficult to imagine an Indonesian president attempting the attacks on democracy that Putin undertook with such ease and public quiescence. Indonesian leaders know they could not succeed.

Conclusion

Russia and Indonesia share important similarities as well as crucial differences in their political trajectories leading up to and following democratic transitions, and concerning the role the mass public plays in this process. Authoritarian regimes, including highly repressive regimes in the twentieth century, ruled both countries for most of their histories. In both, mass protest and calls for democratic reform helped bring about authoritarian collapse. And with regard to mass participation and activities that constrain elite actions, the first years after authoritarianism collapsed in each country looked very similar.

Russia and Indonesia's political trajectories diverged, however, following their respective democratic transitions. The level of mass behavior in constraining elites also varied in these two cases. Russia's political openness peaked during its transition to democracy and remained stable for several years before gradually moving back toward authoritarianism. During the 1990s, Russians experienced meaningful political rights and civil liberties. Although the 1993 Constitution granted considerable power to the executive, the State Duma and regional executives constituted important loci of independent political power, and regularly held the president in check. During this period, Russians had ample opportunity to constrain elites and to push for an expansion and strengthening of nascent democratic institutions by building opposition parties and engaging in contentious politics. Yet they chose not to. When Vladimir Putin came to power in 2000, he had little trouble introducing reforms that recentralized power, and he gradually used legislative mechanisms to reform political institutions until they no longer constituted a democratic system. These changes all occurred without mass mobilization in defense of political rights and freedoms. As a result, democracy failed to survive in Russia.

Indonesia, by contrast, has extended and deepened political rights and civil liberties since its 1999 transition to democracy. Mass political participation has played a key role in pushing democratization forward.

Indonesians join and participate in political parties at much higher rates than Russians, which has ensured that multiple viewpoints are represented in the legislature, providing a constant check on the president. When political elites have behaved in ways that challenge democratic principles, Indonesians have not been afraid to take to the streets. This ongoing political participation has constrained elites and pushed democracy forward.

The following chapter describes the specific patterns in political participation that fostered democracy's survival in Indonesia and its collapse in Russia.

3

Elite-Constraining Participation
and Democracy's Survival

As the previous two chapters demonstrate, the failure of democracy in Russia and its success in Indonesia cannot easily be explained by the structural differences between these two countries or by their different histories. In this chapter, I discuss how patterns of political participation constitute the crucial link between structural and historical factors, on one hand, and the survival of democracy, on the other. In particular, I find that mass political participation that is *elite-constraining* – the dominant pattern of participation in Indonesia – facilitates democracy's survival. In contrast, *elite-enabling* patterns of participation – which are widespread in Russia – jeopardize democracy.

By analyzing trends in nonvoting political participation since political liberalization in Russia and Indonesia, this chapter shows that Russian citizens failed to sustain participatory behaviors that constrain political elites, while Indonesians have been more successful in doing so. Moreover, Russians embraced participatory acts that empowered existing elites – regardless of these elites' commitment to democracy. Consequently, the survival of democracy varied in these two regimes over time. Without a citizen base holding ruling figures accountable in Russia, governing elites were able to chip away at newly liberalized institutions and roll back democratic gains to the point where elections were no longer fair or free enough to "throw the rascals out." In Indonesia, meanwhile, strong and sustained engagement in elite-constraining acts has made it harder for political elites to overstep their mandates. Such participation leads to greater competition in the political arena, which has facilitated democracy's survival.

In this chapter, I first conceptualize political participation and discuss how political participation can play a causal role in democracy's survival.

I then analyze trends in nonvoting political participation in Russia and Indonesia using several public opinion surveys. These trends are further investigated through an examination of open-ended interviews with Russian and Indonesian citizens. This chapter's final section describes how patterns in political participation shaped regime-level outcomes in Russia and Indonesia.

Political Participation and Democratization

Conceptualizing Political Participation

There is no consensus about how much political participation is necessary for democracy or which forms of participation facilitate the survival of democracy in transitioning regimes. In this book, I adopt Joan Nelson's definition of political participation as "action by private citizens intended to influence the actions or the composition of national or local governments" (1979, p. 8). This definition is sufficiently general to apply to polities that are not fully democratic, yet precise enough to establish clear boundaries for operationalization.

Studies of advanced democracies have generally divided political participation into two categories: conventional and contentious (Barnes et al., 1979; Brady, 1999; Harris & Gillion, 2010; Norris, 2007). Conventional activities include voting, organizing and developing political parties, contacting elected officials to express concerns (henceforth "contacting"), voicing political criticism through media outlets, and engaging in political campaign activities. Contentious political activities, on the other hand, are inherently disruptive, such as demonstrations, riots, and acts of civil disobedience.

As Pippa Norris has suggested, dichotomizing between conventional and contentious political activities in advanced democracies is dated since many modes of protest activism have become mainstream (2007, p. 639). In advanced democracies, we have little reason to expect that the most common acts of contentious politics are targeted against a country's political regime rather than against specific government policies. Yet the distinction between conventional and contentious activities remains meaningful for nascent democracies. Regimes that are emerging from authoritarianism are unlikely to have a history of peaceful, civil protest. In these contexts, the risk associated with contentious political acts may be high – or at least unknown.

For example, scholars have generally categorized signing petitions as a form of contentious politics. Yet the extent to which signing petitions is contentious depends on a regime's degree of political openness. In more authoritarian contexts, signing a petition is a risky act that could result in significant consequences for those involved, such as Charter 77 in Czechoslovakia. Yet in most democracies, signing petitions does not involve personal risk and can be thought of as a form of contacting that demands less individual effort.

To ensure that the distinction between political participation and other forms of social and civic activity is clear, it is useful to discuss acts *not* included in my conceptualization of political participation. Four categories of activities are closely related to political participation but separate from it:[1] 1) civic, social, and professional activities, such as participating in neighborhood watches or workplace strikes against a private sector employer;[2] 2) consuming political information, such as following media or receiving uninitiated contact from a candidate; 3) talking about politics with other people; and 4) having intentions to participate in political activities.

Each of these four types of activities may ultimately shape an individual's decision to participate in politics, but behavior cannot be classified as political participation until a person takes a specific action to attempt to influence a political outcome. For example, belonging to an environmental organization is not political participation, but circulating a petition demanding that the government investigate environmental pollution is. Similarly, discussing a mayoral election with friends is not political participation, yet attending a rally for one of the candidates is. We must clarify these subtle distinctions in order to avoid conceptual slippage. The variable of interest in this analysis is political participation. If we consider political participation as an outcome to be explained, it is possible that engaging in civic or social organizations, consuming political information, discussing politics, or expressing an intention to participate might indeed play a causal role in determining variation on this outcome. Whether certain civic and social activities might increase the likelihood of an individual participating in politics is an empirical question that can be investigated.

Political participation in authoritarian regimes, though limited in scope compared to democracies, does exist. Both the Soviet and New Order regimes were "mobilizing regimes." In contrast to voluntary forms

---

[1] These issues are all discussed by Brady (1999).

[2] Workplace strikes in Communist countries or in state-owned enterprises border on political participation, since the demands striking workers make are generally targeted to change government policy or influence a political outcome.

of political participation, which citizens undertake on their own initiative, mobilized participation comprises actions the government sponsors and guides to enhance its welfare or legitimize its claim to power (Conge, 1988, p. 241). While voluntary participation comes from below, mobilized participation is dictated by the government, which can impose a cost for nonparticipation. Although different from voluntary acts, mobilized participation provides a source of popular legitimacy for authoritarian regimes and therefore fits within the scope of "actions ... intended to influence the actions or the composition of ... governments." In addition to mobilized participation, authoritarian regimes frequently encourage basic forms of contacting. For example, it was common for Soviet citizens to contact lower-level Communist Party (CPSU) officials regarding problems with public service provisions.[3]

In the Soviet Union and New Order Indonesia, citizens were mobilized by the regime to participate in social, civic, and political life and faced meaningful sanctions if they refused. In both countries, elections were highly orchestrated events devoid of meaningful competition, yet high levels of participation were expected. Consequently, not voting was viewed as an act of defiance. In the Soviet Union, individuals were expected to show their loyalty to the regime by voting in elections, marching in May Day and Revolution Day parades, engaging in government-organized development projects, such as *subbotnik* clean-up days, and fulfilling designated "social responsibilities" (*общественная нагрузка*) aimed at building communism, such as distributing Marxist-Leninist literature or assisting with labor union organization. In New Order Indonesia, citizens were expected to vote for Golkar every five years and to assist in top-down development projects, but to otherwise stay demobilized.

Elites in both the Soviet Union and New Order Indonesia feared what would happen if the masses were left to their own devices, and countered this perceived threat by involving citizens in "coproduction" (Roeder, 1989). Writing about the Soviet model of development pre-Gorbachev, Philip Roeder describes coproduction as a way of forcing the de-participation of society by substituting citizen involvement in the implementation of government decisions for participation (1989, pp. 859–861). In Russia and Indonesia, citizens were marshaled to carry out specific tasks, such as providing voluntary labor for development projects, as a way of gauging support and identifying non-compliers

---

[3] For more details on citizen participation in the Soviet Union, see Bahry and Silver (1990); DiFranceisco and Gitelman (1984), Friedgut (1979).

who could be penalized (Bowen, 1986; Friedgut, 1979; M. Lane, 2008; Roeder, 1989). The repercussions of not participating were severe in both the Soviet Union and Indonesia. An individual or her family members could be prevented from advancing professionally, gaining admission to schools or universities, or receiving coveted consumer goods.

Political Participation in the Context of Democratization

Studies of political participation have generally focused on either voluntary participation in stable democracies or mobilized participation in nondemocratic contexts. There is significantly less analysis of political participation in countries that have recently experienced a democratic transition. Yet, there are several reasons political participation – particularly nonvoting participation – might play a crucial role in democracy's survival after initial elections. In unpacking the relationship between political participation and democracy's survival, one must consider three issues. First, political liberalization expands citizens' opportunities for political participation. Second, the threat of authoritarian backsliding remains particularly high until all groups accept new democratic institutions and norms as the primary venue for resolving conflicts. Last, the effect of socialization under authoritarianism may influence citizens' likelihood to participate in politics after democratization.

When analyzing political liberalization, scholars have generally focused on institutional effects, overlooking the broadening of opportunities for mass political participation that emerge after a democratic transition. While the expansion of possible forms of participation varies across polities, at least two new arenas are generated. First, political liberalization opens electoral competition to a broader range of actors, enabling individuals to form, join, and support political parties that were not previously allowed. Second, a relaxation of controls on speech and association broadens opportunities for airing public criticism of elite actions, such as writing critical media articles and engaging in peaceful demonstrations.

The hallmark of a democratic transition is the completion of an initial round of fair and free elections (O'Donnell & Schmitter, 1986). For democracy to survive after the first election, political elites must hold fair and free elections at regular intervals. Yet the governing periods between elections give newly elected elites chances to undermine the civil liberties and procedures designed to ensure that subsequent elections will be fair and free. Under these circumstances, political liberalization requires ongoing citizen oversight between elections to hold elites accountable, which is accomplished via elite-constraining political participation.

How can political participation constrain elites? First, participation in the development of opposition political parties promotes competition. Campaigning for a specific candidate or party, carrying out tasks related to the party's work, or attending a rally are activities that spread information about potential governing elites, thereby making elections more competitive. It is important to recognize that the intent behind individuals' decisions to undertake these actions does not affect their status as elite-constraining. People could be paid party canvassers or attend rallies out of curiosity rather than to convey support. What makes the actions elite-constraining is that they foster a competitive political environment and convey that citizens have alternatives to sitting officeholders. In the classic typology on dimensions and modes of political activity elaborated by Sidney Verba, Norman Nie, and Jae-on Kim, campaign activity is considered "high pressure" and "conflictual" (1978, p. 55). Without feasible opposition on the political scene, governing elites do not face a credible threat of removal from political power.

Second, acts of contentious politics raise awareness about policy disagreements and draw attention to elites' misconduct. These acts are inherently public in nature and attract the attention of both citizens and elites. Public scrutiny constrains elites, who must consider how acts of contentious politics might affect their political livelihoods. Writing critical letters or articles for publication in mass media, though not a form of contentious politics, constrains elites in a similar way – by facilitating public awareness and scrutiny of elites' actions. Additionally, demonstrations, civil disobedience, and citizen oversight activities can send important signals to opposition leaders about their potential bases of support. Such signals help foster an organized opposition, which is necessary if elections are to remain competitive. These tasks are all elite-constraining.

Not all forms of political participation inherently constrain elites. Some activities enable elites to maintain and even expand their political authority. The Russian public, for example, did not simply withdraw from political participation. Rather, as this chapter demonstrates, Russians engaged heavily in elite-enabling behavior, which has empowered Russian political leaders who do not adhere to the letter or spirit of democratic institutions.

One form of elite-enabling behavior is particularized contacting of public officials. According to the Verba-Nie-Kim typology, contacting is a "low-pressure" and "nonconflictual" form of participation (1978, p. 55). In a democracy, elected officials are responsible for representing their constituents' interests, both through policymaking and providing basic constituent services. In theory, when elected officials do this work effectively, their constituents reward them with reelection. When they represent their constituents poorly, they are voted out. In this context, contacting representatives is a way the public can hold the government accountable. Yet citizen contact with public officials is not exclusive to democracies. All political regimes require some mechanism for soliciting feedback in order to diffuse social pressure and to ensure popular compliance with regime commands.[4] A political representative can respond positively to a constituent appeal, thus generating support for the representative, but not necessarily behave in a way that promotes democratic institutions. Consequently, contacting is essentially elite-enabling – it can generate the resource of public support for a representative to use without necessarily strengthening democracy.

Some forms of political participation can be alternately elite-constraining or elite-enabling depending on the context. Participatory acts related to party-building and elections shift from being elite-constraining to elite-enabling based on the party or candidate supported. Political party work is elite-constraining when it is aimed at building opposition. Yet, when carried out in support of a hegemonic party, campaigning for a candidate, party-building, and attending party rallies are elite-enabling. Similarly, votes against incumbents aim to constrain them, while votes for them are enabling.

Additionally, violent contentious acts, such as riots, armed incursions, and terrorism are not always elite-constraining. While such actions challenge incumbent supremacy, their violent nature generally compels custodians of power to exercise considerable authority to maintain public order and protect civilians. In such scenarios, elites can be either constrained or empowered depending on public opinion about the violence and how it is managed. For example, as described in Chapter 2, Boris Yeltsin's handling of the 1991 coup attempt in Moscow strengthened his political power.

Neither the Soviet Union nor New Order Indonesia permitted the kinds of conventional and contentious political participation that occur in democracies. Throughout most of Soviet history, individuals could vote in local council elections, but these elections were uncontested and amounted to validating the single CPSU-approved candidate. Although elections in New Order Indonesia featured multiple parties, coercion

---

[4] For example, see discussion of filing complaints in China in Chen (2008), Dimitrov (2010), O'Brien and Li (1995, pp. 756–783), and Thireau and Linshan (2003, pp. 83–103).

and severe restrictions on party activity ensured Golkar victories, and Suharto never faced an opponent in executive elections. While voting and contacting were available under the authoritarian and democratizing regimes in Russia and Indonesia, meaningful development of opposition parties, competitive campaigns, and nonviolent demonstrations are forms of political activism that became permissible only after political liberalization.

As post-Soviet Russia and post-Suharto Indonesia demonstrate, individuals in a democratizing country often have meaningful experience with political participation, albeit in an authoritarian context. Consequently, the forms of participation and citizens' expectations of their usefulness likely differ from what we see in established democracies. We must consider this participatory legacy when analyzing recently democratized countries, even though most of our theories about participation in democracies do not account for the influence of previous regime type. Citizens in new democracies do not approach political participation devoid of expectations. Rather, they have been socialized by the experience of living under authoritarianism and participating in mobilized politics.

Socialization under authoritarianism could influence citizens' participation after a democratic transition in several ways. First, past behavior frequently conditions future behavior. For example, if an individual voted in the past, she is more likely to vote in the future (Campbell, 2006; Fowler, 2006; Gerber, Green, & Shachar, 2003; Jennings & Niemi, 1981; Plutzer, 2002). Likewise, if an individual avoided political confrontation in the past, he is less likely to invite it in the future. We can envision how this behavioral axiom might unfold in voting. Classical democratic theory assumes people vote according to their preferences. Yet, if individuals are habituated to voting in elections without choices, they might be more inclined to vote at random or vote out of a sense of patriotism or duty than to express their political preferences. Similarly, people's expectations of how the government will respond to citizen actions are also conditioned by past experiences. Perceptions that certain acts (such as circulating petitions, writing letters to the media, or holding peaceful demonstrations) are dangerous or inefficacious do not change immediately when a regime changes. Thus, we have little reason to expect that people will embrace these acts as regular, recurring forms of participation in the early years of a democratic regime.

In sum, the effect of socialization under authoritarianism creates a paradox for political participation in democratizing regimes. After experiencing authoritarianism and mobilization politics, individuals in new democracies are likely cautious about engaging in expanded forms of political participation, such as supporting opposition parties and staging acts of contentious politics. Yet, if the level of voluntary participation in opposition party development and citizen oversight does not increase following the introduction of fair and free elections, new institutions become vulnerable to elite abuse. Left unchecked, leaders of nascent democracies (most of whom were themselves socialized in an authoritarian regime) can undermine the electoral process in numerous ways, such as restricting the circulation of information, blocking the development of opposition parties, and misusing state resources to ensure popular support for incumbents (Levitsky & Way, 2010).Participation in elite-constraining activities, such as political party development, citizen oversight activities, and contentious politics, keep political elites' antidemocratic behavior in check. These acts facilitate political competition and sustain democratization. Indonesia has experienced this outcome. Indonesians embraced new opportunities for political participation, pouring energy into the development of a competitive political party system and a robust protest movement. These tasks placed political elites under considerable public scrutiny and prevented them from undermining newly acquired democratic institutions. Consequently, elections have remained competitive in Indonesia and contributed to democracy's survival.

In contrast, if elite-enabling participation – such as contacting public officials – remains the only vigorous form of nonvoting political participation in a democratizing regime, it is more difficult for competitive political opposition to develop, and public scrutiny of elite actions remains minimal. Under these circumstances, elites are well positioned to rescind democratic reforms. I argue that this dynamic in Russia – citizens' reliance on contacting public officials and their failure to expand into other forms of political participation – explains how the country's fledgling democracy reverted to authoritarianism a decade after political liberalization. Empowered by high levels of popularity and left unchecked, the Kremlin under Vladimir Putin clamped down on freedom of speech and assembly, raised barriers to political party development and civil society organization, and intimidated potential sponsors of the opposition. It accomplished these tasks with public quiescence because Russians, on the whole, had not embraced elite-constraining acts.

The remainder of this chapter uses public opinion data and original interviews to demonstrate how elite-enabling patterns of political participation predominated in post-Soviet Russia, while elite-constraining participation was more prevalent in post-Suharto Indonesia.

Measuring Political Participation

Political participation is a behavior, not an attitude. Because participation requires a physical act, we might expect it to be relatively easy to measure. The only form of participation that lends itself to simple measurement, however, is voting. In any given election, an official body has a register of all eligible voters and tallies all votes cast. Yet there is no centralized way of gathering information about the number of letters or phone calls public officials receive, the number of volunteers or paid staff involved in political campaigns, or the number of individuals who attend political protests. In order to investigate nonvoting political participation, we must rely on self-reported activities captured in public opinion surveys.

Lack of comparable survey data creates an obstacle to analyzing nonvoting political participation across countries and over time. Fortunately, numerous, high-quality public opinion surveys have been conducted in Russia dating back to the end of the Soviet period. Russians' attitudes and behaviors have been documented and analyzed to a much greater extent compared to other political communities that have experienced political transition in the past twenty-five years. Questions about Russian political participation have varied across surveys, however, making it difficult to compare results over time. Although Russian surveys rarely focused on nonvoting political participation, several included relevant questions. I draw on information from three sets of surveys – the World Values Survey (WVS), the Russian Election Study (RES), and the Survey of Soviet Values (SSV). The WVS allows us to look at changes in contentious politics from 1990 to 2006, the RES measures participation in conventional political acts from 1995 to 2004, and the SSV gives us a baseline of conventional activity in 1990, near the end of the Soviet era.

Examining nonvoting political participation in Indonesia, however, is more problematic due to the absence of data. In Indonesia, few surveys of any kind exist, and most of those that do are not publicly available for scholarly analysis. The cross-national surveys that include Russia and Indonesia offer only a few questions on acts of contentious politics, leaving us with no direct comparative data for campaign and party activities or contacting public officials. There are only two surveys I can use to analyze nonvoting political participation in Indonesia, the East Asian Barometer (EAB) and the WVS. The East Asian Barometer, which includes measures of conventional and contentious political participation, has been conducted over two stages in several Asian countries (including Indonesia in the second wave in 2006).⁵ The WVS, which includes measures of contentious politics, surveyed Indonesia in 2001 and 2005.

In addition to these surveys, I also rely on information gathered through my interviews with fifty Russian and fifty Indonesian citizens.

Nonvoting Political Participation in Russia and Indonesia

Conventional Participation in Russia

The SSV and the RES provide indicators for examining conventional participation in Russia. Since it was conducted in 1990, the SSV measures Russian political participation prior to democratization. The principal investigators of the study (James L. Gibson and Raymond M. Duch) used a four-stage stratified random sampling technique to establish a respondent pool that would be representative of the European territories of the USSR. Among the respondents, 59.8 percent (N = 933) resided in Russia. While this sample cannot claim to be representative of the territory that currently comprises the Russian Federation, it is among the best available surveys for measuring political attitudes and behaviors in the late Soviet period.

The SSV includes two measures of nonvoting conventional participation that establish a baseline for considering Russians' level of participation during the late Soviet period after *glasnost'*. A sizeable percentage of survey respondents answered "yes" to two separate questions about contacting public officials at various levels of government.⁶ In sum, 27.9 percent of respondents living in Russia had contacted a government official. Few cross-national public opinion surveys ask questions about contacting public officials, making it impossible for us to gauge Russia compared to other countries. But a study of political participation conducted in seven countries several years earlier found a range of particularized contacting of between 2 percent in Nigeria to 38 percent in

---

⁵ Information about the surveys and an online data analysis tool are available at www .jdsurvey.net/eab/eab.jsp. The raw Indonesian survey data were received after submitting an application.

⁶ The survey asks, "Have you ever personally gone to see, or spoken to, or written to some member of the local authorities or some other person of influence in the community about some need or problem?" and "What about some representatives or government officials outside of the Raion area – on the city, regional, republic or all-union level? Have you ever contacted or written to such a person on some need or problem?"

the Netherlands (Verba et al., 1978). Among the countries included in the study, Yugoslavia was the only one with a Communist regime, exhibiting a contacting rate of 20 percent.

There is no way to establish a precise measure for party development work in the late Soviet period, especially since the Communist Party was the only party allowed to compete in the 1989 elections for the Congress of People's Deputies and the 1990 election for the Russian parliament (Hale, 2006, pp. 29–31). So-called public organizations, which often supported independent candidates, were allowed to compete in these elections, but these groups are better understood as either organized aspects of civil society or political movements (Fish, 1995). As Henry Hale (2006) has argued, while the 1990 races for the Russian parliament were indeed competitive, they featured little political organization or coordinated activity outside of CPSU structures. Many of these groups did engage in acts of political participation, however, such as volunteering for campaigns.

How did conventional political participation change after the collapse of the Soviet Union? The RES, initiated by Timothy Colton and other collaborators in 1995–1996, provides several measures for participation in conventional political activities from 1995 to 2004. Modeled on the American National Election Study, the RES initially conducted a three-wave panel survey in parallel with Russia's national election cycle.[7] I use data from the surveys conducted in 1995–1996, 1999–2000, and 2003–2004. The 1995–1996 survey includes a starting sample of 2,841 respondents, the 1999–2000 survey starts with 1,919 respondents, and the 2003–2004 sample starts with 1,648 respondents. The RES is a useful instrument for measuring political participation since the question wording is generally consistent between the different years.

The RES provides measures for both party development work and contacting. First, the survey asks respondents four questions about participation in both Duma and presidential electoral campaigns. Respondents are asked if they participated in the collection of signatures, supported or organized an electoral campaign, attended an election rally or assembly, or donated money to a campaign. Table 3.1 reports the results for participation in the 1995–1996, 2000–2001, and 2003 election campaigns.[8]

---

[7] Respondents were interviewed before the December Duma elections, after the Duma elections, and after the springtime presidential elections. The 2003–2004 RES included only two survey waves, eliminating the first preelection survey due to budgetary constraints.

[8] The 2003–2004 survey asks only about the Duma campaign and does not ask about collection of signatures.

TABLE 3.1. *Participation in Campaign Work in Russian Election Study*

	1995 Duma Campaign (%)	1996 Presidential Campaign (%)	1999 Duma Campaign (%)	2000 Presidential Campaign (%)	2003 Duma Campaign (%)
Participate in collection of signatures	2.8 (N = 2,768)	4.0 (N = 2,450)	2.6 (N = 1,838)	2.0 (N = 1,747)	—
Agitate or otherwise help in the organization of an electoral campaign	2.9 (N = 2,766)	3.3 (N = 2,450)	2.1 (N = 1,838)	1.7 (N = 1,746)	4.0 (N = 1,637)
Attend any election rallies or assemblies	4.1 (N = 2,771)	4.5 (N = 2,451)	5.6 (N = 1,838)	3.7 (N = 1,747)	5.5 (N = 1,638)
Donate money to an election campaign	0.1 (N = 2,771)	0 (N = 2,453)	0.1 (N = 1,838)	0.2 (N = 1,747)	0.2 (N = 1,639)
Engaged in at least one of the above activities	7.9 (N = 2,764)	7.9 (N = 2,449)	7.8 (N = 1,838)	5.8 (N = 1,746)	7.6[†] (N = 1,637)

† Includes agitating, attending rallies, and donating money.

Table 3.1 shows several broad trends in campaign and party development work that are consistent across elections. The most common form of participation is attending election rallies or assemblies, followed by collecting signatures, agitating or organizing a campaign, and donating money. One way to look at levels of participation is to consider the percentage of individuals who engaged in at least one of these activities. This percentage remained rather constant at 7.9 percent across elections until the presidential election of 2000, when it dropped to 5.8 percent.[9]

Participation levels returned to more than 7 percent in the 2003 Duma elections.[10] The percentage of individuals agitating reached its highest level in 2003 (4 percent), and the percentage of individuals attending rallies also returned to a level of more than 5 percent after falling in 2000. In fact, participation in these two activities is highly correlated for 2003 (r = 0.40). In probing this small resurgence of activism more closely, an interesting pattern emerges. If we look at the vote choice of individuals who engaged in preelection activities in 2003, we find that more than 50 percent of those who campaigned or rallied voted for the pro-Kremlin United Russia party, and almost 80 percent of individuals who engaged in one of these acts voted for Putin in the 2004 election. These patterns suggest that most surveyed individuals who engaged in party development in the early 2000s were not building opposition parties, but carrying out work in support of Putin's regime. In other words, their activities were elite-enabling, not elite-constraining.

Did the same people tend to participate in multiple activities or campaigns in Russia during this period? Within each election, participation in different forms of campaign work is correlated, although the strength of the correlation varies from election to election. The acts that are most highly correlated across elections are collecting signatures and supporting or organizing a campaign. Curiously, the individuals who participated in preelection activities for the Duma are not necessarily the same individuals who engaged in presidential campaign activities. While both the Duma and presidential campaigns in 1995–1996 attracted political participation from 7.9 percent of respondents, the percentage who participated in either is much higher at 14.5. In 1999–2000, 11.0 percent

[9] This drop might be related to the unusual timing of this election, which took place three months ahead of the anticipated election schedule as a result of President Yeltsin's surprise resignation on December 31, 1999.

[10] Because the question about participating in the collection of signatures was not asked in the 2003 survey, it is possible that the statistic of 7.6 percent underestimates the percentage of citizens who engaged in preelection participation.

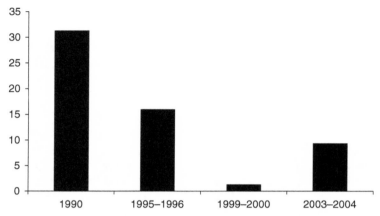

FIGURE 3.1. Percentage of survey respondents who contacted public officials, 1990–2004.

of respondents engaged in either the Duma or presidential campaigns. The decline in activism between these two election periods is statistically significant.[11]

What about contacting? Analyzing patterns in contacting over time is more challenging as the number and wording of survey questions on contacting have varied over successive waves of the RES. Figure 3.1 shows the percentage of respondents who engaged in some form of contacting over time, based on available indicators. The statistics in Figure 3.1 suggest that contacting has declined considerably since the late Soviet era. Due to the variability in number of indicators and question wording for each of these measures, we cannot view these statistics as precise measures, only as general proxies for contacting practices.[12]

---

[11] A Welch's two-sample T-test found the difference in percentages of the population participating in either campaign in 1995–1996 and 1999–2000 to be statistically significant at p < 0.001 (t = 3.98).

[12] Generally speaking, we would expect that the more questions asked about contacting, the broader the cross-section of activities citizens will report engaging in. When a survey includes only one question about contacting, such as the 1999–2000 RES, we cannot say with certainty that the increase in contacting levels in 2003–2004 is not the result of a broader number of activities the survey is capturing. In order to circumvent differences in number of indicators, we can look at the RES questions asking specifically about contacting one's Duma representative, which show the following percentages of contacting: 4.5 percent in 1995–1996, 1.3 percent in 1999–2000, and 4.5 percent in 2003–2004. The number of individuals seeking out the specific aid of their Duma representatives did not increase from the mid-1990s to the mid-2000s.

Based on the RES measures for party development work and contacting, we see a mixed picture of conventional Russian political participation over the second half of the 1990s. Generally speaking, party
development appears to have declined slightly between 1996 and 2003.
We did not see an expansion of participation in political parties or campaigns as Russians gained experience with elections. In fact, we saw a
contraction. Moreover, as the foregoing analysis indicates, evidence suggests that by 2003, most Russians engaging in party development work
were supporting the party in power – an elite-enabling activity – not seeking to broaden political competition. While we cannot compare change
over time in precise terms, the percentage of Russians contacting public
officials appears to have declined substantially since 1990.

The RES data show no meaningful correlation between people who
engage in party development and people who contact public officials.
Additionally, the 1995–1996 RES data show that the correlation between
acts of conventional and contentious politics is also weak, suggesting that
those who engage in conventional acts are not necessarily inclined to
partake in contentious acts and vice versa.[13] In total, 26.1 percent of
respondents participated in some form of nonvoting conventional participation in 1995–1996, dropping to 12.0 percent in 1999–2000 and
increasing to 16.5 percent in 2003–2004. If we look back to our only
solid measure of conventional participation from the 1990 SSV, contacting government representatives (27.9 percent), it appears that participation in conventional activities declined between 1990 and 2004. In sum,
even though political liberalization created opportunities for party development work, Russians did not embrace this activity on a large scale.
Moreover, it appears that their engagement in the most prominent form
of conventional participation – contacting – declined during this period
of political opening.

Contentious Politics in Russia

Data from the WVS, a cross-national survey conducted in more than
eighty countries on every continent in five waves since 1981, allow us
to investigate Russian engagement in contentious politics. Russia has
been included in four iterations of the WVS: 1990 (N = 1,961), 1995
(N = 2,040), 1999 (N = 2,500), and 2006 (N = 2,033). The WVS asks
several questions about contentious acts, including signing petitions,

---

[13] The strongest correlations among the Russian data are between signing petitions and
rallying for the Duma (r = 0.14) and demonstrating and rallying for the Duma (r = 0.13).

attending lawful demonstrations, joining in boycotts, and occupying buildings (WVS Integrated Questionnaire, questions E025, E026, E027, and E029).

Table 3.2 shows the percentage of Russian respondents who have engaged in these acts. Unfortunately, an imprecise translation of the word "demonstration" in the WVS Russian-language survey reduces the validity of this question as a measure for evaluating contentious politics. The Russian-language questionnaire uses the term *demonstratsiya* for "demonstrations," a word more commonly associated with the pro-regime demonstrations and parades held in the Soviet Union in commemoration of May Day and the October Revolution. Joining these "demonstrations" is an example of the mobilized political participation that was common in the Soviet Union. It is likely that many respondents, when answering this question, were thinking about participation in these sorts of demonstrations, not in acts of peaceful political protest – which is usually expressed in Russian with the word *miting*.[14] Bearing this difference in mind, we must approach the WVS data on demonstrations with caution. Indeed, for all four WVS waves the Russian level of participation in lawful demonstrations is higher than the global average, which is suspicious. It seems likely that this question captures recollections of the mobilized demonstrations of the Soviet era rather than genuine, contemporary political protest. Nevertheless, it is worth taking into account as a measure of nonvoting political participation.

The WVS presents some interesting trends. First, leaving aside the question about attending demonstrations, petition signing is the most common form of contentious politics Russians engage in, and this holds across all four waves of the survey. This pattern is consistent with the results of the 1995–1996 RES questions on contentious politics. It is also true of the WVS global averages, which range from a low of 26.1 percent of all survey respondents signing petitions in the last survey wave to a high of 43.1 percent of all survey respondents signing petitions in the

---

[14] Several questions from the 1995–1996 RES provide useful measures to validate the WVS responses. The 1995–1996 RES asked if respondents had ever "signed a declaration, announcement, or petition," "participated in a demonstration against the actions of the government," or "joined a boycott." In contrast to the WVS, the RES used the word *miting* to articulate "demonstration." The RES found that 7.7 percent of respondents signed a petition; 1.7 percent participated in an antigovernment demonstration, and 0.3 percent joined a boycott. While the WVS found higher levels of participation for all of these acts in 1995, the only instance in which the difference is dramatic is for demonstrations. The 2003–2004 RES asks respondents if they have "taken part in a protest, march or demonstration" in the past five years. Only 1.7 percent of respondents answered "yes."

TABLE 3.2. *Participation in Contentious Politics in Russia (WVS)*

	1990 (%)	1995 (%)	1999 (%)	2006 (%)
Signed petition	29.6	10.8	11.7	8.2
	(N = 1,756)	(N = 1,906)	(N = 2,335)	(N = 1,893)
Attended lawful	33.0	21.1	23.9	15.4
demonstrations	(N = 1,814)	(N = 1,943)	(N = 2,405)	(N = 1,922)
Joined in boycotts	4.4	2.3	2.5	2.4
	(N = 1,669)	(N = 1,908)	(N = 2,325)	(N = 1,891)
Occupied a	0.8	0.5	0.7	–
building[a]	(N = 1,641)	(N = 1,900)	(N = 2,306)	
Engaged in signing	34.5	12.4	13.6	9.7[c]
petition, joining	(N = 1,601)	(N = 1,817)	(N = 2,196)	(N = 1,861)
boycotts, or				
occupying a				
building[b]				

[a] This question was not asked in the Fifth Wave.
[b] Attending demonstrations is excluded from this measure due to the questionable validity of the measure as a result of an inaccurate translation into Russian language.
[c] Includes only signing a petition or joining in boycotts.

1989–1993 survey wave. Yet, as discussed earlier, there is only a minimal distinction in democratic political contexts between signing a petition and writing a letter to a political leader. In some respects, we might consider petition signing in these polities as another form of contacting.

Second, acts of contentious politics in Russia are only weakly correlated, suggesting that different individuals tend to participate in different forms of contentious action. The strongest correlation exists between signing petitions and joining boycotts.[15] Last, we see a gradual decline in acts of contentious politics in Russia. In 1990, nearly 30 percent of Russians recalled having signed a petition. By 2006, only 8.2 percent did. In 1990, more than one-third of the Russian population recalled signing petitions, joining boycotts, or occupying buildings. By 2006, fewer than one in ten individuals reported engaging in these activities. With the exception of attending lawful demonstrations, Russian averages for all other forms of activities are lower than the WVS averages for each year the survey was conducted. For example, the percentage of all WVS respondents engaging in boycotts ranged from 8.2 to 9.6 percent over the four survey waves, while in Russia the percentage never exceeded 4.4.

[15] r = 0.19 in 1990; r = 0.27 in 1995; r = 0.30 in 1999; and r = 0.23 in 2006.

Conventional and Contentious Participation in Indonesia

The absence of public opinion data at the end of the New Order period prevents us from establishing a benchmark for Indonesian nonvoting participation at the onset of democratization. Secondary scholarship, however, can help fill some gaps.

The most comprehensive analysis of political participation in Indonesia to date was conducted by Saiful Mujani at the Center for the Study of Islam and Society (Pusat Pengkajian Islam dan Masyarakat, PPIM) at the State Islamic University in Jakarta. Under Mujani's leadership, PPIM conducted two large-scale surveys in 2001 and 2002 that are close to nationally representative.[16] Mujani analyzes the results of these surveys in his doctoral dissertation, *Religious Democrats: Democratic Culture and Muslim Political Participation in Post-Suharto Indonesia* (2003). Mujani's dissertation statistics provide the best baseline for evaluating both conventional and contentious mass participation during Indonesian democratization's early years, but one caveat is in order. Because Mujani's research question focused on the relationship between Islam and democracy, his analysis only includes respondents who self-identify as Muslim. While this group includes nearly 90 percent of Indonesians, the inclusion of Christians, Hindus, Buddhists, and other religious minorities might change these baseline figures.

Mujani's findings offer an insightful, if partial, picture of nonvoting political participation.[17] On the whole, the activity that engages the largest percentage of Indonesians is campaign and party development work – participation that is elite-constraining. According to the PPIM surveys, 30 percent of Indonesians attended campaign events and 13 percent distributed leaflets for candidates or parties. Ten percent of Indonesians engaged in contacting a public official and 7 percent protested. Because these data are aggregate percentages, there is no way to ascertain whether the same individuals are participating in multiple types of activities. We should anticipate some overlap, for example, between individuals engaged in campaign and party promotion activities. But, ultimately, it is clear that a relatively vibrant participatory life had taken root in Indonesia

---

[16] Mujani writes that the 2001 survey represented 87 percent of the country's national population, while the 2002 survey covers the full population with the exception of Maluku (2003, p. 51). The sample sizes of the two surveys are N = 2,012 for the 2001 survey and N = 2,321 for the 2002 survey.

[17] Mujani also analyzes participation in community meetings and working to solve community problems in his measures of political participation. These are excluded here due to their potential overlap with indicators of civil society.

during the first four years following Suharto's resignation, offering several potential constraints on elite actions.

The East Asian Barometer (EAB), conducted in Indonesia in 2006, allows us to investigate conventional and contentious political participation almost a decade after democratization began. The EAB asks several questions that measure contacting, party development work, and contentious politics. On contacting, a three-part question asks whether individuals have ever contacted a "government employee," "a government official who is higher up," or "an elected official, such as a member of the DPR, DPRD, or president" (EAB Questionnaire Indonesia). I use the latter two parts of this question to measure contacting. I exclude the first part because its wording, which does not specify making a complaint or seeking specialized assistance, makes it impossible to determine whether individuals who answered "yes" to contacting a "government employee" (*pegawai pemerintah*) were engaging in political participation or simply trying to receive a standard service that requires bureaucratic interaction, such as obtaining an identification card. Indeed, 50 percent of respondents answered "yes" to this question, which seems remarkably high unless it includes people who interacted with bureaucrats regarding routine matters.

The EAB includes two questions about campaigning and party development work, asking whether individuals attended any campaign events and whether they helped or worked for a campaign or party in 2004, the year of the most recent national elections prior to the survey.

The survey also asks two questions that measure contentious politics. The first asks whether individuals attended a demonstration or protest march. The second asks whether they had ever used force or violence for a political cause. Unfortunately, the EAB does not have a clean indicator to measure petition signing. The survey includes a question that asks whether individuals have ever "gotten together with others to raise a public issue and sign a collective statement (petition),"[18] yet this wording suggests a level of organization that is much more involved than signing a petition organized by others. The question wording is also ambiguous regarding the object of the collective action. It is conceivable that a person answering "yes" to this question could have in mind a simple apolitical neighborhood or community activity, such as establishing guidelines

---

[18] In the Indonesian language: "Bersama-sama warga lain mengangkat sebuah masalah yang menjadi kepentingan umum dan menandatangani sebuah pernyataan bersama (petisi)."

for holiday celebrations. Due to this question's ambiguity, I am excluding it from analysis.

Table 3.3 displays the percentages of Indonesian EAB respondents who participated in each of these activities. The second column provides the percentages of individuals who participated in the specific acts listed, while the third column provides the overall percentages of individuals who engaged in the categories of contacting, party development work, and contentious politics. Party development work had the largest percentage of respondents, as nearly 27 percent of survey respondents had participated in some sort of campaign or party work during the 2004 election season. In particular, nearly 24 percent of respondents had attended a campaign activity or rally held by a party or candidate.

The second most common form of participation was contacting, followed by contentious acts. Generally speaking, these numbers are similar to those in Mujani's analysis of the 2001–2002 PPIM surveys. In both the PPIM and EAB surveys, party development work was the category of nonvoting participation that drew the largest percentage of Indonesians. Due to differences in question wording and Mujani's exclusion of non-Muslim respondents from his analysis, we cannot say whether the slightly lower percentages of participation found in the EAB constitute a genuine decline or are a consequence of question wording and sample factors.

In total, 42 percent of the EAB respondents engaged in some form of nonvoting participation. The 649 individuals who engaged in at least one nonvoting act averaged 1.6 acts. Among respondents, 35 percent had only ever engaged in conventional acts of political participation, 2 percent had only ever engaged in contentious acts, and 5 percent reported participating in both. The EAB data suggest that Indonesians are engaging in conventional forms of democratic participation while also continuing to protest policies they dislike. On the whole, as in the Russian data, engagement in conventional and contentious political participation is only weakly correlated.[19] Elite-constraining forms of participation predominate: 20 percent of Indonesians have contacted public officials, but nearly 27 percent have engaged in party work and almost 7 percent have been involved in contentious acts.

---

[19] The strongest correlations are between activities within the same subcategory. The strongest correlation among all acts is between responses to the two questions about contacting higher-level officials and contacting elected officials ($r = 0.44$).

TABLE 3.3. *Nonvoting Political Participation in Indonesia (EAB 2006)*

	Percentage	Percentage per subcategory
Contacting		20.2
Contacted officials at a higher level	18.1 (N = 1,595)	(N = 1,590)
Contacted elected representatives in the DPR, DPRD, or the president	8.1 (N = 1,589)	
Campaign and party development work		26.8
Attended a campaign activity held by a party or candidate in 2004	23.6 (N = 1,585)	(N = 1,585)
Helped or worked for a candidate or party in 2004	9.3 (N = 1,598)	
Contentious politics		6.6
Attended a demonstration or protest march	6.4 (N = 1,594)	(N = 1,586)
Used force or violence for a political cause	0.3 (N = 1,585)	
Total		
Engaged in at least one of the above forms of participation		41.8 (N = 1,575)

Note: The statistics in this table are taken from the following EAB questions: Q074, "In the past three years, have you never, once, or more than once contacted officials at a higher level because of personal, family, or neighborhood problems, or problems with government officials and policies?" Q075, "In the past three years, have you never, once, or more than once contacted elected representatives in the DPR, DPRD or the president because of personal, family, or neighborhood problems, or problems with government officials and policies?" Respondents who answered "once" or "more than once" are included in the statistics for the previous two questions; EAB question Q029, "During the election campaigns in 2004, did you attend a campaign activity held by a party or candidate?" Q031, "During the election campaigns in 2004, did you help or work for a candidate or party?" Respondents answering "yes" are included in the statistics for the previous two questions; QII88, "Here is a list of actions that people sometimes take as citizens. For each of these, please tell me whether you, personally, have never, once, or more than once done any of these things during the past three years." Respondents reporting that they "attended a demonstration or protest march" are included in this statistic; QII89, "Here is a list of actions that people sometimes take as citizens. For each of these, please tell me whether you, personally, have never, once, or more than once done any of these things during the past three years." Respondents reporting that they "used force or violence for a political cause" are included in this statistic.

The WVS from 2001 and 2006 allows us to look at change in contentious political behavior in Indonesia over time (see Table 3.4). Several trends are worth noting. First, we see that a larger percentage of Indonesians report attending lawful demonstrations than report signing petitions or engaging in other contentious political acts. Second, the

TABLE 3.4. *Indonesian Participation in Contentious Politics (WVS)*

	2001 (%)	2006 (%)
Signed petition	5.4	6.1
	(N = 866)	(N = 1,758)
Attended lawful demonstrations	11.4	14.0
	(N = 934)	(N = 1,856)
Joined in boycotts	2.9	3.5
	(N = 939)	(N = 1,796)
Occupied a building[a]	4.0	–
	(N = 922)	
Engaged in signing petition, demonstrating, boycotts, or occupying buildings	16.4	18.8[b]
	(N = 876)	(N = 1,768)

[a] This question was not asked in the Fifth Wave.
[b] Includes only signing a petition, demonstrating, or boycotting.

percentages of Indonesians engaging in all forms of contentious political acts increase over time. In 2001, 16.4 percent of respondents engaged in at least one form of contentious politics, while in 2006 the figure had increased slightly to 18.8 percent. Last, the percentage of WVS respondents reporting engagement in protest behavior is considerably higher than the percentages reported in the PPIM surveys and the EAB survey, which were conducted in the same years as the WVS. These differences may be due to variation in sample size (the WVS sample is smaller) or sampling frame (the WVS sample excluded several provinces included in the PPIM and EAB surveys). If we set aside the question of which survey provides the best measure of overall protest activity, we can say that within the population sampled in the WVS, a slight increase in contentious political activity occurred during Indonesia's first eight years of democratization.

Comparing Evidence from Public Opinion Surveys

Although there are few directly comparable survey questions for analyzing nonvoting political participation in Russia and Indonesia, we can gauge general trends in the data by considering functionally equivalent measures gathered from each survey. Table 3.5 compares the percentages of respondents in Russia and Indonesia who engaged in at least one form of nonvoting participation according to the SSV, RES, and EAB, as well as the percentages who engaged in the specific categories of contacting, campaign and party development work, and contentious politics. We must be cautious in interpreting these statistics. As mentioned earlier, question

TABLE 3.5. *Comparisons of Russian and Indonesian Nonvoting Participation*

	Russia 1990 (SSV)	Russia 1995–1996 (RES)	Russia 1999–2000 (RES)	Russia 2003–2004 (RES)	Indonesia 2006 (EAB)
Participated in any nonvoting participation (%)[a]	27.9 (N = 924)	32.5 (N = 2,399)	12.0 (N = 1,725)	17.2 (N = 1,341)	41.8 (N = 1,575)
Contacted (%)[b]	27.9 (N = 924)	16.0 (N = 2,101)	1.3 (N = 1,836)	9.4 (N = 1,321)	20.2 (N = 1,590)
Campaign and party work (%)[c]	–	14.5 (N = 2,442)	11.0 (N = 1,727)	7.6 (N = 1,637)	26.8 (N = 1,585)
Contentious politics (%)[d]	–	1.9 (N = 2,764)	–	1.7 (N = 1,489)	6.6 (N = 1,586)

[a] Includes respondents who participated in any of the nonvoting acts listed in the survey. See Tables 3.1 and 3.3 and Figure 3.1 for indicator details.

[b] Includes respondents who had answered "yes" to any of the contacting indicators listed in the survey. See Tables 3.1 and 3.3 for indicator details.

[c] Includes respondents who engaged in any of the campaign or party development indicators listed in the survey. See Tables 3.1 and 3.3 for indicator details.

[d] Includes 1995–1996 RES respondents who had reported that they had "participated in a demonstration against the actions of the government" or "joined a boycott"; 2003–2004 RES respondents who had "taken part in a protest, march, or demonstration" in the past five years; and EAB respondents who had "attended a demonstration or protest march" or "used force or violence for a political cause."

wording varied across different surveys, as did the number of questions asked about each type of activity. We would expect that a larger number of questions about specific activities would elicit a larger number of positive replies from survey respondents. The survey with the largest number of indicators is the 1995–1996 RES, while the survey with the smallest number of indicators is the 2003–2004 RES.

Bearing in mind the limitations mentioned earlier, Table 3.5 provides us with some useful comparative information. First, nonvoting political participation is much more widespread in Indonesia than in Russia. More than 40 percent of Indonesians engaged in some form of nonvoting participation in 2006, which is considerably higher than the percentage observed in any Russian survey, including the 1995–1996 RES, which asked a broad array of questions about participation. Second, participation in party development work is much higher in Indonesia than in Russia. More than one in four Indonesians reported participating in party or campaign-related activity in 2006. This percentage is higher than the level of party development work observed at any point in Russia's post-Soviet history. Last, the percentage of the population who engages in contentious politics appears to be significantly higher in Indonesia than in Russia.

Several tentative conclusions about trends in political participation following Russia's and Indonesia's introduction of democratic institutions emerge from these surveys. First, in Russia, participation in campaign and party development peaked in the mid-1990s and failed to expand after the early years of elections. Second, the practices of contacting and petitioning public officials – both common at the end of the Soviet era – appear to have declined during Russia's first post-Soviet decade. Third, participation in acts of contentious politics has dropped after peaking in the late Soviet era.

On the whole, a high percentage of Indonesians has participated in some form of nonvoting participation, and a considerable number of them have engaged in more than one type of activity. Their primary forms of engagement appear to be party development work and contacting. While we cannot say for certain whether engagement in these activities has increased since democratization began in 1998, the available data suggest that participation has not declined. We also see evidence that a stable minority of Indonesians engages in contentious political acts, especially peaceful protests. The percentage of individuals engaging in contentious activities appears to have increased slightly in the post-Suharto era. Collectively, this pluralism in nonvoting participation has resulted in a rather sizeable segment of the Indonesian population taking part in elite-constraining activities between elections.

These trends largely mirror the findings of fifty in-depth interviews I conducted with a quota sample of Russian citizens in 2008 and fifty in-depth interviews held with Indonesians in 2009.

Citizen Interviews and Dynamics of Participation

Citizen Samples and Questionnaire

This section's analysis is based on ethnographic interviews I conducted in Russia and Indonesia. In Russia, I carried out anonymous, open-ended interviews with a quota sample of twenty-five residents of Kazan and twenty-five residents of Krasnoyarsk. I repeated this process in Indonesia, conducting anonymous, open-ended interviews with a quota sample of twenty-five residents of Surabaya and twenty-five residents of Medan. During these interviews, I used a semi-structured questionnaire that gathered comparable data from all respondents. While no two citizen interviews were exactly the same, in each instance I gathered information about respondents' life histories, social and political activities, and opinions on several issues.

In order to measure citizens' participation in political life, I asked directly about their voting frequency and participation in other political activities, such as writing letters to public officials or the newspaper, visiting or calling an elected representative, campaigning for a candidate, participating in a political party, signing petitions, and demonstrating or protesting. My citizen interviews provide sketches of individuals' political participation over time. These sketches allow me to closely examine factors that influence nonvoting participation, and provide additional information that cannot be gathered from broader surveys, such as frequency of participatory activity, changes over time within the same individual, and the content of citizen appeals and petitions.

In addition to average citizens, I also interviewed more than seventy scholars, analysts, and representatives of political parties and mass voluntary organizations in Russia and more than seventy analogous figures in Indonesia. These individuals provided elite and expert perspectives on political participation in their respective countries. Both the citizen and elite interviews provide valuable information about the possible mechanisms connecting attitudes and behaviors to political participation, as well as citizens' possible motivations for choosing to engage or not engage in particular acts.

Russia: Decline in Nonvoting Participation

My citizen interviews revealed several clues about the nature of nonvoting political participation in Russia. First, consistent with the trends in the survey data, citizens in Kazan and Krasnoyarsk are more likely to engage in contacting than other forms of nonvoting political participation. Second, individuals who contact are more likely to repeat this act than people who engage in other forms of nonvoting participation. Third, the overall volume of political participation appears to have declined over time, particularly in Kazan. Last, individuals seem to choose nonvoting forms of political participation based in part on the actions they perceive as effective, a point I discuss in Chapter 6.

Nineteen of my fifty respondents[20] in Kazan and Krasnoyarsk had engaged in at least one form of nonvoting participation since 1991. Among these respondents, four had campaigned, five had protested, and thirteen had contacted public officials or signed petitions. Consistent with the survey results presented earlier, participation in these different acts is not generally correlated. Only three individuals had engaged in more than one type of nonvoting political participation. In both cities, most participation was fleeting – one campaign, one petition, or one demonstration. Nine respondents had taken part in a nonvoting activity only once.

Frequency of participation also varied across different nonvoting acts. All respondents who had engaged in a political campaign or protest since 1991 only participated in these activities once – they did not develop habits of participating. The only nonvoting political behavior respondents repeated was contacting public officials and signing petitions. For example, all individuals in Kazan who had signed a petition also engaged in some other form of personal contacting. I found that it was not uncommon for an individual who had organized a signature campaign to try multiple avenues of contacting: writing a personal letter, bringing collected signatures to the appropriate government office, and so forth. Additionally, once an individual had a positive response via contacting, she was more likely to repeat it. One thirty-two-year-old Tatar man in Kazan had written three different letters to various government representatives. A thirty-nine-year-old Russian woman in Krasnoyarsk

---

[20] While the citizen samples are not meant to be numerically representative of the Russian and Indonesian populations, I have found that some readers are interested in the frequency with which particular attitudes or behaviors appear in the samples. For this reason, I offer basic information about the number of respondents who hold specific views or engage in certain acts.

had also written three different letters to local officials. Both individuals said that they found contacting an effective way to address their specific problems. Among my respondents, individuals only engaged in protests when they felt a direct sense of personal loss. One respondent participated in protests against the 2005 reform to monetize social welfare benefits, another had attended a protest regarding the reorganization of her labor union, and others had participated in automobile drivers' protests against police misconduct.

Consistent with other survey data, my quota sample indicates that interest in nonvoting political participation has declined in Russia over time. Russian respondents frequently spoke of activities they had engaged in once or twice in the more distant past, often specifically during perestroika or the 1990s. For example, some respondents had campaigned or attended demonstrations in the late 1980s and 1990, but had not engaged in any nonvoting political participation since 1991. The few instances I found of campaign-related work in Kazan since 1991 all occurred before 2000. One thirty-nine-year-old Russian woman had actively campaigned for a coworker who competed in a regional election in 1993. The other campaign participants, a thirty-two-year-old Tatar man and a thirty-nine-year-old Tatar woman, had gathered signatures for parties seeking nomination to the State Duma. While I found examples of more sustained commitment to activism among several leaders in youth branches of Russian political parties – such as the former head of Youth Yabloko, Il'ya Yashin (M-17, interview, February 19, 2008), and one of the leaders of Tatarstan's Youth Communist Party wing (K-7, interview, March 7, 2008) – the trend among my citizen respondents was to participate in party development or contentious acts only once.

My interviews revealed considerable variation in respondents' attitudes toward nonvoting political participation. With regard to contentious politics, many respondents looked at protest activity negatively, believing that in most instances individuals were paid to participate in protests and were not expressing their own preferences. Several respondents who had participated in a protest considered this act ineffective and said that they would not participate again.

Attitudes toward campaign activity were less negative, yet individuals who had previously campaigned showed no signs of repeating this participation. Of the individuals who had engaged in campaign work since the *perestroika* era, all but one had either a personal connection to the person running for office or had engaged in paid campaign work. Interest in campaign and party development work appears to be episodic and often linked to a personal connection or monetary incentive. Of all fifty citizens I interviewed, I did not find a single individual with an ongoing commitment to or interest in helping like-minded candidates reach public office. Moreover, this lack of interest in party development work does not appear to be a consequence of the more recent decline in political openness in Russia, but dates back to the early 1990s when Russian democracy was at its peak.

In contrast to attitudes about protesting and campaigning, Russian respondents were more favorably disposed to contacting and signing petitions. Three individuals each in Kazan and Krasnoyarsk had contacted an official or signed a petition on more than one occasion, and several of them said that they would consider contacting again.

My respondents' patterns of behavior over time speak to the cumulative effects of weak elite-constraining participation and more prominent elite-enabling participation on the political regime. Russians' preference for elite-enabling forms of participation since at least the early 1990s has fostered a system where political elites can respond to constituent needs while simultaneously inhibiting political competition and avoiding electoral accountability. Russians' lack of sustained engagement in elite-constraining participation, such as opposition party development work and contentious politics, has dramatically reduced pressure on political elites to "deliver" democracy.

Indonesia: Pluralistic Participation in Parties and Protests

My interviews with Indonesian citizens also confirmed several aspects of nonvoting participation observed in the survey data. First, generally speaking, participation in conventional and contentious political activities is not correlated. Rather, different activities attract the participation of different subsets of the population. While student organizations serve as important recruiting grounds for protest politics, a broader cross-section of Indonesian society, especially less-educated citizens, are frequently drawn into political party activities. Second, Indonesians who have engaged in some form of nonvoting political participation are likely to participate in political activity on an ongoing basis. Third, although some individuals who had been active in nonvoting participation soon after regime change were no longer regular participants in political activity by 2009, a considerable number of respondents described continued engagement in conventional or contentious participation.

About one-third of my respondents in Surabaya and Medan had engaged in at least one form of nonvoting participation since Suharto's resignation in 1998. In contrast to the Russian sample, I found that a considerable number of Indonesian respondents had engaged in nonvoting political participation more than once since the end of authoritarianism. Moreover, many were regular participants. Half of the respondents in Medan and Surabaya who had engaged in any form of nonvoting participation had repeated this activity more times than they could count. The frequency of participation varied across types of activities, with protestors and contactors repeating participation more than those who had engaged in campaign and party work.

Protests attract many regular participants. Of the individuals who had protested, almost all had participated in more than one protest, and several reported protesting on a regular basis. For example, a twenty-two-year-old university student in Medan estimated that he protested about five times a year. A thirty-nine-year-old who had been involved in the labor movement in Medan recalled protesting about once per month in 1999. Ongoing participation was particularly pronounced among student activists, who tended to engage in a combination of protesting and group-based contacting. For example, when I asked one twenty-two-year-old Javanese student leader in Surabaya how often he participated in protests, he responded, "Very often. I'm waiting at any moment. It could happen three times in one week." These patterns of contentious political participation differ dramatically from those in Russia.

Similarly, all of my Indonesian respondents who had contacted a public official had done so multiple times – more than they could recall. In most instances, they would prepare a letter on behalf of a specific group and then either deliver this letter in person or follow up with an in-person appeal. In contrast to contacting in Russia, however, I found no examples of individual appeals among Indonesian respondents. In every instance in which an Indonesian respondent described contacting a public official, a group to which the respondent belonged initiated this contact. These groups included an ethnic Batak cultural group, two different student organizations, a racketeering "youth group,"[21] and a group of labor activists.

The different contacting dynamics demonstrated by my Russian and Indonesian interview samples mirror the distinction between particularized and social contacting introduced by Sidney Verba and Norman Nie (1972). Particularized contacting involves issues relevant only to the

---

[21] During the New Order regime, several state-sanctioned or military-affiliated youth groups developed reputations as *preman* – or gangster – organizations. For more background, see Ryter (2001).

constituent or his immediate family, to which a government response would have little direct impact on others in the society, whereas social contacting comprises issues that are more public in nature and affect a significant segment of the population (Verba & Nie, 1972, p. 66).

My interview data suggest that contacting in Surabaya and Medan is primarily social, reflecting an exchange between civil society groups and the state rather than an interaction between a private citizen and a public official. Consequently, for these Indonesians, the group dynamic of contacting allows this form of participation to border on elite-constraining. Because political elites are approached by groups, rather than individuals, they face a different set of constraints in choosing how to respond to these appeals.[22] Contacting in Kazan and Krasnoyarsk, meanwhile, represents a mix of both social and particularized contacting, with a stronger emphasis on the latter.

In contrast to their experiences with protesting and contacting, my Indonesian respondents exhibited greater variation in the frequency of their participation in party development work. Among the seven individuals who had engaged in some form of campaign or party work, four had done so only once. Two of these individuals once attended a campaign rally, one had handed out campaign materials for a party in exchange for cigarettes, and one had assisted in a campaign in 1999. The other three individuals described ongoing party work – a feature that was completely absent among my Russian respondents. One is an active member of the Indonesian Democratic Party of Struggle (PDI-P) who regularly engages in party development work. Another is a former PDI-P activist who had regularly assisted the party's campaigns until 2004. The third respondent has no party affiliation, but regularly attends different party rallies or carries out low-level campaign work.

These patterns of behavior can aggregate up to the societal level in ways that advance democratization. On the whole, Indonesians prefer elite-constraining forms of participation – engaging in acts of contentious politics and party development work. Even their standard approach to contacting, which takes place more commonly among groups rather than

---

[22] Curiously, I found that petition signing is not common among Indonesian respondents. One Indonesian scholar noted that many Indonesians were skeptical about signing group documents because signature campaigns were employed in earlier periods as a way to seize land from less literate populations (NS-2, interview, July 2, 2009). None of my respondents raised this point in our interviews, but the presence of such a historical memory may steer some populations away from organizing signature campaigns as a form of political participation.

individuals, approaches the elite-constraining realm. These forms of activism encourage competition among existing political elites and potential candidates. They also regularly compel political elites to respond publicly to criticism and unpopular policies, which helps ensure that democratic institutions hold elites in check.

Political Participation and Democracy's Survival

Elite-Enabling Participation in Russia

As both the survey and interview data demonstrate, Russian nonvoting political participation in the post-Soviet era has generally been elite-enabling, primarily via repeated acts of contacting. Based on information from my interviews, petition signing in the post-Soviet Russian context is more aptly described as a form of contacting than as an act of contentious politics. Most respondents described signing petitions regarding public service provisions, such as problems with local bus services or utilities. These petitions were usually designed as a general appeal to the local authorities and signatories did not view them as controversial or adversarial in nature. When I created a category combining petition signing with contacting an official via a personalized letter or office visit, three-fourths of all my Russian respondents' nonvoting political activities since 1991 involved these forms of contacting. Russians' strong preference for contacting over other forms of political participation enabled elites to garner public support without extending (or even upholding) nascent democratic institutions.

Contacting public officials regarding constituent services takes place in both democracies and non-democracies. Authoritarian regimes regularly rely on information from citizens to ensure that public satisfaction is high enough to guarantee popular compliance. The practice of contacting public officials with specific complaints was common in the Soviet Union, as seen in the SSV results earlier in this chapter. The CPSU was decentralized down to the district level, and lower-level administrators frequently fielded complaints about public services or state-sponsored social benefits. If these administrators failed to ensure the requisite services, individuals often sought redress at a higher level of jurisdiction, including direct appeals to the CPSU General Secretary (Bittner, 2003).

Contrary to popular Western perceptions, these appeals did not necessarily fall on deaf ears or lead to repression. One of my Krasnoyarsk respondents provided a colorful example of Soviet responsiveness to direct appeals when she shared the following story about how she ended up contacting public officials when her husband was sent to fight in Afghanistan:

We had nowhere to live here and ended up living in my grandmother's kitchen, where my mother also lived. We were there about six months and no one did anything for me – I went to all of the places that are supposed to manage these affairs. Then my husband wrote me a letter from Afghanistan and said, "Write to the Central Committee [of the CPSU]." And I wrote a letter directly to Brezhnev describing this and that to him, my husband is so-and-so, etc., and my children have nowhere to live, and if you cannot guarantee my children and me housing, then send my husband back from Afghanistan.... I sent the letter in the mail. And after some time I came home one day and my mother said, "The military was here. They said they'd come again or you could go yourself." I ran to the place where they deal with military housing, and they started in on me, "Why did you write there? Why didn't you come to us? You should have come to us immediately." I said, "I was already here. I came here, there, to the generals, everywhere." They gave us a two-room apartment. I did not expect this outcome.

The notion that the national leader is the protector of Russians' inherent rights and the ultimate arbiter of perceived injustices persists in post-Soviet Russia, as can be seen with Vladimir Putin's annual call-in show. This tradition began in 2001 when Putin was president, and has continued through 2016, even after Putin's move from president to prime minister in 2008.[23] The show, which allowed individuals to ask Putin questions via telephone or email, took place shortly before the New Year's holiday. The prescreened questions represented a mix of inquiries about particular policies and specific appeals to the leader regarding local-level problems. For example, the December 2009 call-in show included a live link-up with the industrial town of Pikalevo, an area that had attracted headlines earlier in the year when residents blocked off a federal highway to protest against local officials who had failed to deliver on promises of back pay from closed factories. Putin traveled to Pikalevo in June 2009 to calm the protest, chastising the owner of one of the bankrupt factories – oligarch Oleg Deripaska, who otherwise has good relations with the Kremlin – in a televised meeting in which Deripaska was forced to sign an agreement to reopen his factory. Putin reprised his role as the people's savior during the call-in show: he told Pikalevo residents that he would return to their town to sort out the situation, if necessary (Whitmore, 2009).

Direct appeals to national leaders are extreme examples of Russians' contacting public officials to address specific concerns. Moreover, the

[23] From 2001 until 2011, the event was held in December as a lead-up to the year's end. The show was not held in December 2012, but began to be held again annually in April starting in 2013.

concerns Russian citizens raise in these exchanges today are similar to the grievances registered with the CPSU in the Soviet era. For example, more than half of the public appeals my respondents in Krasnoyarsk made involved housing – a signature campaign to prevent the construction of a medical research facility next to an apartment building, a petition regarding an apartment building's heating system, and a petition against locating a police station in an apartment building. Another pragmatic constituent appeal came from university students who mounted a signature campaign requesting that the city government expand the number of bus lines serving their university's campus. In many respects, these appeals fit the description of social contacting Verba and Nie outlined (1972).

Yet, these more general forms of social contacting among my Russian respondents were similar to the directly personal appeals in a particular way: the individuals who carried them out did not view them as political participation. For example, the respondent who had organized the signature campaign against the medical facility – a fifty-two-year-old Russian woman who had previously belonged to the CPSU – was adamant that her appeals in this case involved a "private issue," not a political one. This finding is consistent with Soviet-era appeals for addressing personal problems that developed as a consequence of state policy, such as poor-quality housing or work appointments, what Wayne DeFranceisco and Zvi Gitelman term "covert participation" (1984). The view that political participation in Russia is not actually "political" extends to other forms of participation as well. In an interview with a democratic activist in Kazan, I asked about the small waves of localized protests visible across Russia in the early 2000s regarding housing issues, automobile rights, and construction-related fraud. He noted that participants in these activities do not even think about their protest activities as "politics." Rather, they are about "concrete demands" (K-5, interview, February 29, 2008).

The fact that Russians view social contacting as no different from personal appeals has potentially important implications for other forms of political participation. Verba, Nie, and Kim have found that social contacting tends to correlate with other modes of activity aimed at general social issues, such as electoral and campaign participation, while particularized contacting does not – a finding numerous cross-national studies have confirmed (1978). In connecting Verba and colleagues' finding to Soviet Russia, Roeder commented that particularized contacting does not engender or sustain the type of skills that transfer effectively to other forms of political participation, namely "an ability to empathize, generalize, abstract, or defer reward" (1989, p. 865). By 2008, the modal forms of participatory behavior among Russian citizens did not seek to constrain elites' power, but rather appeal to their good graces with hopes that elite power will enable a desirable outcome.

A reliance on contacting to mediate citizen–elite interactions in a democratizing regime opens the door for several potential outcomes, all of which have different implications for democracy's survival. When complaints (either social or particularized) are raised via contacting, the official has the opportunity to respond to the criticism as he chooses. He is not immediately placed on the defensive, and is given the opportunity to react in a manner more advantageous to his political standing. If a public official responds favorably to constituents' appeals, the constituents who issued the complaint may reward the official with electoral support. This is how democracy works in its most simple form.

Yet whether public officials' responses to constituent appeals help preserve democratic rights and freedoms depends on two other factors. First, regardless of how the official resolves the complaint, the entire process does not necessarily generate broad public attention to the official's performance. Consequently, while ongoing acts of contentious politics such as protests generate public scrutiny that can constrain elites, contacting alone does not. Second, as responsive authoritarian regimes have demonstrated, it is possible for officials to meet some public demands without strengthening democratic institutions and practices. One would expect officials who do a poor job responding to constituent demands to lose votes over time (a process we are starting to see in local Indonesian elections). But it is also possible that public officials could resolve basic local and regional management problems (such as housing and transportation) in a way that voters deem satisfactory without otherwise increasing political competition, transparency, or civil liberties. In other words, these officials can be responsive without facilitating democracy's survival. We have observed this dynamic in Putin's Russia.

Elite-Constraining Participation in Indonesia
In contrast to Russians, Indonesians' primary forms of political participation have been elite-constraining. My citizen interviews reflect evidence from public opinion surveys that Indonesians engage in party development work at a high level and are also regularly involved in acts of contentious politics. Moreover, my interviews demonstrate that a broad cross-section of Indonesian society is involved in political participation, which suggests that elite-constraining activism is not confined to a small, educated minority. Indonesian students and former students regularly

engage in acts of contentious politics, while a broader range of citizens participate in campaigns and party development work. Last, Indonesians tend to repeat these elite-constraining activities, which influences the aggregate level of political participation in the polity.

Among my citizen respondents, high levels of education strongly correlated with participation in protests and contacting. Highly educated Indonesian citizens have taken advantage of political liberalization to engage in contentious politics. They focus on activities that grab headlines, apply pressure on political elites, and influence public opinion. Their activism places constraints on the range of options political elites can pursue without losing legitimacy. While the university student population is small as a percentage of the overall population, the regularity of its protest activity translates into a situation where political elites are pressured on an ongoing basis.[24] As I discuss in Chapter 4, Indonesian students participate in civil society at a high rate and are also extremely social. Their networks facilitate political recruitment, particularly for acts of contentious politics and citizen oversight. Moreover, the cyclical nature of student life means that there is a constant influx of new students who take up the mantle of protesting as others reduce their activism.

Yet students are not the only active citizens. Others, particularly those of a lower socioeconomic status, are drawn to traditional party work and campaign activities. Among the respondents in my interview sample who had engaged in any campaign or party work, only one had a high school diploma. In fact, half of these individuals had less than an elementary school education. In contrast, none of my respondents with a university degree had participated in any campaign or party-building activities.

Indonesians with less income and education are frequently drawn into campaign work in exchange for token gifts, including cigarettes or T-shirts. Others attend campaign rallies not because they support a particular candidate, but because they hope to receive small souvenirs or are looking for entertainment. Such motivation was certainly the case for two of my respondents – one in Surabaya and one in Medan. The Surabaya respondent was a pedicab driver with an elementary school education earning less than $100 a month – a marginalized socioeconomic category. To him,

---

[24] According to the UNESCO Institute for Statistics, as of 2007 an estimated 17 percent of the Indonesian population of tertiary age is enrolled in higher education. According to data from the 2005 Inter-Census Survey in Indonesia (SUPAS), which does not make a clear distinction between students enrolled in university degree programs and those holding degrees, less than 1 percent of the Indonesian population aged nineteen and older holds tertiary degrees.

it was not important which party or candidate held a rally nearby. All that mattered was whether he might receive some free food or a T-shirt. These small tokens had more immediate material value for him than the money he might make pedaling people around in his pedicab over a two-hour period. This respondent did more than attend rallies – he voted in all elections. Therefore, while this particular individual's functional view of campaign rallies may differ from our classical notion of political participation, his attendance put him in contact with information and could trigger a positive association with a candidate or party. Regardless of one's motivations for going to a rally or campaign event, involvement in these activities – widespread among Indonesians – draws individuals into the political process and strengthens electoral competitiveness, enhancing democracy's viability.

These activities are elite-constraining as they foster political competition among potential elites and thus reinforce fair and free elections as the primary institution for holding elites accountable. New actors, including opposition candidates and parties, can expand their support base and attract new volunteers and members through these forms of interaction and participation. In turn, elections can become more competitive, making it harder for elites to avoid scrutiny or ignore critiques. Such trends replicated throughout society could have important implications for political life. Namely, if individuals from lower socioeconomic classes are not marginalized from the democratic process, but rather comprise a meaningful segment of the politically active population, there is a greater likelihood that their views will be represented in public policy and that the democratic regime will develop widespread legitimacy.

The effects of the fluid relationships between Indonesian political parties and the population are visible in the dynamism of the Indonesian party system. While party membership is not widespread in either country, the percentage of the population belonging to a political party is considerably higher in Indonesia than Russia. According to the 2005 WVS, 5.1 percent of Russian respondents reported political party membership, compared to 16.4 percent of Indonesian respondents and 16.2 percent of all WVS respondents. If we compare the most prominent opposition parties in each subnational region studied here using membership figures offered by party representatives, we see that Indonesia has a higher level of opposition party activism. For example, in Tatarstan, the Communist Party of the Russian Federation (KPRF), the most formidable opponent of the pro-Kremlin United Russia Party, had only 1,075 registered members in 2008 for a regional population of 3.8 million (roughly 0.03 percent of the population) (K-6, interview, March 1, 2008). In Krasnoyarsk, the KPRF and the nationalist Liberal Democratic Party of Russia (LDPR) each had about 5,000 members for a regional population of approximately 3 million (about 0.17 percent of the population for each party) (Kr-12, interview, November 10, 2008; Kr-13, interview, November 11, 2008). In contrast, in East Java (population 34 million), the Islamist-oriented Prosperous Justice Party (PKS) reported 60,000 card-carrying members (0.18 percent of the population), PDI-P reported 2 to 3 million members (between 5 and 9 percent of the population), and the National Awakening Party (PKB) reported 7 million members (20.6 percent of the population) (EJ-8, interview, June 6, 2009; EJ-5, interview, June 4, 2009; EJ-11, interview, June 8, 2009).

The difference in levels of participation in traditional party work between Russia and Indonesia are immediately visible when one visits regional party headquarters in the two countries. Indonesian party offices are bustling with people, even on Saturdays. In contrast, Russian party offices (other than United Russia's offices) are regularly empty or only lightly staffed. Calls to party headquarters in Russia are rarely answered, and finding party activists to interview usually requires personal connections. In short, while Russia's lack of participation in party development work has impeded the development of a robust party system, Indonesians' widespread and sustained engagement in party work has helped make political parties the centerpiece of political competition in the country.

While few of my Indonesian citizen respondents reported contacting public officials, all Indonesian political party representatives I interviewed said they receive a large number of citizen appeals. These appeals cover a broad range of topics, but often involve some form of public assistance. When asked whether citizens approach the party for assistance, a representative of the Prosperous Justice Party (PKS) in Yogyakarta said, "Almost every day there are people who come to express their aspirations. For example, there is a citizen who is sick, but does not have a public health card (KMS), and PKS will facilitate getting them one. They come to the office or to our homes or find us another way" (Y-2, interview, May 5, 2009). Officials from all political parties I interviewed shared similar stories.

These exchanges, as well as material assistance that parties occasionally provide to specific villages or neighborhoods, generate possibilities for the maintenance of patron–client relationships between political parties and local communities. Curiously, none of my fifty citizen respondents talked about approaching a party or other official for assistance with public services. While it is possible that none of my respondents had contacted a party or official for direct aid, it is also possible that they did not view these interactions as a form of political participation. Whether these interactions are political or personal, however, is of little concern to the question at hand. The fact that Indonesians contact different political parties to address their needs, as opposed to simply contacting the public officeholders, gives parties the opportunity to compete with each other for public support, whether through particularistic or programmatic approaches (Kitschelt & Wilkinson, 2007).

The broad, pluralist range of nonvoting political activities Indonesians engage in have successfully constrained elites in large part because citizens repeat them. In contrast to Russians, Indonesians show considerably more ongoing participation in elite-constraining acts. This distinction is regularly overlooked, in part because our primary instrument for studying nonvoting political participation – public opinion surveys – usually cannot capture repetition. Most survey questions ask whether an individual has ever engaged in a task, or ask about participating during a particular time frame. While these questions help us understand the overall percentage of a population who participates, it tells us nothing about whether their engagement is singular or ongoing. Such survey questions provide a cross-section for a moment in time, but cannot capture longitudinal trends within the same person.

Yet the overall amount of participation in a polity differs dramatically depending on whether 25 percent of the population engages in one political act per year or half a dozen acts per year. Take contacting, for example. Consider a situation where a legislator receives five letters from an individual representing an organized group and one letter from a private citizen. Which of the two letter writers does this legislator anticipate is following his actions more closely? Is he more likely to incur an electoral cost by ignoring the first constituent, who clearly represents multiple voters, or the second constituent, who does not? Repetitive contacting places greater constraint on a political leader than singular contacting. A similar example can be drawn from contentious politics. Which act constrains a leader more – a protest of 1,000 individuals lasting a single day, or one repeated over ten days? Repetition of nonvoting political acts draws greater public attention to political disagreements, thereby making it harder for legitimately elected leaders to behave in illegitimate ways. Indonesians' repetition of conventional and contentious acts has made it impossible for the presidents of post-Suharto Indonesia to act like Russia's Vladimir Putin. Indonesian political leaders are already aware which political moves are off the table.

Conclusion

This chapter presented several key findings. First, Russian nonvoting political participation on the whole has declined over the past twenty years while Indonesian participation has remained steady. Second, Russians have preferred contacting public officials – an elite-enabling form of participation – over the elite-constraining activities of political party development and contentious political acts that predominate in Indonesia. Third, Russians have generally participated in elite-constraining activities only once if at all, while Indonesians have developed habits of participation in party work and protest. Last, these differences in Russian and Indonesian preferences for participation have had system-level effects over time, with Russians failing to constrain political elites from rolling back democratic rights and institutions while Indonesians have held elites in check.

The following chapter will examine the underlying factors that contribute to the different patterns in political participation that have evolved in Russia and Indonesia.

4

Testing the Model

Predicting Nonvoting Political Participation

Chapter 3 discussed patterns of nonvoting political participation in Russia and Indonesia. I now turn to analyzing the factors that contribute to the variation observed in these countries. As the previous chapters have demonstrated, patterns in nonvoting political participation in Indonesia and Russia after the collapse of authoritarian regimes affected the extent to which political elites were constrained. Political liberalization in both countries transformed the political opportunity structure for citizens, as activities forbidden under authoritarianism were now permissible. In this type of environment, high levels of elite-constraining participation protect democracy, while high levels of elite-enabling participation empower officeholders to maintain popular support while weakening nascent democratic institutions. In this chapter, I examine several factors that might explain why elite-constraining participation dominates in Indonesia and elite-enabling participation is preferred in Russia. I argue that variation in engagement in civil society, feelings of political efficacy, and political trust are the primary determinants of the patterns of nonvoting participation observed in Russia and Indonesia. The remaining chapters of this book will examine each of these variables in closer detail.

In the first part of this chapter I discuss institutional constraints that may influence political participation, arguing that none of these is sufficient to explain the differences we see between Russia and Indonesia. I then estimate a series of statistical models using public opinion surveys to demonstrate that civil society engagement, a sense of political efficacy, and political trust are all robust predictors of nonvoting political participation in Russia and Indonesia. The last section of this chapter describes how the micro-level differences between Russians and Indonesians have macro-level effects on regime type.

Constraints on Political Participation

Which factors contribute to the different patterns of nonvoting political participation in Russia and Indonesia? There are two approaches to this question. The first, which has received more attention from comparative politics scholars, considers institutions and the incentives they provide for political participation. In this section, I will outline several primary arguments for how the structure of political institutions shapes the mass participatory responses described in Chapter 3. The second approach, which is more common among political behavior scholars, emphasizes diffusion of individual attributes across society and the extent to which factors such as popular attitudes influence political participation. While the institutional approach explains some of the trends in Russian and Indonesian political participation, I believe that a more complete picture emerges when we incorporate insights from the behavioralist approach, which I elaborate in the second half of this chapter and the remaining chapters of this book.

Russia scholars are quick to identify two institutional factors that may correspond to Russians' low levels of nonvoting participation. The first factor is the impact of mobilized participation from the Soviet era. Some scholars have posited that since Russian citizens are no longer required to participate in mobilized activity, they have little interest in engaging in overtly political acts. Additionally, the Soviet experience left Russians distrustful of political institutions, including political parties, thereby making them less likely to engage in party development work (Howard, 2003; White & McAllister, 2004).

While I do not dispute these observations, the political participation patterns I detected in both national-level surveys and my citizen interviews cast doubt on the notion that a history of mobilized participation serves as the primary cause of Russians' low levels of elite-constraining behavior. If Russians' participatory exhaustion and lack of trust in institutions are sufficient to explain Russians' low levels of political participation, we should see different patterns of behavior emerging. First, Russians who had greater experience with Soviet-era mobilized participation should have lower than average rates of participation in contemporary Russia. Yet both survey data and my interview evidence suggest the reverse is true. A lack of participation and cynicism is particularly pronounced among *younger* cohorts – those respondents who were socialized primarily (or exclusively) in the post-Soviet period. Second, the experience of mobilized Soviet participation does not appear to have uniformly dampened interest in voluntary participation. I encountered several respondents who did not feel forced to participate in pro-Soviet regime activities, but rather fondly remembered the sense of community this participation created. Third, the legacy of mobilized participation cannot account for the peaks observed in Russian political participation. If a history of mobilized participation dampens engagement in a free polity, we should see an increase in participation over time as the population moves away from its Soviet history and younger individuals make up a larger segment of the politically active population. Yet both contentious and conventional voluntary political acts peaked in Russia's early years of political liberalization and declined. Last, if Russian citizens inherited negative views about political participation because of their Soviet experience, why do they engage in contacting, a common form of nonvoting participation in Soviet times?

The second institutional factor that post-Soviet scholars have offered as an explanation for low levels of Russian political participation is the country's weak political party system. The post-Soviet Russian system of governance provided few incentives for building strong political parties (Hale, 2006). Russia's first president, Boris Yeltsin, refused to join a political party, arguing that the president should be above party politics. As Hale demonstrates, Russian electoral markets developed without a strong party system due to the presence of meaningful "party substitutes" in the forms of financial industrial groups and regional political machines (2006, pp. 150–196). This system supplied candidates with the administrative and ideational capital necessary to win competitive elections, thereby fulfilling an important function normally provided by parties. Yet supporting electoral campaigns is not political parties' sole function. Parties also aggregate citizen interests for representation and mobilize citizens to vote based on these interests. With elite-led networks – rather than mass political parties – structuring electoral competition, the public cannot do as much to enhance the competitiveness of elections. Over time, elections become hollow, as we have observed in Russia.

Indonesia also exhibits institutional features that may influence nonvoting political participation. As discussed earlier, Indonesians experienced mobilized participation under the New Order. This experience, however, does not appear to have depressed participation in the post-Suharto era. A second, more relevant factor is the presence of a coherent party system.

From the perspective of governance, the Indonesian political system is wrought with party fragmentation and failed coalitions (Reilly, 2007; Sulistyo, 2002). Yet few observers would doubt that a system of coherent, identifiable parties exists, providing an important avenue for nonvoting participation.

One factor that has facilitated a coherent party structure in Indonesia is the inheritance of a multiparty system from the authoritarian New Order regime, which differed substantially from Russians' experience with the Soviet Union. The presence of multiple parties under the New Order should not, however, be misconstrued as political pluralism. The Indonesian Democratic Party (PDI) and the United Development Party (PPP) were not allowed to have party branches at the local level; the government screened their leaders and candidates for acceptability; and party members were frequently corrupted or co-opted (Liddle, 1978, 1985). Only the pro-Suharto Golkar party could win the majority in elections and hold political control, making New Order Indonesia effectively a single-party regime.

The presence of multiple parties, however, had an unintended, beneficial effect for democratization: it provided an organizational structure that reformists could utilize once democratic reforms were introduced. Even though Golkar was the only party allowed to hold even a modest amount of power in New Order Indonesia's mostly rubber-stamp legislature, PDI and PPP were allowed to hold some seats, and their formal presence made them visible to Indonesian citizens. They developed party organizations and networks over time, as well as name recognition. Consequently, when genuine multiparty competition was introduced in 1999, the PPP and PDI inherited a structure and political symbols that were valuable resources for connecting with the electorate and engaging in genuine political opposition. Indeed, Golkar and PDI-P (the successor to PDI) still have the largest and most formidable party organizations in the country. This picture stands in stark contrast to the Soviet Union, where the CPSU was the only political party allowed to exist for more than six decades. When multiparty competition became permissible in Russia in the early 1990s, all parties and electoral blocs other than the Communists were starting from scratch. The lack of a "usable past" (Grzymała-Busse, 2002) made it difficult for them to establish a presence and rapport with the electorate.

A second, more important factor contributing to Indonesia's party system development is the country's electoral laws. Indonesia combines proportional representation in the national legislature (DPR) with a presidential system where presidential and vice presidential candidates must be nominated together by a party or coalition with either 20 percent of seats in the DPR or 25 percent of the popular vote in the most recent DPR election. These laws have prevented elites seeking national office from sidestepping party structures. The party formation and presidential nomination laws share a common logic in that they advantage parties with cross-regional support and put parties at the center of all levels of political competition.

The coherent party system in Indonesia has likely facilitated Indonesians' participation in campaigns and party development. Yet this factor alone does not explain the broad range of nonvoting political participation observed in Indonesia. First, the presence of parties is not a sufficient condition to ensure that Indonesians will engage in party development work. Rather, the presence of a coherent system and mass participation in that system are reciprocally related. Indeed, Indonesia's robust party system is, in part, a consequence of high levels of citizen engagement in party work. Additionally, while a coherent party system may facilitate party development work, this factor appears unrelated to Indonesians' ongoing engagement in contentious political activities. Institutional factors alone, therefore, cannot explain political participation patterns in Indonesia.

Similarly, the weak party system in Russia does not, by itself, explain the country's political participation patterns. It may influence Russians' preference for contacting over other forms of political participation. Seeing little utility in trying to influence political outcomes by working through political parties, citizens might view contacting as a more reliable method to effect change. But, low levels of party development work are not only a consequence of Russia's weak party system, but also a cause of it. Although Putin's antidemocratic restrictions have hampered party work since 2004, few constraints hindered political party work in the 1990s. Russians had opportunities to build and support political parties, but efforts to do so were minimal and had flagged by the end of the decade (Hale, 2006; Stoner-Weiss, 2002). Legacies of forced participation and low trust in institutions carried over from the Soviet period are not sufficient to explain the lack of mass interest and effort in party-building in the early 1990s. Many former communist countries across Eurasia – including the Czech Republic, Hungary, and Poland – have overcome histories of mobilized participation and popular distrust to build more robust party systems.

Institutional factors alone do not explain why Russians have embraced elite-enabling forms of participation while Indonesians have adopted elite-constraining modes of action. Several classical studies in political participation have found relatively stable trends regarding the individual-level attributes that facilitate greater participation (Almond & Verba, 1963; Milbrath & Goel, 1977; Verba & Nie, 1972). Generally speaking, individuals with higher levels of education and income tend to participate in politics more frequently than those with fewer resources. Given Russia's higher level of industrialization, socioeconomic development, and rates of educational attainment, Russians should have greater resources to devote toward political participation than Indonesians. Yet we see the opposite.

My citizen interviews revealed that several other individual-level factors contribute to the variation in patterns of political participation between Russians and Indonesians: levels of civil society engagement, citizens' sense of political efficacy, and the levels and objects of political trust. Chapters 5, 6, and 7 describe in detail the differences – both quantitative and qualitative – in each of these variables and analyze how they influence political participation and its constraint on elite actions. Yet, before analyzing specific variables, it is useful to determine whether an empirical relationship exists between these variables and nonvoting political participation.

Statistical Hypothesis Testing: RES and EAB

Subsequent chapters describe the impact of my three independent variables on political participation through an analysis of citizen interviews in Russia and Indonesia. In this section, I test the validity of my argument by examining correlations among indicators from the 1995–1996 Russian Election Study (RES) and the East Asian Barometer (EAB). These are the only surveys examined in this book that include measures on all of my independent variables and measures of nonvoting political participation. The purpose of these statistical analyses is not to provide an exhaustive explanation for all variation in nonvoting political participation found in the two surveys. Rather, my goal is to demonstrate that the argument I build in the remaining chapters through a medium-N analysis of open-ended interviews is substantiated in large-N statistical analysis using a nationally representative population.

For both the RES and EAB, I estimate logistic regression models to test the performance of my three independent variables – civil society engagement, sense of political efficacy, and political trust – in predicting elite-enabling and elite-constraining participation in Russia and

Indonesia. I first briefly discuss the indicators used to measure my independent variables and then summarize the findings of my models.

As Chapter 5 discusses in greater detail, civil society is defined as the autonomous, intermediary stratum of society that exists between one's home and the state. In order to measure civil society engagement in the 1995–1996 RES, I rely on questions about membership in voluntary associations. The survey asked respondents if they belong to one of fifteen different organizations (RES 1995–1996, post-Duma election questionnaire, question 11). I use this information to create a dummy variable ("member"), which is scored "1" for anyone belonging to at least one organization and "0" for those respondents not belonging to any organizations. Just more than 42 percent of respondents belonged to at least one organization. I found a similar measure in the EAB to gauge civil society engagement. The EAB asks respondents if they are a member of any organizations (EAB, question Q019). Respondents who answered "yes" are coded as "1" and those who answered "no" are coded as "0" on the "member" variable. A total of 30.9 percent of survey respondents answered "yes" to this question.[1]

Political efficacy, analyzed in greater detail in Chapter 6, gauges one's beliefs about the impact an individual and others like him can have on the political process. In both the RES and the EAB, I measured political efficacy by creating two scales comprised of responses to two survey questions. The RES questions are statements to which respondents reply that they "fully agree," "agree," "waver," "disagree," or "fully disagree." The first statement is: "People like me have no say in what the government does" (RES 1995–1996, post-Duma election questionnaire, question 21(7)). The second statement is: "In my opinion, I am well prepared to participate in political activity" (RES 1995–1996, post-Duma election questionnaire, question 21(8)). The "efficacy" scale generated from these two questions ranges from 0 to 1, where "1" corresponds to the highest degree of efficacy. A person with a score of "1" "fully disagrees" with the first statement and "fully agrees" with the second statement. The two EAB questions that measure efficacy are also statements to

---

[1] While the level of membership using this measure is lower for Indonesia than for Russia, it is necessary to consider that the question wording differs between the two surveys. The RES provided respondents a list of organizations, while the EAB asked if a respondent was a member of any organization. This latter question formulation sets a higher bar for establishing membership status. For comparing membership levels between Russia and Indonesia, we should rely on the World Values Survey measures provided in Chapter 5, in which the question was worded the same way in both countries.

which respondents can "strongly agree," "somewhat agree," "somewhat disagree," and "strongly disagree." The first statement is, "People have the power to change a government they don't like" (EAB, Question QII103), and the second is, "I think I have the ability to participate in politics" (EAB, Question Q126). I averaged responses to the two questions to create an "efficacy" scale ranging from 0 to 1, in which "1" is the highest possible level of efficacy.

Both surveys provide questions that gauge political trust. In particular, the RES asks, "Tell me if you fully trust, trust, mistrust, or completely mistrust," and then lists several institutions, including the president of Russia, the government of Russia, the State Duma (national legislature), the regional administration, and the local administration (RES 1995–1996, post-Duma election questionnaire, question 25). The EAB question is worded as follows: "I'm going to name a number of institutions. For each one, please tell me, how much trust do you have in them? Is it a great deal of trust, quite a lot of trust, not very much trust, or none at all?" Respondents were asked about the presidency, the national government, the DPR (national legislature), and the regional government (EAB Questions QII07, Q008, Q010, and Q014). For both the RES and EAB questions, I recoded each response to fall between 0 and 1 on a four-point scale where "0" equals "completely mistrust" in the RES and "none at all" in the EAB and "1" equals "fully trust" in the RES and "a great deal of trust" in the EAB. I also averaged responses to all political objects to create a composite measure of trust in political institutions.

In order to test the effect of these independent variables on predicting a respondent's likelihood of engaging in nonvoting political participation, I estimated multiple logistic regression models that regress these variables on three different dependent variables that correspond to the three types of nonvoting political participation explored in this book: contacting public officials, campaign and party development work, and contentious politics. The dependent variable in each of these cases is coded "1" for individuals who engaged in an activity in one of the three categories and "0" for those who did not.

For every dependent variable in the two surveys, I estimated five models (for a total of thirty models), each of which included a different measure of political trust – either trust in a specific political object, such as the national government, or a composite measure that averages trust across the different objects. In addition to the independent variables described earlier, I included three control variables in the logistic regression models: age (measured in years), sex (male = 0 and female = 1), and high school degree (no high school degree = o and high school diploma = 1). These demographic variables are all hypothesized to exert independent effects on political participation. On the whole, cross-national evidence suggests that conventional participation increases with age, while contentious activity is concentrated among young adults; men participate at higher rates than women; and individuals with at least a secondary education are more likely to participate. Moreover, there are good reasons to think that these variables correlate with my independent variables as well. Cross-national evidence generally shows that women are more active in associational life than men, and that education both increases efficacy and can attenuate political trust. Therefore, in order to measure the full effects of my independent variables, it necessary to include these socioeconomic controls.

Scholarship on political participation has identified numerous other variables hypothesized to influence decisions to participate. In their study of political participation in the United States, Verba and Nie investigated political interest, exposure to political information, and political knowledge in addition to numerous questions about specific policy issues (1972). Studies of voting behavior – including research on post-Soviet Russia and post-Suharto Indonesia – consider partisan identification, attitudes about current conditions, and candidate evaluations (Campbell et al., 1964; Colton, 2000; Colton & Hale, 2009; Colton & McFaul, 2003; Liddle & Mujani, 2007; Miller & Shanks, 1996). These variables are excluded here because my interview data did not reveal marked differences between Indonesians and Russians on these topics. Consequently, while some of these attitudes might correlate with decisions to participate in Russia and Indonesia, they are unlikely to help us understand why elite-constraining patterns of participation obtain in Indonesia and elite-enabling patterns obtain in Russia. The simplified models estimated here aim to substantiate the causal model developed through qualitative evidence.

Table 4.1 summarizes the general findings from the thirty logistic regression models.[2] Each row corresponds to an independent or control variable in the models, and each column corresponds to a dependent variable. For each instance when an independent or control variable is statistically significant at the level of .05, I have placed a "+" sign in the cell if the correlation is positive and a "−" sign if the correlation is negative. If the cell is blank, no statistically significant relationship between the independent and dependent variables obtains.

---

[2] The complete results of the regression analyses can be found in Appendix 4.

TABLE 4.1. *Summary of Logistic Regression Analyses of Nonvoting Political Participation in RES and EAB*

	Russian Election Study (RES)			East Asian Barometer (EAB)		
	Contacting	Party and Campaign Work	Contentious Politics	Contacting	Party and Campaign Work	Contentious Politics
Associational member	+	+	+	+	+	+
Efficacy scale	+	+	+	+	+	+
Political trust	+[a]	+[b]				−[c]
Age				+	−	−
Female	+			−	−	−
High school degree	+	+	+	+		+

[a] Only trust in the presidency is statistically significant and positive; other trust indicators are not significant.
[b] Trust in all political objects except the presidency is statistically significant and positive.
[c] Trust in all political objects is statistically significant and negative.

127

Table 4.1 provides empirical support for the argument outlined in the forthcoming chapters. Even when controlling for socioeconomic factors, associational membership is a statistically significant predictor of engaging in the elite-constraining activities of party development work and contentious politics in both Russia and Indonesia. While civic engagement is not a statistically significant predictor of contacting in Russia (a finding consistent with my theoretical expectations), it correlates positively with contacting in Indonesia. This correlation between civic engagement and contacting in the EAB, however, reinforces trends observed in the interview data described in Chapter 3, where I found that contacting in Indonesia tends to occur more often as an outgrowth of group-based, rather than individual-based, activism.

Efficacy is a statistically significant and positive predictor of all forms of nonvoting political activity in both the RES and EAB. As discussed in Chapter 6, when individuals believe elite-enabling activity (such as contacting) is efficacious, they are more likely to undertake it. When citizens believe elite-constraining participation (such as working with opposition parties and engaging in acts of contentious politics) is efficacious, they take part in it. These dynamics are present in both countries, yet, as my interview data show, Russians are more inclined to see contacting as efficacious while Indonesians view protesting as efficacious.

As Chapter 7 elaborates, existing scholarship offers conflicting expectations about the relationship between political trust and participation. On one hand, higher levels of trust are thought to stimulate participation. On the other hand, levels of *distrust* rather than trust are thought to fuel participation. Therefore, it is unsurprising that trust variables perform the most ambiguously in my statistical models in Table 4.1.

Trust in the president is a statistically significant and positive predictor of contacting in Russia, which is consistent with my finding that Russians place considerable trust in specific individuals over impersonal institutions. Thus, it is unsurprising that citizens who place a high level of trust in the president might participate by contacting. Trust in institutions *other* than the presidency is a statistically significant and positive predictor of campaign and party work in Russia, which supports the claim that trust in institutions stimulates political participation. In Indonesia, however, trust is not a statistically significant predictor of contacting or party work. Rather, a statistically significant, *negative* relationship exists between trust in institutions and contentious politics. In this particular case, distrust does appear to stimulate Indonesian protest activities. This group of findings is consistent with the results of my citizen interviews, where connections between political trust and nonvoting political participation were less clear than the relationships between participation and civic engagement and participation and efficacy.

While Table 4.1 speaks to the validity of my argument for explaining trends in nonvoting political participation in both Russia and Indonesia, these results also identify a few differences between the two countries regarding the demographic control variables. Age is not a statistically significant predictor for any form of nonvoting political participation in Russia, while it correlates negatively with participation in Indonesia. In other words, once we take into account education and my independent variables, age is no longer a distinguishing characteristic for predicting political participation in Russia, but the propensity to participate declines in Indonesia with age. Being a woman is a statistically significant predictor of contacting in Russia, but otherwise sex does not predict other forms of participation there. In Indonesia, however, being a woman is a statistically significant predictor of *not* participating in any form of nonvoting political participation. Last, having a high school degree correlates positively with party work and contentious politics in Russia, and with contacting and contentious politics in Indonesia. My interviews revealed similar trends: the educated dominate protest activities in both countries, and party and campaign work is common across all educational groups in Indonesia.

In sum, the multiple logistic regression analyses of the 1995–1996 RES and 2006 EAB provide additional support for my argument that patterns in nonvoting political participation in Russia and Indonesia can be explained by the countries' different levels of engagement in civil society, beliefs about political efficacy, and political trust.

Connections between Civil Society, Efficacy, and Trust

The logistic regression models in the previous section test the causal story outlined in Figure 1.3, examining the independent effects of each variable. This causal story is, in many respects, a simplified account of a more complex set of relationships. For example, as Chapter 6 discusses, the relationship between one's sense of efficacy and political participation is reciprocal: a belief that an act is efficacious will increase the likelihood that one will engage in it, while a participatory experience that yields a desirable outcome is likely to increase efficacy as well. Subsequent chapters discuss the causal effects of civil society engagement, political efficacy, and political trust on political participation. Yet it is also possible that these three independent variables *interact* with each other in ways that influence political participation. For example, we can hypothesize that individuals who feel more efficacious are more likely to trust political institutions and are more inclined to engage in civil society. Individuals who trust institutions may also be more likely to engage in civil society, and so on.

I examined the interrelationships between these variables by calculating correlation coefficients using the RES and EAB indicators described earlier. Contrary to what we might expect, the correlations between these indicators are not particularly strong in either survey. The highest correlation in the RES is between efficacy and trust in the State Duma ($r = 0.05$). In the EAB, the strongest positive correlation is between civic organization membership and trust in the regional government ($r = 0.08$). In contrast to the Russian data, the EAB shows a negative correlation between efficacy and trust variables, although the relationships are very weak – the strongest negative correlation is between efficacy and trust in the regional government ($r = -0.08$). The weakness of this correlation precludes us from saying with any confidence that as Indonesians' sense of efficacy increases, their level of trust decreases. On the whole, however, the weak correlations between civil society engagement, political efficacy, and political trust suggest that these concepts are generally not dependent on each other.

We have little reason to believe that these variables interact with each other in a way that precludes them from being considered as independent factors that each contributes to participatory behaviors in its own way. The results of the regression analyses from both surveys show that civil society engagement, political efficacy, and political trust are statistically significant predictors of nonvoting political participation, even when controlling for demographic variables. The following section explores the implications of these findings by comparing the probability of engaging in elite-constraining participation in Russia and Indonesia.

Predicting Elite-Constraining Activity

Table 4.1 summarizes the logistic regression models' findings: we only see which variables are statistically significant and the direction (positive or negative) of the association between the independent variables and nonvoting political participation. This information tells us nothing about which independent variables produce the strongest effects in predicting nonvoting political participation, or whether the variables have a stronger effect in predicting outcomes in one country or the other. On the whole, Table 4.1 shows that the effect of civic engagement, political efficacy, and political trust on nonvoting political participation is quite similar in Russia and Indonesia. If the effect of these variables is similar in both countries, why is elite-constraining participation more widespread in Indonesia than Russia? Part of the answer lies in aggregate-level differences we see in levels of associational memberships, perceptions of efficacy, and political trust between the two countries.

In this section, I compare the effects of the different independent and control variables on nonvoting political participation. I examine the magnitude of effects between variables in the same models and compare the effects of the variables between Russia and Indonesia. This analysis further substantiates my argument that the widespread diffusion of associational membership and high levels of political efficacy facilitate elite-constraining participation at a higher rate in Indonesia than in Russia.

One cannot compare logistic regression coefficients derived from different surveys. Moreover, comparing logit coefficients within the same model is of limited utility since the models are nonlinear and the effect of the variables changes with the value given to each independent variable. For these reasons, it is helpful to calculate predicted probabilities for hypothetical individuals based on estimated models. By definition, a probability is measured from 0 to 1. If an event has the probability of 1, it will definitely occur; if 0, it definitely will not occur. Thus, the closer a probability is to 1, the greater the likelihood an event will occur. In the cases investigated here, the predicted probabilities gauge the likelihood that an individual will contact a public official, engage in party or campaign work, or participate in contentious politics. By calculating predicted probabilities, I can change the value assigned to different independent variables and examine how the likelihood of engaging in nonvoting political participation changes as a result. Additionally, I can calculate predicted probabilities for RES and EAB models that include the same functionally equivalent indicators for the independent and control variables in each survey and compare how the probabilities differ between the two countries. This information helps us ascertain the strength of particular variables in influencing participatory outcomes.

Tables 4.2 and 4.3 display several predicted probabilities based on a basic model estimated for each dependent variable in both surveys ("Model 1" in each of the tables in the Appendix). This model includes variables for associational membership, the efficacy scale, the average trust composite variable, and the control variables for age, sex, and high school

TABLE 4.2. *Predicted Probabilities for Engaging in Nonvoting Political Participation, Holding Efficacy and Trust Constant*

	RES: High School Degree/ No Associational Membership	EAB: High School Degree/ No Associational Membership	RES: No High School Degree/ No Associational Membership	EAB: No High School Degree/ No Associational Membership	RES: High School Degree and Associational Member	EAB: High School Degree and Associational Member
Contacting Public Officials						
Male	0.36	0.30	0.34	0.11	0.39	0.50
Female	0.43	0.17	0.40	0.06	0.45	0.33
Party Work						
Male	0.13	0.35	0.08	0.37	0.21	0.50
Female	0.12	0.19	0.07	0.20	0.20	0.30
Contentious Politics						
Male	0.10	0.10	0.05	0.05	0.15	0.21
Female	0.10	0.07	0.05	0.03	0.15	0.14

These predicted probabilities are based on the results of logistic regression models that include independent variables for age, sex, high school degree, associational membership, efficacy, and trust in political institutions. They are based off of "Model 1" in the tables in the Appendix. The probabilities above are calculated for a thirty-year-old individual with values for efficacy and political trust held at their means.

TABLE 4.3. *Predicted Probabilities for Engaging in Nonvoting Political Participation Varying Efficacy and Associational Membership*

	Contacting RES	Contacting EAB	Party Work RES	Party Work EAB	Contentious Politics RES	Contentious Politics EAB
Efficacy = 1 Membership = 1	0.51	0.69	0.46	0.73	0.35	0.47
Efficacy = 1 Membership = 0	0.48	0.49	0.32	0.60	0.25	0.28
Efficacy = 0 Membership = 1	0.33	0.30	0.13	0.26	0.09	0.07
Efficacy = 0 Membership = 0	0.31	0.15	0.07	0.16	0.06	0.03

These predicted probabilities are based on the results of logistic regression models that include independent variables for age, sex, high school degree, associational membership, efficacy, and trust in political institutions. They are based off of "Model 1" in the tables in Appendix. The probabilities above are calculated for a thirty-year-old male with a high school diploma. The value for political trust is held at the mean.

education. The predicted probabilities in Table 4.2 are calculated for a thirty-year-old individual with values for efficacy and political trust held at their means. Sex, education, and associational membership are varied in the rows and columns so that we can evaluate the effect of changes in these variables. In other words, Table 4.2 compares how likely a thirty-year-old Indonesian and a thirty-year-old Russian (whose senses of efficacy and political trust are equal to the average levels in their societies) are to engage in a particular form of nonvoting political participation.

Table 4.2's first four columns compare predicted probabilities for an individual who does not belong to any organizations. The final two columns provide predicted probabilities for an individual with a high school diploma who belongs to at least one organization. Not surprisingly, on the whole, individuals who have completed high school are more likely to participate in all forms of nonvoting political participation. The one exception is Indonesians' engagement in party work. Here, the predicted probability for a man to participate is 0.02 points higher if he does not have a high school degree. This negligible difference in predicted probabilities is consistent with findings from my citizen interviews in Indonesia, where I observed that individuals with incomplete education regularly participate in party development work. This finding is somewhat at odds with the basic tenets of modernization theory, which posit that education correlates positively with political participation – a relationship found generally true in most studies of participation.

The different role sex plays as a predictor of political participation in Russia and Indonesia is evident in Table 4.2. The hypothetical thirty-year-old Russian woman has a higher predicted probability of contacting a public official than the thirty-year-old Russian man, regardless of education level and civil society engagement. Differences in predicted probabilities for other forms of participation are negligible for Russian women and men. In all instances in Table 4.2, the hypothetical thirty-year-old Indonesian woman has a lower predicted probability of participating in a nonvoting activity than the hypothetical thirty-year-old Indonesian man. In some cases the differences in predicted probabilities are negligible, such as engagement in contentious politics for individuals with a high school degree who do not belong to any organizations (difference is 0.03). In other cases, however, the predicted probability for male engagement is dramatically higher than for female participation. Among Indonesians in the survey population who have a high school degree and belong to at least one association, men are significantly more likely than women to engage in party work (difference is 0.20).

Consistent with my expectations from the qualitative interview data, the predicted probabilities for contacting public officials are higher in Russia than in Indonesia. This finding holds true across both sexes and regardless of high school education. The reverse phenomenon is observed when we examine party work: Indonesian men and women are more likely to engage in this form of participation than Russians, regardless of education level. Contrary to what we might expect, however, the predicted probabilities that an individual will engage in an act of contentious politics are very similar in both Russia and Indonesia.

If we compare predicted probabilities across different forms of political participation within the same survey, we find further evidence that Russians are more likely to engage in elite-enabling activities while Indonesians are more apt to choose elite-constraining forms of participation. Regardless of the values given to education, sex, or associational membership, the highest predicted probabilities for nonvoting political participation among RES respondents are for contacting public officials. A thirty-year-old Russian woman with a high school degree who does not belong to any associations has a predicted probability of contacting a public official of 0.43. The same woman has a predicted probability of 0.12 of engaging in party work and of 0.10 for participating in a contentious act. In other words, if this particular woman engages in nonvoting political participation, the probability that she will contact a public official – an elite-enabling form of participation – is significantly higher than the probability that she will opt for an elite-constraining activity.

On the whole, the highest predicted probabilities for nonvoting political participation among EAB respondents are for party work. A thirty-year-old Indonesian man with a high school degree and no associational memberships has a predicted probability of engaging in party work of 0.35, higher than his predicted probability for contacting (0.30) or participating in contentious politics (0.10). In contrast to Russians, Indonesians who participate in nonvoting political behaviors have a higher probability of engaging in party work – an elite-constraining activity – than in the elite-enabling activity of contacting.

Table 4.2's final two columns are perhaps the most interesting. We see here that the effect of belonging to at least one association has a greater impact in the probability of participating in nonvoting behavior in Indonesia than in Russia. For example, an Indonesian man with a high school degree is 0.20 more likely to contact public officials if he is a member of an association. The difference for the analogous Russian man is only 0.03. The differences are also substantial for party work: the predicted probability for an Indonesian man with a high school degree increases from 0.35 to 0.50 if he belongs to an association. In contrast, the predicted probability for the Russian man only increases from 0.13 to 0.21. These results suggest that associational membership's impact on raising the probability that an individual will engage in nonvoting participation is actually stronger in Indonesia than in Russia. It is also worth noting that the category of person with the highest predicted probabilities of nonvoting participation is an Indonesian man with a high school degree who belongs to at least one organization. This individual has a probability of 0.50 – a one-in-two chance – of contacting a public official or engaging in party work.

Table 4.3 compares predicted probabilities for a thirty-year-old man with at least a high school degree whose level of political trust is held at the mean, while allowing associational membership and efficacy levels to vary. Each row represents a different combination of associational membership levels and political efficacy, moving from a hypothetical scenario in which the citizen belongs to at least one association and has the highest possible level of efficacy to a scenario in which the citizen does not belong to any associations and has the lowest possible level of efficacy. Each column represents a different form of nonvoting participation.

Given the high and positive relationships displayed in Table 4.1 between both political efficacy and associational membership and most of the dependent variables, it is unsurprising that the first row in Table 4.3 exhibits the highest predicted probabilities for all models and that the predicted probabilities decline as we move down the rows. When we hold efficacy constant at its highest level, we see that the predicted probability of participation for the Indonesian man is greater than the predicted probability for the Russian man for all forms of nonvoting political participation, even contacting. Only when we estimate that efficacy levels are at their lowest possible value does the hypothetical Russian man stand a greater chance of contacting a public official than the Indonesian man does. When efficacy levels are held at zero, the hypothetical Russian man also has a slightly higher chance of engaging in contentious politics than the Indonesian man, but the predicted probability for both is quite low, below 0.10. For party development work, the predicted probabilities for the Indonesian man are always higher than for the Russian man, irrespective of level of efficacy or associational membership. For example, an Indonesian man who belongs to at least one organization and has the highest possible level of efficacy has a predicted probability of 0.73 of engaging in party work, while a Russian man with the same attributes has a predicted probability of only 0.46. Even an Indonesian man who does not belong to any organizations and feels he has no efficacy stands a nearly one-in-six chance of engaging in political party work, more than double the probability for a similar Russian man.

Comparing the differences in predicted probabilities for the first two rows and the bottom two rows, it appears as though belonging to an association has a stronger predictive power for nonvoting political participation in Indonesia than in Russia. For example, for a Russian man with an efficacy score of 1, belonging to an association increases the probability he will engage in contentious politics from 0.25 to 0.35. The increase for an analogous Indonesian man is almost twice as great (from 0.28 to 0.47). By comparing the differences in predicted probabilities for the first and third rows and the second and fourth rows, it also appears as though efficacy has a stronger impact on predicting Indonesian than Russian behavior. For example, a thirty-year-old Indonesian man with a high school degree who belongs to at least one association and expresses high levels of efficacy has a predicted probability of engaging in party work that is 0.47 higher than the same individual who has a low sense of efficacy. In contrast, the difference for an analogous Russian man is only 0.33. On the whole, higher efficacy levels have a more dramatic effect on the predicted probability of engaging in nonvoting participation than do higher levels of association membership. This pattern is true for the predicted probabilities in both surveys, but the effect is more dramatic in Indonesia.

A final point worth noting regarding Table 4.3 is that in all but four cases, the predicted probabilities of Indonesian action are higher than the predicted probabilities of Russian action for the same activity. In fact, when efficacy is high, the hypothetical Indonesian man in this scenario has a greater likelihood of contacting or engaging in party work than of *not* doing these activities. In sum, efficacy levels and associational membership appear to have a stronger impact on political activism in Indonesia than in Russia, thereby increasing the likelihood that elite-constraining participation will be more widespread in the former than the latter. It is worth reminding the reader that the Russian data analyzed here are from 1995–1996 – before the onset of Russia's authoritarian decline. Russians' sense of efficacy in this period could not be influenced by Putinism, nor could their level of engagement in civil society be constrained by limitations on organization that came into place in the 2000s.

Diffusion Differences

The next three chapters of this book use a variety of data, both qualitative and quantitative, to demonstrate three important aggregate-level differences between Russians and Indonesians. First, the level of civil society engagement is significantly higher in Indonesia than in Russia. As of 2006, Indonesians belonged to an average of 2.77 associations while Russians belonged to 0.77 associations. Second, political efficacy in Indonesia is higher than in Russia. The functionally equivalent efficacy scales I created from the RES and EAB data found that Russians in 1995–1996 had an average efficacy score of 0.32, while Indonesians in 2006 had an average score of 0.51. Third, while both Russians and Indonesians express a broad range of perspectives regarding political trust, on the whole Indonesians are more trusting of abstract political institutions than Russians are. The more widespread diffusion of these characteristics in Indonesia than in Russia has fostered a higher level of elite-constraining political participation in Indonesia, contributing to the survival of its democracy.

Another factor meriting consideration is the meaningful demographic differences between the two countries and the impact these differences have on patterns of nonvoting political participation. First, the average age of Indonesians is considerably lower than that of Russians. If we compare the average ages of respondents in the RES and EAB (all of whom were at least seventeen years old), the average age of Indonesian respondents is 7.6 years younger (39.4 years) than that of Russian respondents (46.8 years). Second, educational attainment is higher in Russia than Indonesia. While about 71 percent of RES respondents have at least a high school degree, only 32 percent of EAB respondents do. Last, because of the dramatic male-female life expectancy gap in Russia, women constitute a higher percentage of the population there than in Indonesia, where men and women each comprise roughly half of the population.

These demographic differences have several potential consequences for political participation. First, because age correlates negatively with participation in Indonesia, we can expect to see more political engagement among younger segments of the population. This demographic group is acquiring more education, thereby strengthening the diffusion of civic skills. For example, 29 percent of EAB respondents over the age of thirty have a high school education, while 40 percent of those under the age of thirty have one. Levels of associational membership are also higher among those with more education. As a result, the predicted probabilities estimated in the previous section have a strong possibility of fostering elite-constraining participation among a segment of the Indonesian population that is increasing in size. In Russia, by contrast, participation does not correlate with age, and the most common form of political activism is elite-enabling contacting, which is most commonly performed by women with at least a high school education. In other words, little about the demographic picture in Russia has fostered or is likely to foster increased participation in elite-constraining activities.

In addition to demographic differences that serve to amplify the effects of higher levels of civil society engagement, political efficacy, and trust in institutions among Indonesians than Russians, two other macro-level qualitative differences contribute to these countries' patterns of nonvoting political participation. First, as Chapter 6 demonstrates, both Russians and Indonesians select nonvoting acts they believe to be efficacious. Russians, however, find that elite-enabling activities are more effective than elite-constraining activities for achieving desired ends. Second, as discussed in Chapter 7, while both Russians and Indonesians place more trust in individuals than institutions, the leaders earning Russians' trust have attacked democracy, while those earning Indonesians' trust have advanced it.

Conclusion

By conducting statistical tests with public opinion data from the Russian Election Study and the East Asian Barometer, this chapter has revealed several important findings. First, civil society engagement, feelings of efficacy, and political trust are only weakly correlated among respondents in both Russia and Indonesia, although all three variables demonstrate independent effects on nonvoting political participation. Civil society engagement and political efficacy are strong predictors of nearly all forms of nonvoting participation in Indonesia and Russia. The effects of political trust are not as clear: higher levels of trust contribute to participatory behavior for contacting and party work in Russia, while distrust fuels contentious politics in Indonesia. Last, by calculating predicted probabilities of participation using functionally equivalent models from the two surveys, we reach two important conclusions about patterns of participation in Russia and Indonesia. First, the highest probabilities of participation in Russia are for elite-enabling activities, while the highest probabilities of participation in Indonesia are for elite-constraining activities. Second, while all three of my independent variables have a statistically-significant effect on participation, the effect of civil society engagement and efficacy appear stronger in Indonesia than Russia.

The models in this chapter provide evidence for my argument that differences in nonvoting political participation in Russia and Indonesia can be explained by variation in levels of civil society engagement, feelings of political efficacy, and political trust. While the statistical tests conducted here show that my key independent variables predict respondents' decisions to engage in acts of political participation in large-N nationwide surveys, there are limits to what we can gain from these models. While they can validate the presence of particular trends on a national scale, they do not enable us to parse out the qualitative differences between the participatory acts Indonesians and Russians practice. They cannot tell us why individuals choose one act over another, how civil society engagement leads to political participation, which types of activities individuals deem as efficacious, or how trust can be translated into elite-enabling vs. elite-constraining action. Answers to these questions require different data, which will be explored in the next three chapters.

Appendix

Below are the full set of tables for the logistic regression models of data from the 1995–1996 Russian Election Study (RES) and the 2006 East Asian Barometer (EAB). These models provide the results for Table 4.1. Model 1 for each of these tables is the basis for the results in Tables 4.2 and 4.3.

Logistic Regression Models for Contacting in 1995–1996 RES

	Model 1	Model 2	Model 3	Model 4	Model 5
Constant	−1.09***	−1.07***	−1.22***	−0.98***	−0.96***
	(0.28)	(0.27)	(0.20)	(0.27)	(0.27)
Age (years)	0.001	0.002	0.001	0.002	0.002
	(0.004)	(0.004)	(0.004)	(0.004)	(0.004)
Female	0.27**	0.27**	0.27**	0.27**	0.27**
	(0.10)	(0.10)	(0.10)	(0.10)	(0.10)
High school	0.09	0.10	0.10	0.09	0.09
	(0.13)	(0.13)	(0.13)	(0.13)	(0.13)
Member	0.10	0.10	0.10	0.10	0.10
	(0.10)	(0.10)	(0.10)	(0.10)	(0.10)
Efficacy	0.74**	0.75**	0.72**	0.75**	0.76**
	(0.28)	(0.28)	(0.28)	(0.28)	(0.28)
Trust in institutions (5-question average)	0.34 (0.26)				
Trust in government		0.27 (0.22)			
Trust in president			0.74*** (0.20)		
Trust in State Duma				0.08 (0.23)	
Trust in regional administration					0.01 (0.22)
McFadden's R-squared	0.007	0.007	0.012	0.007	0.007
Count R-squared	0.591	0.590	0.590	0.590	0.591

N = 1,689
* p < 0.05, ** p < 0.01, *** p < 0.001.

Logistic Regression Models for Contacting in EAB

	Model 1	Model 2	Model 3	Model 4	Model 5
Constant	−3.50***	−3.51***	−3.61***	−3.64***	−3.71***
	(0.46)	(0.43)	(0.43)	(0.42)	(0.45)
Age (years)	0.03***	0.03***	0.03***	0.03***	0.03***
	(0.01)	(0.01)	(0.01)	(0.01)	(0.01)
Female	−0.70***	−0.70***	−0.70***	−0.70***	−0.71***
	(0.15)	(0.15)	(0.15)	(0.15)	(0.15)
High school	1.26***	1.27***	1.28***	1.26***	1.28***
	(0.15)	(0.15)	(0.15)	(0.15)	(0.15)
Member	0.86***	0.86***	0.85***	0.85***	0.85***
	(0.15)	(0.15)	(0.15)	(0.15)	(0.15)
Efficacy	1.66***	1.67***	1.67***	1.69***	1.68***
	(0.47)	(0.47)	(0.47)	(0.47)	(0.47)
Trust in institutions (4-question average)	−0.43 (0.41)				
Trust in government		−0.46 (0.32)			
Trust in president			−0.24 (0.32)		
Trust in DPR				−0.20 (0.28)	
Trust in regional administration					−0.06 (0.32)
McFadden's R-squared	0.136	0.136	0.135	0.135	0.135
Count R-squared	0.794	0.796	0.793	0.796	0.792

N = 1,341
* p < 0.05, ** p < 0.01, *** p < 0.001.

Logistic Regression Models for Campaigning and Party Work in 1995–1996 RES

	Model 1	Model 2	Model 3	Model 4	Model 5
Constant	−3.65***	−3.55***	−3.39***	−3.54***	−3.59***
	(0.42)	(0.41)	(0.40)	(0.41)	(0.41)
Age (years)	0.004	0.01	0.01	0.004	0.004
	(0.01)	(0.01)	(0.01)	(0.01)	(0.01)
Female	−0.02	−0.03	−0.01	−0.02	−0.02
	(0.15)	(0.15)	(0.25)	(0.15)	(0.15)
High school	0.57**	0.57**	0.55**	0.56**	0.56**
	(0.20)	(0.20)	(0.20)	(0.20)	(0.20)
Member	0.59***	0.60***	0.60***	0.59***	0.58***
	(0.15)	(0.15)	(0.15)	(0.15)	(0.15)
Efficacy	1.77***	1.79***	1.79***	1.75***	1.77***
	(0.39)	(0.39)	(0.39)	(0.39)	(0.39)
Trust in institutions (5-question average)	0.94* (0.38)				
Trust in government		0.65* (0.31)			
Trust in president			0.37 (0.29)		
Trust in State Duma				0.72* (0.33)	
Trust in regional administration					0.79* (0.32)
McFadden's R-squared	0.046	0.044	0.042	0.044	0.045
Count R-squared	0.841	0.841	0.841	0.841	0.841

N = 1,525
* $p < 0.05$, ** $p < 0.01$, *** $p < 0.001$.

Logistic Regression Models for Campaigning and Party Work in EAB

	Model 1	Model 2	Model 3	Model 4	Model 5
Constant	−0.87*	−0.71*	−0.74*	−0.89*	−0.98*
	(0.39)	(0.36)	(0.37)	(0.36)	(0.38)
Age (years)	−0.03***	−0.03***	−0.03***	−0.03***	−0.03***
	(0.01)	(0.01)	(0.01)	(0.01)	(0.01)
Female	−0.88***	−0.87***	−0.87***	−0.88***	−0.87***
	(0.13)	(0.13)	(0.13)	(0.13)	(0.13)
High school	−0.10	−0.11	−0.10	−0.08	−0.09
	(0.14)	(0.13)	(0.13)	(0.14)	(0.14)
Member	0.62***	0.62***	0.62***	0.62***	0.61***
	(0.13)	(0.13)	(0.13)	(0.13)	(0.13)
Efficacy	2.05***	2.04***	2.04***	2.04***	2.08***
	(0.43)	(0.43)	(0.43)	(0.43)	(0.43)
Trust in institutions (4-question average)	0.18 (0.37)				
Trust in government		−0.12 (0.28)			
Trust in president			−0.05 (0.28)		
Trust in DPR				0.24 (0.26)	
Trust in regional administration					0.32 (0.29)
McFadden's R-squared	0.066	0.066	0.066	0.067	0.067
Count R-squared	0.728	0.728	0.728	0.730	0.726

N = 1,332
* $p < 0.05$, ** $p < 0.01$, *** $p < 0.001$.

Logistic Regression Models for Contentious Politics in 1995–1996 RES

	Model 1	Model 2	Model 3	Model 4	Model 5
Constant	−3.22***	−3.30***	−3.22***	−3.28***	−3.33***
	(0.46)	(0.45)	(0.44)	(0.45)	(0.45)
Age (years)	−0.003	−0.003	−0.003	−0.003	−0.003
	(0.01)	(0.01)	(0.01)	(0.01)	(0.01)
Female	0.03	0.03	0.03	0.03	0.03
	(0.16)	(0.16)	(0.16)	(0.16)	(0.16)
High school	0.69**	0.69**	0.69**	0.69**	0.69**
	(0.24)	(0.24)	(0.24)	(0.24)	(0.24)
Member	0.47**	0.46**	0.46**	0.46**	0.46**
	(0.16)	(0.16)	(0.16)	(0.16)	(0.16)
Efficacy	1.67***	1.67***	1.67***	1.68***	1.67***
	(0.42)	(0.42)	(0.42)	(0.42)	(0.42)
Trust in institutions (5-question average)	−0.32 (0.41)				
Trust in government		−0.10 (0.33)			
Trust in president			−0.33 (0.32)		
Trust in State Duma				−0.18 (0.35)	
Trust in regional administration					−0.04 (0.35)
McFadden's R-squared	0.038	0.038	0.039	0.038	0.038
Count R-squared	0.891	0.891	0.891	0.891	0.891

N = 1,726
* p < 0.05, ** p < 0.01, *** p < 0.001.

Logistic Regression Models for Contentious Politics in EAB

	Model 1	Model 2	Model 3	Model 4	Model 5
Constant	−1.16	−1.64**	−1.56*	−1.91**	−1.88**
	(0.67)	(0.61)	(0.63)	(0.62)	(0.65)
Age (years)	−0.05***	−0.05***	−0.05***	−0.05***	−0.05***
	(0.01)	(0.01)	(0.01)	(0.01)	(0.01)
Female	−0.48*	−0.50*	−0.50*	−0.50*	−0.55*
	(0.24)	(0.24)	(0.24)	(0.24)	(0.23)
High school	0.77***	0.81***	0.90***	0.77***	0.81***
	(0.23)	(0.23)	(0.23)	(0.23)	(0.23)
Member	0.82***	0.78***	0.85***	0.75***	0.80***
	(0.23)	(0.23)	(0.23)	(0.23)	(0.23)
Efficacy	2.48***	2.54***	2.54***	2.55***	2.37***
	(0.74)	(0.74)	(0.74)	(0.73)	(0.73)
Trust in institutions (4-question average)	−2.48*** (0.61)				
Trust in government		−1.88*** (0.47)			
Trust in president			−1.82*** (0.48)		
Trust in DPR				−1.11** (0.42)	
Trust in regional administration					−0.94* (0.47)
McFadden's R-squared	0.138	0.138	0.135	0.124	0.119
Count R-squared	0.931	0.931	0.931	0.930	0.930

N = 1,340
* p < 0.05, ** p < 0.01, *** p < 0.001.

5

Tocqueville Revisited

Civic Skills and Social Networks

Chapter 4 demonstrated the correlations between civil society engagement, political efficacy, political trust, and nonvoting political participation in both Russia and Indonesia. Each of these variables helps explain why elite-constraining behavior is more prevalent in Indonesia than in Russia. Yet the distinct political participation patterns in these countries are not only a consequence of different levels of civil society engagement, political efficacy, and political trust, but they also result from important qualitative differences in the character of these variables in Russia and Indonesia. This chapter focuses on civil society engagement. Chapters 6 and 7 examine Russians' and Indonesians' beliefs about political efficacy and political trust. Cross-national variation on these three factors explains why Indonesians expanded elite-constraining participation, while Russians did not.

This chapter revisits Alexis de Tocqueville's concept of civil society and its relationship to democracy. I apply the civic voluntarism model Sidney Verba, Kay Schlozman, and Henry Brady developed in *Voice and Equality* to explain how Indonesia's and Russia's varying levels of civil society engagement have influenced political participation following political liberalization. I argue that dense social interactions, measured by sociability and participation in associational life, stimulate elite-constraining political participation. In Indonesia, social and civic engagement has fostered the transmission of meaningful civic skills to the population. Indonesians have used these skills to organize opposition parties and contentious political acts. The absence of an analogous transfer of civic skills in Russia made it much harder for citizens to constrain elites.

This chapter contains four sections. First, I introduce my conceptualization and measurement of civil society and analyze ways in which civil society might influence democracy. I also outline civic voluntarism as a mechanism that links civil society to democracy's survival following political liberalization. The second section places Russia's and Indonesia's levels of civil society engagement and informal social interactions in a cross-national framework, revealing that Russian levels of engagement are far below the global average while Indonesian levels are far above it. Third, I show that Russians and Indonesians participate in different types of associations, and these differences have meaningful implications for recruitment into elite-constraining political participation. This chapter's final section analyzes the structure and norms of Russian and Indonesian civil society to show that Indonesians have succeeded in mobilizing the key resources of time, money, and civic skills to activate new forms of political participation, while Russians have not.

Civil Society, Democratization, and Civic Voluntarism

Linking Civil Society and Democracy's Survival

Theorists have long viewed civil society – defined here as the autonomous, intermediary stratum of society between the household and the state – as an important factor in supporting democracy. A robust civic life can limit the state's power when autonomous organizations inform political elites about societal demands and serve as "watchdogs" against elites' abuse of power. Civil society can broaden the flow of information between citizens and stimulate political participation by mobilizing supporters and recruiting new political leaders from civic circles. Tocqueville viewed voluntary associations as "schools of democracy" providing citizens with opportunities to learn the norms and skills necessary to take an active role in government.

Although many scholars view civil society as beneficial for democracy, the precise mechanism by which it makes this positive impact remains unclear. Advanced democracies generally have a more robust voluntary associational life than authoritarian political systems, where voluntary organizations face substantial constraints on their actions. It is unsurprising that we find less vibrant associational life in countries with less open political regimes, but this correlation is not evidence of causation.

If we consider causality within the specific context of democratizing regimes, most hypotheses about the role of civil society can be lumped into two broad approaches. The first focuses on individual-level attitudes and behaviors that, when aggregated, contribute to system-level effects. This approach builds on Tocqueville's notion of "schools of democracy." Two of the most prominent scholars taking this approach are Robert Putnam (1993, 2000) and Ronald Inglehart (1997), who both emphasize that civil society engenders people's sense of trust and civic engagement, which can facilitate purposive political participation. The second approach focuses on institutions as the units of analysis – namely on voluntary associations as intermediary organizations that aggregate and communicate popular interests. These associations provide citizen feedback to policymakers outside of elections.

These two approaches are not incompatible – it is possible that both mechanisms might have a causal effect on democracy. In both approaches, the link posited between civil society and democracy is indirect. Individual-level benefits from civil society engagement first affect an intervening variable – such as trust or sense of efficacy about political participation – which then influences people's interaction with political institutions. Institutional-level benefits from active voluntary associations must also be translated through an intervening variable – a constraint on the actions of political elites – which then influences whether democratic institutions and practices are perpetuated. Failure to acknowledge the indirect nature of these mechanisms can impede research on the link between civil society and democratization. If we look only at the direct relationship between levels of civil society and democracy at a single point in time, we may conclude that civil society does not affect democracy's presence or absence. Yet such a relationship may exist, one that is more complex than can be gleaned from a straightforward two-stage model that neglects intermediate steps along the causal chain.

Both approaches posit that civil society influences democracy via a multistage process that involves linkages between individual-level and societal-level behavior. For this reason, the relationship between civil society and democracy may be more salient at certain periods of democratization than others. More specifically, perhaps engagement in civil society is most relevant in the early stages of political liberalization. It is precisely during this stage, when the rules of the game and the political opportunity structure are in flux, that public pressure groups have the greatest likelihood of influencing the character of future institutions and practices. My argument emphasizes the interaction between civil society engagement and new opportunities for political participation that emerge as a result of political liberalization. The strength of civil society becomes causally important only when the political environment provides space for collective action that is not burdened with risk.

Additionally, most scholars who have posited a relationship between civil society and democracy have focused on established democracies, not newly democratizing regimes. It is possible that civil society's role in a democratizing system might be similar to its role in an established democracy, but the specific context of newly acquired political and civil liberties might also enhance the causal importance of civil society on democracy's trajectory.

As previously discussed, until all stakeholders accept newly liberalized political institutions and norms as "the only game in town" (Linz & Stepan, 1996), they are particularly vulnerable to elite abuse, and authoritarian backsliding remains a constant threat. At the same time, however, political liberalization creates new opportunities for political participation that can be used to hold political elites accountable between elections and make elections more competitive. Under these circumstances, robust civil society engagement can facilitate elite-constraining participation that mobilizes against elites' attempts to encroach upon political and civil freedoms. If civil society groups do not utilize the new political opportunity structure to apply pressure on elites, authoritarian backsliding can and often does occur.

Moreover, holding elites accountable is an iterative process. When elite-constraining behavior facilitates greater elite compliance with democratic norms and institutions, subsequent efforts on behalf of reform and accountability are bolstered. We see this dynamic in post-Suharto Indonesia, where citizens' organizations have established a pattern of building on previous successes in constraining elites. Likewise, individuals whose early mobilization efforts fail are less likely to exploit newly won political freedoms and institutions to mobilize in the future. Without mass efforts to constrain political elites, elites can and do roll back political freedoms, as the post-Communist Russian experience illustrates.

Civic Voluntarism in the Democratization Context

The civic voluntarism model – which Verba, Schlozman, and Brady developed in *Voice and Equality* – links involvement in voluntary associations with political participation in long-standing democracies. The authors find that individuals generally become active in politics when they have resources to participate and are part of a network where they can be recruited to participate. In the civic voluntarism model, apolitical civic and social organizations constitute an important locus where individuals acquire the resources that enable them to participate in politics and the social networks that often recruit them to participate. In this chapter, I first use the civic voluntarism model to examine how individuals become active in political life. I then extend the model beyond Verba, Schlozman and Brady's focus on long-standing democracies to illuminate how civil society affects the fate of democratization in polities that have recently experienced political opening, such as Russia and Indonesia.

Even though the civic voluntarism model has primarily been applied to advanced democracies, its causal logic remains relevant for democratizing regimes. By considering civic voluntarism together with the expansion of political participation opportunities generated by political liberalization, we can trace the causal processes linking civil society's vigor to democratic survival. First, individual-level involvement in civil society facilitates participation in political life. This connection is particularly relevant in the context of democratization, when new avenues for political activity emerge. If individuals are involved in civil society at a high rate in a given country, there is a greater probability that participation in these new realms of political activity will also be high, yielding more elite-constraining participation. As a result, competition among elites will be greater and officeholders' power will be circumscribed.

As Chapter 3 discussed, the crucial mechanism that links civil society engagement to democracy's survival is patterns of nonvoting political participation – namely, the widespread expansion of elite-constraining activities (which provide mass support for political opposition and public exposure of elite actions) instead of elite-enabling activities (which bolster incumbents). Indonesia's dense civil society offers a series of networks where citizen activists can be recruited for party work and contentious political acts. Russia's frail civil society, in contrast, has inhibited the expansion of elite-constraining participation. Moreover, Indonesian civil society transmits civic skills and norms of voluntary participation and charitable giving to citizens that are channeled into elite-constraining political participation.

Measuring Civil Society

How can we assess the overall volume of civil society in a given country or region? Until recently, the most common measure was to count organizations, either by collecting registration information in a given location during a particular interval or by looking at other signs of formal organizational structure – such as an office, phone number, or website. This approach presents many problems for cross-national research. A focus on registration emphasizes the legal face of an organization without considering its actual level of activity. It overestimates associations that exist only on paper and fails to consider groups that are highly structured but not officially registered, thereby creating a bias toward registered groups in measurement. Approaches that gather formal indicators of civil society organizations also make it nearly impossible to compare data across societies, because rules for registration and distribution of information vary greatly across countries.

An alternate measure of civil society looks at individual-level participation in associations as reported in public opinion surveys. By focusing on individuals' behavior rather than formal indicators of organizational structure, this approach emphasizes the vitality of associational life and is likely to include participation in voluntary and social organizations that lack offices and phone numbers.

Measuring individual-level participation in associational life provides us with little information about the relationship between civil society and the state. It tells us nothing about whether one type of organization might be more influential than another, or about whether civil society as a whole is efficacious in affecting particular outcomes. These issues, however, are not central to my research. The principal question in this chapter is how citizens' civil society engagement influences their political participation. Therefore, individual-level engagement in associational life suffices as a measure of civil society.

A second methodological consideration is determining which types of activities fall under the rubric of civil society. While a full discussion of this issue is beyond the scope of this chapter, two points of contention are particularly relevant to my study. The first involves how much organizational formality and structure must be present for an activity to be considered part of civil society. Most scholars hold that an activity must take place in a formal organizational or associational setting in order to be considered part of civil society. In this conceptualization, informal gatherings of friends and spontaneous social movements are not part of civil society. Yet, for individuals providing information to public opinion surveys about their associational memberships – the information I use to measure civil society – this distinction between formal and informal is blurred. For example, is a group of individuals who gather every Saturday afternoon in the same place to play football a formal association, even if the group has no name, appointed leader, or formal structure, and is united only by the players' agreement to play together at an appointed time and place? The aspect of civil society that interests us as a possible mechanism for fostering democratization is participation in group activities, not the formal structure of a group. The experiences individuals have through participation in associational life are what matter, and there is little reason to believe that experiences in an informal football group or formal football club differ vastly in this respect.

Is a closed-shop union an element of civil society? If all workers in an enterprise must be members of a union, their participation may not be fully voluntary. As long as the union is autonomous from the state and maintains a formal structure and membership, however, most scholars would consider it an element of civil society. Yet it is possible that a person who acknowledges union membership in a survey has never actively participated in the organization, other than paying dues. If we emphasize organizational formality in measuring civil society, our results would not register the football player's participation but would count the union member's. Such a measure is not an accurate reflection of Tocqueville's conception of the voluntary organizational sociability that binds individuals into a community and fosters collective goals. By considering only formal membership as a proxy for civic engagement, we may overlook the most relevant aspect of civil society for democratization: voluntary interpersonal interactions in organized settings.

The second point of contention involves associations' autonomy from the state. While state-sponsored organizations can hardly be expected to play a watchdog role, even state-sponsored civil society groups can foster democracy indirectly by encouraging participation and the development of civic skills. Youth recreational sports leagues, for example, may receive government funding, but they also play a civil society role by promoting engagement and leadership, qualities that can foster democracy. Since we are examining the indirect link between civil society and democracy, it behooves us to consider civil society's formality and autonomy in flexible terms. Flexibility is especially necessary when studying postcommunist countries, most of which have a relatively short history of autonomous associational life and a long history of extensive citizen experience in formal, state-sponsored associations.

Several scholars incorporate greater flexibility into the notion of civil society by focusing on a related concept: social capital (Fukuyama, 2001; Paxton, 2002; Putnam, 2000). Like civil society, social capital has many different definitions, but generally comprises non-monetary forms of interaction that generate resources that can be used to influence others. Some scholars view social capital as a concept that is broader than civil society since it encompasses both participation in formal associational life and informal social interaction (Howard, 2003). Others note that social capital is used more narrowly than civil society to emphasize particular features that facilitate cooperation, such as friendship networks, norms, and social trust (Smidt, 2003, pp. 4–6). While such features are undoubtedly important to the study of civic life, they are not the only aspects of social interactions that may generate resources for democratization. For example, the acquisition of participatory skills and potential recruitment into political life may be just as important.

Consequently, we should consider a broad range of linkages between civic engagement and democratization, including attention to informal social interactions, which may help us gauge civil society's vibrancy. One can hypothesize that individuals who socialize with greater frequency are more likely to form associations. Alternatively, perhaps belonging to a larger number of associations increases an individual's frequency of informal social interactions through broader social networks. Untangling the causal arrow between formal and informal participation in social life is not possible with observational data, and is not necessary for the purposes of this analysis.

I provide information on both associational memberships and informal social interactions in Russia and Indonesia. I leave aside the question of whether my measure of informal social interactions can be considered "social capital." Given the measurement challenges outlined earlier, paying attention to both formal associational life and informal social interactions helps us create a portrait of civil society that most closely resembles the autonomous, self-initiated sphere of activity Tocqueville described.

Cross-national Benchmarks: Russia and Indonesia as Outliers

Comparing Levels of Civic Engagement

In evaluating any public's level of civil society engagement, it is necessary to establish a comparative benchmark. The most comprehensive cross-national data set that includes measures for civil society is the World Values Survey (WVS).[1] The WVS gathers data in a decentralized manner, occasionally leading to differences in the quality of sampling and interviewing

---

[1] Data files and questionnaires for the World Values Survey can be downloaded from www .worldvaluessurvey.org. The Fourth Wave data used in this chapter were downloaded in July 2008 and the Fifth Wave data were downloaded in February 2009.

across countries. Despite these shortcomings, it provides some of the best data for measuring individual-level indicators of civil society.

The WVS asks respondents about their participation in various formal organizations. The wording of this question, however, has changed over different waves of the survey. In the Second Wave (1989–1993) and Fourth Wave (1999–2004), respondents were given a list of thirteen different organizations and asked if they were a member of these organizations. In the Third Wave (1994–1999) and the Fifth Wave (2005–2008), respondents were given a list of eight or nine different organizations and asked if they were an active member, an inactive member, or not a member of these organizations. These differences in question wording make it impossible to analyze precise change in civil society engagement over time. At best, we can compare the levels in different countries within the same survey wave.

The WVS' Fifth Wave provides data from the largest cross-section of geographic locations and is the only WVS poll to include data on organizational membership in Indonesia. I calculated average membership rates for each country in the data set by summing the number of active and inactive memberships for each individual and dividing by the total number of valid responses in each country's survey. The end result is a variable that measures civil society engagement and ranges from 0.15 in Jordan to 5.58 in India, with a mean among all respondents of 1.69. Indonesia's average membership level is 2.55 and Russia's average level is 0.77.

Only ten countries in the entire WVS have higher average membership rates than those observed in Indonesia. Among all WVS respondents, 62.6 percent belong to at least one organization. Among Indonesians the figure is 83.8 percent, while among Russians it is only 35.7. Both Indonesia and Russia deviate from the global norm, but in opposite directions.[2]

Variation in Association Types: Religious Organizations vs. Unions
Table 5.1 displays Indonesian and Russian membership rates in different types of organizations. Cases in which the Indonesian or Russian levels of participation are substantially higher or lower than the WVS mean are circled.

---

[2] Numerous studies have identified low levels of participation in associational life in the post-Communist world (Howard, 2003; Rose, 2009). Among the eight post-Communist cases included in the WVS, the average membership rate is 0.84, significantly below the average for all WVS respondents. Considerable variation exists within this group, though, ranging from a low of 0.28 in Romania to a high of 1.43 in Slovenia. Only Romania and Bulgaria have lower average membership rates than Russia.

TABLE 5.1. Organizational membership in Russia and Indonesia (WVS 2005–2008)

Organizational type	WVS sample (%)	Indonesia (%)	Russia (%)
Religious organization	41.1 (N=70,633)	67.0 (N=1,987)	11.1 (N=2,007)
Sport or recreational organization	26.6 (N=70,372)	23.7 (N=1,967)	13.6 (N=2,015)
Art, music, or educational organization	19.8 (N=70,204)	30.2 (N=1,958)	10.4 (N=2,015)
Labor union	16.4 (N=69,959)	9.2 (N=1,949)	17.6 (N=1,999)
Political party	16.2 (N=70,048)	16.4 (N=1,955)	5.1 (N=2,012)
Environmental organization	13.2 (N=70,036)	36.9 (N=1,956)	4.7 (N=2,013)
Professional association	15.6 (N=69,841)	27.9 (N=1,946)	7.7 (N=2,003)
Humanitarian or charitable organization	17.7 (N=70,000)	33.4 (N=1,948)	5.7 (N=2,013)
Consumer organization	10.2 (N=68,661)	11.1 (N=1,924)	3.9 (N=2,009)

As Table 5.1 demonstrates, Indonesians have high rates of membership across a variety of organizational types. The only two areas where Indonesians have membership rates below the global average are in recreational organizations and labor unions, the latter of which is certainly a product of the repression of labor organization in Indonesia following the purges of the Communist Party of Indonesia (PKI) in the late 1960s. Indonesians exhibit especially high rates of participation in religious, environmental, professional, and charitable organizations.

Russians, meanwhile, have low rates of participation in most types of organizations. Their levels of participation are below the global average for every type of organization except labor unions. Yet it would be misleading to view this statistic as evidence of a vibrant labor movement in Russia. High rates of labor union participation are an artifact of the Soviet era, when all workers were required to belong to unions and unions were the primary institution for allocating social benefits. Most Russians who belong to a labor union today are members of the Federation of Independent Trade

Unions of Russia (FNPR), the successor of the Soviet-era trade union to which almost all workers were required to belong. If we break down the membership rate of WVS respondents into active versus inactive members, only 3.4 percent of Russians are active union members, compared to 14.2 percent who are inactive. We must bear this distinction in mind when considering the high levels of labor union membership in Russia.[3]

Differences between Indonesians' and Russians' levels of participation in organizations are dramatic. In most cases, the percentage of Indonesians participating in an organization is more than double (and sometimes triple or quadruple) the percentage of Russians participating in the same type of organization. Indonesians and Russians also tend to belong to different types of organizations. As Table 5.1 demonstrates, the most common type of organization to which Indonesians belong is religious (67 percent). Moreover, of the respondents who belong to at least one organization in the Indonesian WVS sample, more than 80 percent belong to a religious organization. In contrast, only 11 percent of Russians belong to a religious organization. As discussed earlier, Russians' dominant form of participation in associational life is nominal union membership. In the Russian WVS sample, 48 percent of the individuals who reported belonging to at least one organization were members of a union. In fact, 24 percent of individuals belonging to at least one organization were only union members; they did not belong to any other organizations.

This variation in types of associational memberships could have important consequences for democratization. According to the civic voluntarism model, involvement in civil society facilitates political participation when individuals develop civic skills that can be transferred into political activism. Some types of associations, including religious groups, are better at generating civic skills than others (Verba, Schlozman, & Brady, 1995).

Change in Russian Civil Society over Time: 1990–2006

The WVS provides only a single snapshot of Indonesians' participation in associations, but it furnishes data on Russia dating back to 1990. While it would be desirable to compare all these statistics directly, the differences in question wording discussed earlier make such a comparison vulnerable to response biases. We can make a more precise comparison by grouping

---

[3] Additionally, the Labor Code reform of 2000–2002 severely curtailed the bargaining and organizational power of Russian trade unions. Consequently, unions lost much of what potential they developed in the 1990s for demanding elite accountability. While trade unions have played an important role in democratization in several cases – most famously Poland – Russian trade unions are not robust, truly autonomous organizations.

data from the 1990 and 1999 surveys together, and then grouping data from the 1995 and 2006 surveys together, since the question wording was identical in these specific years.

The data from 1990 and 1999 show a considerable decline in both Russians' average number of memberships and the percentage of individuals belonging to at least one organization. While nearly 71 percent of Russians belonged to at least one association in 1990, less than half of survey respondents were members of associations by 1999. Similarly, the average membership rate dropped from 0.98 to 0.37. The decline in organizational engagement mainly reflected a weakening in labor union membership, which dropped by two-thirds during this nine-year interval. Participation in political parties, community organizations, youth organizations, and women's organizations also fell. Declining participation in these groups is presumably related to the collapse of the Communist Party of the Soviet Union (CPSU) and its myriad of auxiliary organizations. Since participation in these organizations was not necessarily voluntary before 1991, it is difficult to assess whether participation in associational life in 1990 Russia accurately captures the condition of civil society. Nevertheless, it is clear that once individuals were free to join or not join different types of organizations after the collapse of the Soviet Union, Russians' engagement in associational life declined rather than expanded.

Comparing data from 1995 and 2006 provides rather curious findings. First, Russians' average membership rate rose from 0.66 to 0.77, suggesting that Russian participation in associational life increased between the mid-1990s and the mid-2000s. Yet the percentage of individuals belonging to at least one organization actually declined during this same period, from 48.2 percent to 35.2 percent. If we consider these two statistics together, it appears that fewer Russians are participating in associational life, but individuals who do participate are joining more organizations. Indeed, if we compare participation in different types of organizations, we see an increase in every type of association between 1995 and 2006 except labor unions. The percentage of respondents belonging to a labor union declined from 40 percent in 1995 to 18 percent in 2006.

It is interesting to note that Russians' average membership rate increased even after the government placed meaningful restrictions on civil society activity during this period. Even though Russians' civil society participation was below the global average in 2006, their average membership rate was higher than during the 1990s, a period of greater freedom in the country. Therefore, Russia's low level of civil society engagement is probably not exclusively a consequence of greater restrictions on civil liberties.

The trends over four waves of WVS data on associational memberships in Russia provide useful information. First, with the Soviet Union's collapse, overall participation in associational life declined. Even if the associations Soviet Russian respondents belonged to in 1990 were not autonomous, they did provide a structured forum for interpersonal interactions that in many instances disappeared with the associations. Second, despite increased authoritarianism and greater restrictions on freedom of association in Russia between the mid-1990s and the mid-2000s, participation in associational life actually increased during this period. Even taking this increase into consideration, however, Russians' overall levels of engagement remain well below the global average.

Comparing Informal Social Interactions
Four WVS questions provide particularly useful data for comparing Russians' and Indonesians' informal social interactions. These questions ask how often people spend time with friends, colleagues from work, people from their religious organization, and people from sports, voluntary, or service groups (WVS Integrated Questionnaire, questions A058-A061). For each question respondents may answer "weekly," "once or twice a month," "only a few times a year," or "not at all." These questions were not asked in the WVS' Fifth Wave (2005–2008), so my analysis relies on data from the Fourth Wave (1999–2004), which contains responses from 70,694 individuals in sixty-four countries.

I rescaled each response to range from 0 to 1, with "0" representing "not at all" and "1" representing "weekly." I then constructed a "sociability index," which averages individuals' scores from these four sociability questions. The end result is a variable that ranges from 0 to 1, where "0" corresponds to an individual who spends no time with people from these four realms of social life (1,202 people in the sample) and "1" corresponds to an individual who spends time weekly with people from all four realms (2,001 people in the sample). The distribution between these two extremes roughly resembles a bell curve with a mean of 0.49, which translates to spending time with individuals from three of the social realms approximately once per month.

If we average across all individuals in a country's sample, we can generate a measure for a country's average sociability. The country with the absolute lowest level of sociability is Russia, with a score of 0.30, which equates to interacting with friends once a month and individuals from two other realms a few times a year. The country with the absolute highest sociability score is Indonesia with 0.79, which equates to spending time every week with individuals from two of the social realms and time every month with individuals from the two other realms. Similar to the trend we observed with participation in associational life, both Indonesia and Russia deviate dramatically from the global norm of social interaction. In fact, they constitute the most and least sociable populations in the data set.

Using measures of associational memberships and informal social interactions to examine civil society cross-nationally, it is clear Indonesians are extremely sociable and participate regularly in associational life. They meet often with friends, colleagues, and other community members. The average Indonesian belongs to more than two organizations, and the majority of Indonesians belong to a religious organization. In contrast, the average Russian belongs to less than one organization and inactive membership in a closed-shop union is the modal form of civil society engagement. Indonesia's civil society is extraordinarily rich and dense. Russian communities lack analogous structures and patterns of behavior.

Civil Society in Russia and Indonesia: Citizen Interviews

Russia: Low Levels of Civic Engagement

Russians' low levels of engagement in associational life and informal social interactions, as exhibited in national surveys, were reflected in my citizen interviews as well. Among my Russian respondents, half were current or former union members, but none actively participated in union activities. In fact, when I asked respondents if they belonged to any organizations, none volunteered union membership – they revealed their nominal union membership only when I specifically asked about it. Aside from union membership, only one quarter of my Russian respondents belonged to any organizations, and only two were members of more than one organization.

Other than union membership, the most common form of associational activity among my Russian respondents was participation in recreational, cultural, or sports organizations, including choirs and martial arts clubs. Most of these cultural and athletic groups meet weekly or biweekly. In several instances, these "groups" were not associations per se, but regular dance or sports lessons at the same facility with the same participants. Such groups generally do not have roots in the Soviet past and reflect some of the more typical ways in which Russian society has embraced greater freedom in the private sphere. I also asked respondents about the frequency of their social interactions and used this information to divide them into three categories of sociability: high, medium, and low.[4] Sociability levels were higher in Krasnoyarsk than in Kazan, but collectively, most Russian respondents exhibited "medium" levels of sociability.

The sparseness of civil society in Russia revealed from my interviews is consistent with other scholars' findings. Both Marc Howard (2003) and Richard Rose (2009) have noted the persistence of informal friendship networks in the post-Communist region in general and in Russia specifically. The sociability measures I constructed are not intended as a proxy for the informal networks Howard and Rose described. My indicators measure frequency of social interactions, not reliance on particular relationships for acquiring or accessing needed resources, a concept requiring additional information to gauge. Thus, I would not interpret Russia's low sociability scores as evidence contradicting Howard and Rose's findings.

My interview questions did not seek to determine the strength of informal friendship networks. In general, though, I found that the Soviet-era social and economic structures that gave rise to these networks – such as employment practices that allowed for considerable leisure time, a shortage of consumer goods, and the absence of a private housing market that limited mobility – have changed in ways that may weaken their persistence.

My Russian interview respondents over the age of thirty-five frequently volunteered that they did not have as much leisure time as before and were unable to meet friends and former classmates as frequently. Dramatic decreases in leisure time began in the early 1990s when Russia embarked on its transition to a market economy. During this period, the average Russian found her wages did not keep pace with the cost of living and the social benefits she received in the Soviet welfare state were quickly evaporating. These circumstances created a new set of unmet household needs that cut into Russians' free time. Few of my respondents regularly visited friends in their homes – the most common form of social interaction during the Soviet era.

---

[4] Individuals coded as "high" socialized with friends or neighbors on a daily basis or socialized with them regularly and participated in at least one weekly organized activity. Individuals coded as "medium" socialized with friends or neighbors regularly or socialized with them rarely but participated in at least one weekly organized activity. Individuals coded as "low" did not socialize regularly with friends or neighbors.

Second, markets for renting and purchasing housing have developed, increasing residential mobility. Consequently, individuals are not developing the close ties with neighbors that were common in the Soviet era. A fifty-eight-year-old Russian homemaker in Krasnoyarsk reflected on these points when I asked whether she paid visits to friends or neighbors:

> I practically never go for visits. It seems to me that few people now make visits, except for young people.... Before, it was a given that neighbors were very close. Now, many people rent apartments. Before, we didn't have this – people waited in line [to receive an apartment]. Now, people come and go, come and go.

Last, increasing income inequality in Russia appears to make some individuals more self-conscious about their economic position and to influence their feelings about maintaining contacts with acquaintances who now have a higher (or lower) income.[5] A thirty-nine-year-old female police administrator in Kazan described the challenges these circumstances present:

> It was easier to visit people [during the Soviet era]. You just went to their houses. Now, you need to think about it, because if you go for a visit, they will lay out a table. And maybe they won't have anything to put on it. Before, everyone had some jam, would boil potatoes, and then there would be tea. What would you have with tea? Well, we all had cookies because they were rather cheap. We didn't buy expensive cookies! These interactions were much easier.... So there is some nostalgia, specifically regarding personal relations. Then, it seems to me, I had more free time. Work was a little bit different, and there was more free time. Now, everything is so busy, you don't make visits because there is no time.

My interview respondents cited limited free time, greater residential mobility, and consciousness about income differences as factors contributing to a decline in their social interactions. These factors may be eroding previously robust informal networks as well.

My Russian interviews reveal several arenas of *inaction* in Russian associational life. None of my respondents was an active member of any organizations with a political or policy-oriented agenda. One individual had joined the United Russia party, but did not actually attend meetings or events related to the party. Additionally, participation in religious groups and student organizations is largely absent in Russia. As Table 5.1 reveals, the most common form of organizational membership

---

[5] According to the Bank of Finland Institute for Economies in Transition, Russia's Gini score at the time the Soviet Union dissolved was 29 (2008). According to the UNDP's 2009 *Human Development Report*, the Gini score for Russia in 2009 was 37.5, indicating a rise in income inequality.

cross-nationally is religious – with 41 percent of WVS respondents belonging to a religious organization. The survey data show that Russia is well below this norm. Only one of my fifty Russian respondents participates in a religious group – a young Orthodox Christian man in a Bible study group.

Low levels of participation in religious groups are undoubtedly linked to the Soviet policy of forced atheism, which effectively destroyed religious communities and the social relationships that emanate from them. In effect, Soviet policy on religion, which was implemented more forcefully in Russia than other Soviet republics, incapacitated the most common mass-based voluntary organization that existed prior to Communism – worship groups. Consequently, very few parents passed on traditions of public worship to their children. When I asked respondents if their parents observed religious practices during the respondents' childhoods, they often responded, "This was not done. It was forbidden." Yet several respondents recalled clandestine religious practices within their homes, usually instigated by grandparents who were alive in the prerevolutionary era.[6] One forty-eight-year-old Tatar woman recalled that her parents "read the Muslim prayer (*namaz*). When my grandmother was alive, she taught us how to read the Muslim prayer. It was a secret. Each person in his or her home." To the extent that religious activity persisted during the Soviet period, it became a private, rather than communal, act. After the Soviet Union's collapse in 1991, Russian citizens were granted freedom to practice religion. Organized religion has revived in post-Soviet Russia, but fewer than 5 percent of Russian citizens attend religious services at least once per week (World Values Survey 2005). Only four of my fifty Russian respondents (two Russian Orthodox women, one Russian Orthodox man, and one Muslim man) fit this description.

Russia also lacks vibrant student organizations, which are often a visible component of civil society in other countries, including Indonesia. Although the education level in Russia is much higher than in Indonesia, and nearly half of my Russian respondents had a university education, Russian student organizations do not play a meaningful role in the country's associational life. The Russian students I interviewed participated in associational life at a higher rate than the non-student population, yet they did not belong to well-organized, politically active student organizations (like one sees in Indonesia). For example, one Russian student belonged to a choir, another to a weekly discussion club, and a third

---

[6] These stories were most common among older individuals, particularly Tatar Muslims.

to an English-language club. Two of these three groups were not affiliated with a university.

In the Soviet era, the Communist Youth League (the Komsomol) supervised all student activity in Russia, and its demise has created something of an organizational vacuum for Russian youth. Under *glasnost'* the Komsomol became an important training ground for pro-democracy activists. Multiple interviews in Kazan revealed that discussions among students at Kazan State University and student activism in the Komsomol were the genesis of several grassroots movements that emerged in Tatarstan in the late 1980s, including the Russian cultural movement and the pro-democracy organization Equal Rights and Lawfulness. Indeed, there is evidence that student activism facilitated political participation in Russia in the early years of democratization, but this activism was not sustained over time. Russian student activism of the late 1980s and early 1990s appears to have died with the Komsomol and no other institutions have filled the void. Some clubs can be found in Russian universities, but nothing like the energized Indonesian student organizations I discuss later.

In Soviet Russia, there were no civic organizations independent of the Communist Party. Civic organizations *did* exist in all realms of life, from scouts to unions and professional associations to hobby clubs. Yet they were all established, licensed, and supervised by the CPSU. When the Soviet Union collapsed and the CPSU dissolved, virtually the entire structure of societal organization folded as well. In several instances, motivated activists formed independent organizations from the remnants of former Soviet groups, but the central premise for organizing civil society had disappeared. Russians were left to regroup almost from scratch, and not all had the skills, interest, or wherewithal to build civil society anew.

Indonesia: Robust Religious, Community, and Student Organizations

My Indonesian respondents exhibited considerably higher levels of engagement in associational life and informal social interactions than my Russian respondents. More than half of my fifty Indonesian respondents belonged to at least one organization, and about one-quarter belonged to more than one. As for informal social interactions, almost half of my Indonesian respondents fell into the category of "high" sociability. Only eleven of my fifty respondents exhibited "low" levels of sociability. The high level of civic engagement in Indonesia is largely a consequence of robust participation in religious, community, and student organizations. My Indonesian respondents mirrored my Russian respondents in that few were members of explicitly political organizations. Only two belonged to political parties, although several were members of student groups that were regularly recruited into political action, a point I discuss later.

Consistent with the WVS findings, the most common type of organization my Indonesian respondents belonged to was religious. Muslim respondents were frequently members of prayer groups (*pengajian*). Most Muslim prayer groups were organized in the immediate locality; neighbors on the same street usually participated in the same *pengajian* group. In accordance with Muslim tradition, *pengajian* groups were segregated by sex. Considerable variation existed in how often groups met, from once or twice per month to several times a week. Groups meeting more regularly usually rotated meetings among members' homes, while groups that met less often usually convened at the mosque. The size of *pengajian* groups varied, with most ranging from thirty to sixty participants. *Pengajian* groups served as more than a form of organized worship. In addition to coming together to pray and study the Qur'an, participants – also neighbors – visited with each other and shared community news. Guest speakers – usually scholars of Islam – frequently came to *pengajian* meetings, providing opportunities for sharing information about religious and family life.

My Christian respondents in Indonesia, particularly Protestants, often belonged to Bible study, song, and prayer groups. Participants attended group meetings in addition to Sunday services at their parishes. Christian religious groups were generally organized by specific denomination, and members usually attended a group close to their home.[7] Christian religious groups typically met two or three times per week, sometimes in their parishes and sometimes at parishioners' homes. In many instances, these groups were integrated by sex, although there sometimes were specific groups for young people or students. Like *pengajian* groups, Christian religious groups were very social. In addition to participating in religious activities, members visited with each other and shared community news. The size of Christian religious groups also varied. Groups meeting at parishes often numbered fifty or more participants, while groups gathering at members' homes were generally smaller.

---

[7] Considerable variation exists in Medan regarding ethnic and confessional heterogeneity within neighborhoods. Some neighborhoods are predominantly Javanese, Chinese, or Tamil, but many working- and middle-class neighborhoods are quite diverse. For example, in the district of Polonia, I interviewed a Javanese Muslim, a Tamil Buddhist, a Batak Karo Catholic, and a Minahasan Protestant – all of whom lived within a short motorbike ride from each other.

In addition to neighborhood-level religious groups, Indonesian civil society is heavily influenced by the two prominent mainstream Muslim social organizations, Muhammadiyah and Nahdlatul Ulama (NU). Muhammadiyah and NU are large, hierarchically organized mass organizations that engage in a wide range of social, educational, and religious activities.[8] Muhammadiyah, which means "followers of Muhammad," was founded in 1912 in Central Java as a reform organization focused on education, health, and the poor. Emphasizing rule-governed practices rather than focusing on individual leaders, Muhammadiyah developed an extensive organization across the country that included schools that provided a full array of subjects beyond religious education. In response to the growing strength of Muhammadiyah, in 1926 traditionalist leaders formed Nahdlatul Ulama, which means "Revival of Religious Scholars." Like Muhammadiyah, NU developed into a large organization aimed at providing educational and social services for adherents. Yet the heart of the NU organization consists of religious leaders (*kiai*) and the network of Islamic boarding schools (*pesantren*) they operate (Pringle, 2010).

These two organizations are currently the largest civic organizations in Indonesia. Although NU and Muhammadiyah differ in their ideological views and religious practices, both organizations are Islamic groups that engage in social welfare provision by sponsoring schools, hospitals, and religious teaching. While there are differences in how these associations are organized, both have a hierarchical structure that links village-level organizations up to a national coordinating body, and both have systems for leadership development. While exact membership numbers for these groups are unavailable, as of the year 2000, Muhammadiyah estimated having more than 25 million members nationwide (Hefner, 2000). NU is larger, with more than 30 million members (Pringle, 2010, p. 114). According to Robert Pringle, approximately one quarter of the Indonesian population belongs to Muhammadiyah or NU. As my interviews indicated, there are also considerable numbers of individuals who are not official members of these organizations, but consider themselves adherents.

NU estimates that about 25 million individuals in East Java (70 percent of the region's population) belong to the organization (EJ-4, interview, June 3, 2009; EJ-10, interview, June 8, 2009). Five of my respondents in Surabaya volunteered that they or their families participated in

---

[8] An extensive literature describes significant differences between these two organizations. For more detail, see Doorn-Harder (2006) and Asyari (2009).

NU, although several other *pengajian* participants likely belonged to NU-organized prayer groups. One Javanese respondent from Medan noted that she participated in Muhammadiyah[9] and belonged to a Muhammadiyah *pengajian*.

A second common form of associational membership Indonesian respondents mentioned is Family Welfare Groups (PKK) and neighborhood associations (RT/RW). Both of these organizations were intimately linked with the New Order regime and provided the state with a clear mechanism for promoting development goals and maintaining social oversight at the village and neighborhood levels. Since the collapse of the New Order, however, both the PKK and RT/RW have lost their overtly political character and have become much more autonomous organizations.

The PKK was initiated as a top-down women's group in the 1970s with the goal of promoting health, education, and household-level economic advancement among Indonesian families. Under Suharto, women's positions within the PKK were determined by their husbands' positions in the national bureaucracy (Marcoes, 2002). The PKK was (and still is) structured from the top level of government all the way down to the neighborhood level. At the neighborhood level, the wife of the head of the RT was automatically the head of the neighborhood PKK (Perkasa & Hendyito, 2003). This method for determining leadership positions within the PKK, which gave no consideration to a woman's specific abilities, and the top-down design of development programs, generated extensive criticism of the PKK as a vehicle for female empowerment (Marcoes, 2002; Wieringa, 1992). Since the New Order ended, however, PKK positions are no longer determined by a husband's status, and PKK volunteers have greater opportunities to determine the organization's activities (Perkasa & Hendyito, 2003). PKK volunteers carry out a range of activities, including promoting literacy, organizing nutrition classes, teaching small skills and crafts, and implementing Indonesia's family planning program. While the PKK is not autonomous from the state, women who join the organization and carry out its programs are all volunteers. My interview respondents who belonged to the PKK saw their role as providing important services to neighbors and communities and valued their participation.

---

[9] While East Java is the stronghold for NU, Muhammadiyah is more prominent in Central Java. Both organizations were founded in Java and are more active there than on the outer islands.

The system of neighborhood associations (RT/RW) began under Japanese occupation during World War II and, like the PKK, was also structured to provide the government with a link down to the neighborhood level. Several households are organized into "neighbors' associations" (*rukun tetangga* or RT), and each RT selects a chairperson. Multiple RT units are organized into "citizens' associations" (*rukun warga* or RW). All RT chairpersons participate in the RW to which they are designated and select the RW chairman (Logsdon, 1974). Historically, RT/RW chairpersons have carried out basic administrative duties, such as registering births, deaths, and changes in residency. While RT/RW chairpersons were not formal civil servants, the organization provided the state with information about population flows, and the state could easily use RT/RW organizations to exercise social control and mobilize pro-regime activities. During the Suharto period, the neighborhood association system monitored citizens and mobilized them for elections in addition to organizing and providing important municipal services (Dwianto, 2003; Kurasawa, 2009). In the post-Suharto era, neighborhood associations have transitioned to operating as meaningful community organizations that serve to represent neighborhood members. The RT/RW organizes neighborhood watches and community celebrations, and can also help communicate local concerns to the government, allowing members to participate in bottom-up decision making (Kurasawa, 2009). Similar to *pengajian* groups, PKK groups and RT/RW are comprised of individuals living in the same location. It is not uncommon that the same groups of neighbors participate in several of these organizations, developing community relationships that are reinforced in multiple settings.

While my respondents in both Surabaya and Medan mentioned participation in religious groups, the PKK, and the RT/RW, two other types of organizations were also common among ethnic Batak residents in Medan. The first are mutual assistance associations (*serikat tolong-menolong*, or STM), which provide members with a form of collective insurance. STM members are committed to help neighbors, particularly in organizing traditional Batak ceremonies for weddings and funerals.[10] The second organization, the *marga*, refers to kinship networks to which Bataks belong based on their patrilineal descent. According to William Frederick and Robert Worden (1992), the *marga* has evolved into "a

---

[10] Relatively little has been written about *serikat tolong-menolong*. Based on my interviews in Medan, it appears that these organizations are prevalent among Christian Bataks and are based on place of residence. I found no evidence of STM organizations existing among Muslim Batak communities.

flexible social unit" among contemporary Batak. They note that "Batak who resettle in urban areas, such as Medan and Jakarta, draw on *marga* affiliations for financial support and political alliances." Several of my Batak respondents in Medan described attending monthly *marga* meetings. They see their *marga* associations not as extended family networks, but rather as a formalized social unit that brings together individuals with a shared cultural interest.

All Indonesian community associations described earlier existed during the Suharto regime, and most have been present in Indonesia for generations. In the case of the PKK and RT/RW, Suharto's New Order regime provided an important institutional structure, but these associations survived the Suharto era and have now adapted to conditions of greater autonomy. Even though the New Order regime was oppressive, it did provide meaningful space for civic organization around apolitical aims, and this legacy has served as an important resource for Indonesians in the post-Suharto era. Indeed, I found that most of my Indonesian respondents belonged to organizations that were allowed to exist under the New Order rather than to newly established groups, suggesting that the connection between civic engagement and political participation in Indonesia is less a consequence of new organizations emerging as a result of political liberalization, and more likely stems from opportunities to develop and transfer civic skills to new arenas of political activity.

In addition to formal associations, urban life in both Surabaya and Medan exhibits other forms of structured community cooperation that reflect practices common in regional villages, namely *arisan* and *gotong-royong* activities. *Arisan*, the Indonesian term used to describe rotating credit associations, are present in many Surabaya and Medan neighborhoods and serve economic and social functions. Eleven of my Indonesian respondents belonged to *arisan*. Most *arisan* participants are women; only one male respondent from either city participated in an *arisan*.[11] Most groups meet monthly, and *arisan* participation correlates positively with associational memberships and sociability in both cities.

Gotong-royong, the Indonesian term frequently translated into English as "reciprocity" or "mutual aid,"[12] takes on a very concrete meaning in

---

[11] Several men in each city also noted that their wives belonged to women-only *arisan*, which have been organized regularly by the PKK. Many individuals noted that there were also family *arisan* in their communities open to both men and women.

[12] The term originates from the Javanese verb *ngotong*, which means "several people carrying something together." It gained national symbolic prominence when Sukarno discussed it in a speech in 1945 (Bowen, 1986).

urban neighborhoods, as it typically involves cleaning and maintenance of shared space. The practice of *gotong-royong* in urban neighborhoods builds on a long tradition in rural villages that emphasizes the duty of members to serve the broader community and provide labor for tasks that require a critical mass, such as harvesting crops, constructing roads or buildings, or preparing for important rituals (Bowen, 1986; Soemardjan, 1963). Neighborhood associations generally plan *gotong-royong* activities at regular intervals, and, historically, social pressure to participate is high (Perkasa & Hendyito, 2003). The frequency of *gotong-royong* activities varied considerably across my respondents' neighborhoods. Some individuals participated every weekend, while others reported that *gotong-royong* activities happened only a few times per year.

Curiously, one can find a Soviet-era analogy to *gotong-royong* activities in the *subbotnik* – regular Saturday clean-up and beautification projects carried out in Soviet neighborhoods, schools, and workplaces, usually before major holidays. Many of my Russian respondents old enough to remember *subbotnik* activities recalled them fondly for the social opportunities they provided. Several respondents remembered that after the work was done, they would have picnics or other social activities. Based on my interview findings, the *subbotnik* appears to have died with Communism in Kazan and Krasnoyarsk. Additionally, I found no post-Soviet examples of other structured community activities among Russian respondents in these cities. In spite of Russia's history of community organizing around neighborhood beautification projects, the absence of neighborhood-level community organizing in contemporary Russia stands in stark contrast to Indonesia, where such activities continue under democracy.

While neighborhood-based associations are the most common form of organization among Indonesians, Indonesians with higher levels of education and professional employment participate in a broader set of social networks, including student and professional associations. After growing up in neighborhoods where their parents engaged in vibrant associational lives, young Indonesians who enter university tend to engage in a large number of associational activities.

Student activism has an illustrious history in Indonesia, dating back to the anticolonial movement that gave birth to the 1928 "Youth Pledge" – which proclaimed the ideals of one motherland, one nation, and one language. Student organizations in Indonesia have a history of independence from both the state and universities. Students organized with relative ease during the first decade of the New Order regime until major uprisings in 1974 and 1978 led to repression of student activism. When restrictions inhibited campus-based student activities, many students formed study groups that allowed them to keep student networks alive. During the mid-1980s, different student groups in Java began coordinating with each other. After *keterbukaan* (openness) began in the early 1990s, students became more active and more political. New organizations emerged, coordination between groups in different cities intensified, and involvement became more widespread.

In the 1990s, student activism evolved into a formidable anti-Suharto force.[13] Some students, such as those who belonged to the visible and popular People's Democratic Party (Partai Rakyat Demokratik, PRD), promoted radical changes. The PRD (which was repressed for its activism) and other student groups began organizing poor people in rural and urban areas, with the goal of criticizing the New Order regime regarding land disputes and labor conditions. Other student organizations were based on religious identification, and while not explicitly political, could be mobilized for political ends. The largest of these groups, the Islamic Students Association (HMI), had an estimated membership of 150,000 in 1986 (Aspinall, 2005, p. 133) and close relations with the New Order regime. Other student organizations, which had acted primarily as religious and social groups in the 1980s, began to criticize the regime in the 1990s.

These groups played an important role in mobilizing discontent across different social spheres and organizing protests that ultimately brought down Suharto. One thirty-year-old former student activist in Surabaya who protested against Suharto said student activism was the key factor behind Indonesia's democratization. When describing Suharto's resignation, he said:

> The reaction at this time was euphoric – there was joy because he fell. For thirty-two years, the people of Indonesia did not feel comfortable with Suharto's power. This all was a blessing for students; therefore there was a feeling of satisfaction when Suharto stepped down. The students of PRD triggered democracy by criticizing Suharto.

In the years since Suharto's resignation, Indonesian student groups have maintained a high level of organization and activity. The three university students in my interview sample all belonged to student organizations. The two Javanese students belonged to the Movement of Muslim

[13] The information in this paragraph draws heavily from details in Aspinall (2005), chapter 5.

Students of Indonesia (Pergerakan Mahasiswa Islam Indonesia, PMII) and the one Batak student belonged to a student organization as well as a Batak regional organization. The twenty-two-year-old Javanese student leader of PMII in Surabaya described the organization's regular activities, which include a mix of discussion, political activism, and community service:

> About twenty to twenty-five people have a discussion twice a week. On Monday it is about Islam, and on Thursday about current political events or the government's actions.... Now, group members are discussing the eviction of residents at Strenkali.[14] There is housing for [those evicted] on the Bantaran Kali, and members help there. There are children who have lost their homes, and members help out there.

Not surprisingly, student activism correlated strongly with participation in protests and contacting among my Indonesian respondents. Among those who had participated in demonstrations related to topics other than the labor movement, all were students or former students who had engaged in political protest as an outgrowth of their participation in student organizations. Among those who had contacted public officials, all but one had at least some university education. Student groups – including those that do not have an explicitly political purpose – frequently mobilized members to participate in demonstrations and letter-writing campaigns. The two students who belong to PMII were recruited into protest action specifically through this organization. The student leader of PMII quoted earlier told me that the organization is politically neutral in that it does not involve itself in party politics or support a specific party.[15] Yet many of the organization's activities could certainly be described as political participation. For instance, PMII has one specific unit dedicated to writing letters to the media. Organizing demonstrations is another frequent activity. When the government raised fuel oil prices, PMII held up to three demonstrations in a week in Surabaya.

In contrast to the religious and neighborhood associations centered on one's place of residence, student organizations introduce participants to a broader range of social networks that persist following graduation. Aspinall describes Indonesian student activism as "an apprenticeship for

---

[14] This interview took place several days after several hundred residents of the Strenkali riverbank community living on contested land were evicted from their homes. The Association of Residents of the Surabaya Strenkali (PWS) will be discussed in greater detail later in this chapter.

[15] Historically, however, PMII is associated with NU, which has a long history of political involvement in Indonesia.

middle-class political activism of all stripes," noting that student leaders of the 1980s moved on to NGOs and other organizations while maintaining connections with their former student networks (2005, p. 129). Like neighborhood-based social networks, student and professional networks provide important arenas for political recruitment.

My citizen interviews in Russia and Indonesia confirmed several survey data trends on civil society while also providing additional detail about how social and civic interactions can be mutually supportive. In comparing the pictures of civic engagement in these two countries, we see some similarities. First, sociability did not vary by sex or religious denomination in either country.[16] Second, individuals with higher levels of sociability in both Indonesia and Russia tend to belong to more clubs and associations. Thus, general tendencies about who joins organizations and the correlation between informal social interactions and associational membership are similar in both countries. The primary difference between these two cases is the overall *level* of civic participation. Indonesians are more sociable than Russians on average and overall rates of membership are higher in Indonesia. The mean level of organizational membership for my Indonesian respondents was 1.05, and individuals with high sociability levels belong to an average of 1.54 groups. The mean level of organizational memberships for Russian respondents was much lower – 0.35. The overwhelming majority of Russian respondents did not belong to any organizations, and even Russians with high sociability levels participated in an average of only one group.

Authoritarian Legacies and Civil Society

Experiences under authoritarianism and following the collapse of the New Order and Soviet regimes influenced the landscape of organizational life in Indonesia and Russia in different ways. Just as political liberalization increases opportunities for political participation, it also fosters conditions that may be conducive to apolitical associational life. Relaxation of controls over speech and association in post–New Order Indonesia and post-Soviet Russia created opportunities for the emergence of new types of organizations, including human rights and environmental organizations, student groups, and religious associations. Nevertheless,

---

[16] The WVS data confirmed this finding – no statistically significant differences appeared in sociability levels between Christians and Muslims in either country. In my Medan citizen sample, however, sociability levels were higher among the ethnic Batak. In a sample of this size, it is not possible to separate out the effects of ethnic group compared to education since the Batak are overrepresented among the highly educated.

Indonesia started this process from a more advantageous position than Russia.

In Indonesia, many – though not all – organizations were largely autonomous from the New Order regime, even if the regime did limit the activities these groups could safely engage in. More important, the religious, community, and student organizations that existed under the New Order remained more or less intact as the country began democratization. In the post-Suharto era, membership in these organizations has remained high. Additionally, Indonesian organizational activity expanded in some areas that were prohibited under Suharto, including human rights, environmental protection, and democracy promotion. Thus, at the onset of democratization, Indonesia already had a robust associational life that had opportunities to expand as a result of political liberalization.

In contrast, the Soviet Union did not permit the establishment of any autonomous organizations, which hampered the development of voluntary associations in Soviet Russia. Yet the Soviet Union was not void of organizational life: Soviet citizens, including most of my respondents who had reached adulthood during the Soviet era, participated in numerous sanctioned organizations. The collapse of the Soviet Union brought about the disintegration of many of these organizations, such as the Komsomol, women's councils, and official professional groups. Scholars of post-Communist civil society frequently overlook this fact. We emphasize the non-voluntary nature of Soviet associational activity to such an extent that we presume individuals would not have joined these associations if given a real choice. Although there is no way to measure voluntary versus coerced membership in Soviet associational life, it would be incorrect to assume that all association members joined exclusively because of pressure. Several of my citizen respondents valued their activity in the Komsomol, trade unions, and other Soviet-era organizations and felt a void when these structures did not transfer to the post-Communist era. For a considerable segment of the population, the associational life it had known largely disappeared, leaving those individuals who had enjoyed participating in state-sponsored organizations (and who did not view their activity as forced or formal) without a ready alternative. These individuals – although not the majority of the population – experienced a sense of loss and were not prepared to create new, autonomous associations. The concept was completely foreign and in some instances appeared subversive.

Additionally, the Soviet policy of forced atheism and the destruction of religious communities have likely impeded Russian civil society development in nonreligious spheres as well. While the specific relationship between religious practice and civil society engagement has not been explored extensively in a cross-national context, evidence from specific cases – including Indonesia – suggests a strong link. For example, as discussed earlier, the Islamic organizations NU and Muhammadiyah play an important role in Indonesian civic life, and have served as fertile ground for political participation. No analogous organizations exist in Russia. One reason for the absence may be confessional, as Orthodox Christianity lacks a tradition of mass-based religious organizations seen more commonly in Muslim communities. Yet the legacy of religious repression is likely a factor as well.

This legacy may also have hindered civil society development in Russia by blocking communal worship as a focal point for engendering broader civic engagement. Regular participation in communal worship practices brings individuals into contact with a greater number of people, increasing their exposure to other types of activities. My respondents in both Surabaya and Medan (Muslims and Christians) who attended religious services at least once per week had a higher average level of associational memberships than those who did not.

Although autonomous activity was prohibited in the Soviet era, greater opportunities for civil society engagement emerged in Russia in the early 1990s. Russians could form virtually any type of association, and while the number of registered nongovernmental organizations mushroomed in the 1990s (Sundstrom, 2006, p. 14), Russians did not develop a habit of civic engagement. Engagement in associational life – though higher in the mid-2000s than in the mid-1990s – remains low compared to other countries. The Russian case demonstrates that relaxation of control over associations does not automatically generate high levels of citizen involvement in associational life.

Antecedent regime conditions clearly shaped the level of civil society in Russia and Indonesia when political liberalization began. The effects of state monopolization of civic life and the state destruction of organized religious groups undoubtedly conditioned Russians' low levels of engagement in civil society. In contrast, associational pluralism under the New Order facilitated a sphere of independent, voluntary action separate from political life in Indonesia, which certainly contributes to Indonesia's higher levels of civic engagement after authoritarianism. The impact of these different legacies is perhaps most evident in the defining characteristics of the civic engagement demonstrated by my Russian and Indonesian respondents: most engaged Indonesians belonged to religious, community, and neighborhood organizations that existed long before democratization, while most engaged Russians belonged to recreational groups that lacked Soviet roots.

Overall, perhaps the best way to think about the impact of Soviet social repression on Russian civil society is as a conditioning cause: it has conditioned the low level of civic engagement in post-Communist countries. These societies likely had more terrain to travel in building robust civil societies than those that emerged from non-Communist authoritarian regimes that tolerated limited pluralism. But experience has shown that formerly Communist countries are quite capable of making up for the civil society deficit from the Communist era. Based on the data available from the WVS, numerous post-Communist regimes – such as Albania, Macedonia, and Slovenia – have overcome their legacies of state monopolization of civic life to develop robust civil society engagement. Thus, the fact that Russia and Indonesia started from different places with regard to building associational life did not necessarily predetermine that a weak civil society would persist in Russia. It also did not guarantee that Russians would fail to embrace elite-constraining participation or that Indonesians would seize it.

Linking Civil Society Involvement to Civic Voluntarism

Resources and Networks for Political Participation
How does variation between civil society engagement in Indonesia and Russia contribute to the adoption of elite-constraining or elite-enabling participation? The civic voluntarism model provides an analytical framework to understand how a robust civil society often makes citizens better equipped to utilize expanded opportunities for political participation in a liberalizing political system. This model emphasizes three interconnected features: motivation, capacity, and connectedness. Specifically, a citizen must be motivated to participate, capable of participating, and part of a network through which she can be recruited to participate (Verba et al., 1995, pp. 3–6). Russians and Indonesians differ on all of these dimensions, even though in both countries the political opportunity structure changed in the 1990s to create new spaces for political activity. After liberalization, Russians exhibited – and continue to exhibit – low levels of interest in civic participation, and many of my respondents demonstrated no motivation to engage in political activism. As the data on social interactions show, Indonesians are plugged into a larger number of active social networks than are Russians, which provides them with greater opportunities to be recruited into political participation.

While differences between Indonesians' and Russians' levels of motivation and connectedness are straightforward, the issue of participation capacity merits closer analysis. In explaining participation capacity, Verba, Schlozman, and Brady emphasize the need for individuals to have access to resources in the forms of time, money, and civic skills to facilitate participation in political life. The organization of Indonesian civil society equips individuals to activate these resources through both the norms of participation and the structure of associations. Associational life in Indonesia relies on two resources that are useful to political life: volunteer labor and charitable giving. In other words, Indonesians are used to giving both time and money to civic causes. This norm has facilitated mass support for opposition parties, promoting political competition. Additionally, Indonesian associations prioritize leadership training and community organizing – two features that encourage the development and transfer of civic skills from one domain to another.

Russian civil society, in contrast, does not exhibit the characteristics that help to generate individual capacity for political participation. Volunteer labor and charitable giving are not standard practices among Russians, and the absence of these resources has inhibited the growth of opposition parties. Russia also lacks strong mass-based civil society associations. Organizations that do exist are generally small and centered on a few enthusiastic activists. Although the CPSU had a system for training leaders, this system did not survive the collapse of communism. While some Russians have acquired civic skills through participation in civic and educational life, the number of people who apply these skills to elite-constraining political participation is too small to engender system-level effects.

The following sections discuss the resources of time, money, and civic skills and analyze how they have affected political participation and democracy's survival in Indonesia and Russia.

Time: Volunteer Work

The first resource Indonesians develop through engagement in civil society is the norm of providing voluntary labor. Indonesians' participation in women's groups, neighborhood associations, charitable organizations, and mass religious societies speaks to their high rates of voluntarism. Indonesians who participate in religious organizations also regularly volunteer their time for charity or service work. When asked how he spends his free time, one thirty-two-year-old Batak Protestant man in Medan replied, "I am a servant of God in my church, therefore I carry out many social activities at the church." He is a church elder, a responsibility that involves two meetings a week on top of his regular participation in worship and prayer groups.

Examples of volunteer activity abounded in my Indonesian citizen interviews. One Javanese woman in Surabaya nearing age fifty who has an elementary school education runs a free after-school program with her daughter for neighborhood children out of her house. The children, who come from poorer families, practice reading, writing, and other activities. Another respondent, a thirty-five-year-old Javanese woman in Medan with a high school degree and a low-level administrative job, spends an average of ten hours a week participating in volunteer work and voluntary associations. She is the head of her local neighborhood association, the head of the local volunteer health services program (Posyandu), and deputy head of the local PKK chapter. At these groups, her volunteer tasks range from preparing the local polling station for elections to coordinating neighborhood women's bulk purchase of rice. A third respondent, a forty-nine-year-old Malay factory worker in Medan with only five years of schooling, voluntarily coaches three different neighborhood youth soccer teams almost every day after work. What is remarkable about these three respondents is just how unremarkable they are among Indonesians. These individuals, who give frequently of their time, are typical of their peers and neighbors.

Indonesians have a well-established tradition of voluntary service that derives from the *gotong-royong* and other mutual help practices in villages, where norms of reciprocity were integral to a community's success. Suharto's New Order regime capitalized on these norms to mobilize labor in support of the regime's developmental goals. While New Order dictates for development have largely faded into the background, it is clear that volunteers are responsible for a significant portion of village- and neighborhood-level social activism, as both Indonesian and international development agencies have frequently indicated.

Such activism is largely absent in Russia. I found committed volunteers among my Russian respondents, but in much smaller numbers. In fact, only three individuals among my fifty respondents volunteered any time. One sixty-nine-year-old Russian woman from Kazan who is a retired factory worker described several volunteer tasks she has taken on over the years, including organizing the clean-up of her apartment block yard and serving as the "building monitor" (equivalent to a building co-op manager and liaison to city services). A thirty-nine-year-old midwife voluntarily gave talks on sex education and health topics at schools. The one Russian respondent who belongs to a Bible study group was trying to start a charitable organization among his fellow parishioners, but noted that this was difficult due to low levels of voluntarism. These examples of volunteering, however, were exceptional among my Russian respondents.

In Indonesia, norms of voluntarism are not limited to neighborhood-level initiatives. One example of higher-level organization is the Council of the City of Surabaya (Dewan Kota Surabaya). Though similar in name to the city's legislative body – the Regional Representative Council (Dewan Perwakilan Rakyat Daerah, DPRD), the Council of the City of Surabaya is a private, unofficial nongovernmental organization. It was started in 2003 by a group of Surabaya artists and professionals with the goal of improving the city. More than 160 professional associations have been involved in the Council, which never registered as a formal non-governmental association. The Council runs its activities out of donated office space and volunteers carry out all activities.

The Council has engaged in a variety of projects, most of which involve using members' professional skills, contacts, and expertise to advocate on behalf of more vulnerable citizens. One of the Council's projects is to ensure the government fulfills its promise to earmark 20 percent of the state budget for education. Council members work with families and students to draft letters of complaint when students do not receive benefits to which they are entitled, and then arrange to deliver these letters to the appropriate authorities. The Council has also worked with marginalized social groups, such as the villagers who were displaced as a result of mud volcanoes in East Java and the Association of Residents of the Surabaya Strenkali (Paguyuban Warga Strenkali Surabaya, PWS). PWS has been in a protracted battle with local and regional governments about the community's right to land use (EJ-12, interview, June 5, 2009; see also Some, Hafidz, & Sauter, 2009).

In Russia, examples of volunteers propelling more organized forms of civic engagement are less common. Even prominent national human rights organizations like the Union of the Committees of Soldiers' Mothers of Russia (henceforth Soldiers' Mothers) and Memorial have a difficult time recruiting volunteers (M-14, interview, February 21, 2008; Kr-11, interview, November 10, 2008). The Soldiers' Mothers, who first organized in 1989, monitor the Russian military, attempt to ensure human rights are maintained in the armed forces, and assist families of conscript soldiers if these soldiers' rights are violated. According to a member of the Soldiers' Mothers' leadership, the group has about 300 committees with an estimated 2,500 volunteers throughout Russia

(M-14, interview, February 21, 2008). Most volunteers are mothers of current or former soldiers.

Memorial, an organization that investigates human rights abuses in contemporary Russia and from the Soviet past, was also founded in 1989. Like the Soldiers' Mothers, many Memorial volunteers have a personal connection to the organization's cause. A leader in the organization's Krasnoyarsk branch said that everyone working for Memorial in Krasnoyarsk is a volunteer. He said the volunteers span three generations: Soviet-era dissidents, who do not have family members who suffered political repression; volunteers ranging in age from forty to sixty, many of whom had family members who were victims of political repression; and a few young volunteers up to age thirty (Kr-11, interview, November 10, 2008).

The Soldiers' Mothers and Memorial examples provide further testimony to the lack of widespread voluntarism among Russians, as these prominent and long-standing organizations struggle to attract volunteers. Lesser-known organizations have even more difficulty attracting and maintaining volunteers.

The absence of a norm of volunteering in Russia stands in sharp contrast to the picture in Indonesia, where individuals view voluntary activity as a natural extension of community membership. The most visible effect of the difference in norms of voluntary labor involves political parties. In Indonesia, volunteers, not paid administrators, carry out most lower-level party organizational work – such as recruitment, campaign work, and social outreach. For example, a representative from the Prosperous Justice Party (Partai Keadilan Sejahtera, PKS), which boasts 60,000 members in East Java, noted that the party has about 100 paid administrators for the region and relies on volunteer labor for most activities (EJ-8, interview, June 6, 2009). Indonesian voluntarism in charitable and social organizations – like PKK, NU, and Muhammadiyah – often leads to voluntary commitments of time to political causes. This is one reason Indonesia has developed a broad range of organized and competitive opposition parties. In contrast, political parties in Russia have failed to develop strong voluntary reserves, inhibiting the development of a competitive party system.

Money: Autonomous Self-Financing
Indonesia also enjoys advantages over Russia in autonomous self-financing. Indonesia's two largest mass organizations, NU and Muhammadiyah, are entirely self-financed. Although active members of both organizations are

expected to pay dues, collection of dues varies across locales. Consequently, most of these organizations' financing comes from donations and revenue-generating activities. In-kind transfers for development projects are common (EJ-3, interview, June 2, 2009; EJ-10, interview, June 8, 2009).

Examples of autonomous self-financing are evident in smaller-scale initiatives as well. For example, the nongovernmental Council of the City of Surabaya operates in member-donated office space. Members of the Association of Residents of the Surabaya Strenkali (PWS) began a recycling and trash-collecting program to raise money for bringing their homes into accordance with government regulations. In another example, one of my Surabaya respondents, a thirty-year-old food stall vendor who slept on a bench behind his wok, described the merchant association he belonged to: neighborhood vendors contribute 10,000–15,000 rupiah to the association per month (about $1 to $1.50), and this money is available as insurance or loans for participating members. It can be used to improve one's stall or purchase a new piece of equipment. According to the respondent, whose monthly income was less than $50, "This has indeed become an association that is serious. Without it, we [small traders] could not get by."

While Indonesian associations large and small have developed strategies to finance their activities, Russian associations struggle to support themselves. For example, the Krasnoyarsk branch of Memorial lacks a steady revenue stream and relies primarily on in-kind resources. A local firm provides the group with an office in its building, a computer, and Internet access. The organization receives occasional grants from Russian and international donors for projects, but this support is sporadic. The Soldiers' Mothers representative I interviewed described the organization's financial situation in similar terms, in that the group as a whole has no general finances, relying on occasional project grants and donated office space.

It is surprising that civil society organizations in Russia, a country with a middle level of economic development, have a harder time raising money than similar organizations in Indonesia. In 2008, Russia's GDP at purchasing power parity neared $15,000, while Indonesia's was less than $4,000 (UN Development Program). Indonesia is a much poorer country, yet none of the organizations I interviewed complained about financial struggles. What prevents Russian civil society from developing? Repression is clearly one factor. In April 2006, a new federal law regulating nongovernmental organizations went into effect. This law made it much more difficult to register an NGO and to receive foreign financial support.[17] Moreover, other aspects of the Russian Civil Code and taxation law place heavy burdens on NGOs, thereby decreasing the incentives for both donors and recipients to establish a system of charitable giving. In order to reduce reliance on foreign grant-making agencies, Russia's Public Chamber[18] established annual grant competitions for Russian associations starting in 2006. These grant competitions transfer up to 1.5 billion rubles (approximately $50 million) of state money into Russian civil society each year, making the Russian government – not private citizens – the largest financial backer of associational life in the country (Human Rights Watch, 2009; Richter, 2008). The grant competitions have raised concerns of bias against organizations that have criticized Kremlin policy (Human Rights Watch, 2009) and have undoubtedly reduced the likelihood of a robust, independent civil society developing.

The perception that charitable giving has political implications in Russia can be seen in smaller-scale ventures as well. One former candidate for local office in Krasnoyarsk described a failed attempt to organize an outing at local theaters for children in the city's orphanages. Several local businesses he approached for sponsorship favored the idea, but said that they could not support it since city officials had not explicitly approved it (Kr-3, interview, November 1, 2008). These business owners did not want their donations to be perceived as hostile to local officials. According to this individual, Russian businesses do not necessarily lack a spirit of charity, but they cannot exercise it openly. Rather, they wait for the government to request their participation or assistance in particular tasks, such as providing resources for a New Year's celebration or donating goods to schools and orphanages. In these instances, of course, businesses feel compelled to give, fearing negative repercussions if they do not.

While the 2006 law that increased repression of civil society has certainly had a negative impact on charitable giving, Russian organizations' fundraising struggles date further back. Many analyses of Russia's burgeoning civil society in the 1990s note the difficulties associations encountered in financing their activities (Lussier & McCullaugh, 2009; Sperling, 1999; Sundstrom, 2006). In particular, organizations had a hard time obtaining support from private, domestic sources. Large, professionalized NGOs relied on foreign grants, while smaller, local organizations

---

[17] For good overviews of the regulations and their impact on NGOs, see Human Rights Watch (2009), Richter (2008), and International Center for Not-for-Profit Law (2006).

[18] The Public Chamber was founded in 2005. It is a consultative committee comprised of 126 members, one-third of whom are appointed by the president. These members in turn elect representatives from public associations.

depended on state assistance, including in-kind transfers of items such as meeting space.

The difficulty Russian civil society has encountered in financing its activities may be rooted in Soviet-era attitudes and behaviors that have persisted in the post-Communist context. The first is citizens' continuing belief that the state should be the main source of financial support for civic initiatives. Similarly, because individuals expect the state to support these activities, private individuals and businesses do not fund them. Third, both political elites and business owners still do not view the civic realm as a sphere of truly autonomous activity. The state continues to dictate how associational life is financed – either through large-scale Public Chamber grants or through compelling local businesses to make small donations – and thereby influences which organizations survive. In the absence of a norm of individual- and household-level giving, the state controls most of the purse strings for Russian civic life.

In Indonesia, norms for self-financing of civil society lead to a very different outcome. Unlike Russians, Indonesians are accustomed to parting with fixed sums of money for a collective benefit. This custom increases an individual's willingness to pay dues to a more structured organization, such as a political party. Most of the party members I interviewed described a system of dues paying that finances party work. Parties that win seats in the national and local legislatures receive a fixed sum in public financing that is proportional to the number of seats they receive, but this assistance is inadequate for parties to mount effective political campaigns. Consequently, most parties require that each of the party's legislative representatives donate a portion of his or her salary to the party. The same is true for representatives of regional legislatures. A representative of PDI-P in East Java explained that each active member is expected to make a contribution to the party for presidential campaigns. The level of the expected donation is decided in a meeting at the city or regional level (EJ-5, interview, June 4, 2009). Parties frequently redistribute money across provinces in order to invest in party development in areas where their representation is weaker. These forms of self-financing are an important augmentation to donations from business elites, and have helped build a competitive political party system in Indonesia.[19]

---

[19] This system has come under extensive criticism for facilitating "money politics," or the direct use of financial incentives to influence parties' electoral and legislative agendas. For a thoughtful critique, see Mietzner (2007).

Like Russian civic organizations, Russian political parties struggle to raise funds. Throughout the 1990s, they failed to develop an independent base of small and medium-sized donors. During this period, people could freely donate to parties, but political parties were either unwilling or unable to establish serious resource bases. Since they were able to draw campaign resources from non-party sources, candidates were less interested in seeking donations for ongoing party organizations. As Stoner-Weiss (2002) points out, the politically and economically powerful in Russia have demonstrated no interest in party-building. Consequently, only parties that received backing from the Kremlin have had the monetary resources to launch effective campaigns. At the regional level, funding for political competition came from competing industrial groups outside of the party structure (Hale, 2006). In the absence of a mass-based party system where members' dues provide basic financing, or where active volunteers cultivate outside donors, Russian opposition parties flounder financially.

In my interviews with leaders from all of Russia's major political parties in Krasnoyarsk Krai and Tatarstan, I found that a party's level of financial support was directly correlated to its representation in the State Duma. As the party of power, United Russia received both the most federal support for political parties in office and the Kremlin's blessing for donations by the business community. The party's relative wealth is evident in the vibrancy of its regional offices, which have more paid staff and modern facilities than other parties' offices. Other parties rely heavily on the federal support they receive from being in the parliament. Duma deputies are provided three paid assistants and an official reception space in their home district, complete with a phone line and Internet connection. These resources are crucial for parties other than United Russia, and these parties often pool their Duma deputies' resources to facilitate party-development work.

Even though Russia is a richer country than Indonesia, Russia's greater wealth does not translate into philanthropy for civic or political causes. Moreover, the persistence of attitudinal and behavioral legacies from the Soviet era perpetuate a view that the state should provide the financial resources for civic life – and that it has a right to intervene in the financing of associational life and charitable initiatives. This norm has had negative consequences for opposition parties and, by extension, political competition in Russia. Indonesia's relative poverty, on the other hand, has not hindered the self-financing of associational life. Indonesians are accustomed to contributing money to social and civic initiatives, a norm that has helped the country's opposition parties.

The Islamic tradition of alms-giving (*zakat*) may influence the widespread giving among the Indonesian population. While none of my interlocutors mentioned this specifically, it is likely that this tenet of Islamic faith has become internalized and habituated such that it influences broader-scale giving as well.[20] This norm has played a role in political parties' successful autonomous self-financing, which has helped the party system develop into a viable institution for political competition.

Civic Skills: Leadership Training and Community Organizing

The civic voluntarism model's third key resource for political participation is civic skills. Verba, Schlozman, and Brady define civic skills as "the communications and organizational abilities that allow citizens to use time and money effectively in politics" (1995, p. 304). They argue that individuals who possess civic skills are more likely to be effective when they become involved in politics and find political activity less daunting. Similarly, civic skills help individuals to use the resources of time and money more effectively.

Civic skills are acquired through life experience, especially educational and workplace experiences. Given Russia's significantly higher rates of educational attainment and workforce professionalization, it is reasonable to expect that Russians would have more extensive civic skills than Indonesians. Yet voluntary associations and religious groups also provide forums for acquiring civic skills, and these organizations are more widespread in Indonesia than Russia. Indeed, I have found that the structure of Indonesian associations facilitates civic skills development by virtue of associations' commitment to leadership development and community organizing. An analogous dynamic is absent in Russia.

Many local-level Indonesian organizations – women's groups, *pengajian*, and church groups – are part of larger organizational structures that include a system of leadership training. For example, many *pengajian* groups I encountered in Surabaya were affiliated with NU, which has its stronghold in East Java. According to the regional NU leaders I interviewed, anyone can become an NU member, but members cannot advance in the organization without receiving an education in NU ideology and organizational management. After this training, a member becomes a "cadre" (*kader*) and is permitted to take on leadership responsibilities. If a cadre remains in the NU structure and continues to take on

---

[20] For a discussion on alms-giving as a possible explanation for cross-national differences in social inequality, see Fish (2011), chapter 6.

an active role, he can become an "official" (*pengurus*) of the organization. Muhammadiyah and the PKK have similar leadership-training programs.

Both NU and Muhammadiyah are officially apolitical and do not support any specific political party.[21] Yet following the collapse of the New Order, members of both organizations established new political parties. Some NU members followed their long-time leader, Abdurrahman Wahid, to form the National Awakening Party (Partai Kebangkitan Bangsa, PKB), and Muhammadiyah members formed the National Mandate Party (Partai Amanat Nasional, PAN) under the leadership of former Muhammadiyah chairman Amien Rais. More than a decade after these parties were founded, their primary members and supporters still come from NU and Muhammadiyah adherents, even as the mass organizations self-consciously maintained a clear organizational distinction between themselves and the parties their members embraced.

According to a top PKB "official" in East Java, 80 percent of the party's members belong to NU (EJ-11, interview, June 8, 2009). Moreover, all of the party's leaders are NU members who received NU leadership training. Because of the close informal relations between NU and PKB, as of 2009 PKB had not developed its own leadership-training program. The experience of NU and PKB is a clear example of civic skills transferring directly to political participation – PKB activists rose through the party's ranks based on their apolitical participation experiences in NU.[22] Additionally, active NU members were often invited to participate politically in PKB.

A similar dynamic is evident in Indonesia's smaller-scale civic organizations. For example, *pengajian* groups often host guest speakers, and political candidates frequently seek audiences with *pengajian* to meet voters. Half of the Muslim women in my Medan citizen sample said candidates from different parties had visited their *pengajian* groups prior

[21] Both organizations have long histories of political involvement in Indonesia. NU was a political party from 1952–1973, when it was forced along with other Islamic parties to form the United Development Party (Partai Persatuan Pembangunan, PPP). In 1984, NU withdrew from PPP and adopted the official apolitical position it maintains to this day. Muhammadiyah members were heavily involved in the 1950s parliamentary-era Masyumi party. For more on these organizations' political roles, see Mujani and Liddle (2004).

[22] Starting in late 2008, PKB became embroiled in internal party conflicts, resulting in a sharp decline in the party's vote share in national and regional elections in 2009. According to my PKB informant in East Java, the absence of a cadre-development program specifically for the party contributed to these conflicts. Going forward, PKB aimed to create its own leadership-training program to ensure that promotion within the party would be based on performance in goals and activities specific to the party's development.

to the 2009 legislative election. Coordinating a speaker for one's local prayer group is an example of an apolitical civic skill that easily transfers into the political sphere.

Similarly, neighborhood association leaders who organize monthly *gotong-royong* activities can apply those same skills to mobilizing neighbors to register complaints about inadequate public services. A clear example of this transfer of skills comes from the marginalized residents from Surabaya's Strenkali riverbank community. With help from students and human rights NGOs, residents facing forced relocation organized the Association of Residents of the Surabaya Strenkali (PWS). The association, which boasts 1,500 members, convinced the provincial government to change its relocation policy to one of community redevelopment. The provincial government approved proposals PWS submitted for developing sustainable and ecological riverside communities.

During this campaign, PWS received assistance from the nongovernmental Council of the City of Surabaya. The Council's involvement is another example of how civic skills – especially more advanced professional skills among lawyers and the business elite – can be utilized for political activity, such as writing letters, contacting elected officials, and organizing forums for public discussion. Moreover, Council members' volunteer efforts have promoted greater political participation among citizens with lower income and less education – precisely the population that is less likely to acquire civic skills through school and professional opportunities.

Student organizations also cultivate leadership development and community organizing skills. The Surabaya student who is a leader in the inter-university PMII – which is associated with NU – described the organization's leadership-training process:

Students who are not yet members of PMII are given training and are then able to become members of PMII. There are stages that one has to go through to become a new member of PMII. A basic member must then go through another process to become a cadre of PMII. Anyone may become a member of PMII, but not everyone can become a PMII cadre, because becoming a cadre requires loyalty toward the organization. [Among about sixty members] only about fifteen will become cadre. You must always be ready for the organization.

Student organization leaders develop skills that help them convince their peers – who tend to join organizations not to become political activists, but to acquire a sense of community – to write letters, sign petitions, and demonstrate in the streets. Student leaders can also use these skills to train and organize other populations who have less exposure to nonvoting political activity, such as the Strenkali neighborhood residents who formed PWS.

In contrast, Russian civil society lacks a system of leadership training and community organizing. This situation differs dramatically from the Soviet era, when the CPSU had an extensive leadership-training program (which was, of course, highly politicized) that began from the elementary school Young Pioneer scouts and continued through workplace leadership-training programs. Indeed, ample evidence from my interviews and other studies shows participation in the former Communist Party or its auxiliary organizations provided people with important skills, networks, and access to infrastructure (Fish, 1995; Grzymała-Busse, 2002; Hale, 2006). In political terms, the main initial beneficiary of these skills and networks was the Communist Party of the Russian Federation (KPRF), which provided the most formidable opposition in Russia during the 1990s. In the past decade, however, as the KPRF's political clout has declined, the pro-Kremlin United Russia party has succeeded in appropriating several of the former CPSU's organizational techniques, including a leadership-training program (K-17, interview, March 13, 2008; Kr-20, interview, November 26, 2008). Many party representatives I interviewed in Kazan and Krasnoyarsk volunteered that lack of leadership training presented a significant obstacle to party development. In general, parties lack committed, reliable, and competent members who can work on outreach and other tasks. This attitude was expressed by representatives of the KPRF, the Liberal Democratic Party of Russia (Liberalnaia Demokraticheskaia Partiia Rossii, LDPR), and among sympathizers of United Russia.

Thus, while Russian citizens may possess civic skills acquired from educational and workplace experiences, they activate these skills selectively in a political context. Although Russians use civic skills to contact public officials, they do not use these skills to engage in elite-constraining political participation. In contrast, the structure of Indonesian civil society, which emphasizes leadership training and community organizing, facilitates civic skills development among the population and creates opportunities to use these skills for elite-constraining political activities.

Networks of Recruitment: Religious Society, Civil Society, and Political Society

The preceding discussion has argued that the norms and structures of Indonesian civil society have helped Indonesians acquire and utilize resources that facilitate political participation – namely, time, money, and civic skills. In contrast, the structure of Russian civil society – which is marked by low levels of voluntarism and little autonomous fundraising – hinders the activation of civic skills and their application to political participation. The final component of the civic voluntarism model – networks of recruitment for political participation – also bodes well for Indonesia and poorly for Russia. Verba, Schlozman, and Brady find that Americans who are active in apolitical civic institutions – such as churches and unions – are especially inclined to accept invitations to participate in political activities. I found a similar dynamic among Indonesians, but not among Russians.

In Indonesia, the overlapping social networks of religious organizations, women's groups, neighborhood associations, student organizations, and structured cooperative activities like *arisan* and *gotong-royong* form the basis of a dense civil society. Indonesians' informal social interactions and participation in formal associational life offer opportunities for political recruitment and foster political engagement. Some recruitment networks are very straightforward: members of NU and Muhammadiyah, for instance, fall into direct lines of recruitment for participation in PKB and PAN party activities. For example, one female Minangkabu respondent from Medan with only two years of elementary education participates in a weekly *pengajian* group affiliated with Muhammadiyah. She had consistently voted for PAN-endorsed candidates in national elections over the past decade. In addition, members of student organizations are frequently recruited to participate in acts of contentious politics. Other associations, such as the Council of the City of Surabaya, perform advocacy work, encouraging nonvoting political participation among the communities receiving assistance. Yet, there are also extensive recruitment opportunities through day-to-day interactions just by virtue of the fact that Indonesians have such extensive social connections. Even if formal organizations' aims and interactions are not explicitly political, the density of these social networks and their importance in neighborhood life facilitate mobilization for political participation. Moreover, frequent interaction and cooperation in shared goals often expose individuals to political information, stimuli, and contrasting opinions. This dynamic is particularly important during political liberalization, when voters are evaluating different perspectives and selecting representatives in a newly competitive political environment.

Such linkages are largely absent in Russia, where fewer overlapping social networks evolve out of participation in religious, neighborhood, student, and professional life. This is not to say that some Russians do not resemble Indonesians in their levels of social interaction and civic engagement. But while these more social individuals are a visible segment of Russian society, they do not constitute the majority of Russian citizens. These more active Russians tend to engage in groups that reflect their hobbies and interests, which are often not located near their residences. The ways Russians engage in civil society offer fewer opportunities to develop dense networks of social relations, and consequently these networks cannot be mobilized as easily for political or civic causes.

In both Indonesia and Russia, political parties conduct social outreach programs to attract new supporters. One important difference, however, is that this patronage is more widespread in Indonesia and comprises parties of all political persuasions. Where the state has failed to provide public goods, political parties step in as service providers with the hopes of winning public support. For example, the Prosperous Justice Party (Partai Keadilan Sejahtera, PKS) in East Java and Golkar in Yogyakarta both have ambulances that residents can use for emergency transportation to the hospital. PKS and PAN in East Java have distributed food, clothing, and other aid to needy residents.

During the period under investigation in Russia, however, only the United Russia party, with its intimate ties to the Kremlin, had sufficient resources to provide social services. For example, the Tatarstan branch of United Russia has its own charitable fund supporting "economic, cultural, and social programs that correspond with the goals and tasks" of the party (Tatarstan Regional Branch website https://tatarstan.er.ru/). This foundation has financed popular initiatives like the Naberezhnyi Chelny City Center for Children's Creative Works. Such displays of patronage reinforce the image of United Russia as intertwined with regional and national political organs.

While political parties' direct provision of goods and services constitutes an obvious attempt to win popular support, subtle forms of service provision linked to political recruitment also exist. For example, in East Java many local executives belong to NU and bring NU's attention to their community's specific needs. NU sometimes uses these connections when promoting certain programs in a particular region, which can result in NU-sponsored programs that are similar to government programs (EJ-10, interview, June 8, 2009). A local government might support *pesantren* (Islamic schools), for example, by providing the salary for a teacher of *aji* (Qur'an reading). When a leader's political and civic identities overlap, it can be difficult for citizens to discern the source of his authority in a given situation, and conflicts of interest may emerge. Nevertheless, trusted civic leaders have the opportunity to recruit individuals into political causes.

In Russia in 2008, however, the pro-Kremlin United Russia was the only party that regularly recruited new people into political activism. While little information is readily available about the party's growth in membership, my interviews suggest that the spread of United Russia membership in recent years closely parallels recruitment in the Soviet period. During President Putin's second term (2004–2008), enterprise directors often joined United Russia and strongly encouraged subordinates to join as well. These employees saw job security as contingent on party membership. A United Russia party insider noted young people share this view and see party membership as a way to advance their careers (K-17, interview, March 13, 2008).

These differences in civic engagement levels, civil society organizational structures, and networks of recruitment in Indonesia and Russia shape the different patterns in nonvoting participation that have taken root in these two countries. Indonesians' extensive participation in civic life and overlapping social networks provide frequent opportunities to be recruited into elite-constraining political acts. Russians, by contrast, exhibit associational membership rates well below the global average and have significantly fewer informal social interactions. Russians' chances of being recruited for elite-constraining political participation are much lower than Indonesians'.

Conclusion

Variation in civil society engagement in Russia and Indonesia influenced the patterns of political participation that obtained in these two countries following political liberalization. While both countries experienced an increase in organizations that were prohibited from operating freely under authoritarianism – human rights groups, environmental organizations, and so forth – my argument is not that such groups expanded more broadly in Indonesia than in Russia. Rather, I argue that civic engagement as a whole – including in organizations that existed under authoritarianism – is higher in Indonesia than in Russia. Once the political opportunity structure in both countries changed to make collective action in the political arena both acceptable and safe, levels of civil society engagement became meaningful in shaping *how* the new political opportunity structure would be utilized. Thus, to the extent that organizational pluralism existed under Indonesia's New Order, this factor would not have facilitated democratization *until* the political opportunity structure changed to admit new forms of collective political action.

By applying the civic voluntarism model to Indonesia and Russia, we see how Indonesia's dense social networks and active civic life can be channeled into participation that constrains elites and improves democracy's chances for survival, while an analogous pattern did not obtain in Russia. Leadership development and community organizing experience confer useful civic skills to participants in civil society. These skills constitute a resource that can be deployed in the elite-constraining forms of political participation that have expanded following the collapse of an authoritarian regime. Additionally, norms of volunteer labor and charitable giving in Indonesia provide resources for political activity. Indonesians' access to all three aspects of the civic voluntarism model – time, money, and civic skills – has facilitated their participation in formal party politics, oversight activities, and contentious politics.

Low levels of civic and social engagement in Russia, however, have limited the extent to which individuals could be recruited to participate in new arenas for political activism under political liberalization. While Indonesians could be called upon to donate labor and money to both civic and political causes, Russians failed to muster these resources on a large scale. As a result, Russian political parties lack the resources to mount meaningful political opposition and watchdog groups remain weak. Additionally, while the structure of associational life in Indonesia facilitates the acquisition and transfer of civic skills, Russian civic life is more atomized. Consequently, Russians' civic skills are not activated in the political process beyond the narrow scope of contacting officials.

As the next two chapters demonstrate, Russia and Indonesia's differences in civic engagement and civil society norms are not the only factors that contribute to variation in the countries' patterns of political participation. Russians and Indonesians' beliefs about political efficacy and political trust also align in ways that foster elite-constraining participation in Indonesia and elite-enabling participation in Russia.

Appendix

Countries Included in World Values Survey

Argentina (2006); Australia (2005); Brazil (2006); Bulgaria (2006); Burkina Faso (2007); Chile (2006); China (2007); Colombia (2005); Cyprus (2006); Egypt (2008); Ethiopia (2007); Finland (2005); France (2006); Germany (2006); Ghana (2007); Great Britain (2006); India (2006); Indonesia (2006); Iran (2005); Italy (2005); Japan (2005); Jordan (2007); Malaysia (2006); Mali (2007); Mexico (2005); Moldova (2006); Morocco (2007); Netherlands (2006); New Zealand (2004); Peru (2006); Poland (2005); Romania (2005); Russia (2006); Rwanda (2007); Serbia (2006); Slovenia (2005); South Africa (2007); South Korea (2005); Spain (2007); Sweden (2006); Switzerland (2007); Taiwan (2006); Thailand (2007); Trinidad and Tobago (2006); Turkey (2007); Ukraine (2006); United States (2006); Vietnam (2006); Zambia (2007).

6

Political Efficacy and "Throwing the Rascals Out"

Chapter 5 showed that Russians' and Indonesians' civil society engagement varies both in terms of volume and in types of organizations citizens join. Ultimately, Indonesians' numerically greater and broader-ranging experiences with formal associational life and informal social interactions increase the chances they will acquire civic skills and apply them to elite-constraining political participation to a greater extent than Russians do. Civil society engagement, however, is not the only factor that facilitates elite-constraining participation. Individuals who believe political party work and acts of contentious politics are efficacious are more likely to participate in them. Likewise, individuals who believe that contacting public officials is the best avenue to effect change are more inclined to engage in elite-enabling participation.

This chapter explores the relationship between citizens' sense of political efficacy and a regime's democratic survival. Through a comparative analysis of survey data and citizen interviews, I highlight three primary findings. First, Indonesians feel more confident about their ability to influence political outcomes than do Russians, engendering a higher overall level of political participation. Second, individuals select participatory acts based on their perceived efficacy. Russians' perception that contacting is more efficacious than contentious political acts and opposition party work facilitates elite-enabling behavior as the modal form of nonvoting participation, leaving political elites relatively unconstrained. In contrast, Indonesians' view that elite-constraining activities are more efficacious contributes to their greater participation in party development work and contentious politics. Similarly, while both Russians and Indonesians vote in elections at high levels, Indonesians are more inclined to perceive their elections as fair and influential in determining political outcomes. Their perception about the efficacy of elections may influence their decisions about involvement in political campaigns and in supporting the political opposition. Additionally, if citizens perceive elections as efficacious, they are less likely to tolerate actions that interfere with elections' integrity. In contrast, Russians who vote for incumbents out of a sense of civic duty enable the elites who have undermined democracy to stay in power.

Third, because the relationship between political efficacy and political participation is reciprocal, events that occur in the early years of democratization can have an outsized impact on perception of efficacy in later years. To be clear, identifying the causal roots of citizens' perceptions of political efficacy is beyond the scope of this book, and I do not contend that early experiences with democratization are the sole or even primary cause of attitudes about efficacy in later years. Yet the relationship between attitudes about political efficacy and political participation is inherently reciprocal. Individuals choose *whether* to participate and *how* to participate based on their beliefs about the efficacy of participatory actions. When specific outcomes confirm one's beliefs, one's sense of efficacy is likely to increase. Conversely, when a participatory act does not yield the desired outcome, one's sense of efficacy can decline, making further participation less likely. This reciprocal relationship places a spotlight on the early experiences a population has with democratic institutions and practices. Populations who effectively "throw the rascals out"[1] see the efficacy of their votes firsthand. Populations who confirm the status quo – even if the reigning government has high levels of public support – are less inclined to perceive meaningful differences between authoritarian and democratic elections. Likewise, populations who remove a government through peaceful protest are more likely to understand the power of their numbers.

This chapter has four parts. First, I discuss the concept of political efficacy, its relationship to political participation, and the specific link between attitudes about political efficacy and democratization. I then present comparative measures of political efficacy in Russia and Indonesia based on surveys and my interviews with Russian and Indonesian citizens.

[1] This phrase originated from a campaign slogan, "turn the rascals out," that Horace Greeley used in his 1872 campaign against incumbent Ulysses S. Grant for the presidency of the United States. According to *American Sayings: Famous Sayings, Slogans, and Aphorisms* by Henry F. Woods, the phrase came from Charles A. Dana, an editor from the New York *Sun* who became a fierce critic of Grant after breaking with him in 1869 (Woods, 1945, 1949).

This chapter's third section looks at Russian and Indonesian attitudes toward elections and their efficacy. In the final section, I explore the reciprocal relationship between perceptions of efficacy and political participation during the early years of democratization in Russia and Indonesia.

Political Efficacy, Participation, and Democratization

Linking Political Efficacy and Democracy's Survival

Political efficacy is measured at the individual level and, in contrast to participation and civil society, is rarely thought of in aggregate terms. Yet the diffusion of specific attitudes about political efficacy within society can play an important role in democracy's survival by facilitating or inhibiting engagement in elite-constraining political participation. Differences in feelings of political efficacy in Indonesia and Russia help explain Indonesians' greater effectiveness at constraining elites.

I define political efficacy as the beliefs about the impact an individual and others like him can have on the political process. This definition is similar to Angus Campbell, Gerald Gurin, and Warren Miller's famous definition (Campbell et al., 1954), but removes language about the importance of performing one's "civic duties." A similar concept of political efficacy articulated by Gabriel Almond and Sidney Verba in *The Civic Culture* (1963) is "subjective competence." According to these authors, a "subjectively competent" individual believes he can exert influence on government officials (Almond & Verba, 1963, pp. 136–137). Robert Lane and other scholars disaggregate the concept of political efficacy into two dimensions, internal and external efficacy (1959). Internal efficacy refers to individuals' perception that they can understand and participate in politics, while external efficacy is the belief that political activities can influence government actions. These two dimensions of efficacy may be related, but an individual can have a high sense of internal efficacy and a low sense of external efficacy, or vice versa.

Studies of political participation have long emphasized political efficacy as a resource that can motivate individuals to take action (A. Campbell et al., 1964; Rosenstone & Hansen, 1993). The correlation between one's sense of political efficacy and political participation has been well established in the study of democratic politics (Almond & Verba, 1963; A. Campbell et al., 1964; A. Campbell et al., 1954; Rosenstone & Hansen, 1993; Verba et al., 1995). Several works have demonstrated the reciprocal relationship between efficacy and participation (A. Campbell et al., 1964; Finkel, 1985; Pateman, 1970): someone who has political efficacy is more likely to take an active part in politics, and an individual who has participated in politics is more likely to feel efficacious.

A valuable critique of the purported causal relationship between political efficacy and participation contends that one's sense of political efficacy can never be fully separated from the political context he inhabits. Carole Pateman (1989) argues that individuals' sense of efficacy is shaped by their own evaluation of how well a system responds to citizens' demands and how closely it aligns to their beliefs about how a democracy should look. Ann Craig and Wayne Cornelius (1989) maintain that efficacy is not solely an individual characteristic, but an attitude produced in part by the effectiveness of the government structure. In applying these critiques to the specific cases of Russia and Indonesia, we might ask whether Indonesians' higher levels of efficacy emanate from closer congruence between their expectations of government responsiveness and actual outcomes than found among Russians.

It is logical to ask if Russians have lower levels of efficacy simply because they are living in an authoritarian regime. If so, then the argument I present here might appear tautological: authoritarianism depresses efficacy, which in turn depresses participation, which in turn facilitates authoritarianism. Undoubtedly, the weak sense of efficacy my interview respondents exhibited in 2008 was partially shaped by the dearth of accessible options for effecting political change in the Putin era. Yet, as I show throughout this chapter, my argument is more nuanced than the circular logic just described. First, one's level of efficacy is not solely the product of system accessibility. Russians revealed low levels of efficacy even at the highpoint of political openness in the 1990s, suggesting that factors other than authoritarian backsliding account for low levels of efficacy in later years. Second, Russians' sense of efficacy is not simply high or low, but rather depends on the specific political action involved. My interviews demonstrated that many Russians feel efficacious about contacting public officials, but do not see voting as particularly effective.

I argue that qualitative differences in *how* efficacy fosters elite-constraining or elite-enabling participation are of greater importance than overall levels of efficacy in explaining the different participatory outcomes in Russia and Indonesia. A variety of factors (including system responsiveness) shape efficacy levels, but individuals' perceptions of which acts are more efficacious determine how they will participate. The subsequent choice of acts fosters patterns of elite-constraining or elite-enabling participation. If my goal were to understand the causes of variation in political efficacy, then it would be necessary to find a way to fully measure the extent to which level of political openness affects efficacy levels in Russia and Indonesia. Yet, because my argument relies primarily on qualitative differences, the fact that political context contributes to the types of acts individuals perceive as efficacious does not constitute a tautology – there is no a priori reason to know what types of activities individuals will prefer.

Political Efficacy in the Democratization Context
Most studies of political efficacy examine long-standing democracies. Investigations of political efficacy in countries that have recently experienced a democratic transition are uncommon. Yet our knowledge of the reciprocal relationship between efficacy and participation gives us good reason to hypothesize that early experiences under democracy may influence subsequent attitudes about political efficacy. Three issues are central to the relationship between political efficacy and democracy's survival: 1) the role political participation played in bringing about the collapse of the previous authoritarian regime; 2) the outcomes of multiple democratic elections in the early years following a transition; and 3) the socialization effect of authoritarianism on citizens' perceptions of efficacy.

In both the Soviet Union and New Order Indonesia, mass mobilization played a key role in removing authoritarian regimes. In the Soviet Union, public pressure for greater political openness contributed to the introduction of competitive elections and, ultimately, to the USSR's dissolution. Widespread protests in Indonesia forced Suharto's resignation and the introduction of fair and free elections. Thus, Russians and Indonesians were not simply handed an opportunity for democratic governance – they pushed for it. One might expect that these experiences of hastening authoritarian collapse would, at least initially, engender a sense of efficacy.

This sense of efficacy can be attenuated, however, by early experiences with democratic elections. Both Steve Fish (1998) and Michael McFaul (2002) contend that the outcome of initial elections in the post-Communist region is a strong predictor of democracy's survival at later stages. If the forces that engineered the collapse of Communism won an initial election and used their mandate to push for more reform, democracy was more likely to endure. According to Samuel Huntington, for an "emergent" democracy to become a "stable" democracy, it must undergo two peaceful and democratic turnovers of ruling parties (1991, pp. 266–267). A single turnover is not sufficient: a new administration often reintroduces authoritarian rule after one change in power. These studies share the conclusion that early transfers of power to the opposition can make political elites more committed to elections as the means to determine access to political power.

For voters, elections can shape attitudes about efficacy. Similar to when protests bring down an autocrat, elections that bring the opposition to power serve as meaningful examples of how citizens' political participation effects change. Alternatively, when early democratic elections merely validate the status quo – proving similar to elections under authoritarianism – they do not elevate citizens' perceptions of efficacy. While initial elections regularly bring opposition parties to power, the outcome of subsequent second and third elections may be of greater importance for engendering political efficacy. The case of Russia demonstrates that the inability to bring about a transfer of power via elections early in a democratic regime may contribute to a decline in voting participation and reduce trust in elections. While Russia's first presidential elections of June 1991 brought opposition to power with the victory of Boris Yeltsin, subsequent executive elections never produced a transfer of power. For these reasons, I hypothesize that Indonesians' experience in observing peaceful turnovers of power through elections has made them more likely than Russians to view voting as efficacious. The final section of this chapter elaborates this supposition.

Finally, previous experience in authoritarian regimes likely influences political efficacy in a democratizing regime. As Chapter 2 discussed, individuals in both the Soviet Union and New Order Indonesia were expected to engage in mobilized participation and vote in authoritarian elections that were not fair, free, or competitive. While voter turnout has gradually declined in these two countries in the post-Soviet and post-Suharto eras, it remains more than 60 percent in both countries for legislative and presidential elections, much higher than in advanced democracies that lack compulsory voting rules.

We cannot infer from high voter turnout that individuals who vote believe that voting is efficacious. Scholars have argued that individuals vote for a variety of reasons, including a sense of civic duty (Riker & Ordeshook, 1968), to show allegiance to a specific party (Fiorina, 1976), and to support specific moral ideals (Gutmann, 1993). While each of these explanations was offered in the context of democratic elections, the same factors can apply to voting in authoritarian elections as well. Authoritarian regimes frequently hold elections in an attempt to legitimate dictatorial or military rule to either the international community or domestic constituents. Some citizens vote in these elections because they fear repercussions if they do not have evidence of having voted. Yet citizens participating in these elections may also come to believe that they are voting out of a sense of civic obligation, patriotism, or to show allegiance to the ruling regime. For example, 43 percent of respondents to a 1996 survey in Jakarta said that participating in elections was an obligation, not a right (Center for the Study of Development and Democracy, 1996). These same attitudes may persist under democratization. As I discuss later, many of my Russian respondents said it is important to show support to the regime by voting in an election even when the outcome is known in advance. Thus, we need to explore more than just voting rates to understand whether individuals see voting and elections as efficacious.

Measuring Political Efficacy

In contrast to voting and civil society engagement, which can be measured using indicators other than self-reported behavior, political efficacy can only be measured by public opinion surveys and interviews. The most frequently used measures of political efficacy in American politics come from the efficacy scale originated in the Michigan Election Studies and repeated by the American National Election Studies. The questions ask how "people like me" view their capacities for political involvement, emphasizing the subjective content of attitudes about efficacy (Lipset & Schneider, 1983, pp. 383–384). Another method is Almond and Verba's subjective competence scale (1963), which highlights specific types of interactions between an individual citizen and political institutions by asking respondents about their comprehension of local politics and expectations in exerting influence. Verba, Schlozman, and Brady adopted a similar approach to measure political efficacy in *Voice and Equality*, querying respondents about how they would be treated if they brought a complaint to a member of the local government and how much influence they felt that "someone like you" can have on government decisions. Another approach for measuring efficacy is to ask respondents how prepared they feel to participate in politics or to ask them how they could influence the political system and then code open-ended responses based on whether respondents could name a strategy.

Although scholarship has demonstrated that Lane's distinction between internal and external efficacy is empirically valid, not all measures of efficacy can easily be categorized as estimating one or the other dimension. For example, the question "Suppose the central government is debating a decision that could be very disadvantageous to you. Do you think that you could do anything to influence this debate or decision?"

is ambiguous with regard to internal vs. external efficacy. A person responding "yes" to this question could have a high sense of both internal and external efficacy. Yet a person answering "no" might fall into one of three patterns vis-à-vis internal and external efficacy. He could have a high estimation of his competencies to participate (internal efficacy), but little confidence that participation could shape the government's decision (external efficacy). Alternately, he might believe that participation is influential, but have little regard for his abilities to participate. Last, he might have low confidence in both his personal competence and the effect of participation on the system. In this question, a "no" response does not illuminate which dimension of efficacy is lacking.

In this chapter, I use a combination of indicators to measure levels of political efficacy among Russians and Indonesians. In analyzing survey data, I rely on the measures available in each survey. Many of these survey questions are worded identically to the Michigan Election Studies and the Almond and Verba surveys, which is further testimony to these early studies' influence. Some (but not all) of these questions provide insight into the internal and external dimensions of efficacy. For my quota-sample interviews with Russian and Indonesian citizens, I asked open-ended questions designed to elicit the clearest responses for ascertaining an individual's sense of political efficacy. I also asked specific questions about how respondents perceived the fairness of elections and their own influence in the electoral process.

Political Efficacy in Russia and Indonesia

Cross-Case Survey Analysis

How do Russians and Indonesians compare on measures of political efficacy? Table 4.1 demonstrated that efficacy was the only variable in my causal model that was a statistically significant predictor of all forms of nonvoting participation under investigation in both Russia and Indonesia. Those data confirm the strong relationship between political efficacy and participation. Yet Russians and Indonesians differ in important ways in both their levels of efficacy and the types of nonvoting participation they deem efficacious. In making the cross-case comparison, I first examine survey data and then analyze information from my interviews with a quota sample of the Russian and Indonesian populations.

Unfortunately, the World Values Survey does not include questions measuring respondents' beliefs about political efficacy, so I cannot analyze how Russians and Indonesians compare to residents of other countries

TABLE 6.1. *Could You Do Anything to Influence a Debate or Decision Taken by the Central Government?*

	Indonesia (%)	Russia (%)
I could be influential	4.6	1.9
I could be influential to some extent	13.4	9.0
I could be just a little influential	12.4	24.7
I could hardly be influential	68.2	60.1
Don't know	1.4	4.4

Keio University Research Survey of Political Society.

with regard to efficacy. The Keio University Research Survey of Political Society provides the only data we have to directly compare political efficacy in Russia and Indonesia.[2] Russia was surveyed in August–September 2005, while Indonesia was surveyed in February–March 2006.

The Keio survey asks two questions that directly measure political efficacy. The first asks, "Suppose the central government is debating a decision that could be very disadvantageous to you. Do you think that you could do anything to influence this debate or decision?" Respondents who said that they could be influential to even a small extent were then asked what they could do to influence the debate or decision. This second question offers a list of more than ten possible responses. Responses to these questions are in Tables 6.1 and 6.2.[3]

Table 6.1 shows that the majority of both Russian and Indonesian respondents do not believe that they could do much to influence the central government's debate or decision. Sixty-eight percent of Indonesians and 60 percent of Russians responded that they could "hardly be influential" in this context. If we look at the responses indicating some sense of efficacy ("I could be influential" or "I could be influential to some extent"), 18 percent of Indonesians responded affirmatively, compared to 11 percent of Russians.

[2] Marginal data from each of the country-level surveys is available through the Keio University Center for Civil Society with Comparative Perspective's online Data Archive at www.coe-ccc.keio.ac.jp/data_archive_en/data_archive_en_csw_download.html (Site consulted April 7, 2010).

[3] The survey includes two other questions that are almost identical to these, but ask respondents how they could influence a debate or decision made by the regional government. Overall the results to the two sets of questions were very similar, suggesting that both Russians and Indonesians perceive similar levels of efficacy for national and regional politics.

TABLE 6.2. *What Could You Do to Influence the Debate or Decision Taken by the Central Government?*

	Indonesia (%)	Russia (%)
Work through groups		
Form a group or organization	28.9	6.7
Take action through a political party	13.2	7.9
Take action through an organization (labor union, industry cooperative, religious organization) to which I belong	30.9	13.8
Contacting		
Ask friends and acquaintances to write letters of protest or to sign a petition	21.1	16.9
Make direct contact with a politician/ politicians or the mass media	5.3	12.6
Write a letter to a politician/politicians	7.2	12.6
Call to see the leaders of or those in positions of influence in all sectors of society	26.3	15.4
Make direct contact with a government official/bureaucrat	6.6	20.5
Legal channels		
Consult a lawyer	0.7	34.3
Appeal to the court	1.3	27.2
Direct action		
Take some kind of direct action	9.9	7.9
Just protest/complain	23.7	14.0
Do nothing	4.6	1.1
Don't know	0.0	16.0
N	152	356

Keio University Research Survey of Political Society.

I have grouped Table 6.2 responses into categories based on the action described. Three questions address seeking solutions through group action, five involve different forms of contacting, two address legal solutions, and two comprise direct action. If we compare Russian and Indonesian responses across categories, we see some interesting parallels between these replies and the political participation patterns described in Chapter 3. These responses also reflect variation in Russian and Indonesian civil society engagement discussed in Chapter 5. First, Indonesians exhibit a considerably higher propensity than Russians to work through a group to solve a problem. As Chapter 5 indicated, Indonesians are much more involved in voluntary organizations and structured community life than

Russians. Thus, we see a correlation between high levels of associational activity and a view that collective action is efficacious.

Second, Russians are much more likely than Indonesians to view contacting public officials as an efficacious way of influencing a central government debate or decision. In Table 6.2, the one item in the contacting category that attracts considerable support from Indonesians is contacting "the leaders of or those in positions of influence in all sectors of society." More than 26 percent of Indonesians selected this item, compared with 15 percent of Russians. The higher percentage of Indonesians selecting this response speaks to the visibility of societal leaders in Indonesia who are indeed separate from the state. In contrast, few such individuals exist in Russia. A final observation is that Russians are much more likely than Indonesians to view legal solutions as politically efficacious.

Political Efficacy in Russian and Indonesian National Surveys

As Chapter 4 noted, the Russian Election Study (RES) and the East Asia Barometer (EAB) contain measures of political efficacy. The Survey of Soviet Values (SSV) also includes questions that help assess political efficacy at the end of the Soviet period. The wording of questions varies across these three surveys, however, as well as across different iterations of the RES. Consequently, these data provide only a general overview of Indonesians' and Russians' views about political efficacy.

The SSV asks two questions that measure political efficacy in the late Soviet period. The first asks, "How much influence do you think people like you can have over local government?" to which respondents could answer, "a lot," "a moderate amount," "a little," or "none at all." More than 66 percent of respondents in the Russian territories said they could not have any influence over the local government, while 22.1 percent said they could have a little influence. The second survey question gauges external efficacy by asking about agreement with the statement: "People like me don't have any say about what the authorities do." Among all respondents, 13.1 percent strongly disagreed or disagreed with the statement, 10.1 percent were uncertain, and 76.9 percent agreed or strongly agreed. In short, it appears as though three out of four Russians in the late Soviet period felt they were incapable of influencing political authorities.

Did Russians' sense of political efficacy increase as people's overall ability to influence political outcomes also increased? This question confronts the reciprocal relationship between one's sense of efficacy and political participation. With the disappearance of the Communist Party's monopoly on political competition and the introduction of civil liberties protecting freedoms of speech, press, and assembly in the early 1990s, Russians' opportunities to participate in the political process and to have their participation influence outcomes increased dramatically. Boris Yeltsin's victory in the Russian presidential election of 1991 is evidence of this change, as is independents and pro-democracy parties' success in the 1993 State Duma elections.

We can examine this question regarding efficacy by consulting the 1995–1996 RES. Respondents were asked if they "fully agree," "agree," "waver," "disagree," or "fully disagree" with two statements. The first is, "People like me have no say in what the government does," which is almost identical to the statement used in the 1990 SSV, allowing us to compare responses across these two surveys. The second statement is, "In my opinion, I am well prepared to participate in political activity." The first statement measures external efficacy, while the second measures internal efficacy. Table 6.3 shows the range of agreement with these statements.

Fifty-two percent of respondents fully agreed or agreed with the first statement, which is nearly twenty-five percentage points lower than the number who agreed with the same statement in the 1990 SSV. While only 13.1 percent of respondents in 1990 disagreed or strongly disagreed with the statement that people have no say in what the authorities do, that number had more than doubled to 31.7 percent by 1995–1996. It appears that Russians' perception of external efficacy increased after the onset of democratization. Nevertheless, the majority of citizens still felt that they had no say over political authorities.

The second statement further confirms that most Russians did not view themselves as efficacious by the mid-1990s. Eighty-five percent of respondents disagreed or strongly disagreed with the statement that they were well prepared to participate in political activity. Taken together, these two statements suggest Russian citizens in the first half of the 1990s believed they had greater political influence than during the Soviet period, but still felt incapable of exercising this influence.

How different are Russians' and Indonesians' perceptions of efficacy? The EAB also includes two questions that measure political efficacy. Respondents were asked if they "strongly agree," "somewhat agree," "somewhat disagree," or "strongly disagree" with two statements. The first gauges external efficacy: "People have the power to change a government they don't like," while the second measures internal efficacy: "I think I have the ability to participate in politics." Responses to these statements appear in the second half of Table 6.3.

TABLE 6.3. *Political Efficacy Measures from RES (1995–1996) and EAB (2006)*

RES (Russia)	Fully agree (%)	Agree (%)	Waver (%)	Disagree (%)	Fully disagree (%)	N
People like me have no say in what the government does	8.9	43.1	16.3	27.0	4.7	2,470
In my opinion, I am well prepared to participate in political activity	0.6	5.3	9.0	45.1	40.0	2,494
EAB (Indonesia)	Strongly agree (%)	Somewhat agree (%)		Somewhat disagree (%)	Strongly disagree (%)	
People have the power to change a government they don't like	11.0	60.4		26.4	2.2	1,501
I think I have the ability to participate in politics	1.6	29.8		63.6	5.0	1,491

More than 71 percent of Indonesian respondents agreed that people have the power to change the government, suggesting a high level of external efficacy among the population. The second statement, "I think I have the ability to participate in politics," is similar in wording to the RES statement, "I am well prepared to participate in political activity." The majority of Indonesian respondents – 68.6 percent – disagreed with this statement. As high as this number is, it is still sixteen percentage points lower than the corresponding number in the Russian survey, suggesting that Indonesians feel better prepared to participate in politics than Russians do. If we take the two EAB measures together, we see that Indonesians have a high estimation of the population's ability to influence political outcomes, but a rather low estimation of their own individual abilities. Thus, they differ from Russians in their overall perceptions of external efficacy, yet share a similar sense of limited internal efficacy.

In Chapter 4, I use the RES's two efficacy measures and the EAB's two efficacy measures to create efficacy scales. For the RES measure, I recoded the first statement, "People like me have no say in what the government does," such that "0" equals "fully agree" and "1" equals "fully disagree." I recoded the second statement, "In my opinion, I am well prepared to participate in political activity" such that "0" equals "fully disagree" and "1" equals "fully agree." I then averaged these two variables to create a scale from 0 to 1 where "0" translates to having the lowest sense of efficacy possible and "1" translates to having the highest possible sense of efficacy. For the EAB measure, I combined the two statements to create a similar scale that ranges from 0 to 1, where "0" is equal to answering "strongly disagree" to both items and "1" is equal to answering "strongly agree" to both statements.

These two scales essentially serve as functionally equivalent measures of efficacy attitudes for Russia in 1995–1996 and Indonesia in 2006, allowing us to compare the mean scores as a way of gauging cross-national differences. Russia's mean score is 0.32, compared to 0.51 for Indonesia. Ultimately, Indonesian citizens' perceived efficacy in the initial years of democratization was higher than Russian citizens' perceived efficacy during their first years of democratization. Explaining this variation is beyond the scope of this book. Yet the countries' differing experiences in elections during the initial years of democratization are one possible cause.

Citizen Interviews: Evolving Attitudes of Political Efficacy

My citizen interviews further highlighted the qualitative differences in Russian and Indonesian perceptions of efficacy. As discussed in earlier chapters, my conversations with a quota sample of citizens in each city were based on a semi-structured questionnaire that I adapted to each locale's specific political context. Over the course of my 100 citizen interviews, I improved my questionnaire by adding new questions and dropping less fruitful ones. My questions about political efficacy evolved more than questions about other topics. The importance of efficacy attitudes became increasingly apparent as I conducted more interviews, compelling me to include additional questions to draw out citizens' thoughts about their potential political influence. Consequently, my measures of efficacy attitudes are leanest for Kazan and richest for Medan.

To measure political efficacy, I first asked how an individual thought she could influence the political system or what she could do if she wanted to influence politics. This question is helpful in two ways. First, it connects the abstract notion of influence to concrete acts. Individuals who can suggest a specific action have a higher sense of efficacy than those who cannot. Second, respondents' answers revealed telling emotions. Individuals with low senses of efficacy often responded with frustration. Those who could suggest concrete actions, meanwhile, did so with a calm voice. Individuals also regularly elaborated on their views about their country's political system when responding to the question. Over time, I added other questions that gauged respondents' attitudes about nonvoting political participation and whether they viewed other forms of participation as potentially effective.

Efficacy in Russia: Varied Perceptions between Regions

My Russian interviews convey three primary findings about the relationship between political efficacy and political participation. First, they confirm the survey measures that Russians have lower political efficacy levels than Indonesians. Generally speaking, I found that Russians' sense of external efficacy presented a greater obstacle to action than internal efficacy. Indeed, Russians' sense of competence is on display regularly in contacting officials. Rather than feeling themselves incapable of engaging in political acts, my respondents' comments reflect the position that the government is unmoved by citizen concerns. Second, Russians view contacting officials as an efficacious form of nonvoting political participation, which helps explain why they frequently select this act. Third, while none of the other attitudes or behaviors I examined differed meaningfully between my interview samples in Kazan and Krasnoyarsk, I noticed a considerable difference in perceived efficacy levels between respondents in these cities. On the whole, Krasnoyarsk residents appear to have a higher sense of political efficacy than Kazan residents. As I discuss in this chapter's final section, I believe these differences are due in part to the two regions' dissimilar experiences with post-Soviet elections.

Compared to my Indonesian respondents, my Russian sample expressed low levels of efficacy. Nevertheless, when asked what they could do if they wanted to influence politics, more than double the number of individuals in Kazan than Krasnoyarsk said they had no way to influence the political system. Among the Kazan group who said they could do nothing, one respondent felt that he could influence politics until the Yeltsin era and another felt one could influence politics during the Soviet era. In these instances, individuals believed that their efficacy had declined over time. Both of these individuals – a fifty-nine-year-old Tatar man with a graduate degree and a forty-eight-year-old Tatar woman with an undergraduate degree – had engaged in some form of nonvoting political participation in the late Soviet period.

When I asked the woman how people could be influential in the Soviet era, she replied, "They listened to us. They respected us." Several respondents shared this view that the Soviet government listened to its citizens more than the current government and that public opinion had greater influence on policy outcomes during the Soviet period. Participants in a series of focus group discussions in central Russia in December 2003 and March 2004 also expressed these attitudes about declining government responsiveness (White, 2005). Participants in Stephen White's study noted that acts such as strikes or letters to the newspaper were viewed as major events in the Soviet era, and consequently the government paid attention and corrected policies. In the post-Soviet era, however, citizens perceive such acts as so common that the government rarely listens to people's demands.

Not only were more individuals in Krasnoyarsk able to suggest concrete strategies to influence politics than their counterparts in Kazan; Krasnoyarsk respondents also offered a broader range of specific actions they believed to be efficacious. These respondents suggested contacting public officials, voting in elections, and joining political parties. Three respondents in Kazan offered similar responses for influencing politics: through fair elections, working with the media, or through collective action. The Kazan respondents quickly added, however, that while these options are efficacious in theory, current circumstances in Russia stymied the influence of such acts.

My Russian respondents' views about the efficacy of specific acts factored into their decisions about engaging in nonvoting participation.

In particular, many respondents cited their belief that contacting a public official is more likely to yield a favorable response than other forms of activity as a reason for engaging in this action. While I found evidence of contacting in both Kazan and Krasnoyarsk, Krasnoyarsk residents were more inclined to see contacting as efficacious. Additionally, my interviews with regional political party leaders and legislators in both cities reinforced the finding that citizen appeals occur at a higher rate in Krasnoyarsk, and are taken rather seriously by local and regional officials.

Interviews with both residents and legislators in Krasnoyarsk suggest that the Krasnoyarsk regional government attends to constituents' appeals, and citizens actually seek out regional deputies and party members to address their problems – phenomena I did not observe in Kazan. When asked if they knew how to contact their Duma and regional legislative representatives, most Krasnoyarsk respondents indicated that their representatives' phone numbers are advertised and that these officials have monthly reception hours. One of the most organized forums for providing constituent feedback is "Putin's public reception (*priem Putina*)," held in the headquarters of the regional branch of the United Russia party.[4] The reception, held three days a week from 10 A.M. to 5 P.M., is organized by a party staff member whose full-time job is to oversee constituent appeals. This person consults with visitors to the reception, instructs them how to direct their appeals to the appropriate level of government, and then follows up. The Krasnoyarsk Putin public reception receives an average of twenty appeals per day. The regional branch analyzes the appeals and sends a monthly report to the central party offices in Moscow. As one party analyst told me, even though United Russia is the party in power, it wants to stay in power, and this can happen only if it succeeds in addressing people's problems and provides a loyal critique to executives and legislators (Kr-22, interview, November 27, 2008).

While the Krasnoyarsk Putin public reception constitutes an especially well-coordinated and well-resourced effort, representatives and staffs from other political parties in Krasnoyarsk also regularly receive phone calls, letters, and citizen visits. For example, a leader of the Krasnoyarsk regional branch of the Liberal Democratic Party of Russia (LDPR) explained that the party has a reception space in downtown Krasnoyarsk

---

[4] Information about the Krasnoyarsk Putin public reception is based on the reception's organization at the time of my fieldwork in fall 2008.

that is open every weekday from 10 A.M. to 6 P.M. (Kr-12, interview, November 10, 2008). The reception is staffed by a law student who keeps a register of every encounter (which I viewed during our interview). The law student often asks reception visitors to write a letter because documentation helps the party resolve a problem. He noted that the party keeps a journal of all appeals and an accounting of the party's follow-up. Both federal and regional laws prescribe timelines (usually thirty days) by which lawmakers must respond to written appeals.[5] According to this LDPR leader, the party's twenty-four deputies working at all levels of government in Krasnoyarsk Krai received a total of 1,500 appeals in 2007. Representatives from the Krasnoyarsk branch of the Communist Party of the Russian Federation (KPRF) described a similar process (Kr-13, interview, November 11, 2008). Political party leaders in Kazan also received appeals from residents. For example, the Yabloko branch in Kazan reported receiving twenty to thirty phone calls per day after sending out a party mailer (K-21, interview, March 26, 2008).

Although public appeals and party responses were significantly less common in Kazan, I still encountered instances where contacting was the preferred method of political activism. For example, activists from the Russian cultural movement in Kazan revealed that they considered writing letters to officials and visiting their offices to be the most effective ways to promote the movement's interests (K-10, interview, March 13, 2008; K-18, interview, March 18, 2008). The letters tend to take two approaches – either asking an official to do something, or providing a statement documenting some form of government inaction. As one of my interlocutors pointed out, republican and federal laws allow a letter writer to take her appeal to a higher authority or go to court if a lower-level official does not respond, and the cultural movement's leaders have taken advantage of this right. In 2002, for instance, the movement's leaders wrote to President Putin due to lower-level agencies' inaction. This letter ultimately led to the opening of a Russian philological high school in Kazan. One movement leader reported personally writing more than 100 letters since 1991. He usually then visits the relevant official to convey the seriousness of the issue. This individual noted that the group's

---

[5] These laws include federal law No. 3-F3, "On the status of a member of the Federation Council and status of a deputy of the State Duma of the Federal Assembly of the Russian Federation," federal law No. 59-F3, "On the order of review of appeals by citizens of the Russian Federation," Tatarstan republican law No. 15-3RT, "On the status of a deputy of the State Assembly of the Republic of Tatarstan," and Krasnoyarsk Krai regional law No. 1–18, "On the status of a deputy of the Legislative Assembly of Krasnoyarsk Krai."

activists are generally well received and find a sympathetic audience for their concerns about "99 percent of the time" (K-18, interview, March 18, 2008).

One activist explained that contacting was the only political avenue open to the cultural movement. This individual noted that party development and advancement within political parties are based on acquaintances, connections, and decisions made in Moscow, not on commitment to particular principles. Therefore, the movement did not find it efficacious to work with local party leaders through a straightforward advocacy of its principles. It had to become a squeaky wheel in the political system by taking its contacting strategy all the way to the president. This leader also emphasized, however, that the cultural movement wants to attract attention to its concerns "without a scandal," which is why it avoids acts of contentious politics.

Overall, individuals in both Kazan and Krasnoyarsk who had participated in some form of nonvoting participation had a higher sense of efficacy and often linked their views about efficacy to their specific participatory experiences. The reciprocal relationship between efficacy and participation is particularly apparent in the case of contacting in Russia. My Russian respondents reported that they were more likely to repeat contacting as a participation strategy after having used it successfully to obtain a specific goal. One thirty-two-year-old Tatar man in Kazan had written three different letters to various government representatives. A thirty-nine-year-old Russian woman in Krasnoyarsk had also written three different letters to local officials. Both individuals said that they found contacting an effective way to address their specific problems.

Efficacy in Indonesia: Closely Tied to Participation

Like my Russian respondents, the Indonesians I interviewed shared a close connection between their experiences with nonvoting participation and feelings of efficacy. In contrast to the Russians, however, my Indonesian respondents feel efficacious about the elite-constraining acts that have promoted democratic outcomes. Indonesian respondents' ideas about how they could influence politics mirrored the forms of political participation and civic engagement discussed in Chapters 3 and 5. Suggestions included discussions and consultations with others, acting through an organization, participating in elections, joining a political party, writing to the newspaper, going to a demonstration, issuing a complaint, and trying to work for social change. Many of these acts are precisely the types of actions that help constrain elites.

Indonesians' perceptions of efficacy and individual experiences in nonvoting political participation are connected. Among the Indonesian respondents who were asked how they could influence politics, all but three who had engaged in some form of nonvoting political participation were able to list a specific act that they believed could be influential. The more involved an individual had been in nonvoting participation, the more strategies of influence he tended to name. For example, a twenty-two-year-old Javanese student activist who regularly engaged in non-voting political participation in Surabaya said, "You can demonstrate, write to the media, or sign a petition to signify the actualization of your opinion." In contrast to my Russian respondents, Indonesian respondents had more direct and ongoing experience with acts of contentious politics and political party organizing. For this reason, it is logical that Indonesians have a higher opinion than Russians about the efficacy of these actions.

Among the few Indonesian respondents who had engaged in nonvoting political participation but said they could not influence politics, the relationship between their specific experiences and attitudes is illustrative of the reciprocal relationship between participation and efficacy. One respondent is a PDI-P sympathizer who had once attended a campaign event in Medan, an act that takes minimal initiative and is as much informative as influential. The other two respondents – a thirty-six-year-old Javanese janitor in Surabaya and a thirty-eight-year-old Minangkabu female factory worker in Medan – had previously participated in labor protests that did not improve their situations. For example, the Surabaya janitor was part of a protest that failed to achieve its goal of raising minimum wages. Had the protest resulted in a favorable outcome, this respondent might have suggested that protesting could be influential.

Like my Russian respondents, Indonesians evaluated different forms of nonvoting political participation in part based on the perceived efficacy of such actions. This connection between attitudes about political participation and efficacy is further evidence of the reciprocal relationship between practicing politics and developing a sense of political efficacy. Indonesian respondents expressed a range of attitudes about political participation, from complete disdain to full support. Yet many Indonesians who had engaged in nonvoting political participation viewed their work as efficacious, which contributed to their continued participation. Because Indonesians are more frequent repeat participants in nonvoting political acts than Russians, there is greater opportunity for their participation to influence their sense of efficacy over time.

Furthermore, Indonesian respondents who had not engaged in non-voting political participation could point to the influence others' activism had on political outcomes. For example, several Indonesians connected protests to Suharto's downfall, and viewed these demonstrations as efficacious. As one thirty-eight-year-old Javanese woman in Medan said, "If there hadn't been the demonstrations [Suharto] would still be in power." When talking about the New Order era, a forty-two-year-old Batak woman who had never engaged in nonvoting political participation noted how demonstrations brought about Suharto's resignation. When later in the interview I asked what could be done if an elected representative failed to uphold his campaign promises, she replied, "Demonstrate – isn't that all we can do?"

While repeat protesters are more common in Indonesia than in Russia, leading to a stable and ongoing presence of contentious politics, my Indonesian respondents expressed mixed views about protesting. Regular protestors noted that this form of participation was the only method they could employ to attract public officials' attention. According to the Surabaya student leader of PMII, "You need to communicate with [legislative] representatives. But, because they are difficult to find, we have demonstrations." A thirty-three-year-old Tamil construction worker in Medan, whose nonvoting political participation was limited to once attending a PDI-P rally, expressed a similar view: "It is very difficult to meet a [legislative] representative. That is why they carry out demonstrations – just to be met by representatives." This perception is grounded in some truth. When discussing his interactions with constituents, a regional legislator in East Java noted that demonstrations often compel representatives to hold meetings with aggrieved citizens (EJ-5, interview, June 4, 2009).

Yet several citizen respondents expressed disapproval of contentious politics. Some critics associate demonstrations with violence, which is logical given the bloodshed that accompanied many protests in recent Indonesian history, particularly during Suharto's last days in power. A forty-six-year-old Javanese fruit merchant in Surabaya expressed this sentiment well: "If I see a demonstration, I do not agree if it contains violence.... It is unreasonable if a demonstration leads to violence, destruction, and results in death." Other respondents distinguished between individuals who protest voluntarily and those who are paid, viewing this latter group negatively. One forty-one-year-old Batak woman who is a lower-level civil servant said: "They can be influential, but I don't join demonstrations because I feel that they are senseless. I know someone who joined a demonstration and received 20,000 rupiah [about $2] for demonstrating."

Respondents also expressed mixed views about contacting. Some view contacting as a more peaceful way to express oneself than protesting. Others expressed skepticism that a letter would "make it to the top." Poorer and more socially marginalized individuals often felt that contacting a public official would be too burdensome given their limited resources. For example, one twenty-nine-year-old Javanese woman in Surabaya with an elementary school education said that while she thought nonvoting forms of political participation could be effective, she herself would never join a protest or visit a public official:

I wouldn't go to a demonstration. It would be too hot and I'd get tired. Representatives' offices are far away. I'd have to find time to travel there, and pay the fare for the bus. Then, if I went, the representative would not listen to me. It would be a waste.

After offering this explanation, she added, "We are little people (*rakyat kecil*). We do not climb to the top." Even individuals with more developed civic skills express reservations about contacting. A thirty-two-year-old Batak construction worker with a high school education in Medan noted, "I feel that I would not go directly to an office because the procedures are rather difficult." This individual is an elder in his Protestant church, the head of the mutual aid society to which he belongs, and is a leader in his *marga* (Batak sub-ethnic patrilineal clan), experiences from which he has acquired considerable civic skills, yet even he viewed contacting public officials as complicated.

Although some Indonesian respondents could not offer an example of how they could influence politics, many named several acts of political influence that help constrain elites. Like Russians, Indonesians' individual experiences with nonvoting political participation appear to influence their efficacy attitudes. Unlike Russians, however, more Indonesians have had positive experiences with elite-constraining participation. This qualitative evidence adds a new layer of nuance to the statistical tests in Chapter 4, which showed that while efficacy was a statistically significant predictor of nonvoting participation in both Russia and Indonesia, it appears to be a stronger predictor of participation in Indonesia than in Russia. Here we can see why: as a result of successful elite-constraining participation, Indonesians are more likely to engage in such acts in the future. This connection between efficacy attitudes and elite-constraining participation has important consequences for democracy's survival as Indonesians are more frequent participants than Russians in these nonvoting acts. Consequently, the boost in efficacy that participation in elite-constraining acts generates can have a multiplier effect that leads to increased and ongoing engagement in the activities that pressure elites to work within democratic institutions and norms.

Elections and Efficacy: Positive and Negative Reciprocal Effects

The Efficacy of Elections

The primary behavioral focus of this book is nonvoting political participation. When considering the relationship between political efficacy and participation, however, it is helpful to consider the impact of voting on efficacy. Voting in elections can be either elite-constraining or elite-enabling. Votes against incumbents aim to constrain them, while votes in favor of them are enabling. Following the onset of democratization, Indonesians have acquired considerable experience with elite-constraining voting, while most Russians have practiced elite-enabling voting.

As Chapter 2 discussed, the Soviet Union and New Order regimes regularly held controlled elections, giving citizens of these countries ample experience with voting in elections that were not fair or free. Competitive elections were gradually introduced on the Russian territories of the Soviet Union starting in 1989. The late Soviet legislative elections, the 1991 Russian presidential election, and the 1993 and 1995 Russian State Duma elections are generally believed to have been free and fair. Indonesia's first post-Suharto competitive election was held in 1999. This election and subsequent national elections in 2004, 2009, and 2014 are generally believed to have been free and fair.

Although an absence of data prevents us from gauging how Russians and Indonesians perceive the efficacy of these early elections, we do have some information about Russians' and Indonesians' attitudes about elections and electoral campaigns. The Keio University Research Survey on Political Society asks, "In general how do you regard voting or election campaigns?" and offers five unusual responses that do not seem to capture a clear attitudinal dimension. Even though the wording of the responses is odd, they constitute a roughly ordinal scale of how much one enjoys voting and campaigns. At one end is the response, "I feel satisfied in voting," and at the other end is, "Sometimes election campaigns appear totally ridiculous to me." Table 6.4 shows how Russians and Indonesians responded.

TABLE 6.4. *In General How Do You Regard Voting or Election Campaigns?*

	Indonesia (%)	Russia (%)
I feel satisfied in voting.	18.6	10.8
I sometimes find election campaigns interesting and fun.	22.6	6.9
I have never found election campaigns interesting or fun, nor have they ever caused me to feel annoyed, nor have I ever disdained them.	40.0	27.8
I sometimes feel annoyed during election campaigns.	6.8	11.8
Sometimes election campaigns appear totally ridiculous to me.	10.0	16.4
None of the above	1.0	22.2
Don't know	1.0	4.2

As Table 6.4 shows, the modal response for both Indonesians and Russians to this question is indifference ("I have never found election campaigns interesting or fun ... "). If we look at the other responses, however, it appears as though Indonesians have more positive views of campaigns than Russians. Nearly 23 percent of Indonesians "find election campaigns interesting and fun," compared with 7 percent of Russians. The percentage of Indonesians who find voting satisfying (18.6 percent) is also higher than the percentage of Russians (10.8 percent). At the opposite end of the spectrum, 28 percent of Russians express negative views of electoral campaigns, compared to 17 percent of Indonesians.

This survey question suggests that Indonesians view voting and electoral campaigns more positively than Russians do. By 2005 and 2006 (the years when the survey was conducted), these two countries had amassed varied election experiences. Indonesians had experienced two fair and free national electoral cycles, including their first direct elections for the presidency. Russia, by contrast, had more than a decade of post-Soviet electoral experience in which each national election was accompanied by a narrowing of competition and the outcomes became less and less uncertain. One would logically expect that recent election disappointments increased Russians' disdain for electoral campaigns.

One way to address this potential endogeneity is to examine Russian attitudes toward voting in the early post-Soviet period and change in these attitudes over time. The RES has asked a question about the efficacy of voting or elections in each of its surveys, although the wording has changed over time. In 1995, RES respondents were asked if they "fully agree," "agree," "waver," "disagree," or "fully disagree" with the statement "Nothing will change in this country as a result of how people vote." In total, 36.4 percent of respondents disagreed or fully disagreed with the statement, compared to 46.5 of respondents who agreed or fully agreed. Even in 1995 – the highpoint of Russian democracy – more Russians viewed elections as ineffective than effective. Thus, Russians' low levels of perceived voting efficacy precede the decline in the fairness and competitiveness of national elections and are not exclusively a consequence of it.

In the 1999–2000 RES, respondents were asked to place themselves on a five-point scale where "1" translates to "voting does not make a difference to the country," and "5" translates to "voting does make a difference to the country." Respondents received a similar question in the 2003–2004 and 2008 RES, when they were asked to place themselves on a five-point scale where "1" translates to "who people vote for won't make a difference," and "5" translates to "who people vote for can make a difference." Thus, the higher one's self-placement on either of these scales, the greater her perception of the efficacy of elections. The mean response for 1999–2000 was 3.63, which dropped slightly to 3.23 in 2003–2004, then remained relatively stable at 3.21 in 2008. Russians' efficacy dropped only slightly between 1999 and 2008, suggesting that Russians' disdain for electoral campaigns likely took root long before the 2006 Keio survey was administered and before the laws and norms that make it harder for the opposition to organize emerged.

It is illuminating to consider the RES responses in light of a 1990 SSV question about elections. At the time of the SSV survey, the only competitive election Soviet respondents had experienced was the 1989 Congress of People's Deputies election, in which multiple candidates (but not multiple parties) were allowed to compete. Respondents were asked, "How much do you feel that having a government elected instead of appointed makes it pay attention to what the people want?" Among all respondents, 12 percent replied, "not much," while 48 percent replied "some" and 39 percent answered "a good deal." The percentages for respondents in Russian territories are almost the same. In 2008, the New Russia Barometer (NRB) asked a similar question, "Do you think having regular elections makes politicians do what people want?" Table 6.5 compares the 1990 SSV and the 2008 NRB responses, and the differences are remarkable. Only 8 percent of NRB respondents replied "to a large extent" and

TABLE 6.5. *Russian Attitudes about Elections as Constraint on Elites*

"How much do you feel that having a government elected instead of appointed makes it pay attention to what the people want?"	1999 (SSV %)	"Do you think having regular elections makes politicians do what people want?"	2008 (NRB %)
		None at all	26
Not much	12	Not very much	30
Some	48	To some extent	35
A good deal	39	To a large extent	8
N	1,354	N	1,601*

* The total number of interviews conducted in the NRB was 1,601. The published data report does not include the number of valid responses for this specific question, which may have been lower.

35 percent answered "to some extent," while 56 percent of respondents replied "not very much" or "none at all" (Rose, 2008, p. 11). Russian citizens in the late Soviet era viewed elections as a potential mechanism for attracting the government's attention to their needs. Yet, as survey data show, once they experienced more elections, Russian citizens became less convinced that the ballot could make a difference in their lives.

In sum, Russians' experience with elections in the post-Soviet era did not increase their sense of voting's efficacy. Yet, Russians' low sense of efficacy about voting is not simply a consequence of the increased authoritarianism of the 2000s, but can be traced back to the mid-1990s when Russian elections were fair, free, and competitive.

Citizen Interviews: Connecting Perceptions and Experiences

The differences between Indonesian and Russian attitudes toward elections revealed in the survey data are further confirmed in my citizen interviews. As mentioned earlier, I expanded my questions about elections and their efficacy over the course of my interviews. About halfway through my interviews in Kazan, the first of my four case studies, I began to measure respondents' views about the fairness of elections by asking whether they thought official election results correspond with the way people actually voted. Starting in Krasnoyarsk, my second case study, I asked respondents if it was important to vote in elections. If they answered affirmatively, I asked why. I also asked if they believed that voting in elections could influence political decisions. My interviews in Surabaya and Medan included all these questions.

Russian Attitudes about Elections: A "Dirty Business"

Like most Russian citizens, my respondents voted at high rates. Only three respondents had never voted. Twelve individuals in Kazan talked about whether elections were honest and had reliable results. Of this group, only two said elections were honest and that official results correspond with how people actually voted. Most respondents were much more skeptical. In some cases, individuals felt the overall outcomes are accurate but that the percentages are off. In other cases, individuals view elections as a "dirty business." A thirty-two-year-old Tatar sociologist expressed an "absence of faith in honest elections" – a sentiment many shared. He last participated in a federal election in 2000, when he voted against acting President Vladimir Putin. "Elections will be falsified. I've turned cold toward elections," he said. In contrast to Kazan, Krasnoyarsk residents are split in their views about the honesty of elections. About half of my Krasnoyarsk respondents said official election results correspond with how people voted.

Although my quota sample sizes are too small to make definitive statements about differences between the two cities, it seems highly likely that respondents in Krasnoyarsk view their elections as more honest than did respondents in Kazan. I believe this variation is related to these cities' different experiences with post-Soviet elections, a topic I explore in this chapter's final section.

Most of my Krasnoyarsk respondents believe it is important to vote in elections, and a considerable number agreed that voting can influence political decisions. Attitudes about the honesty of official election results and the influence of voting on political decisions are also correlated. Almost all the individuals who believe that official election results are accurate also see voting as an effective way of exerting influence.

Generally speaking, attitudes about the importance of voting and the efficacy of voting are also correlated in Krasnoyarsk. If individuals believe voting can influence political decisions, they also view voting as important. Conversely, if they do not think voting can be influential, they do not see it as important. Some individuals, however, see voting as important, but do not think it influences political outcomes. Two respondents noted that voting only confirmed decisions others had already made, creating an impression of democracy. Others qualified their statements – saying in general voting is important, but that here it makes no difference.

Respondents offered several explanations for why voting is important. While some connect it directly to determining who is in power, others see voting as a civic obligation or a way of expressing one's opinions.

In short, not all reasons respondents gave for why voting is important specifically involve electing leaders. In one example, a fifty-nine-year-old Russian social worker noted that it was important to vote to ensure that someone else does not use one's ballot to commit electoral fraud.

My interviews show that in Krasnoyarsk, participation in nonvoting political acts does not appear to correlate with attitudes about the honesty of elections, the importance of voting, or the efficacy of voting. There is a positive correlation, however, between voting frequency and opinions about the accuracy of official election results. Likewise, my respondents who believe that voting is important or can affect political outcomes are regular voters, while those who do not share these views vote less often.

Russian attitudes about the efficacy of elections exemplify the reciprocal nature of efficacy and participation. Russians who view voting as efficacious are more likely to vote, and they are also more likely to view election results as honest. In contrast, those who question the accuracy of official election results are less likely to vote or see voting as influential. Indeed, the absence of integrity in the electoral system is, in part, what makes them feel inefficacious. In this instance, we see how the reciprocal relationship between participation and efficacy attitudes can have a multiplicative effect on overall levels of political participation. A small dose of manipulation can have a sizeable impact on citizens' sense of efficacy and their willingness to vote in future elections.

Indonesian Attitudes about Elections: "Now there is Freedom"
Even though Russians and Indonesians both vote at high rates, they express considerably different views about elections. Indonesians are more likely than Russians to believe that voting is important and can influence political decisions.

My Indonesian respondents, like most of their fellow compatriots, are ardent voters. About two-thirds of my respondents have voted in almost every election since 1999. Only five had never voted – and two of these had only recently reached voting age. Almost all respondents believe it is important to vote in elections. Most respondents who expressed this view also believe that voting in elections can influence political outcomes.

Considering how almost all my Indonesian respondents view voting as important, it is not surprising that this attitude does not necessarily correspond with voting practices. Respondents who never vote, or vote only occasionally, view voting as important, and two of the three individuals who do not consider voting important vote in almost all elections. The same pattern exists for attitudes about the efficacy of voting. Even individuals who rarely or occasionally vote see voting as efficacious, and the one individual who does not share this view votes in most elections.

Residents of Surabaya and Medan exhibited different opinions, however, about the accuracy of election results. About half of the respondents in Surabaya believe that official election results correspond with how people vote, compared to nineteen out of twenty-four respondents in Medan. Among those who question the official tally, however, they rarely doubt the overall validity of the results, which they see as generally reflecting the people's will. Most individuals who doubt the honesty of official election results believe it is important to vote in elections and that voting can influence political outcomes. Thus, despite the imperfections they see in the electoral system, these individuals perceive the efficacy of elections as rather high.

While the small size of my interview sample may account for the differences in attitudes observed between Surabaya and Medan, it is also possible that a 2008 election controversy in East Java contributed to increased skepticism among Surabayans. In 2008, East Java held its first direct election for governor. The first round of voting in July included five candidate pairs. The second round in November between the top two candidates, Soekarwo and Khofifah, proved very close, with the official results displaying a difference of only about 60,000 votes among more than 15 million votes cast (Mawuntyas & Wibowo, 2008). Investigations into electoral fraud revealed widespread irregularities in three districts on East Java's Madura Island. In December the Constitutional Court annulled the official election results and called for the election to be rerun in two districts within sixty days, and for a recount of ballots in the third district within thirty days (Indra Harsaputra, 2008). The results from the rerun election and recount were as close as the initial election results, and the electoral commission validated Soekarwo's victory with 50.1 percent (Indra Harsaputra & Nugroho, 2009).

The drama of these elections played out in full view of the public and was covered widely in the Indonesian media. Even after Soekarwo was sworn in as governor in February 2009, allegations of fraud and mismanagement sullied the regional electoral commission's reputation. In particular, there was widespread concern that the 2009 national elections would include similar irregularities. These concerns were confirmed when the official voter list for the April 2009 DPR elections in Indonesia proved inaccurate, excluding many voters. The omission appeared to be a result of gross negligence or ineptitude, not malfeasance. An additional 5.2 million voters were added to the voting list by the July 2009 presidential election to correct for these inaccuracies (Komisi Pemilihan Umum website www.kpu.go.id/).

My Surabayan respondents referred to these events when asked whether official election results accurately reflect how people vote. One twenty-six-year-old Javanese homemaker with a professional degree expressed this view: "Many were not able to vote [in April] because their names were not listed; also candidates gave money so that you would vote for that candidate. I do not trust these elections." Only three respondents in Surabaya intimated egregious forms of falsification, such as the buying and selling of votes or direct manipulation by political parties. Other respondents, however, seemed to believe that official results were not "100 percent" accurate. Some noted that the "differences are not big," or that there was some playing with the numbers "at the top."

Indonesian respondents offered several opinions about why voting is important. Most answers, however, emphasized that voting determined the country's leaders and who would be in government. The twenty-two-year-old Javanese student leader of PMII in Surabaya suggested that voting supersedes any other activism he engages in: "In my opinion, yes, it is important [to vote]. Because in casting our votes we are also determining the fate of our nation." Several respondents linked their vote choice to their views about what they wanted for their country. Others noted that voting was their right or their obligation. As a thirty-four-year-old unemployed Batak man in Medan noted, "It is a waste of your vote if you don't choose [a candidate]."

In fact, the most striking difference in my Russian and Indonesian respondents' attitudes about efficacy is their views about elections and what is at stake in them. Even Russians who believe that official election results are honest and that it is important to vote do not express much enthusiasm about elections. Indonesians, by contrast, voice considerable pleasure in their freedom to "be political" (*berpolitik*). One seventeen-year-old Batak man in Medan voted for the first time in Indonesia's presidential elections a couple of weeks before our interview. When I asked what he thought of the experience, he replied, "There was a feeling of great freedom, where I felt that democracy meant something to me."

The freedom Indonesians feel in elections comes, in part, from the end of the unofficial requirement to support Golkar, the party Suharto used to control Indonesian society for almost three decades. Several respondents expressed this view, including those too young to have been politically active in the New Order era. A twenty-five-year-old Javanese clerical worker with a junior-high school education in Surabaya offered,

"Now there is freedom. Before, civil servants needed to vote for Golkar." A thirty-year-old Javanese/Madurese man with an elementary school education who runs a small food stall in Surabaya noted, "My parents voted, but for Golkar. Before there was a lot of pressure and you had to vote for Golkar. Now you are free to choose."

In sum, Indonesians' and Russians' attitudes about elections and the efficacy of voting exhibit both similarities and differences. On the whole, Indonesians are more likely than Russians to see voting as important and to view their votes as directly determining the leadership of their country, which in turn establishes policies that affect them. Russians, by contrast, are less likely to view voting as politically determinative. Last, while I observed variation in attitudes between residents in Kazan and Krasnoyarsk and Surabaya and Medan regarding the honesty of official election results, on the whole my Indonesian respondents tend to trust their election results more than Russians do. Even when they do not trust election results, Indonesians are more likely to attribute inaccuracies to incompetence and mistakes than to blatant falsification.

Indonesians' and Russians' different attitudes reflect, to a certain degree, variation in these countries' electoral practices. In Indonesia, there is evidence of mistakes happening in the course of elections, but little proof of organized fraud. Indonesian attitudes about the accuracy of election results reflect their criticism of the incompetence of some electoral officials while also accepting the legitimacy of results. In Russia, however, elections have become more orchestrated in the past several years, discouraging competition and raising public suspicion about outcomes. Since 2004, political aspirants have faced an environment in which access to the media is highly unequal, harassment of political opposition has increased, and pressure to vote for the pro-Kremlin United Russia has become more overt. These conditions contributed in part to the wave of protests that broke out in Russia following the December 2011 State Duma elections (see Chapter 8). Several scholars have identified multiple "fingerprints" of electoral fraud in Russian federal elections from 1996 to 2008, including a dramatic increase in districts reporting turnout of more than 90 percent, suspicious shifts in patterns of support away from opponents and in favor of the pro-Kremlin candidate, as well as a clear trend in new votes gained by increases in turnout (Lukinova, Myagkov, & Ordeshook, 2011; Myagkov, Ordeshook, & Shakin, 2009). Yet these more recent developments' impact on Russian attitudes about the efficacy of elections should not be overstated. Until 2004, Russian elections exhibited considerable levels of competition. Nevertheless, as the survey data demonstrate, Russians' views about the efficacy of elections did not increase as they gained more experience with competitive elections.

How "Throwing the Rascals Out" Increases Efficacy

Mapping Citizen Responses to Election Experiences

Examining early post-authoritarian elections helps us understand the potential impact of these elections on political efficacy in subsequent years. In the years following Russia and Indonesia's transitions to democracy, their national elections led to dramatically different outcomes. If we apply Huntington's two-turnover test to these cases, Russia fails and Indonesia passes. Indonesians have voted an incumbent political executive out of power, while Russians never have. In Russia, most political power is concentrated in the presidency. Consequently, turnover in the party that holds a plurality in the State Duma does not signify a change in power. Opposition came to power in Russia in the form of Boris Yeltsin, who was elected Russian president in 1991 and reelected in 1996. He resigned in late 1999, forcing early presidential elections. Acting President Vladimir Putin was elected with nearly 53 percent of the vote in March 2000, and was reelected with 71 percent of the vote in March 2004. Constitutionally prohibited from running for a third consecutive term, Putin endorsed First Deputy Prime Minister Dmitrii Medvedev as his successor in 2008. Medvedev handily took 71 percent of the vote in the March 2008 election. In 2012 Putin once again ran for election, capturing 64 percent of the vote. In sum, Russian national elections have never transferred executive power away from the incumbent political force.

At the time of its democratic transition, Indonesia had a quasi-parliamentary system in which the president was elected indirectly by the parliament. In this context, opposition came to power in Indonesia following the 1999 DPR elections. As Chapter 2 discussed, the Indonesian Democratic Party of Struggle (PDI-P) won a plurality of seats in this election, but a coalition of smaller parties propelled the head of the National Awakening Party (PKB), Abdurrahman Wahid, to the Indonesian presidency. After Wahid's unsuccessful first two years as president, large numbers of Indonesians participated in demonstrations demanding the president's resignation. In July 2001, the People's Consultative Assembly (MPR) voted to dismiss Wahid and replace him with Vice President Megawati Sukarnoputri, the head of PDI-P. In 2004, Megawati ran as the incumbent in the first direct elections for the Indonesian presidency. She lost to Susilo Bambang Yudhoyono and peacefully turned over power. In this sense, Indonesia passed Huntington's two-turnover test quickly – within six years after the end of authoritarianism.

Indonesians' success at forcing Abdurrahman Wahid's removal from power in 2001 and unseating Megawati in the 2004 presidential elections helped strengthen their sense of political efficacy. Russians, however, have never unseated an incumbent president or anointed "successor." Every Russian presidential election since 1991 has validated the status quo, by either reelecting sitting presidents (1996 and 2004) or endorsing the incumbent's preferred candidate (2000, 2008, and 2012). I find that Indonesians' and Russians' different electoral and protest experiences in the early years of democratization have contributed to the variations in their perceptions of efficacy.

To test my hypothesis about the importance of early election outcomes, I examine Russian subnational variation in gubernatorial elections, held in Russia from 1996 to 2005. While some gubernatorial elections[6] validated incumbent governors who were appointed by Boris Yeltsin, others resulted in turnovers of power. The cases of Tatarstan (of which Kazan is the capital) and Krasnoyarsk Krai demonstrate this difference. While Tatarstan never removed a sitting regional executive or had competitive elections for the position, Krasnoyarsk held three competitive gubernatorial elections, one of which resulted in the removal of an incumbent. Thus, while Kazan residents have never seen their votes remove an incumbent from executive power at any level of government, Krasnoyarsk residents have used elections to bring about a change in the regional executive.

As the previous two sections have shown, my respondents in Kazan and Krasnoyarsk displayed differences in efficacy measures. Respondents in Krasnoyarsk display a greater overall sense of efficacy than respondents in Kazan and are also more likely to trust official election results. My samples in both cities were selected to be generally representative of the ethnic, educational, and occupational variation found in each region. I found no differences in opinions based on ethnic identification, and citizens of the same educational status or occupational sphere shared similar attitudes across the two cities. Thus, the differences in attitudes about efficacy cannot be explained by ethnicity, education, income, or other personal differences between respondents in the two cities. One striking

---

[6] The executives of Russia's ethnic republics, including Tatarstan, have the title of "president" rather than governor. For simplicity's sake, when referring to the general process of elections for regional executives, I use the term "gubernatorial," yet when referring to specific executives of Tatarstan, I use the term "president."

difference between respondents in Krasnoyarsk and Kazan, however, aligns with these differences in efficacy attitudes: electoral turnover of the regional executive.

Kazan: Noncompetitive Authoritarian Elections

Kazan is the capital of Tatarstan, one of twenty-one national republics within the Russian Federation. During the early years of post-Soviet Russian federalism, Tatarstan leveraged nationalist sentiment to negotiate the first bilateral power-sharing treaty between the central government and a federal unit, garnering more autonomy than any other region. Tatarstan's power-sharing treaty limited the extent to which Moscow could interfere in regional politics, including efforts at democratization. From 1989 to March 2010, Tatarstan's regional politics were under the control of Mintimer Shaimiev. Shaimiev became the first secretary of the Tatar regional committee of the Communist Party of the Soviet Union in 1989. He successfully adapted the method of single-party political rule to the post-Soviet context, running unopposed as republican president in 1991 and 1996 – violating a federal law that Moscow did not try to uphold until after Vladimir Putin became Russia's president in 2000. In the 1996 election, Shaimiev won 97 percent of the vote and voter turnout was nearly 78 percent (Orttung, Lussier, & Paretskaya, 2000, p. 539). Shaimiev changed Tatarstan's constitution to run for a third term in 2001, although this time he permitted token opposition from four contenders. Shaimiev handily won with nearly 80 percent of the vote (Faroukshin, 2001). After Putin cancelled gubernatorial elections in 2004, he appointed Shaimiev to another term in March 2005. Shaimiev finally stepped down in early 2010, securing the regional executive appointment for his trusted advisor, Rustem Minnikhanov.

My interviews with Kazan residents showed that, as of 2008, Shaimiev was wildly popular. An ethnic Tatar, Shaimiev enjoyed great public support among both Russians and Tatars, and would have likely won multiple terms as regional executive under fair and free elections. Yet Russia's brief experiment with gubernatorial elections failed to bring competitive and free elections to Tatarstan. Consequently, the Soviet tradition of approving a candidate the authoritarian elite had already ordained continued in Tatarstan throughout Shaimiev's tenure in office. Residents of Kazan, therefore, have not experienced competitive incumbent turnover at the national or regional level. According to one opposition figure in Kazan, the biggest "sin" of Yeltsin, Shaimiev, and Putin is that people lost belief in their own power. As a result, he argues, there is no difference between Soviet and contemporary elections (K-16, interview, March 11, 2008). Kazan's lack of experience in "throwing the rascal out" has contributed to my Kazan respondents' low sense of efficacy, as well as their skepticism about the honesty of election results. Krasnoyarsk respondents, meanwhile, expressed higher levels of efficacy attitudes and greater trust in the honesty of election results.

Krasnoyarsk: Incumbent Turnover

Post-Soviet regional elections in Krasnoyarsk have proven significantly more competitive than elections in Tatarstan. Krasnoyarsk held three gubernatorial elections between 1993 and 2002. Each included at least eight candidates in the first round and required two rounds of voting since no single candidate won a majority in the first round.[7]

Krasnoyarsk's first popularly elected governor, Valerii Zubov, stood for reelection in 1998. He was challenged by a popular national-level figure, former Lieutenant General Aleksandr Lebed. After a decorated military career, Lebed entered Russian politics full-time in 1995, heading the party list for the Congress of Russian Communities (KRO) in the 1995 State Duma elections and running for the Russian presidency in 1996, where he finished third with more than 14 percent of the vote. In the Krasnoyarsk gubernatorial race, Lebed led the first election round with 45 percent of the vote, while incumbent Zubov came in second with 35 percent. Lebed emerged victorious in the second round of voting with 57 percent of the votes, as the voters of Krasnoyarsk Krai successfully used elections to vote out an incumbent.

Governor Lebed's death in a helicopter crash in 2002 necessitated a third gubernatorial election in the region – a contest that has earned a reputation in Russia as one of the most competitive regional elections in the country's history. This election's notoriety comes from both the explicit involvement of business interests, as well as the controversy that ensued over the results. The top two candidates to emerge from the first round of voting, chair of the regional legislature Aleksandr Uss (27.6 percent) and governor of Taimyr Autonomous Okrug[8] Aleksandr Khloponin (25.3 percent), were prominent political figures backed by major

---

[7] Information about the number of candidates and their vote share was taken from the Krasnoyarsk Krai Electoral Commission's website http://iksrf.kgs.ru/ under the section "Arkhiv vyborov i referendumov." The site was accessed on March 25, 2011.

[8] Taimyr and Evenk autonomous okrugs were simultaneously parts of Krasnoyarsk Krai and separate subjects of the Russian Federation. In January 2007, the autonomous okrugs were officially merged with Krasnoyarsk Krai to form a single federation subject.

economic concerns.[9] The second round of voting proved very close, with Khloponin coming in first with 49 percent of the votes. The regional electoral commission declared the election invalid and set a date for new elections in March 2003. President Putin then intervened by forcing the region's acting governor to tender his resignation, appointing Khloponin to the post, and prodding the Russian Central Electoral Commission to declare Khloponin's victory final ("Ukroshchenie Stroptivykh," 2002).

The 1998 and 2002 gubernatorial elections in Krasnoyarsk were not paragons of democracy. There are many reasons to question their fairness, including the extensive involvement of financial-industrial groups and the misuse of state resources to facilitate an electoral campaign and obstruct opponents, which were considered particularly prominent in the 2002 race (Hale, 2006; Orttung, 2004; Yorke, 2003). But while these elections were not entirely fair, they were largely free and undoubtedly competitive. Potential candidates were not prevented from participating, and the outcome was not foreordained. In both elections, the result was determined by how people voted.

In sum, residents of Krasnoyarsk experienced three competitive gubernatorial elections in nine years, each of which required two rounds of balloting. In one instance an incumbent was unseated, and in another the narrow victory invited high levels of scrutiny. Even though Russian executive politics at the national level simply validated the status quo, Krasnoyarsk residents saw the efficacy of elections firsthand in regional contests.

My interviews picked up on the influence of competitive gubernatorial elections on people's attitudes about politics and elections. While respondents in Kazan universally loved their regional executive, citizens of Krasnoyarsk expressed a much broader array of views about their leaders. Some, for example, believe that Lebed had dramatically improved conditions in the region. Others view him as an unsympathetic outsider and called him a "*soldafon*," a derogatory term for a person of the military perceived as uncivilized and limited in his abilities. Krasnoyarsk residents expressed a similar range of opinions about Khloponin. Some respondents like that he is young, energetic, and capable, while others view him as a transplant from another region who only cares about his political career. After experiencing competitive elections and seeing the value of their votes, Krasnoyarsk residents do not simply accept the leadership handed to them from above. Rather, they have

---

[9] For an analysis of the role of financial industrial groups in this election, see Hale (2006) and Orttung (2004).

begun to look at leaders in a critical light and are more confident in their capability to determine what kind of leadership they want.

By comparing cross-regional variation in incumbency turnover in Tatarstan and Krasnoyarsk Krai, I have explored the effect of this phenomenon on efficacy attitudes. I find that respondents in Krasnoyarsk, who successfully unseated an incumbent governor via elections, have a higher sense of efficacy than respondents in Kazan, who never saw electoral turnover in executive power. This cross-regional analysis provides strong support for my hypothesis about the differences in efficacy attitudes between Russians and Indonesians. As the data presented in this chapter have demonstrated, Indonesians have a higher sense of efficacy than Russians. Additionally, Indonesians believe that elections can influence political outcomes at a higher rate than Russians do. Indonesians have unseated an incumbent president via election, which I believe has strengthened their sense of efficacy and propelled further political participation. In analyzing the Indonesian and Russian experiences with incumbency turnover in early elections together with the cross-regional cases within Russia, my finding about the relationship between incumbency turnover and efficacy attitudes contributes to our theoretical knowledge about the importance of early elections for democracy's survival.

Conclusion

This chapter has described several important qualitative differences in Russians' and Indonesians' perceptions of political efficacy. Not only do Indonesians on the whole feel more efficacious than Russians; they are also more likely to view key elite-constraining behaviors, such as supporting political parties, demonstrating, and voting for the opposition, as meaningful ways to influence political outcomes. In contrast, Russians view the elite-enabling act of contacting as the most efficacious form of political participation. These attitudinal differences have important implications for the political participation patterns that take shape in Russia and Indonesia. In both countries, individuals are more likely to participate in activities they perceive as efficacious, thus fostering elite-constraining behavior in Indonesia and elite-enabling behavior in Russia.

The public opinion surveys and interviews discussed in this chapter also show that Russian and Indonesian attitudes about voting may be tied to their own experiences. As post-Soviet Russians have gained more practice with elections, they have been less likely to view them as influential. Furthermore, Russians and Indonesians have had very different experiences with elections. While Russian national elections have consistently validated the status quo, Indonesians have successfully voted a presidential incumbent out of national office. Thus, voting in elections in Russia has generally been an elite-enabling act, while in Indonesia voting has further constrained elites.

Analysis of cross-regional differences in perceptions of efficacy in both Indonesia and Russia further highlights the potential importance of early elections in determining attitudes about the efficacy of elections as a mechanism of political influence. In Indonesia, respondents in Surabaya, who expressed concern about irregularities in East Java's first gubernatorial election in 2008, are less likely than respondents in Medan to view official election results as honest. In Russia, Krasnoyarsk's experience of three competitive gubernatorial elections, one of which led to an incumbent turnover, contributes to higher overall levels of efficacy and more positive views about elections among respondents than those expressed by respondents in Kazan. These examples shed light on the reciprocal relationship between efficacy and participation, showing that individuals' experiences participating in politics can have a substantial and lasting effect on efficacy attitudes, fostering something akin to a multiplier effect across society.

Differences in perceptions of efficacy can have important consequences for democracy's survival. First, if individuals view elite-constraining acts of participation as potentially influential, they are more likely to engage in them. Second, if voters believe that election results are fair, that the election's outcome depends on their votes, and that elections have meaningful political consequences, they are more likely to support the continuation of fair and free elections – a key feature of democracies. They are also more likely to speak up against elections that are not fair and free, demanding accountability from elites that guards against electoral fraud.

Last, as the cross-national pairing of Russia and Indonesia and the cross-regional comparison between Kazan and Krasnoyarsk show, the competitiveness of elections early in the democratization process can influence how citizens in democratizing regimes view the efficacy of elections. When elections simply validate elites' leadership choices, citizens are less likely to view them as important or protest when their integrity is violated. In contrast, when elections are a respected mechanism for effecting change, individuals are more likely to defend them. Citizens become more invested in the process when they see that their votes can throw a rascal out.

7

Political Trust and Regime Legitimacy

Chapter 6 showed that differences between Indonesians' and Russians' perceptions of political efficacy influence citizens' preferences for elite-constraining or elite-enabling participation. We also saw that incumbent turnover in early democratic elections can have important implications for a population's subsequent sense of political efficacy. Ultimately, political efficacy and participation are individual-level factors that have system-level consequences.

Another individual-level attitude that influences democracy's survival is political trust. This chapter analyzes how qualitative differences in the nature of political trust have strengthened democracy in Indonesia and undermined it in Russia. Drawing on my open-ended interviews with Indonesian and Russian citizens and comparable survey data, this chapter emphasizes four key points. First, political trust is higher among Indonesians than Russians. Second, both Russians and Indonesians tend to trust individuals more than institutions. Third, citizens' evaluations of leaders' performance are closely linked to political trust. Indonesians' and Russians' similarities on these second and third points, however, have led to very different outcomes. Russians have placed considerable trust in leaders who have rolled back democratic gains, while Indonesians have trusted leaders who promote democracy. Fourth, trust can influence political participation in ways that affect democracy's survival. When people who have low levels of political trust still engage regularly in elite-constraining participation, elites are held in check. When low trust keeps people away from the polls and out of the streets, however, the voice of opposition often becomes more muted. Ultimately, democracy's survival depends on which political actors receive the population's trust and whether they use this trust to advance democratic norms and institutions.

In this chapter, I first provide a theoretical overview of the relationship between trust and democracy and consider the specific case of trust in the context of democratization. The second section examines my citizen interviews in Indonesia and Russia to establish a general sense of political trust in these countries. Bearing in mind the patterns from the qualitative interviews, I then investigate survey data on trust in political institutions in Indonesia and Russia. The final section demonstrates how differences in political trust in these two countries facilitated the expansion of elections in Indonesia and their contraction in Russia.

Trust and Democratization

Linking Trust and Democracy's Survival

Trust is studied widely in the field of political behavior. As Margaret Levi and Laura Stoker describe, "Trust is relational; it involves an individual making herself vulnerable to another individual, group, or institution that has the capacity to do her harm or to betray her. Trust is seldom unconditional; it is given to specific individuals or institutions over specific domains" (2000, p. 476). Trust involves a belief that the trustee – whether another person or an institution – will act on one's behalf in a way that observes expected norms. Thus, trust is a belief in the reliability of another individual or institution. Like political efficacy, trust is an individual-level variable that, when aggregated, can reveal information about the prevalence of trusting attitudes within a given society.

Within comparative politics, two sets of hypotheses connect trust to democracy's survival. The first set evolved from Gabriel Almond and Sidney Verba's (1963) argument that interpersonal trust contributes to the development of a "civic culture" that can sustain democracy. Indeed, as Ronald Inglehart's analysis of cross-national data from the early 1990s reveals, levels of interpersonal trust correlate with the survival of democratic institutions (1997, pp. 173–174). In untangling the mechanism between interpersonal trust and democracy's survival, however, more recent scholarship has generally found the link between interpersonal trust and trust in political institutions rather weak (Mishler & Rose, 2001; Newton, 1999, 2001). Individuals' evaluations of political institutions' performance provide a better predictor of trust in these institutions than interpersonal trust does.

A second approach linking trust to democracy has evolved from David Easton's work on political support (1975). Easton hypothesized that support of political institutions and the regime – generally operationalized by looking at measures of trust or confidence in institutions – was central to democracy's survival. Scholars working in the Eastonian tradition have sought to establish a link between trust in democratic institutions and the viability of democracy (Chu et al., 2008; Dalton, 2006; Norris, 1999; Rose, Mishler, & Munro, 2006). The dominant hypothesis is that higher levels of trust in democratic institutions will enhance the legitimacy of the political order, thereby encouraging participation in the political and civic activities that strengthen democratic values and institutions while also discouraging activities that threaten the democratic order. Similarly, lower trust makes democracy more vulnerable. In contrast to the first set of hypotheses mentioned earlier, scholarship that examines political support tends to emphasize trust in political institutions, not interpersonal trust.

While emphasizing different aspects of trust, both the interpersonal trust and political support approaches maintain that trust is connected to democracy via citizens' civic and political behaviors. While some studies examine the relationship between trust and behavior empirically, the mechanism of participation is often implied. Trust is thought to help inculcate values that foster participation and behavioral compliance with government commands, legitimating the democratic regime and facilitating its survival.

Trust in the Democratization Context

In contrast to studies of political participation and political efficacy, which have focused primarily on advanced democracies, scholarship on political trust covers a variety of regime types, including democratizing regimes. Various studies have examined interpersonal trust and trust in institutions, usually with the goal of establishing whether levels of trust in a given society are potential impediments to democracy's survival. Again, the link between trust and participation is usually implied, but not empirically tested.

Scholars have paid less attention to how individuals in democratizing regimes understand trust in specific political institutions. While work on established democracies finds that people generally make a clear distinction between the regime and incumbents (Citrin, 1974; Citrin & Green, 1986), we know little about whether people make a comparable distinction in regimes that have emerged following the collapse of authoritarianism, where most political institutions are new to the public. There are both empirical and theoretical reasons, however, to suspect that citizens in new regimes make fewer distinctions between political offices and the individuals who occupy them. Evidence from qualitative case analyses of democratization in specific countries suggests that the public often conflate officeholders' attributes and attributes of the regime (Fish, 1995; McFaul, 2001a). My research supports this finding, as the overwhelming majority of Russians and Indonesians I interviewed regarded the sitting president and the regime as coterminous. Citizens in new regimes often perceive incumbents as the embodiment of both regime principles and regime performance. Even seventeen years after the collapse of the Soviet Union, I found in 2008 that most Russians were unable to distinguish political institutions, such as the executive and the legislature, from the people who occupy these offices.

Moreover, regimes in the abstract are not responsible for performance: political elites determine policy that subsequently affects regime performance. Public evaluation of this performance is the primary factor that influences trust in a regime's institutions. In early years of regime-building, trust in institutions will be highly dependent, if not perfectly correlated, with attitudes toward specific actors. My citizen interviews in both Russia and Indonesia adhered to this pattern: individuals who viewed their political system positively almost universally trusted the incumbents, while those who evaluated their political systems negatively were less trusting of officeholders.

A second, more theoretical consideration is how citizens' development of a longer-term perspective can affect public perceptions in stable political systems. Citizens in advanced democracies can distinguish between regimes and governments in part because they have experienced a succession of governments within a given regime. This experience provides a basis for comparing how elites implement regime principles and how government performance can vary over time across different administrations. In more established political systems, the relevant comparison for evaluating political institutions' performance is between governments within the same regime. In new regimes, however, the main comparison is often between the old regime and the new regime. For the first several years following regime change, in particular, government performance and regime performance are essentially the same for most citizens. Therefore, we would expect that as citizens experience successive governments within a new regime, the distinction between the regime and the government will become clearer.

The overlap between regime and government performance in the early years of democratization, together with the popular notion that political institutions are equivalent to their incumbents, has implications for how political trust relates to democracy's survival. Namely, citizens' levels of trust in political institutions in the years following an initial democratic transition are likely to reflect their trust in specific incumbents. We have strong reasons to believe that trust in specific incumbents is largely determined by citizens' evaluation of these incumbents' performance. Candidates' anticipated performance has been a strong predictor of vote choice in both Russia and Indonesia (Colton & McFaul, 2003; Liddle & Mujani, 2007; Lussier, 2007; Mujani & Liddle, 2010).

Consequently, citizens' approval of officeholders plays an important role in establishing trust in and legitimacy of political institutions, regardless of whether these institutions uphold the democratic ideals they represent. Citizens sometimes place trust in leaders and institutions that fail to uphold democratic norms and procedures. While these citizens may support democratic ideals in principle, supporting politicians who behave undemocratically prevents the development of trust in the procedures that promote democracy's survival. Under such circumstances, trust actually enhances the legitimacy of authoritarian disregard for democratic institutions and norms. As this chapter describes, this scenario has played out in Putin's Russia.

Measuring Trust

Like political efficacy, trust is generally measured via public opinion surveys. Even though most scholars view trust as occurring along a continuum, closed-ended surveys generally offer ordinal categories of trust, such as "fully trust," "trust," "distrust," or "fully distrust." Yet, as I learned when conducting interviews with Russian and Indonesian citizens, people are more likely to say that they "trust" or "don't trust" an institution or individual without giving a gradation of their views.

For analysis of public opinion data, I rely on the ordinal scales offered in the World Values Survey (WVS), the Russian Election Study (RES), and the East Asian Barometer (EAB). In my citizen interviews, I asked respondents whether they trusted specific institutions. Most people presented dichotomous "yes" or "no" answers, which I use to categorize their different levels of political trust.

Political Trust among Indonesians and Russians

Citizen Interviews: Trust Based on Evaluations of Incumbents

This section investigates trust attitudes displayed by the citizens I interviewed in Surabaya and Medan, Indonesia, and in Kazan and Krasnoyarsk, Russia. In each city, I asked respondents about the president, national legislature, governor, and regional and local councils as political institutions. I also asked about incumbent officeholders as well as previous presidents.[1] After soliciting general opinions about these political objects, I asked if respondents trusted these specific institutions or individuals. In both Indonesia and Russia, I found that only a very small fraction of the population could offer an opinion on political institutions in the abstract; they offered opinions about specific individuals, such as sitting and previous presidents. In general, only university students and some college graduates who closely followed politics could make distinctions between institutions and officeholders.

In many interviews, I asked respondents what they thought of the president or the legislature, without specifying whether I was referring to political institutions or their incumbents. My goal in asking this question in a more general way was to ascertain whether citizens discuss regime institutions or specific individuals when asked about "the president" or "the legislature." Respondents in both Russia and Indonesia tended to discuss specific incumbents. For most respondents, "the presidency" is the sitting president and "the legislature" signifies the representatives currently holding office. It was not uncommon for an Indonesian to respond, "Oh, SBY is good. I like him as president," or for a Russian to respond, "I don't know much about this new president [Medvedev] since he was just elected. I liked Putin as president, though." Consequently, most of the information I gleaned from these interviews analyzes trust in specific incumbents. These results suggest that surveys asking Russians and Indonesians about their trust in specific institutions most likely capture respondents' trust in sitting officeholders (people) rather than political offices and elections (institutions).

Another question in most of my interviews indirectly captures people's trust in political and social institutions. I asked respondents, "If you had a complaint against a state service, or thought that your rights had been violated, where would you turn for help?" Responses to this question

---

[1] In Krasnoyarsk, I also asked about previous elected governors.

depict trust in political, state, and social institutions relative to other possible resources. Individuals are unlikely to rely on a source they distrust. If respondents mention a political institution, we can infer that they exhibit some trust in that institution. Similarly, if individuals suggest turning to family members or friends, such a response is an indicator that these individuals do not have sufficient trust in an impersonal institution to apply to it for help without first conferring with others and gauging additional opinions about different institutions' trustworthiness. Of course, this question is not a perfect measure of political trust. Individuals can (and do) offer responses about sources of assistance unrelated to politics, such as nongovernmental organizations or lawyers. In such instances, respondents are communicating some trust in these apolitical institutions, but this information tells us nothing about whether the same individual trusts political institutions.

The information I gathered from respondent interviews in Russia and Indonesia helped contextualize the relationship between political trust and nonvoting participation revealed in Chapter 4. Those tests showed that political trust was a less consistent predictor of nonvoting participation than were civil society engagement and political efficacy. In Russia, trust in the president was a positive predictor of contacting, while trust in all political objects other than the president correlated positively with party work. In Indonesia, trust in all political objects was a negative predictor of acts of contentious politics. Trust was not a statistically significant predictor of contentious politics in Russia or of contacting or party work in Indonesia. As discussed in Chapter 4, all these relationships have logical interpretations that do not invalidate the importance of trust as a variable. As the information from my interviews reveals, both the similarities and the differences Russians and Indonesians exhibit regarding political trust have resulted in dramatically different outcomes.

Indonesia: High Trust in SBY and Other Executives

Indonesian respondents expressed a range of views about trust. Only one respondent in Surabaya expressed no trust in political institutions or leaders. Most individuals expressed trust in at least one political object. Overall, respondents in both Surabaya and Medan expressed more trust in specific political leaders than in political institutions. A substantial number of individuals in each city expressed trust in Indonesian President Susilo Bambang Yudhoyono (commonly known as SBY), but also some trust for their governor or the previous president, Megawati. Regarding institutions, several people said they trusted the national legislature, the Dewan Perwakilan Rakyat (DPR), or certain political parties.

One constant across almost all respondents was trust in SBY. Some respondents said they trusted SBY, but did not trust Megawati or her predecessor, Abdurrahman Wahid. Respondents' levels of trust aligned closely with their overall evaluation of the political system and satisfaction with political outcomes. High levels of trust in SBY, for example, tended to correspond with satisfaction with his performance in office, particularly relative to Megawati. In several cases, people explicitly made this connection between office and officeholder. A fifty-nine-year-old Javanese man in Surabaya with an elementary-school education noted that all of Indonesia's presidents have been good and said, "If they are all good, why not trust them?"

The DPR is the institution Indonesian respondents criticized most frequently, followed by political parties. One Surabaya respondent, for example, said he trusts executive institutions, such as the presidency and governorship, but does not trust representative institutions, noting that the national and regional legislatures need better people. A twenty-two-year-old Javanese law student in Surabaya expressed a similar view. "The people need representatives in the House, but I personally do not trust the people who are there." A twenty-nine-year-old Javanese woman in Surabaya with an elementary school education expressed views typical for people of her age and educational status: she mostly trusts SBY, but has no trust in the DPR.

I don't like that the salaries of the DPR are high. [DPR representatives] put more importance on their own needs compared to those of the people.... The mission of the DPR is to oversee the welfare of the people. Yes, they need to pay attention to the people, not merely make promises and then not make any changes.

The same respondent offered a similar opinion of parties. When asked if she trusted parties, she responded, "Why trust officials? They look for a position for themselves only; they do not look out for the people." A twenty-five-year-old Javanese man in Surabaya with a junior high school education offered a more cynical view of DPR deputies. "They rarely fulfill their promises, but they use a lot of money to goad people into voting for them. I don't have much trust in the DPR."

Criticism of political parties, as well as mixed levels of trust in parties, is partly related to Indonesians' frustration with the number of parties participating in the country's elections. In the first post-Suharto DPR elections held in 1999, forty-eight parties competed. This number halved to twenty-four in 2004, but increased to thirty-eight in 2009. Virtually all Indonesians I interviewed, regardless of their levels of education and political knowledge, said they found the sheer number of parties overwhelming. Nevertheless, some citizens criticized aspects of the political system while also recognizing that the country's political institutions, including parties, were becoming more democratic. When discussing Indonesia's many parties, a forty-three-year-old Javanese female university instructor in Surabaya noted, "I am confused [by the number of parties], but I am also solid in my choice, and this may be called democracy. We must trust in parties because they are the only vehicle for representing the voice of the people."

Several respondents evaluated the post-Suharto regime in Indonesia positively, and tended to evaluate SBY more favorably than former presidents Abdurrahman Wahid and Megawati. Their evaluations were not entirely positive, however. Respondents articulated various shortcomings, including corruption, weak economic development, and limited opportunities for social advancement. The twenty-two-year-old Javanese student in Surabaya simultaneously articulated support for the regime and criticism of the government:

I feel that the present system [of government] is the best compared to what we had before. All citizens are involved in the election of this president. But there have been problems that have resulted in much disappointment, much injustice, government-led vote engineering, and the right of the people not to vote. In my opinion, this [set of outcomes] is a problem of the [government] administration.

While overall patterns of trust and evaluation of incumbent performance are essentially the same in Surabaya and Medan, respondents in the two cities exhibited differences in their answers regarding where they would turn for help if their rights were violated. In Surabaya, nearly a third of respondents said that they did not know – the most common response to this question. The second most common reply is that respondents would turn to their family or friends for help and advice. One respondent noted that she would seek help through an employer, one would go to the head of the village, and two others would go to the police. Several respondents said they would seek solutions through civil society organizations: neighborhood associations, NGOs, and the legal aid society. Only one Surabaya respondent said she had nowhere to turn for help. These responses emphasize the importance of community organizations as a source of help in Indonesian society. Political and state institutions do not figure prominently among the primary objects individuals trust in moments of crisis. Most respondents indicated that they seek solutions to life's daily problems among family, friends, and extensions of their community – neighborhood associations, employers, and NGOs.

In contrast to respondents in Surabaya, individuals in Medan were more likely to mention a specific institution when asked where they would go if their rights were violated. Only one individual did not know where he would go, and another said she would not go anywhere. The most common answer offered was the police. Others mentioned that they would go through the local government, usually starting with the bureaucracy at the urban ward or village (*kelurahan* or *desa*) or subdistrict level (*kecamatan*). The third most common response was to seek help through legal means, including consulting lawyers or the legal defense group. Only one individual said she would consult her neighbors about where to go.

The differences in responses in Medan and Surabaya suggest that Medan respondents may have a higher level of trust than Surabaya respondents in the police, local bureaucracy, and justice system. With sample sizes as small as these, however, it is impossible to say with certainty that residents of Surabaya and Medan have different levels of political trust, particularly when responses to the other trust questions do not vary across cities. When viewed together, however, these responses suggest that trust is not monolithic in Indonesia.

Consistent with the discussion of contacting and party work in Chapter 4, levels of trust do not appear to heavily influence political participation among respondents in my Indonesian interviews. Chapter 4 also showed that distrust is a predictor of participation in contentious politics. The number of individuals in my interview sample who had engaged in protest, however, was too small to discern any patterns with regard to trust. Individuals in both cities who engage in nonvoting political participation expressed a variety of views about trust, from full trust to no trust. Several individuals who have engaged in nonvoting political participation, however, were able to identify aspects of the political system they do not trust, including the DPR and certain political leaders. My interview data also provided some indication that trust can have an impact on voting. In Surabaya, those who expressed trust in a greater number of political objects appeared to vote with greater frequency than those whose trust was more mixed. Indeed, one thirty-year-old food vendor in Surabaya who has never voted in an election said that, "I have not voted, because I don't have trust [in the political system]. And now I still don't vote." In Medan, however, trust levels among regular voters and those who vote with less frequency were the same.

Establishing clear connections between trust and nonvoting political participation in Indonesia is difficult because trust in different political objects varies considerably within the same individual. The average

Indonesian in my sample trusted the president, but expressed less trust in other political objects. In triangulating the qualitative data from my interviews and the quantitative data from surveys, it appears as though strong levels of trust in a president who has generally upheld democratic norms and procedures, combined with a healthy skepticism in other political institutions, has engendered participation that adequately constrains elites without choking the whole system.

Russia: Distrust in the State Duma, Trust in Putin

Russians' attitudes about political trust were also mixed. In contrast to my Indonesian respondents, however, a considerable number of my Russian respondents expressed explicit distrust in specific institutions, such as the State Duma, regional legislature, and political parties. Indeed, the Duma was the least-trusted political object among my Russian respondents. A forty-eight-year-old Tatar woman in Kazan considered the Duma "empty space," voicing a view of its deputies many other respondents shared: "They speak and speak, but they don't do their job. They are just talk." A second category of citizens expressed trust specifically in President Vladimir Putin and/or their governor, as well as trust in some political institutions such as the Duma. Another common trend among Russian respondents was to trust Putin, but not trust the Duma or the regional legislature. A final pattern evident in Krasnoyarsk, but less so in Kazan, was to trust specific legislators in either the Duma or the regional legislature, but not to trust political parties.

A few respondents articulated an entirely different view of trust. When asked if he trusted the Duma, a fifty-six-year-old Russian man in Krasnoyarsk responded, "Trust them or not, they do what they want." This remark reveals the disdain many respondents feel for the Duma, but also suggests that the speaker sees trust as irrelevant to how deputies govern. Another forty-one-year-old woman who works as a university administrator expressed almost the opposite view, noting, "I should trust my state." In this instance, trust is not a trait that is earned, but granted by virtue of one's position.

Russian respondents also spoke about how their trust in the political system had changed over time. For some individuals, Yeltsin's 1993 military assault on the popularly elected Congress of People's Deputies represented a turning point. A sixty-four-year-old Russian woman in Kazan recalled her shock at the "full destruction" Yeltsin had inflicted. "Who gave them that right?" she asked, still in disbelief that one branch of government had ordered violence against another. Other individuals saw the 1996 reelection of Yeltsin – whose popularity rating in the winter before the election was in the single digits – as evidence that their political system did not have the fair and free elections promised at the onset of democratization. A forty-five-year-old Russian man in Kazan recalled that he lost trust in elections at that time, noting that not a single person he knew had voted for Yeltsin, but Yeltsin still won. Once it became clear that elections were dishonest, he lost trust in them.

Although the Russians I interviewed offered a range of views about political trust, several clear trends emerged. First, similar to Indonesia, the institution least likely to earn respondents' trust was the legislature, both at the national and regional levels. Second, people were more likely to place trust in specific individuals – usually executives, but also specific representatives – than in institutions. Putin generally held a high place of trust among respondents. Citizens in Kazan also placed considerable trust in their republican president, Mintimer Shaimiev. Last, similar to the dynamics among Indonesian respondents, trust levels among Russian respondents closely overlapped with how individuals evaluated specific incumbents' performance. Other scholars have reported similar findings in Russia. Several studies have found that presidential approval in Russia is closely linked to perceptions of economic performance (Mishler & Willerton, 2003; Treisman, 2011), and that satisfaction with the economy is a robust predictor of voting for Putin and United Russia (Colton & Hale, 2009; McAllister & White, 2008).

Respondents in Kazan and Krasnoyarsk did exhibit differences regarding where they would turn for help if their rights had been violated. In Kazan, six individuals out of nineteen did not know where they would turn to, and two individuals said there was nowhere they could go. Of those who named a place they would turn for help, some responded that they would appeal to a political leader or state agency, their employer, or the justice system. One mentioned the police and another said she would turn to her family. Using this measure, we see some evidence of trust in the political system or aspects of the state. In particular, seeking remedy from the justice system and appealing to political leaders had the same level of support among respondents. Nevertheless, the most common response from Kazan respondents was that they did not know where they would turn if their rights were violated.

In contrast, among the twenty respondents who answered this question in Krasnoyarsk, only two said there was nowhere they would go, and no one said that they did not know where to turn. In Krasnoyarsk, the most common response (six respondents) was appealing to the justice system via the court, a lawyer, or the public prosecutor's office. Other individuals said they would apply to public officials, including the mayor and local deputies, some would seek help from friends or family, and two respondents would go to the police. Several individuals would appeal to a civic organization, such as the consumer advocacy group, and one would go to a TV station. These different answers do not necessarily indicate that Krasnoyarsk respondents have higher levels of political trust than respondents in Kazan – similar numbers of people in both cities expressed a willingness to appeal to political authorities. Krasnoyarsk respondents, however, mentioned a larger number and broader range of trust objects, including non-state civic organizations. Again, this small sample size makes it is impossible to say that residents in Kazan are more alienated than their counterparts in Krasnoyarsk. Collectively, however, it appears as though Russians display only modest trust in political objects, but surprisingly higher trust in the judicial system.

The relationship between political trust and political participation among my Russian respondents was not straightforward. On the whole, respondents who expressed trust in a larger number of political objects tended to vote in elections with greater frequency than those who exhibited lower levels of trust. Respondents who did not express trust in any part of the political system appeared to vote with less frequency than those who trusted some individuals or institutions. The relationship between trust and nonvoting political participation was more opaque. Individuals who engaged in some form of nonvoting participation generally expressed less trust in political objects than those who did not participate. Yet, curiously, there did not appear to be any clear patterns with regard to whether people with low trust levels engaged in conventional or contentious behavior. My citizen samples did not provide evidence for the view that low trust levels lead only to contentious (and not conventional) acts, as individuals who expressed no trust in political objects have campaigned, signed petitions, demonstrated, and contacted public officials. My sample does, however, provide support for a broader counter-claim: more trusting individuals are less likely to participate in nonvoting acts. Yet it is important to remember that participation and trust may be reciprocally related: it is possible for individuals to participate and be dissatisfied with the results. Subsequently, their trust in institutions declines.

In sum, my interviews in two Indonesian and two Russian cities revealed four significant details about political trust in these countries. First, citizens in both countries trusted specific leaders, not abstract institutions. Second, their levels of political trust correlated very closely with their evaluations of the political system and their quality of life when specific presidents held office. Third, the political object that received the most criticism in both countries – and the least amount of trust – was the national legislature. Last, attitudes about trust were too complicated to easily and clearly predict political participation. These dynamics obtained in both Russia and Indonesia, with one difference: Indonesians were generally more trusting in political objects than Russians. Only one of my Indonesian respondents could be categorized as distrustful of most political leaders and institutions. In contrast, a quarter of my Russian respondents expressed no trust in any political objects. As the next section demonstrates, survey data support this distinction as well. These trust patterns have important implications for democracy's survival.

Trust in Political Institutions in Indonesia and Russia

Cross-national Survey Analysis

As interviews with Russian and Indonesian citizens showed, most individuals in these countries volunteer opinions about specific incumbents when asked about abstract institutions, such as the presidency or legislature. Nevertheless, most public opinion surveys ask about institutions, not individuals. Careful analysis of these questions can help us gauge trust in different political objects in both countries, compare trust between the countries, examine change in trust over time, and place Indonesian and Russian levels of trust in a cross-national framework.

In its two most recent survey waves of 1999–2004 and 2005–2008, the World Values Survey (WVS) asked questions about people's trust in several political institutions. The question was worded as follows: "I am going to name a number of organizations. For each one, could you tell me how much confidence you have in them: is it a great deal of confidence, quite a lot of confidence, not very much confidence or none at all?"[2] Respondents are then read a list of several types of societal, state, and political institutions. The three institutions from this list that clearly relate to politics are the parliament, the government, and political parties (WVS, Integrated Questionnaire, questions E075, E079, and E080). Table 7.1 compares Russian and Indonesian responses against global averages. The left side of the table compares the Fifth Wave data (2005–2008) and the

---

[2] While most studies in English use the word "trust," in general "confidence" and "trust" are considered largely interchangeable with regard to political institutions.

TABLE 7.1. *Trust in Political Institutions (WVS)*

	Percentages for all WVS respondents (Wave 5) (%)	Indonesia (2006) (%)	Russia (2006) (%)	Percentages for all WVS respondents (Wave 4) (%)	Indonesia (2001) (%)	Russia (1999) (%)
Parliament						
A great deal/quite a lot	39.8	36.7	30.5	41.6	43.0	19.9
Not very much/none at all	60.3	63.3	69.6	58.4	56.9	80.8
	N = 64,452	N = 1,880	N = 1,836	N = 86,193	N = 925	N = 2,288
Government						
A great deal/quite a lot	48.0	56.0	45.2	49.9	52.4	–
Not very much/none at all	52.0	44.0	54.9	50.0	47.7	–
	N = 66,686	N = 1,934	N = 1,927	N = 50,848	N = 966	
Political Parties						
A great deal/quite a lot	27.7	30.6	21.9	32.2	33.1	–
Not very much/none at all	72.3	69.5	78.2	67.8	66.9	–
	N = 64,499	N = 1,900	N = 1,901	N = 46,994	N = 942	

right side of the table compares the Fourth Wave data (1999–2004). In each section of the table, the first column provides global averages from all respondents, the second column looks at Indonesian respondents, and the third column looks at Russian respondents. For ease of interpretation, I have collapsed responses into two categories, one for "a great deal" and "quite a lot" of confidence, and one for "not very much" or "none at all."

Table 7.1 shows that in Indonesia, Russia, and the WVS as a whole, trust in government is higher than trust in parliament or in political parties during the Fifth Wave of the survey. Fifty-six percent of Indonesians trust government, which is higher than the WVS average by approximately eight percentage points. Among Russians, 45.2 percent trust government, which is slightly lower than the WVS average. What about other institutions? Trust in parliament is higher in Indonesia than in Russia, but both countries are below the WVS average. Trust in parties is higher in Indonesia than in Russia. Indonesians' trust in parties is also a bit higher than the WVS average. Russians' trust in parties, by contrast, is significantly lower than the global average. In addition, the percentage of Russians who expressed the lowest confidence in institutions – "none at all" – is considerably higher than the analogous percentage of Indonesians and percentage of overall WVS respondents for all institutions investigated. In 1999, 41.2 percent of Russians expressed no trust in parliament, and in 2006, 37 percent expressed no trust in political parties.

The WVS data suggest Indonesians are more trusting of political institutions than Russians are. These attitudes about trust may help explain why Indonesians engage in more elite-constraining political participation than Russians. If individuals have confidence in political institutions' ability to resolve conflicts, they may become more invested in trying to influence how those institutions operate.

The following two sections examine the WVS survey data together with trust indicators from the East Asian Barometer (EAB) and the Russian Election Study (RES) to establish a more comprehensive picture of political trust in Indonesia and Russia.

Indonesia: High Trust in Political Institutions

If we compare the WVS' Fourth and Fifth waves (Table 7.1), Indonesians' trust in parliament and parties declined between 2001 and 2006, while their trust in government increased. What happened to these institutions during this period? Most significantly, Indonesians voted in parliamentary elections and the country's first direct presidential elections in 2004, and

TABLE 7.2. *Trust in Political Institutions in Indonesia (EAB)*

	Great deal of trust/quite a lot of trust (%)	Not very much trust/ no trust at all (%)	N
President	76.0	24.0	1,559
Central government	68.2	31.8	1,531
DPR	61.2	38.8	1,536
Regional governments	75.2	24.8	1,563

turned out incumbents in both these elections. In the 2004 parliamentary elections, the Indonesian Democratic Party of Struggle (PDI-P) lost its plurality in the DPR, as Golkar became the party with the largest parliamentary representation. And as discussed in the previous chapter, SBY defeated incumbent Megawati in the 2004 presidential election. Since significant incumbent turnover occurred during this period, it would be imprudent to suggest that the WVS data imply a decline in Indonesians' trust for regime institutions per se. Given the connection between incumbent evaluation and trust indicators observed in my interviews, it is very likely that the WVS data reflect Indonesians' evaluation of the changes in government personnel between 2001 and 2006.

Examining the EAB helps establish a more complete picture of trust in political institutions in Indonesia. The EAB asks Indonesians about their trust in the presidency, the central government, the DPR, and the regional government (EAB, questions QII07, Q008, Q010, and Q014). Similar to the WVS, the EAB offers four possible responses, which I have divided into two categories, one expressing a "great deal" or "quite a lot" of trust and the other expressing "not very much" trust or "no trust at all" (Table 7.2).

The EAB and WVS were both conducted in 2006, yet the EAB reports significantly higher levels of trust in the central government and the parliament. The term "parliament" was translated differently in the two surveys, which may explain some differences in the results.[3] Both surveys, however, translated "central government" identically (*pemerintah pusat*). For all four political objects mentioned, the majority of Indonesian respondents in the EAB expressed "quite a lot" or "a great deal" of trust.

---

[3] While the EAB used the specific name of the Indonesian parliament, Dewan Perwakilan Pusat (DPR), the WVS translated this item as the more general *parlemen*.

In the WVS (Table 7.1), a majority of Indonesians expressed "quite a lot" or "a great deal" of trust in the government, but not the parliament.

It is impossible to say which survey provides a more accurate reflection of Indonesians' levels of political trust in 2006. We might want to consider the WVS results a lower bound and the EAB results an upper bound of actual opinion. If so, we can still say that Indonesians' levels of trust in political institutions are generally higher than the WVS global average and higher than the Russian average. It also appears that Indonesians are more inclined to trust than distrust political institutions.

Russia: Trust in Institutions Rebounds with Putin

Since the WVS has included Russia four times since 1990, there is a larger volume of data on trust in institutions for Russia than for Indonesia. Table 7.3 compares Russians' confidence in political institutions from the WVS together with measures on trust in political institutions from the RES. Parliament is the only institution included in all four waves of the WVS. The data tell us that in 1990, just as the Soviet Union initiated political liberalization, a larger percentage of the population was distrustful of parliament than trustful of it. Russians' trust in parliament declined between 1990 and 1995, and dropped even further by 1999. In 1999, 80 percent of the Russian population had no trust or "not very much" trust in parliament, which is about twenty percentage points higher than the WVS average and the analogous levels of distrust in Indonesia. By 2006, Russian confidence in parliament had improved substantially, even though levels were still below the WVS average.

A similar dynamic appears in Russians' trust in government and political parties. Trust in the government improved between 1995 and 2006, even though almost 55 percent of Russians in 2006 expressed little or no trust in the government. Curiously, trust in Russian parties was at its peak in 1990 – when Russians' experience was limited primarily to the Communist Party of the Soviet Union (CPSU). By 2006, when parties had been able to compete in political life for fifteen years, confidence in parties had increased compared to 1995 levels, but the majority of Russians continued to have little or no trust in parties. Taken together, these three measures show that Russians' trust in political institutions is low. Trust was at its highest in the late Soviet period and lowest in the 1990s. By 2006, however, trust in all three institutions discussed in the WVS had improved over trust levels in the 1990s.

The 1995–1996 and 1999–2000 RES asks several questions about trust in political objects (RES 1995–1996, post-Duma election questionnaire,

TABLE 7.3. *Trust in Political Institutions in Russia 1990–2006 (WVS and RES)*

	WVS (%) 1990	WVS (%) 1995	WVS (%) 1999	WVS (%) 2006	RES (%)* 1995–1996	RES (%)* 1999–2000
Parliament						
A great deal/quite a lot	46.9	22.6	19.9	30.5	41.8	
Not very much/none at all	53.2	77.4	80.0	69.6	58.2	
	N = 1,801	N = 1,877	N = 2,288	N = 1,836	N = 2,238	
Government						
A great deal/quite a lot		26.0		45.2	43.2	57.6
Not very much/none at all		74.0		54.9	56.5	42.4
		N = 1,961		N = 1,927	N = 2,386	N = 1,690
Political Parties						
A great deal/quite a lot	45.6	19.4		21.9		34.3
Not very much/none at all	54.4	80.6		78.2		65.6
	N = 1,751	N = 1,845		N = 1,901		N = 1,478
Regional Administration						
Fully trust/trust					51.0	55.5
Mistrust/completely mistrust					49.0	44.5
					N = 2,386	N = 1,598
Local Administration						
Fully trust/trust					53.1	55.3
Mistrust/completely mistrust					46.9	44.7
					N = 2,477	N = 1,696
President of Russia						
Fully trust/trust					33.0	40.3
Mistrust/completely mistrust					66.9	59.8
					N = 2,443	N = 1,636

* The response categories for the RES are a combination of "fully trust" and "trust" for the first row and "mistrust" and "completely mistrust" for the second row.

question 25; RES 1999–2000, post-Duma election questionnaire, question 90). As with the previous surveys, I combine the two highest categories of trust ("fully trust" and "trust") and the two lowest categories ("mistrust" and "completely mistrust") to create a binary measure. Across all four political objects repeated in both RES surveys – the government of Russia, the regional administration, the local administration, and the president of Russia – the percentage of respondents trusting the object of interest increased between 1995–1996 and 1999–2000. Among these four objects, the most dramatic rise came from trust in the government. In 1995–1996, only 43.2 percent of respondents exhibited trust in the government, but by 1999–2000 this figure had jumped to 57.6 percent. In examining differences in trust between the political objects included in the RES, we see that Russians in 1995–1996 had the greatest levels of trust in their local administrations, and the lowest levels of trust in the president (at the time, Yeltsin). In 1999–2000, respondents displayed the highest level of trust in the Russian national government and the lowest level of trust in parties.

It is useful to consider the political environment when WVS and RES polls were conducted, particularly changes in the types of parties that enjoyed public support in different elections. As Chapter 2 discussed, Russian voters in March 1990 elected the Congress of People's Deputies of the Russian Soviet Federative Socialist Republic (RSFSR), which was a republic-level version of the Soviet Congress of People's Deputies elected in 1989. While independent candidates could compete in these elections, the only party with the formal right to compete was the Communist Party of the Soviet Union (CPSU).

This Congress of People's Deputies became the Russian Federation's parliament after the collapse of the Soviet Union in 1991. President Yeltsin and the Congress sparred over several issues during the initial years of democratization, until Yeltsin ordered military force to disband the Congress in October 1993. In December 1993, Russian voters elected a new parliament – the State Duma – and adopted a new Russian Constitution. According to the new constitution, Russia would hold Duma elections at four-year intervals beginning in December 1995.

Thus, by 1995 Russians had experienced two competitive elections for parliament and one violent episode when the president removed a popularly elected parliament from office by force. By 2006, the population had witnessed three more competitive elections to parliament in 1995, 1999, and 2003.

The composition of Russia's parliament changed dramatically between 1993 and 2003. The plurality (41 percent) of 1993 State Duma deputies were independents and representatives from parties who defy ideological categorization, followed by representatives from pro-democracy parties (26 percent), communist-leaning parties (18 percent), and nationalist parties (14 percent). In 1995, representatives from communist-leaning parties had the plurality of seats (42 percent), followed by independents (17 percent), and smaller clusters of reformists, pro-government representatives, and nationalists (about 13 to 14 percent of seats each) (Belin & Orttung, 1997, pp. 114–118). By 1995, the Russian electorate had moved to the left and support for reformist party candidates had declined by half.

Both the WVS and RES asked Russians about their trust in the government and parliament in 1995–1996. The data in Table 7.3 show higher levels of trust from RES measures than from the WVS. These differences may, in part, be a consequence of the fact that Russia held parliamentary elections on December 17, 1995. WVS respondents were polled November 17, 1995 through January 25, 1996. Thus, WVS respondents polled before the election may have a different image of the parliament they are being asked about than those polled after the election. RES respondents were polled December 18, 1995 through January 20, 1996 and may have been thinking more about the newly elected Duma.

Russia's 1999 and 2003 elections showed yet another shift in electoral support, away from left-leaning parties and toward representatives of pro-government parties. By 2003, 62 percent of parliamentary representatives belonged to a party that was part of a pro-government coalition, while only 12 percent of deputies were from communist-leaning parties, 8 percent from nationalist parties, and less than 2 percent from reform parties.[4] If we consider changes in citizens' levels of trust together with these fluctuations in the Duma's composition, the WVS suggests that Russians' trust in parliament first declined when independents and reformists held the plurality, dropped further when left-leaning parties held greater sway, and then rebounded once pro-government parties took a majority of seats. Thus, it appears that Russians have been the most satisfied with parliaments dominated by

---

[4] "Pro-government" parties include United Russia, the Rodina coalition, the coalition of the Russian Pensioners' Party and the Russian Social Justice Party, the coalition of the Party of Russia's Rebirth and the Russian Party of Life, and the People's Party of the Russian Federation. "Communist-leaning" parties include the Communist Party of the Russian Federation and the Agrarian Party. The Liberal Democratic Party of Russia is the only "nationalist" party, and Yabloko and the Union of Right Forces are the two "reformist" parties.

pro-government representatives. Such parliaments emerged in 1999 and have held power ever since. Pro-government parliaments, however, have not been favorable to democracy's survival. As Chapter 2 outlined, the Duma has consistently supported Putin's rollback of democratic institutions since the early 2000s. As numerous scholars have documented, public support for Putin has little to do with democratic values and is largely explained by satisfaction with substantive improvements in living standards. Considerable evidence shows Russians are more concerned with outcomes than procedures, willing to embrace authoritarian means to achieve what they perceive as equitable or "democratic" ends (Lukin, 2009).

RES data about Russians' trust in the presidency also demonstrate the relationship between levels of trust and evaluations of specific incumbents. The 1999–2000 RES asked about trust in interviews administered between December 25, 1999, and January 25, 2000 – both before and after Yeltsin announced his resignation on December 31, 1999. Within this sample, 121 respondents were interviewed when Yeltsin was still president, and 1,515 were interviewed when Putin was acting president. The differences in responses between these two groups are considerable. While only 22.3 percent trusted or fully trusted the president when Yeltsin was in office, 41.7 percent of respondents expressed trust or full trust in the president once Putin took office. Moreover, the percentage of respondents who completely mistrusted the president dropped by half (from 35.5 percent to 18.0 percent) once Putin became acting president.

The WVS and RES data point to two findings on trust. First, Russians' trust in political institutions appears to have dropped considerably in the 1990s and rebounded during the end of the decade and into the twenty-first century. Second, it appears as though trust in institutions may reflect evaluations of incumbents presiding over those specific institutions. When we consider these two findings together with the direction of Russian politics during these survey periods, a clear pattern emerges: Russians' political trust increased once Putin and pro-Putin legislators came to power. Yet these political actors and the policies they promoted contributed to the demise of democracy in Russia.

Regardless of the survey used to measure trust – the WVS, the EAB, or the RES – Russians appear to have lower levels of political trust than Indonesians. Moreover, Indonesian levels of political trust have not decreased dramatically over the course of democratization. In fact, as my citizen interviews demonstrated, Indonesians have high levels of trust in SBY – a political leader who has acted in accordance with democratic norms and has upheld democratic institutions established before his election in 2004. Ultimately, the most significant way in which political trust has influenced the survival of democracy in Russia and Indonesia is through the specific political leaders the citizens in these countries have trusted. Namely, Russians have trusted political leaders who have curtailed democratic institutions, while Indonesians have trusted leaders who have promoted them. In this respect, trust in political leaders is perhaps a more random variable than the other independent variables in this study. There was no way to predict that Russians (who recently lived under an authoritarian Soviet government) would trust the authoritarian Putin while Indonesians (who recently lived under the authoritarian Suharto regime) would trust the pro-democracy SBY.

This chapter's final section traces how trust in specific leaders and policies has contributed to democracy's demise in Russia and its survival in Indonesia by examining an example at the core of democracy: the expansion and contraction of elections.

Expanding and Contracting Elections in Indonesia and Russia

Elections as Indicators of Democracy's Survival

Elections do not necessarily make a regime democratic. Yet elections are a necessary condition of democracy and the expansion and contraction of political offices determined by election rather than appointment are clear benchmarks for determining whether a regime is maintaining democracy. In the years since their initial democratic transitions, Indonesia and Russia have exhibited wildly different policies toward elections. Barriers to entry in Russian elections for the Duma and presidency have increased, gubernatorial elections were cancelled, and elections for local government were not uniformly adopted, contributing to stagnation in local-level democracy. In contrast, Indonesia has dramatically revised the electoral rules for entrance to the legislature, established direct elections for the presidency, and expanded elections for regional and local executives.

My interviews show that both Russians and Indonesians generally support using elections to determine access to power. Yet these two populations have responded differently when threatened with the loss of elections. Russians accepted the cancellation of gubernatorial elections without protest, while Indonesians responded to the 1999 presidential election controversy with a demand for direct elections. In short, Russians have placed considerable trust in leaders who have emasculated democratic institutions – such as Putin – while Indonesians have tended to trust leaders who have adhered to democratic norms and practices.

Indonesia: Supportive of Electoral Expansion

Indonesians have shown strong support for expanding elections. Moreover, the political leaders Indonesians have trusted have introduced and upheld the electoral reforms that are a central feature of Indonesia's democratic survival. Reforms from 1999 to 2001 significantly increased the number of political offices allocated via election, and introduced direct (rather than two-tier) voting for president. Direct elections were not an initial component of the country's democratization. The first post-Suharto presidential elections, held in October 1999, followed the standard procedure of earlier elections, where the People's Consultative Assembly (MPR) elected the president from among its ranks. The 1999–2004 MPR was comprised of the 500 deputies elected to the DPR in the first fair and free elections since 1955, and 200 appointed members from the provinces and various social groups. The controversy that erupted during the MPR's election of a president, however, set the stage for public demands to elect the president directly.

As discussed in previous chapters, the first post-Suharto national parliamentary election in 1999 gave the Indonesian Democratic Party for Struggle (PDI-P), headed by Megawati, a plurality but not a majority of seats. Since PDI-P had the largest share of the popular vote (34 percent), its supporters expected that the MPR would elect Megawati president. Her primary rival for the election was incumbent President B. J. Habibie from Golkar. Yet a coalition of smaller parties, spearheaded by National Mandate Party (PAN) Chair Amien Rais, began to promote Abdurrahman Wahid, leader of the National Awakening Party (PKB), as an alternative to both Megawati and Habibie. When Habibie's candidacy collapsed and Golkar was left without a suitable alternative candidate, the party's representatives threw their support behind Wahid. Consequently, Wahid, whose PKB won only 13 percent of the popular vote in the DPR election, became president, while Megawati, who had more than twice as much popular support than Wahid, was elected vice president.

Public outrage over the election outcome erupted in violence in Jakarta, Solo, and Bali, as well as mass protests in Habibie's home province of South Sulawesi (Thompson, 1999). Indonesian citizens were frustrated by the deal that brought Wahid to the presidency in place of Megawati, providing a strong impetus for reforming the system of indirect presidential elections. A public opinion poll conducted in 1999 asked two questions related to the presidential controversy (Center for the Study of Development and Democracy, 1999, pp. 7–8). The first question asked, "Must the president come from the party that won the elections?" The majority of respondents, 51.7 percent, answered that the president should come from the winning party; 37.2 percent of respondents did not view this as necessary; and 11.1 percent of respondents did not know. The second question was, "Do you agree or disagree with direct elections for the presidency?" The majority of respondents, 53.0 percent, agreed with direct presidential elections, while 30.4 percent disagreed and 16.6 percent did not know.

Support for direct presidential elections increased over time. In 2000, 67 percent of Indonesians supported direct presidential elections, and by 2002 this figure had climbed to nearly 80 percent (International Foundation for Electoral Systems, 2002; Konsorsium Lembaga Pengumpul Pendapat Umum, 2000; LP3ES, 2002). In August 2002, with Megawati as president after Wahid's dismissal in 2001, the MPR amended the Indonesian constitution to allow for direct presidential elections. At the time, Megawati was expected to win reelection easily.

Indonesians have prioritized elections over other budgetary needs. A public opinion poll in 2003 asked Indonesians to evaluate the importance of elections compared to funding for development goals. In a country with a considerable portion of the population living in poverty, the trade-offs between paying for an election or allocating resources to programs for economic development can appear stark. The survey asks, "The upcoming 2004 elections are estimated to cost approximately four trillion [rupiah]. Would you agree or disagree with canceling the 2004 elections and putting these funds towards development?" Fifty percent of respondents disagreed with the proposition of canceling elections, while 25 percent agreed and 25 percent did not know or did not answer the question (Center for the Study of Development and Democracy, 2003, p. 8). Half of Indonesians viewed the electoral process – even when the incumbent was expected to win a second term – as more important than pressing development needs. This attitude represents a significant commitment to democratic procedures in a country where GDP per capita is less than $4,000.

Indonesians' support for direct elections to determine governors and local executives – appointed offices during Suharto's New Order – has also been strong. In 2000, 66 percent of Indonesians wanted direct elections for district and regional executives (Konsorsium Lembaga

Pengumpul Pendapat Umum, 2000). Laws planning for these elections were passed in 2001, the elections were gradually introduced starting in 2005, and by January 2009, 87.1 percent of Indonesians agreed or strongly agreed with direct elections for regional and local executives (LP3ES, 2009, p. 37). Polls conducted in Indonesia between 2001 and 2005 show that an increasingly large percentage of Indonesians believe that they have greater control over the actions taken by local government since the implementation of regional autonomy reforms, which include fiscal and administrative decentralization as well as direct elections for regional and local executives (International Foundation for Electoral Systems, 2005, p. 48).

My interviews with Indonesian citizens validated these survey trends. In the forty-five interviews in which we discussed the topic, thirty-nine respondents favored direct election for executive and legislative offices. While critical of how regional autonomy reforms were implemented, respondents overwhelmingly supported elections for local and regional executives and have come to view direct presidential elections as a fundamental political right. Moreover, I found that for most of my interlocutors, direct elections for political leaders are an integral component of democracy.

Indonesians' resolve to preserve and extend direct elections stands in stark contrast to Russians' general indifference toward the cancellation of gubernatorial elections in 2004. Yet the public's reaction to expanding or abolishing elections in either country was related to trust in political leaders. As the next section describes, Russians' support of Putin's policies and trust in his political decisions was stronger than their support for democracy. In Indonesia, on the other hand, support for Megawati as a presidential candidate in 1999 propelled public demands for a more democratic system. Megawati used that public trust to push for legislation that deepened democracy by expanding direct elections. When she lost these direct elections in 2004, she peacefully left office. Her successor, SBY, implemented the reforms that expanded local and regional elections. While SBY's popularity rating declined in his second term from levels that neared 70 percent, public opinion polls consistently showed that he was regarded as a trustworthy and reliable government official.

Russia: Supportive of Elections in Principle, Indifferent in Practice

Following the Beslan school hostage crisis in North Ossetia in September 2004, then Russian President Putin argued a further restructuring of the political system was necessary to strengthen regional development and to ensure Russian citizens' safety. One reform announced at this time was the abolition of gubernatorial elections. Under the new system, the president would appoint regional executives, who would be confirmed by regional legislatures. The Kremlin argued that it was necessary to have federally appointed regional executives since corruption and greed had penetrated regional governments to such an extent that state security was at risk (Hill, 2005). Even if such a claim were true, abolishing elections is a clear example of democracy being reduced rather than expanded in Russia.

Shortly after Putin announced the cancellation of gubernatorial elections, a poll asked Russians whether they agreed that it was necessary to cancel gubernatorial elections to guarantee the "unity of the state." Among respondents, 48.7 percent fully disagreed or mostly disagreed with this proposition, while 38.0 percent fully agreed or mostly agreed (VTsIOM website). Nearly half the Russian population disagreed with the decision to cancel gubernatorial elections, but there were not mass protests against the decision. While supportive of gubernatorial elections in principle, Russians have hesitated to demand them.

My interview data validated this assertion. I first asked individuals whether executive and legislative offices should be appointed or elected. I then asked specifically about the person's opinion regarding Putin's 2004 decision to cancel gubernatorial elections. Responses to these two questions proved illuminating. With only a few exceptions, respondents supported popular elections for executive and legislative offices. Yet most respondents did not think it was wrong for Putin to cancel gubernatorial elections. Among the thirty-five interviews in Russia where I discussed this topic, only ten respondents (five in each city) criticized Putin's decision.

Many respondents, in contrast, supported the move. Several suggested that the president was in a better position than the people to decide who should govern them. Some noted that Putin was more knowledgeable about potential candidates' qualifications. For example, one fifty-nine-year-old female Russian pensioner in Kazan first agreed that executives should be elected, but then expressed her support for Putin's abolition of gubernatorial elections. "This was correct. Putin knows who to appoint." A seventy-five-year-old retired Tatar Soviet military officer in Kazan expressed a similar view, saying, "It is good if [governors] are elected by the people, but people do not always know who is good to vote for." A fifty-nine-year-old female social worker in Krasnoyarsk thought it would be best if the president appointed the governor and the legislature approved the appointment, noting, "The people don't know who to elect." A fifty-six-year-old Russian laborer in Krasnoyarsk thought that appointing governors was a better way to ensure accountability than elections. If governors are appointed, he noted, they can be removed. For this respondent, elections did not appear to be a sufficient form of accountability.

Other respondents expressed indifference about the cancellation of gubernatorial elections. They noted that Putin had appointed the governor who had been elected by popular vote, so the sitting governor was unchanged. For these respondents, the outcome – who was governor – was more important than the procedures that determine it.[5] One thirty-six-year-old woman who works at a kiosk in Krasnoyarsk rhetorically asked, "What is the difference?" This response is further indication of Russians' prioritization of substantive outcomes over procedure, which has helped elite-enabling behavior in undercutting democracy.

A final group of respondents had a harder time determining their opinion about gubernatorial elections. These individuals supported elections for political office in principle. Yet their convictions conflicted with pragmatic considerations about the state of elections in Russia. For example, a thirty-year-old Russian man who owns an auto repair business suggested that perhaps it makes sense to appoint representatives when the president has a clear sense of what the people want and need and who can fulfill these needs. When different candidates' qualities are less apparent or the people's preferences are unclear, he reasoned, perhaps elections are necessary. Others were even more critical of elections as a mechanism for bringing leaders to office. A twenty-five-year-old Russian repairman in Krasnoyarsk did not necessarily support Putin's decision to end gubernatorial elections, but appeared to show greater trust in him than in the electoral process: "Elections cannot always be trusted. Let it be this way [with governors appointed]. People are bought off with commercials." A thirty-three-year-old Russian male factory worker expressed similar cynicism about elections, noting, "The people never elect anything. They vote to receive a check mark," indicating that they have fulfilled their civic duty.

---

[5] Since the time of my interviews in 2008, both Tatarstan and Krasnoyarsk Krai have received new governors. Tatarstan President Mintimer Shaimiev retired in 2010, and Rustem Minnikhanov was appointed as his replacement. In January 2010, Russian Prime Minister Putin appointed Krasnoyarsk Governor Aleksandr Khloponin to head the new North Caucasus Federal District. Lev Kuznetsov was appointed as Khloponin's replacement. Kuznetsov was replaced by Viktor Tolokonsky in 2014.

Not surprisingly, within my interview sample attitudes about the cancellation of gubernatorial elections correlated with levels of trust. Individuals who believed it was wrong to cancel the elections tended to have low trust in institutions, or a mixed view about trusting individuals and institutions. Those expressing indifference to the cancellation also tended to have little trust in institutions. Respondents who supported Putin's decision to cancel elections or felt there was nothing wrong with this decision tended to have a mixed view of trust – in some cases trusting individuals but not institutions, in other cases trusting some institutions, but not others. These correlations are not perfect, but suggest that perhaps Russian attitudes about trust and the necessity of elections for determining access to regional executive power may be reactive: individuals' responses are formed in part based on their own experiences as observers of the regime's political evolution and the effect political decisions have had on their daily lives.

Research by Aleksei Makarkin (2011) on the Russian social contract supports this position. Makarkin argues that Russians welcomed the right to elect regional and local executives under former Russian President Boris Yeltsin, in part because many of the governors in office when elections were introduced had been appointed by the unpopular Yeltsin. Putin, however, established a social contract that went much further in meeting the population's economic needs, thereby changing the way people perceived political leaders and institutions. According to Makarkin, the population does not want "to risk electing a candidate who might upset the social contract. Whereas a 'bad' president was not trusted with the nomination of local governors, a 'good' president has been able to regain that power with minimal difficulty," and instead of public resentment, the reform "was greeted merely with mild bewilderment which soon turned into approval" (2011, p. 1469).

My conversations with Russians about whether elections should determine access to power, and about the cancellation of gubernatorial elections, reveal several nuances of political trust in the country. First, even though most individuals support elections in principle, there was no outcry over Putin's decision to abolish gubernatorial elections. In many instances, individuals' trust in the president's judgment outweighed their trust in elections as a mechanism for representing the people's interest. Moreover, even when individuals were critical of the decision, their lack of trust in the electoral process led them to conclude that there was little difference between election and appointment. This reaction relates to the second clue about Russians' views of political trust: their opinion of the electoral process is not high enough for them to view the abolition of gubernatorial elections as an infringement of their rights. Third, Russians' thinking about the decision to cancel gubernatorial elections reflects a relatively short-term view of the decision's implications. Rather than expressing concern about a curtailment of democracy, several noted that the method for selecting the governor did not matter as long as the outcome was the same. Additionally, those who supported Putin's decision tended to evaluate presidential appointments in the context of Putin making the decisions, with little regard for what might happen with another individual in office. Russians' response to the cancellation of gubernatorial elections in 2004 is evidence of mass quiescence in the face of authoritarian reversal.

In both Indonesia and Russia, trust in political leaders is a significant factor in the democratization process. What specific leaders did with public trust, however, led to variation in democracy's survival in these two cases. Putin drew on the public's trust to slowly dismantle democratic institutions. In contrast, Indonesia's Megawati expanded direct elections in accordance with popular will, and SBY honored and extended democratic institutions.

Conclusion

This chapter has shown that Indonesians and Russians have important similarities and differences with regard to political trust. First, both Indonesians and Russians tend to view objects of political trust in terms of specific officeholders, not abstract institutions. Second, trust in specific authorities appears to be highly correlated with citizens' evaluation of incumbents' performance in office. Third, the political object that receives the highest degree of criticism – and the lowest level of trust – from both Indonesians and Russians is the national legislature.

Indonesians' and Russians' similarities regarding political trust are generally consistent with theoretical expectations of regimes that have undergone democratization. It is logical that citizens in new regimes will trust individuals more than institutions, and that performance will play a strong role in determining trust. The differences that we see, however, depart from our standard theories about political trust and support.

First, Indonesians have higher levels of trust than Russians. This holds true in both public opinion surveys and in citizen interviews. This higher level of trust partially explains why Indonesians are more likely than Russians to engage in elite-constraining behavior. Since they have higher trust in political institutions, they are more inclined to engage in party development work, and also more likely to mount a credible threat of protest against attempts to infringe upon democratic institutions. In contrast, Russians' low levels of trust in these institutions keep them away from participating to influence the institutions or objecting when elites' infringe upon them.

Second, political trust in Indonesia has remained relatively constant in the post-Suharto era, while political trust in Russia has been more volatile. Analysis of trust indicators over time suggests that Russians' political trust plummeted in the mid-1990s when Yeltsin was president and reformers and communists populated the legislature, but then rebounded once Putin and his pro-government legislators took the policy reins, in no small part because the Russian economy also improved dramatically on Putin's watch. Finally, and most important, Indonesian and Russian leaders have used the public's trust to enact different reforms that are directly relevant to the survival of democracy. While the immensely popular and trusted Putin has dismantled democratic institutions in Russia, the trusted Megawati and SBY have expanded elections and implemented democratic reforms in Indonesia.

Russian and Indonesian political elites have both utilized trust as a resource, but for different policy ends. In the first decade of the 2000s, Russians were willing to relinquish democratic institutions, such as gubernatorial elections and a free press, in return for safety and economic growth. By 2008, it appeared as though the Russian regime's legitimacy was based on political elites' ability to deliver greater economic development and security. In Indonesia, however, the president's legitimacy has consistently derived from winning elections. Trust in democratic procedure makes the cost of elections worthwhile.

Admittedly, no Indonesian equivalent of a President Putin has come to office. The closest Indonesia has come to electing a counter-reformer as president was in 2014 when Prabowo Subianto earned nearly 47 percent of the vote on a platform that called for returning Indonesia to the (un-amended) 1945 Constitution and upending the decentralization reforms that have been a pillar of Indonesian democratization. Yet, as the results of the 2014 election confirm, post-Suharto politics in Indonesia have generally shown that the population has no desire to grant power to an individual who would not adhere to democratic procedures and norms.

In writing about the process of achieving democratic legitimacy, Larry Diamond suggests that legitimation is more than a normative commitment to the ideals of democracy. It also requires routinized, or habituated, behavior on the part of all political actors (1999). In Indonesia, this routinization and habituation is taking place on both the elite and popular levels. Indonesian presidents have found that they must adhere to democratic practices to remain popular, since the public has come to expect elections to determine access to power. While Indonesians are critical of elected officeholders and not always satisfied with candidates, they do not question the legitimacy of democratic elections for determining access to power.

In contrast, as of 2008 the rules and methods of political competition appeared less important to the Russian public. By prioritizing outcomes over procedure, Russians have allowed political elites to hollow out potentially democratic political institutions. Moreover, the non-democratic political system in Russia, which is characterized by an elite-led oligarchy that enjoys broad public support, held a considerable amount of legitimacy among the Russian population. Whether the discontent that began to emerge in the end of 2011 signifies a legitimacy crisis for the Russian regime remains to be seen.

8

Conclusion

Political Participation and the Future of Democracy

The previous chapters provided a cross-case analysis of two "outliers" in democratic theory: post-Soviet Russia and post-Suharto Indonesia. Both countries introduced democratic systems of government at the end of the twentieth century. After several years, however, authoritarianism returned to Russia while democracy survived in Indonesia. Our dominant theories of democratization, which privilege structural conditions such as socioeconomic development and a history of independent statehood, predicted the opposite outcome for both countries.

In accounting for these cases' failures to meet expected outcomes, this book has posited democracy's survival as a product of dynamic interactions between political elites and the mass public. To ensure that democratic institutions and practices endure, citizens must credibly threaten to remove leaders who do not adhere to democratic norms and practices. As Chapter 2 demonstrated through an analysis of critical junctures in the post-transition periods in Russia and Indonesia, elite-constraining political participation is a key factor in communicating this credible threat. When a society's modal form of political participation is elite-constraining, as in Indonesia, politicians learn that their best chances for maintaining political power lie in adhering to democratic rules. When elite-enabling participation dominates, as in Russia, officeholders are provided with resources they can use to undermine democratic institutions and reverse democratic gains.

This concluding chapter summarizes the main findings of the previous chapters and the causal story they present, discusses the implications of these findings for democratization, and briefly speculates on the future trajectories of Russia and Indonesia's political regimes.

Summary of the Findings and Argument

The preceding analysis of post-Soviet Russia and post-Suharto Indonesia shows that the overall volume of elite-constraining political participation does not simply rise and fall with a society's level of socioeconomic development, but is shaped by the contours of the population's civic engagement, perceptions of political efficacy, and political trust. Collectively, these three variables determine whether citizen attitudes and behaviors constrain elite actions, compelling political leaders to act in accordance with democratic institutions and norms as the best strategy for remaining in power. Quantitative and qualitative differences along these three variables explain why Indonesians established alternate sources of power that have constrained sitting elites, while Russians have not.

As Chapter 4 showed through statistical analysis of public opinion data from Russia and Indonesia, civil society engagement, political efficacy, and political trust are all statistically significant predictors of non-voting political participation. Yet democracy's success in Indonesia and failure in Russia is not simply a consequence of the existence of more civic engagement, efficacy, and trust in Indonesia. Rather, qualitative differences in how these variables shaped participatory decisions proved consequential in the development of elite-constraining participation in Indonesia and elite-enabling participation in Russia. The predicted probabilities calculated in Chapter 4 revealed that the highest probabilities for participation in Russia are for elite-enabling activities and the highest probabilities for participation in Indonesia are for elite-constraining activities. Several differences in the dynamics of civic engagement, political efficacy, and political trust between the two countries explain how these different patterns emerged.

First, Indonesians are more civically engaged than Russians. Chapter 5 illustrated that Indonesians display levels of civic and social engagement that are above the global average, while Russians demonstrate below-average levels. Moreover, Russians and Indonesians tend to participate in different types of organizations. Russians prefer sports and recreational activities, which provide fewer opportunities for the development and application of civic skills. In contrast, Indonesians are active in religious, neighborhood, and student organizations, which all serve as training grounds for skill development. Additionally, high levels of social connectivity among Indonesians translate into greater opportunities to recruit people for political acts, thereby enhancing political mobilization. Last, the structure and norms of Indonesian civil society, which emphasize giving one's time and money for the collective good, have served as a resource for developing and maintaining political parties and other intermediary organizations that facilitate political competition during elections. The absence of these norms in Russia, meanwhile, has hindered the country's weak political party system. Ultimately, the structure and norms of Indonesian civil society, as well as the sheer volume of popular engagement, have fostered an expansion of elite-constraining political participation in the post-Suharto era. An analogous phenomenon is absent in Russia.

Second, feelings of political efficacy are more widespread among Indonesians than Russians, particularly with regard to elite-constraining acts. Chapter 6 demonstrated that both Indonesians and Russians tend to select nonvoting acts of political participation based on actions' perceived effectiveness, painting a clear path between efficacy and participation. Yet they view different acts as efficacious. Russians believe that elite-enabling actions, such as contacting public officials, can be influential, while Indonesians are more likely to turn toward elite-constraining acts such as protests and campaigning. These differences in attitudes have contributed to variation in the forms of nonvoting political participation that Indonesians and Russians choose, leading to aggregate-level differences in the countries' levels of elite-constraining participation. Additionally, Russians and Indonesians differ in their attitudes about the efficacy of voting. While both populations vote at high rates, a higher percentage of Indonesians believes that participating in elections will bring positive outcomes, contributing to both a willingness to participate in campaign activity and low tolerance for electoral manipulation. Consequently, Indonesian elites are more effectively constrained by electoral mechanisms than are Russian leaders.

Third, Indonesians display consistently higher levels of political trust than Russians. Political trust in Russia has been much more volatile, dropping considerably in the mid-1990s, but rebounding once Vladimir Putin came to office. Additionally, as Chapter 7 details, both Russians and Indonesians have tended to place trust in specific individuals rather than in institutions. Yet the leaders Russians and Indonesians have trusted have used the public's confidence to achieve dramatically different ends. Emboldened with high levels of trust, Putin chipped away at Russia's nascent democratic institutions without resistance. In contrast, Indonesia's leaders in the post-Suharto era have used public trust to further entrench democracy. Last, while both Russians and Indonesians trust specific individuals more than abstract institutions, trust in political institutions is somewhat higher in Indonesia than in Russia. This higher level of trust contributes to Indonesians' willingness to accept the uncertain outcomes of institutional mechanisms – such as elections and courts – that are the backbone of democratic governance.

These quantitative and qualitative differences in civic engagement, political efficacy, and political trust have facilitated different models of nonvoting political participation in Russia and Indonesia, which have in turn shaped the survival of democracy. Because the participatory acts that enable elites – namely contacting public officials and supporting hegemonic parties – dominated participation in Russia, elites were gradually able to roll back democratic institutions with public quiescence. In fact, as Chapter 7 shows, high levels of trust and support for Putin actually facilitated the president's manipulation of democratic institutions to weaken political rights and civil liberties. In contrast, Indonesians' high levels of elite-constraining participation through party building and contentious politics have pressured political elites to abide by democratic institutions and practices, or face consequences at the ballot box.

This book's causal model, depicted in Figure 1.3, includes three stages. First, individual-level measures of civic engagement, political efficacy, and political trust each have an independent effect on political participation. In particular, high levels of civic engagement foster elite-constraining modes of participation. Similarly, when individuals perceive elite-constraining activities as efficacious, they repeat them. When individuals view elite-enabling participation as efficacious, they select and repeat these activities instead. Last, when political trust is vested in democratic institutions, individuals are more inclined to participate in the elite-constraining activities that influence these institutions. When trust is bestowed instead on an individual leader, the role of mass participation is marginalized. In these circumstances, political trust enables elites to make decisions according to their short-term interests, which may be antithetical to democracy's survival.

Individual-level attitudes and behaviors are aggregated at the second stage of the model, where nonvoting political participation patterns that predominate in a society shape political elites' decision-making environment. When elite-constraining participation predominates, as it does in Indonesia, incumbents and challengers recognize that their range of options for executing power is limited, narrowing the scope of tactics a politician might employ to gain or maintain power. In other words, it becomes harder for a political leader to hollow out democratic institutions. In Indonesia, rulers have come to expect popular resistance. Under such circumstances, it is difficult to envision an Indonesian president even attempting the attack on democratic institutions that Putin achieved in Russia with little resistance. Indonesian leaders know such an approach would likely fail. When elite-enabling participation predominates, as it does in Russia, elites have considerable leeway to undermine democratic institutions and norms. Ultimately, at the third stage of the model, elite decisions within these frameworks determine whether democracy survives.

Implications for Democratization Theory

This book's causal model has several implications for our understanding of democratization theory. First, my findings highlight the importance of the period *after* a democratic transition for democracy's further survival. While scholars have paid considerable attention to the outcomes of initial elections in projecting democracy's further trajectory, I find that the intervals between subsequent elections constitute critical periods during which political elites have incentives to prevent the enactment of democratic reforms that could make it harder for them to retain power. Under such circumstances, there is a functional need for mass political participation to expand in ways that will compel elites to abide by democratic practices and enact further democratic reforms.

Second, these findings indicate a clear role for the mass public in the early years of regime building. As the Indonesian and Russian cases demonstrate, nonvoting political participation can facilitate democratic survival when it constrains political elites in nascent democratic regimes, but it can also foster democratic erosion when it enables and empowers entrenched elites. Getting the institutions "right" is not necessarily sufficient to ensure that democracy will survive – the population needs to consistently prevent political elites from manipulating institutions for short-term gains.

Third, the explanatory account in the preceding chapters challenges conventional understandings of the relationship between macrostructural factors and regime type. Rather than assuming that citizens respond to structural developments in uniform ways, the framework employed in this analysis examines specific actors and their roles in facilitating or obstructing democracy's survival. If we develop a clearer understanding of how macro-structural variables influence the behavior of the specific agents who decide whether to deepen or rescind democracy, we may learn more about whether certain structural variables can ever be considered necessary conditions for democracy. The evidence presented here suggests that perhaps structures are important only to the extent that they foster certain intermediary conditions, which are the real "causes" of democracy's survival.

The genesis of this project was the "outlier" status of both Russia and Indonesia as big, important cases of third wave democratization that predominant regime change theories could not explain. I find a common answer for Indonesia's success and Russia's failure: patterns in nonvoting political participation. Further investigation of this variable in other cases of democratization might lead to greater insights for understanding the regime trajectories of both outliers and typical cases.

Lingering Questions

Nonvoting political participation patterns can explain why democracy succeeded in Indonesia and failed in Russia. The process of unpacking factors that fostered elite-constraining participation in Indonesia and elite-enabling participation in Russia, however, opens up additional questions that cannot be answered within the scope of this project, but that would benefit from further research. First and foremost, what caused the differing patterns in civil society engagement, political efficacy, and political trust in these two countries? We can see how numerous hypotheses quickly emerge as potential answers, ranging from differences in historical conditions, access to resources, and psychological dispositions.

Within the data gathered for this project, however, one possible causal variable stands out: Russians' and Indonesians' dramatically different experiences with organized religion. As Chapter 5 indicated, Indonesians attend religious services at very high rates. The practice of organized religion brings Indonesians into contact with others on a regular basis, and thereby provides them with greater opportunities to develop norms of reciprocity. The potential importance of attendance at religious services as a conduit for engendering civic engagement becomes more persuasive when we consider the low levels of religious practice in Russia. In examining the rates of attendance at religious services for the thirty-three countries included in the 1999–2004 World Values Survey that have undergone a democratic transition since the 1970s, I found that Russia has the lowest rate of attendance at less than 4 percent. At the opposite end of the spectrum, only Tanzania and Nigeria have higher rates of attendance than Indonesia's 64.7 percent.

The covariation between religious practice and civic engagement in Russia and Indonesia raises several questions for further investigation: What effect does religious service attendance have on civic engagement? Are individuals who frequently attend religious services more likely to become involved in civic and political life? Does participation vary according to religious denomination? Fish and Lussier find that while Muslims are no more likely than Christians to attend religious services on a weekly basis, Orthodox Christians are significantly less likely to attend regularly than are Catholics or Protestants (Fish, 2011, ch. 2). This finding has particular resonance for the comparison of predominantly Muslim Indonesia and predominantly Orthodox Russia. Is Indonesia's robust civil society a consequence of its high level of religiosity? Is the deficit in civil society observed in Russia linked to the forced atheism of the Communist era? Is repression of organized religion under Communism another factor that has contributed to the lower levels of civil society observed across the post-Communist region? At present, there are more questions than answers regarding the relationship between religious attendance and civic engagement, but these preliminary speculations suggest a fruitful area for further research.

Whither Russia and Indonesia?

In addition to opening up further queries about democratic theory, this book's empirical findings raise several questions about the further trajectories of Russia and Indonesia's respective political regimes. If we examine Freedom House scores for political openness, there has been relatively little movement in Indonesia and Russia's level of political rights or civil liberties for a decade. In both cases, this stretch of regime stability constitutes the longest period of continuity in the levels of political openness since democratic transitions were completed. Russia has become a stable authoritarian regime, while Indonesia is proving a robust new democracy. The following two sections discuss the prospects for democracy's survival in Indonesia and its revival in Russia.

Indonesia: Corruption and Clientelism

Indonesia has maintained a stable level of political openness that is higher than Russia's level at its democratic peak. Yet the level of democracy in Indonesia is still lower than that of several other third wave democracies, such as Brazil, Ghana, and the countries of Eastern Europe. Moreover, there has been little progress in extending or strengthening political rights or civil liberties in the past several years. Scholars and Indonesians regularly cite corruption, clientelism, and popular discontent as evidence of a lack of democracy within Indonesia (Buehler, 2010b; Hadiz, 2010; Webber, 2006).

Yet several indicators that some perceive as symptoms of a democratic deficit, such as mass protests and clientelistic party relations, may alternately be viewed as signs of a functioning democratic system. As the preceding chapters have argued, peaceful protest communicates useful information to political leaders and can constrain their actions. Moreover, as Herbert Kitschelt and Steven Wilkinson (2007) illustrate, patronage-based, party–voter linkages exist in many countries, including some advanced industrial democracies. These factors alone do not prevent democracy from taking root.

Certain obstacles, however, could hinder Indonesia's further democratic development. First, Indonesia faces meaningful problems with good governance, particularly regarding corruption. While corruption exists in both open and closed regimes, it generally reduces transparency and enhances elites' interests in keeping the polity closed. Moreover, widespread corruption can create inducements for electoral fraud, which in turn hinders democracy.

Former Indonesian President Megawati introduced the Corruption Eradication Commission (KPK), which was further empowered during the presidential tenure of Susilo Bambang Yudhoyono. The KPK has uncovered numerous high-level corruption cases that have resulted in criminal charges. The results of national anticorruption efforts are reflected in Indonesia's steady improvement in Transparency International's Corruption Perceptions Index (CPI). Indonesia and Russia tied in their CPI rankings in 2007, but since then Indonesia has consistently had a better rating.

Yet, for all of the visible, high-profile instances of the KPK rooting out corruption, unscrupulous practices at all levels of government abound. In particular, scholars have pointed to the new opportunities for corruption that have emerged due to the decentralization reforms that were central to extending and expanding democracy. As Freedman and Tiburzi (2012) contend, decentralization has resulted in positive and negative consequences for Indonesian democracy. On the positive side, decentralization led to an expansion of local elections and control, giving citizens greater opportunities to hold the government accountable. On the negative side, these same reforms multiplied occasions for patronage, corruption, and military control. Michael Buehler's research (2010a) shows that while local elections do grant citizens greater agency to throw out ineffective leaders, new leaders are generally drawn from the same pool of elites, leaving patronage-based networks unchanged and drawing decentralized public resources away from their intended aims.

As most observers of Indonesia will attest, the challenge to stemming corruption cannot be overcome simply by institutional reforms, but also requires an adjustment in both public and elite attitudes about the proper use of public office. The enabling role that widespread public tolerance of corruption has on elite behavior is apparent in public reactions to a high-profile corruption case in Medan, Indonesia. In 2008, Medan Mayor Abdillah and Deputy Mayor Ramli Lubis were arrested for graft, found guilty by the Anti-Corruption Court, and sent to prison. My interviews in 2009 revealed that citizens had mixed attitudes about this outcome. Half believed that if the mayor was guilty of corrupt practices, he should be punished, but the other half expressed more conflicted views. This latter group had a generally positive estimation of Abdillah as the city's mayor, and found his conviction troublesome not because he proved corrupt, but because the city was left without capable leadership. These attitudes are testimony to the pervasiveness of corruption in Indonesian life, as well as the widely held expectation that political leaders are likely to be corrupt. Indeed, few respondents viewed Abdillah's conviction as evidence of a moral failing or a lack of commitment to democracy.

These responses to a case where the political regime adhered to the rule of law in fighting corruption – a topic that consistently rates high in Indonesian public opinion polls as one of the country's greatest problems – suggest that Indonesians do not always prioritize democratic procedure over outcome. If citizens tolerate corruption, and even pardon it when popular political leaders carry it out, they are less likely to use democratic institutions as a mechanism for curbing corruption and improving governance. Moreover, if individuals tolerate corruption in political administration, it could interfere with the fairness and freeness of elections. This possibility relates to a second factor frequently cited as an obstacle to Indonesia's further democratization: the pervasiveness of clientelism in electoral politics.

Clientelistic exchanges do not preclude democracy as long as they generate meaningful political competition. However, reliance on patron–client relationships for mobilizing the electorate creates conditions that are conducive to corruption, abuse of power, and fraud, as political aspirants find that they need ever-greater resources to compete effectively for office. Indeed, as mentioned earlier, one of the main criticisms of Indonesia's decentralization policies is that they put considerable resources in the hands of local officials who now have to compete for office, thereby facilitating the spread of so-called money politics (Hadiz, 2010; EJ-11, interview, June 8, 2009). Others have argued that the rise in direct clientelistic exchanges is not so much a consequence of decentralization as an outgrowth of the increase in competitive elections at all levels (EJ-1, interview, May 25, 2009; EJ-10, interview, June 8, 2009; EJ-15, interview, June 6, 2009).

My citizen respondents offered several examples of "money politics," both in terms of direct payments and in gifts of rice, headscarves, prayer rugs, or other items that might be donated to local prayer groups and neighborhood associations. In some instances, the presence of such exchanges contributed to negative feelings about the winners of elections. On the whole, however, my citizen respondents in Surabaya and Medan were generally not influenced by the small sums and gifts common in preelection "money politics." Many viewed such practices as a way in which parties tried to encourage you to vote for them, rather than as a binding commitment of one's vote. For example, a thirty-eight-year-old Javanese woman in Medan described how two parties came to her *pengajian* prayer group before legislative elections. They offered noodles and floor mats to the participants. Other parties came through the neighborhood offering food staples. She noted that after the elections, "many candidates were disappointed because they did not get votes [after providing the gifts]. Stupid candidates." When I asked a fifty-three-year-old Minahasan man if it would be permissible to vote for a candidate other than one he might have accepted money from, he responded, "When there are elections, I have my own choice. Therefore I am not prejudiced by receiving money from another person."

Kitschelt and Wilkinson argue that clientelism can persist only when "politicians have good reasons to expect that the target constituencies for clientelistic bargains will behave in predictable fashion and refrain from opportunism" (2007, p. 8). Absent these conditions, politicians must construct elaborate and expensive surveillance structures to ensure that constituents adhere without free-riding. For this reason, clientelism is more common and effective in smaller communities, where face-to-face interactions are the norm. In large urban centers like Surabaya and Medan, however, compliance is much harder to enforce. Many of my respondents did not feel constrained to vote a particular way by candidates' preelection inducements. In this context, it is questionable whether parties will continue to raise the stakes of "money politics." Programmatic party competition is simply less expensive. Party–voter linkages are only a threat to democracy if they erode meaningful competition, and there is little evidence of this happening in Indonesia.

While widespread corruption and clientelism are not likely to induce democratic erosion in Indonesia, they may inhibit further democratic deepening, particularly if they divert resources away from pressing welfare concerns or otherwise interfere with the government's ability to enact public policy that meets popular expectations. Of greater concern to Indonesian democracy, however, are increasing levels of intolerance for certain religious minorities, such as Christians and followers of Ahmadiyah Islam, who have suffered a growing number of violent attacks in recent years (Arnaz & Pawas, 2011; Freedom House, 2014). While the Indonesian constitution technically guarantees freedom of religion, the government has done little to protect religious minorities. This lack of protections contributed to Freedom House's lowering of Indonesia's civil liberties score in 2013.

Indonesians will ultimately decide whether the country will strengthen political rights and civil liberties by addressing corruption, money politics, and intolerance. While there is little momentum for tackling these specific weaknesses at present, Indonesia's civically engaged population is already endowed with the tools it needs to confront such issues. The country's post-Suharto history provides ample evidence of citizens constraining elites and pushing for further democracy. Indonesia's 2014 presidential election, in which Joko Widodo, a former furniture salesman with no connection to the political or military establishments, emerged victorious over former Suharto son-in-law Prabowo Subianto, is the latest example of Indonesia's commitment to democracy. The election is noteworthy for two reasons. First, Widodo succeeded in reaching national office based on his successful management record as mayor of Surakarta and governor of Jakarta, campaigning against a well-heeled Prabowo coalition that included the backing of several business and media magnates. Second, while Prabowo did not initially accept defeat, he used democratic institutions to appeal the decision, arguing that the election result was mired in widespread fraud. Ultimately, the Constitutional Court ruled that these allegations had no basis and Prabowo backed down. Indonesian presidential candidates have learned that they must play by democratic rules to attain and maintain power.

Russia: Limits of Protest under Authoritarianism

The nascent democracy introduced in Russia in the early 1990s did not survive. In considering prospects for political openness in contemporary Russia, the question is no longer one of democracy's survival, but of the democratization of a stable authoritarian regime. The rise in protest movements that Russia experienced following the December 2011 State Duma elections was initially viewed as a possible first step toward greater political openness. By fall 2012, however, it was clear that while Russians' increase in contentious politics initially forced political elites to soften some aspects of authoritarian rule, the contemporary Russian regime was already too politically closed for street protests to prompt elites into supporting renewed democratization.

The increase in activism in Russia during 2011 and 2012 represented an aberration from the norm of elite-enabling participation that has taken root since the collapse of the Soviet Union. Allegations of major fraud during the December 2011 State Duma elections generated a substantial, though short-lived increase in participation in street protests. Protests in Moscow attracting 100,000 people constituted the largest protests in Russia in twenty years. Protest action continued, though on a smaller scale, across the country throughout the winter and spring, taking on a variety of both sanctioned and unsanctioned forms. The last large-scale protest occurred in the capital on June 12, 2012, "Russia Day," which commemorates Russia's declaration of sovereignty from the Soviet Union. Tens of thousands of protestors participated. A much smaller mass protest was held in September 2012, when thousands gathered in Moscow and smaller numbers of protestors took to the streets in the regions ("Opposition Protests Reported Across Russia, Regional Turnout Modest," 2012).

From December 2011 until Putin's reelection in March 2012, this increase in political participation constrained the elite somewhat, as the government moved away from a strategy of outright repression. The first and most immediate signal that the rise in protests had constrained elites came in the response to the December 2011 demonstrations, which were marked by few arrests and more neutral media coverage ("Russian TV Programme Breaks New Ground in Opposition Protest Coverage," 2011; Walker, 2011). In his annual televised call-in show on December 15, Putin conceded to some token liberalizing steps, such as allowing small political parties to register for elections, loosening the Kremlin's grip over regional politics, and increasing the number of cameras at polling locations to reduce fraud (Abbakumova & Birnbaum, 2011). These proposals were all at least partially enacted before Putin's March 2012 reelection.

This period of retrenchment was tactical, not strategic. No genuine underlying liberalization occurred. These initial measures were designed to prevent further opposition organization, neutralize first-time protestors, and defuse tensions enough to secure Putin's reelection. Once the regime accomplished these tasks, it moved to a position of heightened coercion. Following Putin's inauguration in May 2012, the regime undertook several moves to prevent organization of elite-constraining participation among the opposition. Measures comprise several repressive laws, including one dramatically increasing fines for participating in unsanctioned rallies, one requiring NGOs that receive foreign funding and engage in "political activity" to register as "foreign agents" with the Justice Ministry, one that expands the definition of high treason to potentially target any organization with foreign contacts, an Internet censorship law, a law introducing a single voting day in September that would hamper the opposition's ability to campaign, and amendments to a law that partially re-criminalizes slander or defamation. In addition to these legal restrictions, the regime has sought to silence opposition through the arrest and interrogation of opposition activists and the dismissal and censure of vocal opponents in the State Duma. Attacks on civil liberties continued in 2013 with the adoption of laws that prohibit so-called propaganda of nontraditional sexual relations, creating considerable restrictions on the lives of LGBT citizens. Radio, television, and the Internet came under further regulation in 2014, compelling Freedom House to lower Russia's civil liberties rating.

In another tactical move, Putin granted a series of high-profile amnesties in late 2013, including the release of former business tycoon Mikhail Khodorkovsky, the two artists from the Pussy Riot collective held for their unsanctioned 2012 performance in Moscow's Christ the Savior Cathedral, thirty Greenpeace activists, and four protestors from the May 2012 inauguration demonstrations. These amnesties were largely viewed as an attempt to blunt international criticism of Russia's human rights abuses before the 2014 Sochi Olympics. Indeed, one of the regime's most visible critics, Aleksei Navalny, spent most of 2014 under house arrest.

In analyzing the dynamic between the mass public and the political elite since December 2011, it is clear that the upsurge in elite-constraining protest activity compelled the Russian regime into a brief period of retreat, but it failed to usher in a period of re-democratization. Yet it is important to note that the political environment in which these activities were taking place had changed dramatically from the period of political openness Russia experienced in the early post-Soviet years. It is no longer accurate to think of these protests as elite-constraining participation taking place in a liberalized political system. Rather, Russians in 2011 and 2012 were protesting an authoritarian regime.

For elite-constraining political participation to guard against authoritarian retrenchment, two conditions must adhere. First, there must be enough liberalization within the political system for opposition to mobilize and genuinely compete in elections. In order for the public to limit the range of actions elites can take and still maintain power, it must demonstrate that it can credibly threaten to remove incumbents from office. In an open political system, this credible threat of incumbent removal is achieved by the organization, maintenance, and support of opposition parties and candidates. Yet, in an authoritarian regime such as contemporary Russia, insufficient liberalization for mobilization and organization of electoral competition will substantially diminish participation's ability to foster an elite transfer of power.

Second, elite-constraining activities cannot be limited to intensified pressure for contentious politics. While street protest and civil disobedience do force political elites to be reactive and defensive – which can compel ruling elites to consider policy changes – these forms of participation are not necessarily sufficient to constrain elites over time. Intense, regularized street protest can present such a credible threat if it forces the collapse of a regime through popular revolution, as witnessed in Tunisia and Egypt in 2011. Yet, in most systems where there is some pluralism and competition, elections constitute the primary mechanism for removing incumbents. Moreover, authoritarian regime collapse and democracy's survival are not equal – contentious politics might facilitate the former, but it is not sufficient to guarantee the latter.

Contemporary Russia fails to meet either of these two conditions. There was a period when an increase in both contentious politics and mass support for opposition parties might have constrained political elites in Russia. That period was in the mid-1990s. For the current regime to democratize, incumbent elites must believe that political liberalization is essential to their political survival. At present, there is little indication that those in power hold such beliefs.

Final Thoughts

Political regimes, whether democratic or authoritarian, are not created simply by structures aligning in a particular way. Rather, they are the product of struggles between those who want to govern and those who are governed. Nascent democracies survive when citizens constrain elites from becoming too powerful. They fail when citizens react to elite decisions with quiescence or indifference. Recent attempts at activism in Russia show that once a political regime closes, it is much harder to reopen.

As this book has demonstrated, existing theories for democratization require revision and further testing, as they failed to accurately predict the democratization outcomes in Russia and Indonesia, two of the largest polities within the third wave of democratization. Indonesia – a postcolonial, less industrialized, predominantly Muslim country with unresolved secessionist conflicts – has built a surviving democracy in less than two decades. Yet Russia – an oil-rich, industrialized, former superpower – failed to see its post-Soviet democratic transition through to survival. After years of political and economic upheaval, Indonesians and Russians have reached a comfortable level of equilibrium in their political regimes. How long this equilibrium will hold depends on the dynamic interaction of masses and elites. It is up to these agents to activate democracy.

List of Expert Interview Subjects

In total, approximately 140 scholars, analysts, journalists, and representatives of political parties and mass organizations were interviewed for this project. The list given here is not comprehensive of all expert interviews conducted, but rather only includes those subjects cited specifically in the text.

RUSSIA

Moscow City special administrative district

M-14	Representative from the Leadership of the Union of the Committees of Soldiers' Mothers	February 21, 2008
M-17	Representative from Youth Branch of Yabloko	February 19, 2008

Kazan, Tatarstan

K-5	Scholar and Democratic Activist	February 29, 2008
K-6	Representative from Communist Party of the Russian Federation Regional Leadership	March 1, 2008
K-7	Representatives from Regional Youth Branch of Communist Party of the Russian Federation	March 1, 2008
K-10	Member of Russian Cultural Movement	March 13, 2008
K-16	Opposition Activist	March 11, 2008
K-17	United Russia Political Party Analyst	March 13, 2008
K-18	Member of Russian Cultural Movement	March 18, 2008
K-21	Representatives from Yabloko Regional Leadership	March 26, 2008

Krasnoyarsk, Krasnoyarsk Krai

Kr-11	Representative from Leadership of Krasnoyarsk Branch of Memorial	November 10, 2008

Kr-12	Representative from Liberal Democratic Party of Russia Regional Leadership	November 10, 2008
Kr-13	Representatives from Communist Party of the Russian Federation Regional Leadership	November 11, 2008
Kr-20	United Russia Political Party Activist	November 26, 2008
Kr-22	United Russia Political Party Analyst	November 27, 2008

INDONESIA

Surabaya, East Java

EJ-1	Political Scientist, Airlangga University	May 25, 2009
EJ-3	Representative of Muhammadiyah Regional Leadership	June 2, 2009
EJ-4	Representative of NU Women's Organization Fatayat's Regional Leadership	June 3, 2009
EJ-5	Representative of Indonesia Democratic Party of Struggle Regional Leadership	June 4, 2009
EJ-8	Representative of Prosperous Justice Party Regional Leadership	June 6, 2009
EJ-10	Party Official in NU Regional Leadership	June 8, 2009
EJ-11	Representative of National Awakening Party Regional Leadership	June 8, 2009
EJ-15	Legal Scholar, University of Surabaya	June 12, 2009

Medan, North Sumatra

| NS-2 | Legal Scholar, Institut Agama Islam Negeri Sumatera Utara | July 2, 2009 |

References

Abbakumova, N., & Birnbaum, M. (2011). Putin Makes Few Concessions to Protestors in Broadcast Q&A. *The Washington Post.*

Acemoglu, D., & Robinson, J. A. (2006). *Economic Origins of Dictatorship and Democracy.* New York: Cambridge University Press.

Aglionby, J. (2001). Army Tells Wahid: No State of Emergency. *The Guardian.*

Almond, G. A., & Verba, S. (1963). *The Civic Culture: Political Attitudes and Democracy in Five Nations.* Princeton, NJ: Princeton University Press.

Antlov, H. (2004). Introduction. In H. Antlov & S. Cederroth (Eds.), *Elections in Indonesia: The New Order and Beyond* (pp. 1–17). London: RoutledgeCurzon.

Arnaz, F., & Pawas, Z. (2011). Activists Say Police Allowed Ahmadiyah Attacks. *Jakarta Globe.*

Asmarani, D. (2006a). Indonesia's Unions Split over Labour Law Revision. *The Straits Times.*

(2006b). Mass Protests in Indonesia against Labour Law Changes. *The Straits Times.*

(2006c). Women Outraged by Jakarta's Anti-porn Bill. *The Straits Times.*

Aspinall, E. (2005). *Opposing Suharto: Compromise, Resistance, and Regime Change in Indonesia.* Stanford, CA: Stanford University Press.

(2010). The Irony of Success. *Journal of Democracy, 21*(2), 20–34.

Asyari, S. (2009). *Nalar Politik NU & Muhammadiyah: Over Crossing Java Sentris.* Yogyakarta: LKiS.

Bahry, D. (1993). Society Transformed? Rethinking the Social Roots of Perestroika. *Slavic Review, 52*(3), 512–554.

Bahry, D. and Silver, B. D. (1990). Soviet Citizen Participation on the Eve of Democratization. *Annual Political Science Review, 84*(3), 821–847.

Baker, P., & Glasser, S. B. (2001). Large Rally in Moscow Backs Independent TV: Thousands Gather to Protest Moves By Putin. *The Washington Post.*

Barber, B. (1984). *Strong Democracy: Participatory Politics for a New Age.* Berkeley: University of California Press.

Barnes, S. H., Kasse, M., Allerback, K., Farah, B., Heunks, F., Inglehart, R., . . . Rosenmayr, L. (1979). *Political Action: Mass Participation in Five Western Democracies.* Beverly Hills, CA: Sage Publications.

Belin, L., & Orttung, R. W. (1997). *The Russian Parliamentary Elections of 1995.* Armonk, NY: M.E. Sharpe.

Bertrand, J. (1996). False Starts, Succession Crises, and Regime Transition: Flirting with Openness in Indonesia. *Pacific Affairs, 69*(3), 319–340.

Bird, J. (1998). Indonesia in 1997: The Tinderbox Year. *Asian Survey, 38*(2), 168–176.

(1999). Indonesia in 1998: The Pot Boils Over. *Asian Survey, 39*(1), 27–37.

Bittner, S. V. (2003). Local Soviets, Public Order, and Welfare after Stalin: Appeals from Moscow's Kiev Raion. *Russian Review, 62*(2), 281–293.

Boix, C., & Stokes, S. C. (2003). Endogenous Democratization. *World Politics, 55*(4), 517–549.

Bollen, K. (1979). Political Democracy and the Timing of Development. *American Sociological Review, 44*, 572–587.

(1983). World System Position, Dependency, and Democracy: The Cross-national Evidence. *American Sociological Review, 48*(4), 468–479.

Bondarenko, A., & Migalin, S. (2005). Pensioners Have Lost Faith in Benevolent Government. *Current Digest of the Russian Press, 57*(5), 9.

Bowen, J. R. (1986). On the Political Construction of Tradition: Gotong Royong in Indonesia. *Journal of Asian Studies, 45*(3), 545–561.

Brady, H. E. (1999). Political Participation. In J. P. Robinson, P. R. Shaver, & L. S. Wrightsman (Eds.), *Measures of Political Attitudes* (vol. 2, pp. 737–801). San Diego, CA: Academic Press.

Brady, H. & Kaplan, C. (2007). Public Responses to Elite Changes in the Soviet Union: 1987-1991. Paper presented at the Annual Meeting of the Midwest Political Science Association.

Brady, H. E., & Kaplan, C. (2008). The Development of Mass and Elite Cleavages during the Soviet Transition: 1987–1991. Paper presented at the American Political Science Association Annual Meeting, Boston, MA.

Breslauer, G. W. (2002). *Gorbachev and Yeltsin as Leaders.* New York: Cambridge University Press.

Brown, A. (2010). Perestroika as Revolution from Above. In S. Fortescue (Ed.), *Russian Politics: From Lenin to Putin* (pp. 127–151). New York: Palgrave MacMillan.

Buehler, M. (2010a). Decentralisation and Local Democracy in Indonesia: The Marginalisation of the Public Sphere. In E. Aspinall & M. Mietzner (Eds.), *Problems of Democratisation in Indonesia: Elections, Institutions and Society* (pp. 267–285). Singapore: Institute of Southeast Asian Studies.

(2010b). Indonesia. In Freedom House (Ed.), *Countries at the Crossroads 2010*: Freedom House.

Bunce, V. (2000). Comparative Democratization: Big and Bounded Generalizations. *Comparative Political Studies, 33*(6/7), 703–734.

Campbell, A., Converse, P. E., Miller, W., & Stokes, D. (1964). *The American Voter.* New York: John Wiley and Sons.

Campbell, A., Gurin, G., & Miller, W. (1954). *The Voter Decides*. Evanston, IL: Row, Peterson.

Campbell, D. E. (2006). *Why We Vote: How School and Communities Shape Our Civic Life*. Princeton, NJ: Princeton University Press.

Carnaghan, E. (2007). Do Russians Dislike Democracy? *PS: Political Science & Politics*, 40(1), 61–66.

Center for the Study of Development and Democracy. (1996). *Rakyat & Pemilu: Laporan Pengumpulan Pendapat Umum tentang Kesadaran Masyarakat Jakarta Mengenai Pemilu*. Jakarta: LP3ES.

(1999). *Rakyat & Politik Pasca Pemilu 1999: Laporan Survai Pendapat Umum tentang Politik Pasca Pemilu 1999*. Jakarta: LP3ES.

(2003). *Preferensi dan Sikap Masyarakat tentang Pemilihan Umum*. Jakarta: LP3ES.

Central Intelligence Agency. 2011. *The World Factbook*. Retrieved from www .cia.gov/library/publications/the-world-factbook/.

Chandler, A. (2008). The Social Promise: Rights, Privileges, and Responsibilities in Russian Welfare State Reform since Gorbachev. In T. Lahusen & P. H. Solomon, Jr. (Eds.), *What Is Soviet Now? Identities, Legacies, Memories* (pp. 192–213). Berlin: Lit Verlag.

Chen, X. (2008). Collective Petitioning and Institutional Conversion. In K. J. O'Brien (Ed.), *Popular Protest in China* (pp. 54–70). Cambridge, MA: Harvard University Press.

Chu, Y.-h., Bratton, M., Lagos, M., Shastri, S., & Tessler, M. (2008). Public Opinion and Democratic Legitimacy. *Journal of Democracy*, 19(2), 74–87.

Citrin, J. (1974). Comment: The Political Relevance of Trust in Government. *American Political Science Review*, 68(3), 973–988.

Citrin, J., & Green, D. P. (1986). Presidential Leadership and the Resurgence of Trust in Government. *British Journal of Political Science*, 16(4), 431–453.

Collier, R. B., & Collier, D. (1991). *Shaping the Political Arena: Critical Junctures, the Labor Movement, and Regime Dynamics in Latin America*. Princeton, NJ: Princeton University Press.

Colton, T. J. (2000). *Transitional Citizens: Voters and What Influences Them in the New Russia*. Cambridge, MA: Harvard University Press.

Colton, T. J., & Hale, H. E. (2009). The Putin Vote: Presidential Electorates in a Hybrid Regime. *Slavic Review*, 68(3), 473–503.

Colton, T. J., & McFaul, M. (2003). *Popular Choice and Managed Democracy: The Russian Elections of 1999 and 2000*. Washington, DC: Brookings Institution Press.

Compton, J., & Robert W. (2000). *East Asian Democratization: Impact of Globalization, Culture, and Economy*. Westport, CT: Praeger.

Conge, P. J. (1988). The Concept of Political Participation: Toward a Definition. *Comparative Politics*, 20(2), 241–249.

Court Ruling Ends Government's Authority to Ban Books. (2010, October 14). *Jakarta Post*.

Craig, A. L., & Cornelius, W. A. (1989). Political Culture in Mexico: Continuities and Revisionist Interpretations. In G. A. Almond & S. Verba (Eds.), *The Civic Culture Revisited* (pp. 325–393). Newbury Park, CA: Sage Publications.

Cribb, R. (2001). Genocide in Indonesia, 1965–1966. *Journal of Genocide Research*, 3(2), 219–239.

Dahl, Robert. (1989). *Democracy and Its Critics*. New Haven: Yale University Press.

Dallin, A., & Lapidus, G. W. (Eds.). (1995). *The Soviet System: From Crisis to Collapse*. Boulder, CO: Westview Press.

Dalton, R. J. (2006). *Citizen Politics: Public Opinion and Political Parties in Advanced Industrial Democracies* (4th ed.). Washington, D.C.: CQ Press.

Diamond, L. (1999). *Developing Democracy: Toward Consolidation*. Baltimore, MD: Johns Hopkins University Press.

(2008). The Democratic Rollback: The Resurgence of the Predatory State. *Foreign Affairs*, 87(2), 36–48.

DiFranceisco, W., & Gitelman, Z. (1984). Soviet Political Culture and "Covert Participation" in Policy Implementation. *American Political Science Review*, 78(3), 603–621.

Dimitrov, M. (2010). Building Loyalty as a Strategy for Autocratic Survival: A Comparison of Eastern Europe and China. Paper presented at the American Political Science Association Annual Meeting, Washington, D.C., September 2–5, 2010.

Donno, D., & Russett, B. (2004). Islam, Authoritarianism, and Female Empowerment: What Are the Linkages? *World Politics*, 56(4), 582–607.

Doorn-Harder, P. v. (2006). *Women Shaping Islam: Reading the Qu'ran in Indonesia* Urbana, IL: University of Illinois Press.

Dwianto, R. D. (2003). An Existing Form of Urban Locality Groups in Jakarta: Reexamining RT/RW for the Post-New Order Era. In T. Mizuuchi (Ed.), *Representing Local Places and Raising Voices from Below: Japanese Contributions to the History of Geographical Thought* (pp. 41–60). Osaka, Japan: Osaka City University.

Easton, D. (1975). A Re-assessment of the Concept of Political Support. *British Journal of Political Science*, 5, 435–457.

Emmerson, D. K. (1991). Indonesia in 1990: A Foreshadow Play. *Asian Survey*, 31(2), 179–187.

Faroukshin, M. (2001). Civil Servants on Edge as Shamiev Starts Third Term. *EWI Russian Regional Report*, 6(16).

Feith, H. (1957). *The Indonesian Elections of 1955*. Ithaca, NY: Cornell University Press.

Finkel, S. E. (1985). Reciprocal Effects of Participation and Political Efficacy: A Panel Analysis. *American Journal of Political Science*, 29(4), 891–913.

Fiorina, M. P. (1976). The Voting Decision: Instrumental and Expressive Aspects. *Journal of Politics*, 38(2), 390–415.

Fish, M. S. (1995). *Democracy from Scratch: Opposition and Regime in the New Russian Revolution*. Princeton, NJ: Princeton University Press.

(1998). Democratization's Requisites: The Postcommunist Experience. *Post-Soviet Affairs*, 14(3), 212–247.

(2002). Islam and Authoritarianism. *World Politics*, 55(1), 4–37.

(2005). *Democracy Derailed in Russia: The Failure of Open Politics*. New York: Cambridge University Press.

(2011). *Are Muslims Distinctive?: A Look at the Evidence*. New York: Oxford University Press.

Fish, M. S., & Wittenberg, J. (2009). Failed Democratization. In C. Haerpfer, P. Bernhagen, R. Inglehart, & C. Welzel (Eds.), *Democratization* (pp. 249–267). New York: Oxford University Press.

Fowler, J. (2006). Habitual Voting and Behavioral Turnout. *Journal of Politics*, 68(2), 335–344.

Frederick, W. H., & Worden, R. L. (1992). *Indonesia: A Country Study*. Washington, D.C.: Library of Congress, Federal Research Division.

Freedman, A., & Tiburzi, R. (2012). Progress and Caution: Indonesia's Democracy. *Asian Affairs: An American Review*, 39(3), 131–156.

Freedom House. (2009). *Freedom in the World 2009*. Retrieved from Washington, D.C. www.freedomhouse.org.

(2010). *Freedom in the World 2010*. Retrieved from Washington, DC: www .freedomhouse.org.

(2014). *Freedom in the World 2014*. Retrieved from Washington, D.C.: www .freedomhouse.org.

Friedgut, T. H. (1979). *Political Participation in the USSR*. Princeton, NJ: Princeton University Press.

Fukuyama, F. (2001). Social Capital, Civil Society, and Development. *Third World Quarterly*, 22(1), 7–20.

Gallagher, M. (2002). "Reform and Openness": Why China's Economic Reforms Have Delayed Democracy. *World Politics*, 54(3), 338–372.

Gelling, P. (2010, April 20). Law Banning Blasphemy Is Upheld In Indonesia. *The New York Times*.

George, A. L., & Bennett, A. (2005). *Case Studies and Theory Development in the Social Sciences*. Cambridge, MA: MIT Press.

Gerber, A., Green, D., & Shachar, R. (2003). Voting May Be Habit-Forming: Evidence from a Randomized Field Experiment. *American Journal of Political Science*, 47(3), 40–50.

Gerring, J. (2007). *Case Study Research: Principles and Practices*. New York: Cambridge University Press.

Grzymała-Busse, A. M. (2002). *Redeeming the Communist Past: The Regeneration of Communist Parties in East Central Europe*. Cambridge, UK: Cambridge University Press.

Gutmann, A. (1993). Democracy. In R. E. Goodin & P. Pettit (Eds.), *A Companion to Contemporary Political Philosophy* (pp. 411–421). Oxford: Basil Blackwell.

Hadiz, V. R. (2010). *Localising Power in Post-Authoritarian Indonesia: A Southeast Asia Perspective*. Stanford, CA: Stanford University Press.

Hale, H. E. (2006). *Why Not Parties in Russia? Democracy, Federalism, and the State*. New York: Cambridge University Press.

Harris, F., & Gillion, D. (2010). Expanding the Possibilities: Reconceptualizing Political Participation as a Toolkit. In J. E. Leighley (Ed.), *The Oxford Handbook of American Elections and Political Behavior* (pp. 144–161). New York: Oxford University Press.

Harsaputra, I. (2008). Madura Polling Stations Refuse East Java Election Re-Run. *The Jakarta Post*, December 8.

Harsaputra, I., & Nugroho, I. (2009, January 31). Soekarwo Wins in E. Java for 2nd Time, Khofifah Still Defiant. *The Jakarta Post.*

Hefner, R. W. (2000). *Civil Islam: Muslims and Democratization in Indonesia.* Princeton, NJ: Princeton University Press.

Heifetz, R. A. (1994). *Leadership Without Easy Answers.* Cambridge, MA: Harvard University Press.

Hill, F. (2005). Governing Russia: Putin's Federal Dilemmas. *New Europe Review,* (January). www.brookings.edu/articles/2005/01russia_hill.aspx Retrieved from www.brookings.edu/articles/2005/01russia_hill.aspx

Howard, M. M. (2003). *The Weakness of Civil Society in Post-Communist Europe.* Cambridge, UK: Cambridge University Press.

Human Rights Watch. (2009). *An Uncivil Approach to Civil Society: Continuing State Curbs on Independent NGOs and Activists in Russia.* Retrieved from New York: www.hrw.org/en/reports/2009/06/16/uncivil-approach-civil-society-0 and www.globalpolicy.org/images/pdfs/russia0609web.pdf.

Hundreds of Indonesian Activists Demonstrate against Pornography Bill. (2006, April 24). *BBC Monitoring Asia Pacific.*

Huntington, S. (1991). *The Third Wave: Democratization in the Late Twentieth Century.* Norman: University of Oklahoma Press.

(1993). The Clash of Civilizations. *Foreign Affairs,* 72(3), 22–49.

Indonesian Government, House Agree to Revise Regional Administration Law. (2007, August 23). *BBC Monitoring Asia Pacific.*

Indrayana, D. (2008). *Indonesian Constitutional Reform 1999–2002: An Evaluation of Constitution-Making in Transition.* Jakarta: Kompas Book Publishing.

Inglehart, R. (1997). *Modernization and Postmodernization.* Princeton, NJ: Princeton University Press.

International Center for Not-for-Profit Law. (2006). *Analysis of Law # 18-FZ: On Introducing Amendments to Certain Legislative Acts of the Russian Federation.* Washington DC: International Center for Not-for-Profit Law.

International Foundation for Electoral Systems. (2002). National Public Opinion Survey: Republic of Indonesia. www.ifes.org Retrieved from www.ifes.org

(2005). Public Opinion Survey Indonesia 2005. www.ifes.org Retrieved from www.ifes.org

Jennings, M. K., & Niemi, R. G. (1981). *Generations and Politics: A Panel Study of Young Adults and Their Parents.* Princeton, NJ: Princeton University Press.

Jowitt, K. (1992). *New World Disorder: The Leninist Extinction.* Berkeley: University of California Press.

Kagda, S. (2006, May 2). Indonesian Stocks, Rupiah Rise as Worker Protests Fizzle Out. *The Business Times Singapore.*

Karl, T. L. (1986). Imposing Consent: Electoralism and Democratization in El Salvador. In P. W. Drake & E. S. La Jolla (Eds.), *Elections and Democratization in Latin America, 1980–1985* (pp. 9–36). San Diego: University of California, San Diego, Center for International Studies.

Katznelson, I. (2003). Reflections on Purposive Action in Comparative Historical Social Science. In J. Mahoney & D. Reuschemeyer (Eds.), *Comparative Historical Analysis in the Social Sciences* (pp. 270–301). Cambridge: Cambridge University Press.

Kitschelt, H., & Wilkinson, S. I. (2007). Citizen-Politician Linkages: an Introduction. In H. Kitschelt & S. I. Wilkinson (Eds.), *Patrons, Clients, and Policies: Patterns of Democratic Accountability and Political Competition* (pp. 1–49). New York: Cambridge University Press.

Konsorsium Lembaga Pengumpul Pendapat Umum. (2000). *Suara rakyat untuk wakil rakyat laporan akhir survai nasional tentang masalah politik.* [Jakarta]: Konsorsium Lembaga Pengumpul Pendapat Umum.

Kurasawa, A. (2009). Swaying Between State and Community: The Role and Function of RT/RW in Post-Suharto Indonesia. In B. L. Read & R. Pekkanen (Eds.), *Local Organizations and Urban Governance in East and Southeast Asia: Straddling State and Society.* New York: Routledge.

Lally, K. (1993, October 5). Yeltsin Crushes Hard-Line Foes; Rebel Leaders Jailed. *Baltimore Sun.*

Lane, M. (2008). *Unfinished Nation: Indonesia Before and After Suharto.* London: Verso.

Lane, R. E. (1959). *Political Life: Why People Get Involved in Politics.* Glencoe, IL: The Free Press.

Lee, T. (2002). *Mobilizing Public Opinion: Black Insurgency and Racial Attitudes in the Civil Rights Era.* Chicago: University of Chicago Press.

Lembaga Penelitian, P. d. P. E. d. S. (2002). *Hasil Survei Pengumpulan Pendapat Masyarakat Pemilik Telepon di 18 Kota: Laporan Temuan Pokok.* Jakarta: LP3ES.

(2009). *Konferensi Pers: Survei Preferensi Politik Masyarakat Menjelang Pemilu 2009.* Jakarta: LP3ES.

Levi, M., & Stoker, L. (2000). Political Trust and Trustworthiness. *Annual Review of Political Science, 3*, 475–507.

Levistky, S. and Way, L. (2010). *Competitive Authoritarianism: Hybrid Regimes After the Cold War.* New York: Cambridge University Press.

Liddle, R. W. (1978). The 1977 Indonesian Election and New Order Legitimacy. *Southeast Asian Affairs*, 122–138.

(1985). Soeharto's Indonesia: Personal Rule and Political Institutions. *Pacific Affairs, 58*(1), 68–90.

(2001). Indonesia in 2000: A Shaky Start for Democracy. *Asian Survey, 41*(1), 208–220.

(2007). Indonesia: A Muslim-Majority Democracy. In W. P. Shively (Ed.), *Comparative Governance: Political Structure and Diversity Across the Globe*: New York: McGraw Hill Primis.

Liddle, R. W., & Mujani, S. (2007). Leadership, Party, and Religion: Explaining Voting Behavior in Indonesia. *Comparative Political Studies, 40*(7), 832–857.

Lindberg, S. I. (2006). *Democracy and Elections in Africa.* Baltimore: Johns Hopkins University Press.

Linz, J. J. (2000). *Totalitarian and Authoritarian Regimes.* Boulder, CO: Lynne Rienner Publishers.

Linz, J. J., & Stepan, A. (1996). *Problems of Democratic Transition and Consolidation: Southern Europe, South America, and Post-Communist Europe.* Baltimore, MD: The Johns Hopkins University Press.

Lipset, S. M. (1960). *Political Man: The Social Bases of Politics*. Garden City, NY: Doubleday and Company.

Lipset, S. M. (1994). The Social Requisites of Democracy Revisited: 1993 Presidential Address. *American Sociological Review*, 59(1), 1–22.

Lipset, S. M., & Schneider, W. (1983). The Decline of Confidence in American Institutions. *Political Science Quarterly*, 98(3), 379–402.

Logsdon, M. G. (1974). Neighborhood Organization in Jakarta. *Indonesia*, 18, 53–70.

Lukin, A. (2009). Russia's New Authoritarianism and the Post-Soviet Political Ideal. *Post-Soviet Affairs*, 25(1), 66–92.

Lukinova, E., Myagkov, M., & Ordeshook, P. C. (2011). Metastasised Fraud in Russia's 2008 Presidential Election. *Europe-Asia Studies*, 63(4), 603–621.

Lussier, D. (2007). *The Nature of Mass Communist Beliefs in Postcommunist Russian Political Space*. Berkeley Program for Soviet and Post-Soviet Studies Working Paper Series. Berkeley, CA: Institute for Slavic, East European, and Eurasian Studies.

Lussier, D. N., & Fish, M. S. (2012). Indonesia: The Benefits of Civic Engagement. *Journal of Democracy*, 23(1), 70–84.

Lussier, D. N., & McCullaugh, M. E. (2009). Epidemic Breakpoint: Confronting HIV/AIDS in Russia's Regions. *Problems of Post-Communism*, 56(1), 35–46.

Makarkin, A. (2011). The Russian Social Contract and Regime Legitimacy. *International Affairs*, 87(6), 1459–1475.

Malley, M. S. (2003). Indonesia in 2002: The Rising Cost of Inaction. *Asian Survey*, 43(1), 135–146.

Marcoes, L. (2002). Women's Grassroots Movements in Indonesia: A Case Study of the PKK and Islamic Women's Organisations. In K. Robinson & S. Bessell (Eds.), *Women in Indonesia: Gender, Equity and Development* (pp. 187–197). Singapore: Institute of Southeast Asian Studies.

Marples, D. R. (2011). *Russia in the Twentieth Century*. Harlow: Pearson Education Limited.

Marsh, C. (2002). *Russia at the Polls: Voters, Elections, and Democratization*. Washington, D.C.: C.Q. Press.

Marshall, T. (2000). Citizenship and Social Class. In C. Pierson & F. Castles (Eds.), *The Welfare State: A Reader* (pp. 32–41). Cambridge: Polity Press.

Mawuntyas, D., & Wibowo, K. S. (2008). Soekarwo Wins East Java Governor Election. *Tempo Interactive*, (November 12). Retrieved from www.tempointeractive.com

McAllister, I., & White, S. (2008). 'It's the Economy, Comrade!' Parties and Voters in the 2007 Russian Duma Election. *Europe-Asia Studies*, 60(6), 931–957.

McAuley, M. (1992). *Soviet Politics: 1917–1991*. Oxford: Oxford University Press.

McFaul, M. (2001a). *Russia's Unfinished Revolution*. Ithaca, NY: Cornell University Press.

(2001b). Russian Electoral Trends. In Z. Barany & R. G. Moser (Eds.), *Russian Politics: Challenges of Democratization* (pp. 19–63). Cambridge: Cambridge University Press.

(2002). The Fourth Wave of Democracy and Dictatorship: Noncooperative Transitions in the Postcommunist World. *World Politics*, 54, 212–244.

McGowan, B. (1993, October 11). Yeltsin Exerts Authority over Local Councils. *Courier-Mail*.

McLaren, L. M. (2008). *Constructing Democracy in Southern Europe: A Comparative Analysis of Italy, Spain, and Turkey*. New York: Routledge.

McMann, K. (2006). *Economic Autonomy and Democracy: Hybrid Regimes in Russia and Kyrgyzstan*. Cambridge: Cambridge University Press.

Melville, A., & Lapidus, G. W. (Eds.). (1990). *The Glasnost Papers: Voices on Reform from Moscow*. Boulder, CO: Westview Press.

Meyer, G. (2003). Values, Small Life Worlds and Communitarian Orientations: Ambivalent Legacies and Democratic Potentials in Post-Communist Political Cultures. In D. Pollack, J. Jacobs, O. Muller, & G. Pickel (Eds.), *Political Culture in Post-Communist Europe: Attitudes in New Democracies* (pp. 169–179). Burlington, VT: Ashgate.

Midlarsky, M. I. (1998). Democracy and Islam: Implications for Civilizational Conflict and the Democratic Peace. *International Studies Quarterly*, 42(3), 485–511.

Mietzner, M. (2007). Party Financing in Post-Soeharto Indonesia: Between State Subsidies and Political Corruption. *Contemporary Southeast Asia*, 29(2), 238–263.

(2010). Political Conflict Resolution and Democratic Consolidation in Indonesia: The Role of the Constitutional Court. *Journal of East Asian Studies*, 10, 397–424.

Milbrath, L., & Goel, M. L. (1977). *Political Participation* (Second ed.). Chicago: Rand McNally.

Miller, W. E., & Shanks, J. M. (1996). *The New American Voter*. Cambridge, MA: Harvard University Press.

Miller, T. (n.d.) "Parliament, Coverage by Television. In *Encyclopedia of Television*. Retrieved from http://www.museum.tv/eotv/parliamentc.htm.

Mir i Strana (2007). "Mir i Strana // Na Urovne 'Zhigulei' // Kachestvo Gosudarstva v Rossii," *Delo*, January 22, 2007.

Mishler, W., & Rose, R. (2001). What are the Origins of Political Trust?: Testing Institutional and Cultural Theories in Post-Communist Societies. *Comparative Political Studies*, 34(1), 30–62.

Mishler, W., & Willerton, J. P. (2003). The Dynamics of Presidential Popularity in Post-Communist Russia: Cultural Imperatives versus Neo-Institutional Choice? *The Journal of Politics*, 65(1), 111–141.

Mujani, S. (2003). *Religious Democrats: Democratic Culture and Muslim Political Participation in Post-Suharto Indonesia*. (PhD Doctoral Dissertation), Ohio State University, Columbus, OH.

Mujani, S. & Liddle, R. W. (2004). Politics, Islam and Public Opinion. *Journal of Democracy*, 15(1), 109–123.

Mujani, S., & Liddle, R. W. (2010). Personalities, Parties, and Voters. *Journal of Democracy*, 21(2), 35–49.

Murdoch, L. (2001, April 30). Sit Back and Watch, Wahid Urges. *Sydney Morning Herald*, p. 8.

Muslims Protest 'Porn'. (2006, May 22). *Northern Territory News*, p. 14.23.

Myagkov, M., Ordeshook, P. C., & Shakin, D. (2009). *The Forensics of Election Fraud: Russia and Ukraine*. Cambridge: Cambridge University Press.

Nelson, J. M. (1979). *Access to Power: Politics and the Urban Poor in Developing Nations*. Princeton, NJ: Princeton University Press.

Newton, K. (1999). Social and Political Trust in Established Democracies. In P. Norris (Ed.), *Critical Citizens: Global Support for Democratic Governance* (pp. 169–187). New York: Oxford University Press.

(2001). Trust, Social Capital, Civil Society, and Democracy. *International Political Science Review*, 22(2), 201–214.

Nikitina, L., Klimovich, A., Korablyov, N., & Gordeyeva, Y. (2005). It's Their Last Stand: Pensioners and Veterans Won't Give Up Their Benefits Without a Fight. *Current Digest of the Russian Press*, 57(4), 9–10.

Noorani, A. G. (1977). Repression in Indonesia. *Economic and Political Weekly*, 12(44), 1847–1848.

Norris, P. (2007). Political Activism: New Challenges, New Opportunities. In C. Boix & S. C. Stokes (Eds.), *The Oxford Handbook of Comparative Politics* (pp. 628–652). Oxford: Oxford University Press.

(Ed.) (1999). *Critical Citizens: Global Support for Democratic Governance*. New York: Oxford University Press.

O'Brien, K. J., & Li, L. (1995). The Politics of Lodging Complaints in Rural China. *The China Quarterly*, 143, 756–783.

O'Donnell, G., & Schmitter, P. C. (1986). *Transitions from Authoritarian Rule: Tentative Conclusions about Uncertain Democracies*. Baltimore, MD: The Johns Hopkins University Press.

Opposition Protests Reported Across Russia, Regional Turnout Modest. (2012). *BBC Monitoring Former Soviet Union*.

Orttung, R. W. (2004). Business and Politics in the Russian Regions. *Problems of Post-Communism*, 51(2), 48–60.

Orttung, R. W., Lussier, D. N., & Paretskaya, A. (2000). *The Republics and Regions of the Russian Federation: A Guide to Politics, Policies, and Leaders*. Armonk, NY: M.E. Sharpe.

Ottoway, D. B. (1996, December 22, 1996). Croatian Leader Displays Discontent with U.S.; Tudjman, Key Ally in Balkans, Reportedly Blocked Boeing Deal and Criticized American Envoy. *Washington Post*, p. A31.

Papaioannou, E., & Siourounis, G. (2008). Economic and Social Factors Driving the Third Wave of Democratization. *Journal of Comparative Economics*, 36, 365–387.

Parliament Stormed as Wahid Told to Resign. (2000, November 14). *The Advertiser*, p. 21.

Pateman, C. (1970). *Participation and Democratic Theory*. New York: Cambridge University Press.

(1989). The Civic Culture: A Philosophic Critique. In G. A. Almond & S. Verba (Eds.), *The Civic Culture Revisited* (pp. 57–102). Newbury Park, CA: Sage Publications.

Paxton, P. (2002). Social Capital and Democracy: An Interdependent Relationship. *American Sociological Review, 67*(2), 254–277.

Pepinsky, T. B. (2009). *Economic Crises and the Breakdown of Authoritarian Regimes.* New York: Cambridge University Press.

Pereira, D. (1998, October 20). Keeping Up the Tempo. *The Straits Times.*

Perkasa, V., & Hendyito, M. K. (2003). Inventing Participation: The Dynamics of PKK, Arisan and Kerja Bakti in the Context of Urban Java. In N. Yoshihara & R. D. Dwianto (Eds.), *Grass Roots and the Neighborhood Associations: on Japan's Chonaikai and Indonesia's RT/RW* (pp. 122–185). Jakarta: Gramedia Widiasarana.

Plutzer, E. (2002). Becoming a Habitual Voter: Inertia, Resources, and Growth in Young Adulthood. *American Political Science Review, 96*(1), 41–56.

Pribylovskii, Vladimir. (2005). "Chto Takoe 'Upravlyaemaya Demokratiya:' Kontseptsiya, Istoriya, Rossiiskii Opyt," *Demokratiya v Osade,* March 17, 2005, SOVA Center website (www.sova-center.ru).

President Warns Military Not to Harm Protestors. (2001, March 16). *BBC Summary of World Broadcasts.*

Pringle, R. (2010). *Understanding Islam in Indonesia: Politics and Diversity.* Honolulu: University of Hawaii Press.

Przeworski, A. (1991). *Democracy and the Market.* New York: Cambridge University Press.

Przeworski, A., Alvarez, M. E., Cheibub, J. A., & Limongi, F. (2000). *Democracy and Development: Political Institutions and Well-Being in the World, 1950–1990.* New York: Cambridge University Press.

Przeworski, A., & Limongi, F. (1997). Modernization: Theories and Facts. *World Politics, 49*(2), 155–183.

Przeworski, A., & Teune, H. (1970). *The Logic of Comparative Social Inquiry.* New York: Wiley Interscience, John Wiley & Sons.

Puddington, A. (2015). *Freedom in the World 2015.* Retrieved from www .freedomhouse.org.

Putnam, R. D. (1993). *Making Democracy Work: Civic Traditions in Modern Italy.* Princeton: Princeton University Press.

Putnam, R. D. (2000). *Bowling Alone: The Collapse and Revival of American Community.* New York: Simon & Schuster.

Pye, L. (1968). *The Spirit of Chinese Politics.* Cambridge, MA: Massachusetts Institute of Technology Press.

Reddaway, P. (2010). How Much Did Popular Disaffection Contribute to the Collapse of the USSR? In S. Fortescue (Ed.), *Russian Politics: From Lenin to Putin* (pp. 152–184). New York: Palgrave MacMillan.

Reeve, D. (1985). *Golkar of Indonesia: An Alternative to the Party System.* Singapore: Oxford University Press.

Reilly, B. (2007). Electoral Systems and Party Systems in East Asia. *Journal of East Asian Studies, 7*(2), 185–202.

Remington, T. F. (1989). A Socialist Pluralism of Opinions: Glasnost' and Policymaking under Gorbachev. *Russian Review, 48*(3), 271–304.

(2010). Parliament and the Dominant Party Regime. In S. K. Wegren & D. R. Herspring (Eds.), *After Putin's Russia: Past Imperfect, Future Uncertain* (pp. 39–58). Lanham, MD: Rowman & Littlefield.

Remington, T. F., Smith, S. S., Kiewiet, D. R., & Haspel, M. (1994). Transitional Institutions and Parliamentary Alignments in Russia, 1990–1993. In T. F. Remington (Ed.), *Parliaments in Transition* (pp. 163–170). Boulder, CO: Westview.

Resosudarmo, B. P. (2005). Introduction. In B.P. Resosudarmo (Ed.), *The Politics and Economics of Indonesia's Natural Resources* (pp. 1–9). Singapore: ISEAS Publications.

Richter, J. (2008). *Civil Society in the New Authoritarianism* (35). Retrieved from Washington, D.C: http://ceres.georgetown.edu/esp/ponarsmemos/page/55935.html

Ricklefs, M. C. (2008). *A History of Modern Indonesia Since 1200c.* (4th ed.). Stanford, CA: Stanford University Press.

Riker, W. H., & Ordeshook, P. C. (1968). A Theory of the Calculus of Voting. *American Political Science Review*, 62(1), 25–42.

Risse-Kappen, T. (1991). Opinion, Domestic Structure, and Foreign Policy in Liberal Democracies. *World Politics*, 43(4), 479–512.

Roeder, P. G. (1989). Modernization and Participation in the Leninist Developmental Strategy. *American Political Science Review*, 83(3), 859–884.

Roemer, J. E. (1999). Does Democracy Engender Justice. In I. Shapiro & C. Hacker-Cordon (Eds.), *Democracy's Value* (pp. 56–68). New York: Cambridge University Press.

Rose, R. (2008). *New Russia Barometer XVI: United Russia's Duma Victory.* University of Aberdeen Studies in Public Policy No. 442. Aberdeen, Scotland: Centre for the Study of Public Policy.

(2009). *Understanding Post-Communist Transformation: A Bottom Up Approach.* New York: Routledge.

Rose, R., Mishler, W., & Munro, N. (2006). *Russia Transformed: Developing Popular Support for a New Regime.* Cambridge, UK: Cambridge University Press.

Rosenstone, S. J., & Hansen, J. M. (1993). *Mobilization, Participation, and Democracy in America.* New York: Macmillan Publishing Company.

Ross, M. L. (2001). Does Oil Hinder Democracy? *World Politics*, 53(3), 325–361.

Russian TV Programme Breaks New Ground in Opposition Protest Coverage. (2011, December 11). *BBC Monitoring Former Soviet Union.*

Rustow, D. A. (1970). Transitions to Democracy: Toward a Dynamic Model. *Comparative Politics*, 2(3), 337–363.

Ryter, L. (2001). Pemuda Pancasila: The Last Loyalist Free Men of Suharto's Order. In B. Anderson (Ed.), *Violence and the State in Suharto's Indonesia* (pp. 124–155). Ithaca, NY: Cornell University Press.

Schmitter, P. C., & Karl, T. L. (1991). What Democracy Is ... and Is Not. *Journal of Democracy*, 2(3), 75–88.

Schwarz, A. (1997, July-August 1997). Indonesia after Suharto. *Foreign Affairs*, 76, 119–134.

Sims, C. (2001, January 30). Hints of Graft by Indonesian President. *New York Times*, p. 14.23.

Smidt, C. (2003). Introduction. In C. Smidt (Ed.), *Religion as Social Capital: Producing the Common Good* (pp. 1–18). Waco, TX: Baylor University Press.

Smith, B. (2008). The Origins of Regional Autonomy in Indonesia: Experts and the Marketing of Political Interests. *Journal of East Asian Studies, 8*(2), 211–234.

Soemardjan, S. (1963). Some Social and Cultural Implications of Indonesia's Unplanned and Planned Development. *The Review of Politics, 25*(1), 64–90.

Some, W., Hafidz, W., & Sauter, G. (2009). Renovation Not Relocation: the Work of Paguyuban Warga Strenkali (PWS) in Indonesia. *Environment and Urbanization, 21*(2), 463–475.

Sperling, V. (1999). *Organizing Women in Contemporary Russia: Engendering Transition.* New York: Cambridge University Press.

Stoner-Weiss, K. (2002). Central Governing Incapacity and the Weakness of Political Parties: Russian Democracy in Disarray. *Publius, 32*(2), 125–146.

Sulistyo, H. (2002). Electoral Politics in Indonesia: A Hard Way to Democratize. In A. Croissant, G. Bruns, & M. John (Eds.), *Electoral Politics in Southeast and East Asia: A Comparative Perspective* (pp. 75–99). Singapore: Friedrich Ebert Stiftung.

Sundstrom, L. M. (2006). *Funding Civil Society: Foreign Assistance and NGO Development in Russia.* Stanford, CA: Stanford University Press.

Tarrow, S. (2010). The Strategy of Paired Comparison: Toward a Theory of Practice. *Comparative Political Studies, 43*(2), 230–259.

Thireau, I., & Linshan, H. (2003). The Moral Universe of Aggrieved Chinese Workers: Workers' Appeals to Arbitration Committees and Letters and Visits Offices. *The China Quarterly, 50*(7), 83–103.

Thompson, E. C. (1999). *Indonesia in Transition: The 1999 Presidential Elections* (9). Retrieved from www.nbr.org

Thousands of Indonesians Demonstrate against Labour Law Changes. (2006, April 6). *BBC Monitoring Asia Pacific.*

Thousands of Indonesians Demonstrate in Demand of Anti-Porn Law. (2006, June 7). *BBC Monitoring Asia Pacific.*

Tilly, C., & Tarrow, S. (2007). *Contentious Politics.* Boulder, CO: Paradigm Publishers.

Treisman, D. (2011). Presidential Popularity in a Hybrid Regime. *American Journal of Political Science, 55*(2).

Tsai, K. S. (2007). *Capitalism Without Democracy: The Private Sector in Contemporary China.* Ithaca, NY: Cornell University Press.

Uhlin, A. (1997). *Indonesia and the "Third Wave of Democratization".* New York: St. Martin's Press.

Ukroshchenie Stroptivykh. (2002, October 5). *Novye Izvestiia.*

United Nations Development Program. Human Development Indicators. Retrieved February 3, 2011.

United Nations Development Program. (2009). *Human Development Report 2009.* Retrieved from http://hdr.undp.org/.

United States Department of State. (2010). Background Note: Indonesia. Retrieved from www.state.gov.

Verba, S., & Nie, N. H. (1972). *Participation in America: Political Democracy and Social Equality.* Chicago: University of Chicago Press.

Verba, S., Nie, N. H., & Kim, J.-o. (1978). *Participation and Political Equality.* Chicago: University of Chicago Press.

Verba, S., Schlozman, K. L., & Brady, H. E. (1995). *Voice and Equality: Civic Voluntarism in American Politics.* Cambridge, MA: Harvard University Press.

Walker, S. (2011, December 14, 2011). Why the Russian Revolution is Being Televised at Last. *The Independent.*

Webber, D. (2006). A Consolidated Patrimonial Democracy? Democratization in Post-Suharto Indonesia. *Democratization, 30*(3), 396–420.

White, S. (2005). Political Disengagement in Post-Communist Russia: A Qualitative Study. *Europe-Asia Studies, 57*(8), 1121–1142.

(2011). *Understanding Russian Politics.* Cambridge: Cambridge University Press.

White, S., & McAllister, I. (2004). Dimensions of Disengagement in Postcommunist Russia. *Journal of Communist Studies and Transition Politics, 20*(1), 81–97.

Whitmore, B. (2009). In Annual Call-In Show, Putin Leaves Open a Return to the Presidency. *Radio Free Europe/Radio Liberty.*

Wieringa, S. (1992). Ibu or the Beast: Gender Interests in Two Indonesian Women's Organizations. *Feminist Review, 41,* 98–113.

Woodard, C. (1996, December 10). As in Nearby Serbia, Dissent Rumbles in Croatia. *Christian Science Monitor,* p. 14.23.

Woods, H. F. (1945, 1949). *American Sayings: Famous Phrases, Slogans and Aphorisms.* New York: Duell, Sloane and Pierce.

World Bank. World Development Indicators. Retrieved January 6, 2011 www.worldbank.org

Yorke, A. (2003). Business and Politics in Krasnoyarsk Krai. *Europe-Asia Studies, 55*(2), 241–262.

Index

Abdillah (mayor of Medan, Indonesia), 272
Aceh conflict (Indonesia), 72–73
Ahmadiyah Muslims in Indonesia, 274
Almond, Gabriel, 196, 200–201, 233
American National Election Studies, 200
Arab Spring (2011), 277
arisan (rotating credit associations in Indonesia), 169, 189
Asian Financial Crisis (1997–98), 53, 56
Association of Residents of the Surabaya Strenkali (PWS), 179, 181, 187–88
authoritarianism
    backsliding into, 1–3, 7, 10–11, 17, 41, 58, 61–67, 76, 78, 82, 86, 137, 150, 159, 219, 236, 253–54, 261, 264, 270, 275–76, 278
    civil society engagement under, 148
    contacting of public officials under, 109–12
    elites and, 15–16
    Indonesia's New Order regime and, 3, 6, 49–52, 254
    institutions under, 42
    legacies of, 6–7, 40, 85–86, 119–22, 173–76, 184, 199–200
    political efficacy under, 197
    political participation under, 6, 15–16, 80–82, 85–86
    protests as a means of overthrowing, 198–99
    socialization under, 21, 82, 85–86
    in the Soviet Union, 44–45, 254

Suharto and, 6–7, 49–50, 52
Sukarno and, 49–50

Bali (Indonesia), 74–75
Batak ethnic group (Indonesia)
    community organizations among, 107, 168–69
    interviews with members of, 38–39, 107, 165n7, 177, 214–15, 223
    in Medan, 30, 38–39, 168–69, 173n16, 177–78
    sociability levels among, 173n16
Beslan school massacre (Russia, 2004), 63, 257
boycotts, 47, 63, 94–95, 100
Brady, Henry
    civic skills defined by, 185
    civic voluntarism model and, 147, 150–51, 177, 189
    on measures of political efficacy, 200
    on resources for political participation, 177
    Soviet public opinion studies and, 47
Brazil, 9–10, 270
bupati (local lords in Indonesia), 48

campaign work. *See* political campaign work
Center for the Study of Islam and Society (PPIM) survey data, 96, 98, 100
Central Electoral Commission (Indonesia), 73

Central Electoral Commission (Russia), 229
Charter 77 movement, 80
China, 13, 15, 84n4
The Civic Culture (Almond and Verba), 196, 233
Civic Forum (Czech Republic), 55
civic skills
　civic voluntarism model and, 151, 157, 185
　civil society engagement's development of, 19, 148, 151, 153, 157, 169, 177, 185–89, 192, 194, 215, 265
　definition of, 185
　educational attainment and, 138, 185
　elite-constraining political behavior and, 188, 192, 194
　in Indonesia, 147, 151, 177, 185, 188–89, 194
　leadership training and, 177, 185–88, 192
　political participation facilitated by, 185–87, 215
　in Russia, 177, 185, 188–89
　work experience and, 185
civic voluntarism model (Verba-Schlozman-Brady)
　advanced democracies and, 150–51
　capacity and, 176–77
　civic skills development and, 151, 157, 185
　connectedness and, 176–77, 189
　democratization and, 147, 151
　in Indonesia, 147, 151, 176–77, 192
　motivation and, 176–77
　in Russia, 147, 151, 176–77, 192
civil society engagement
　in advanced democracies, 148, 150
　associations' autonomy from the state and, 153, 182
　association types and, 155–57, 265
　authoritarian legacies' impact on, 173–76, 184
　in authoritarian societies, 148, 174
　civic skills development and, 19, 148, 151, 153, 157, 169, 177, 185–89, 192, 194, 215, 265
　definition of, 19, 148
　democracy and, 24, 28, 147–50
　democratization and, 15, 19–20, 60, 148–51, 153–54, 157, 191, 265, 267, 269–70
　education levels' impact on, 138–39, 170

elite-constraining political participation and, 2, 18–20, 128, 131, 148–51, 176, 265–67
gender as a factor influencing, 126, 134
global averages of, 148, 155
in Indonesia, 19, 21, 108, 113, 124, 127–28, 130–40, 147–48, 150–51, 154–57, 164–81, 183, 185–92, 194, 203–4, 212, 215, 240–41, 265–67, 269, 273
labor unions and, 60, 153, 156–58, 160
measures of, 124, 148, 151–55
money as a resource for, 180–85, 265–66
neighborhood associations and, 167–68, 265
organizational formality and, 152–53
political efficacy and, 21, 130, 136, 139, 149, 203–4, 212
political participation and, 2, 18–21, 24, 118, 125, 127–31, 135–37, 139–40, 147–53, 172, 176, 191, 238, 265, 267
political trust and, 21, 130, 240–41
professional organizations and, 156, 170, 179
religious organizations and, 156–57, 162–63, 165–67, 171–72, 177–79, 185–89, 215, 265, 269–70, 273
in Russia, 19, 21, 60, 86, 124, 127–28, 131–40, 147–48, 151, 154–64, 173, 175–83, 188–92, 194, 203–4, 265–67, 269
sociability and, 147, 153, 173
social capital and, 153–54
social networks and, 19, 113, 151, 154, 172–73, 176, 190–92
time as a resource for, 177–80, 265–66
Tocqueville on, 147–49, 153–54
World Values Survey data on, 154–59, 163
Colton, Timothy, 26n6, 89
Communist Party (China), 15
Communist Party (Russia; KPRF)
　civic skills development and, 188
　elections for parliament (1995) and, 59
　elections for president (1996) and, 59–60
　in Krasnoyarsk Krai, 115, 211
　political minority status of, 64, 114
　public receptions held by, 211
　in Tatarstan, 105, 114–15
　youth wing of, 105

Communist Party (Soviet Union; CPSU)
Central Committee of, 44–45, 47
civil society organizations administered
by, 164
collapse of the Soviet Union and, 158, 164
contacting officials in, 81, 109–11
coup attempt (1991) by hardline
members of, 54, 84
elections for Russian president (1991)
and, 53–54
general secretary of, 45, 109–10
Komsomol youth organization in, 46,
164, 174
leadership training and, 177, 188
Politburo of, 45–46
political monopoly of, 3, 44–45, 47, 60,
89, 121, 204, 249, 251
political repression and coercion by,
6–7, 45
Communist Party of Indonesia (PKI),
48–49, 70, 156
Communist Youth League (Komsomol;
Soviet Union), 46, 164, 174
Congress of People's Deputies (Soviet
Union's parliament), 46–47, 89, 218,
242, 251
Constitutional Court (Indonesia), 70,
73–74, 222, 274
contacting public officials
age as factor influencing, 127, 141–42
in authoritarian regimes, 109–12
civic skills and, 187, 192
civil society engagement's impact on,
127–28, 132–33, 135–36, 141–42
in Communist China, 15
education levels' impact on, 113, 127,
129, 132, 139, 141–42, 172
elite-enabling nature of, 2, 18, 79, 83–84,
86, 109, 112, 117, 135, 139, 230, 267
gender as factor influencing, 127, 129,
132, 134, 139, 141–42
in Indonesia, 85, 96–102, 107–9, 115–16,
127–29, 132–33, 135–37, 142, 172,
203–4, 215, 238
interview data regarding, 103–4
particularized *versus* social forms of,
107–9, 111–12
political efficacy and, 104–6, 122,
127, 133, 141–42, 194, 197, 203–4,
208–12, 215, 266
political trust and, 238

in Russia, 89, 92–93, 101–2, 104–11,
117, 120, 122, 127–29, 132–36, 139,
141, 192, 194, 197, 203–4, 208–12,
230, 238, 266–67
in the Soviet Union, 81, 85, 88–89, 93,
109–10, 120
contentious politics. *See also* protests
age as factor influencing, 127, 145–46
in authoritarian countries, 79
civil society engagement's impact on, 19,
127–28, 132–34, 137, 145–47, 151
conventional political participation's
correlation with, 93, 98, 106, 122
democracy and, 271
education levels' impact on, 113, 127,
129, 132, 134, 145–46
elite-constraining nature of, 18, 43, 83,
86, 98, 111, 113, 116–17, 267, 277
examples of types of, 79
gender as a factor influencing, 127, 132,
134, 145–46
in Indonesia, 41, 51, 74–76, 96–102,
106–8, 112–13, 117, 122, 127–29,
132–33, 135–37, 139, 147, 151,
172–73, 192, 203, 212–14, 238, 241,
262, 266–67
political efficacy and, 127–28, 133,
145–46, 194, 198–99, 203, 212–14, 266
political trust and, 127–28, 139, 145–46,
238, 240, 262
in Russia, 67, 76, 93–95, 101–2, 104–5,
107, 111, 127, 132–33, 135–37, 145,
194, 203, 238, 275, 278
Corruption Eradication Commission (KPK,
Indonesia), 271
Council of the City of Surabaya (volunteer
organization), 179, 181, 187, 189
Crescent Star Party (PBB; Indonesia), 72
Croatia, 62
Czech Republic, 55, 122

Dahl, Robert, 7–8
democracy. *See also* democratization
civil liberties and, 7–9
civil society engagement and, 24, 28,
147–50
contentious politics and, 271
Dahl's criteria for, 7–8
elections and, 2, 7, 43, 195, 254
good governance and, 41–42
"guided democracy" and, 3, 48–49, 61

democracy (*cont.*)
  institutionalization of the rules of, 8, 43
  legitimacy and, 262–63
  the middle class and, 12, 24
  political trust and, 233–34
  socioeconomic development and, 7, 11–14
Democratic Party (PD; Indonesia), 72, 74
Democratic Russia Movement (DRM),
  53–54
democratization. *See also* democracy
  authoritarian backsliding and, 1–3, 7,
    10–11, 17, 41, 58, 61–67, 76, 78, 82,
    86, 137, 150, 236, 253–54, 261, 264,
    270, 275–76, 278
  civic voluntarism model and, 147, 151
  civil liberties and, 11, 14
  civil society engagement and, 15, 19–20,
    60, 148–51, 153–54, 157, 191, 265,
    267, 269–70
  corruption and, 4–5, 271–74
  cross-national statistical analysis of, 22–23
  democratization theory and, 2–8, 11–12,
    14, 22, 28, 264, 268–69, 278
  "deviant" cases in, 2–3, 11, 22, 264,
    269, 278
  elections and, 3, 8, 11, 14, 16–17, 82, 85,
    195, 198–99, 216, 225–26, 229–32,
    243, 254–61, 263, 268
  elite-constraining political participation
    and, 2, 5, 11, 16–20, 41–42, 78, 82,
    86, 118, 138, 215–16, 264–65,
    267–68, 277–78
  elite-enabling political participation and,
    5, 42–43, 78, 83–84, 86, 112, 118,
    264, 268
  Freedom House scores as measure of,
    1, 10
  hydrocarbons and, 4–5
  independent statehood history and, 2–5,
    14, 28, 264
  in Indonesia, 2–6, 10–11, 21, 24–25, 28,
    40–42, 67–78, 85, 96, 100, 102, 113,
    118, 121, 151, 171, 191, 207, 225–26,
    254, 261–64, 267–74, 278
  intervals between elections and, 17, 82,
    268
  the middle class and, 13, 24
  modernization and, 4, 22–23
  Muslim-majority countries and, 4–6
  political efficacy and, 19–20, 194–200,
    205, 231–32, 265, 267, 269

  political institutions and, 8, 11, 14–15,
    268
  political opportunity structure and, 21,
    118, 150–51, 191–92
  political trust and, 19–20, 28, 232–36,
    261–62, 265–67, 269
  post-Communist countries and, 6
  regionally focused case studies of,
    22–23
  religions and, 5
  in Russia, 2–7, 10–11, 21, 24–25, 28,
    40–42, 54, 58–63, 76, 78, 85, 93, 102,
    118, 151, 164, 175–76, 191–92, 205,
    207, 225–26, 229, 243, 251, 253–54,
    261–64, 268–70, 274–78
  socioeconomic development and, 2–3,
    12–14, 22–23, 264
  in the Soviet Union, 45–46
  "third wave" of, 1–2, 5, 8, 12, 23,
    269–70, 278
demonstrations. *See* protests
Deripaska, Oleg, 110
deviant-case selection, 2, 22
DPD. *See* Regional Representatives Council
  (Indonesia)
DPR. *See* House of Representatives
  (Indonesia)
Duch, Raymond, 88
Dutch East Indies Company, 48
dwifungsi ("twin functions") doctrine
  (Indonesia), 50, 69, 71

East Asian Barometer (EAB)
  civil society engagement measured by,
    124, 127–28, 132–33
  contacting measured by, 97–99, 101,
    127–28, 132–33, 142
  contentious politics acts measured by,
    97–101, 127, 132–33
  political efficacy measured by, 124–25,
    127–28, 138, 204–7
  political participation measured by,
    87–88, 100, 123, 127–30, 132–33,
    142, 144
  political party–development work
    measured by, 97–99, 101, 127,
    132–33, 144
  political trust measured by, 125, 127,
    236, 247–49
  predicted probability data from,
    131–37

East Java gubernatorial elections (2008), 222–23, 231
Easton, David, 234
Egypt, 1, 277
Election Law and the Law on Political Parties (Russia), 63–64
elections
  authoritarian regimes and, 85, 195, 199–200, 216
  clientelism in, 115–16, 272–74
  democracy and, 2, 7, 43, 195, 254
  democratization and, 3, 8, 11, 14, 16–17, 82, 85, 195, 198–99, 216, 225–26, 229–32, 243, 254–61, 263, 268
  elite-constraining *versus* elite-enabling forms of, 84, 216, 231
  for Indonesian parliament (1955), 48
  for Indonesian parliament (1971), 49
  for Indonesian parliament (1997), 52
  for Indonesian parliament (1999), 57, 216, 225, 255
  for Indonesian parliament (2004), 72, 216, 248
  for Indonesian parliament (2009), 74, 187, 216, 222–23
  for Indonesian parliament (2014), 216
  for Indonesian presidency (1968), 49
  for Indonesian presidency (1998), 52, 56
  for Indonesian presidency (1999), 57, 255
  for Indonesian presidency (2004), 3, 72, 217, 225–26, 248
  for Indonesian presidency (2009), 74, 216
  for Indonesian presidency (2014), 216, 274
  Indonesians' attitudes toward, 196, 199–200, 212, 216–17, 221–24, 230–31, 254–57, 261, 263, 266, 273
  political efficacy and, 20, 28, 194–200, 209, 212, 216–32, 266
  political trust in, 241, 255–62
  for Russian parliament (1993), 59, 205, 216, 251
  for Russian parliament (1995), 59, 90–91, 216, 251–52
  for Russian parliament (1999), 90–92, 251–52
  for Russian parliament (2003), 62, 90–91, 251–52
  for Russian parliament (2007), 65
  for Russian parliament (2011), 65, 275

  for Russian presidency (1991), 53–54, 199, 205, 216, 225
  for Russian presidency (1996), 59–60, 90–91, 225–26, 228
  for Russian presidency (2000), 42, 90–92, 225–26
  for Russian presidency (2004), 42, 58, 63, 225–26
  for Russian presidency (2008), 65, 225–26
  for Russian presidency (2012), 65, 225–26, 275–76
  Russians' attitudes toward, 196–97, 199, 216–21, 224–25, 227–31, 254–55, 257–61, 263, 266
  in the Soviet Union (1987), 45–46
  in the Soviet Union (1989), 46, 89, 216, 218
  in the Soviet Union (1990), 53, 89, 251
elite-constraining political participation
  in authoritarian countries, 16
  civil society engagement and, 2, 18–20, 128, 131, 148–51, 176, 265–67
  democratization and, 2, 5, 11, 16–20, 41–42, 78, 82, 86, 118, 138, 215–16, 264–65, 267–68, 277–78
  elections and, 17, 74, 84, 86, 114, 216, 231, 266, 277
  in Indonesia, 5, 17–20, 41, 44, 68–69, 74–78, 86–87, 96–98, 103, 108–9, 112–18, 122–23, 126, 131, 135, 138–39, 147, 150, 177, 188, 191–92, 194, 212, 215–16, 230–31, 247, 261, 264–65, 267, 269
  political campaign work and, 18, 83–84, 114
  political efficacy and, 2, 19–20, 128, 131, 194, 196–97, 212, 215–16, 231, 265–67
  political party–development work and, 18–20, 43, 83–84, 86, 96, 98, 114, 117, 128, 177, 267, 277
  political trust and, 2, 19–20, 247, 261, 265, 267
  predictions regarding, 130–37
  in Russia, 44, 63, 66–67, 106, 117, 119, 128, 131, 215, 230, 265, 267, 276
elite-enabling political participation
  contacting public officials as, 2, 18, 79, 83–84, 86, 109, 112, 117, 135, 139, 230, 267

elite-enabling political participation (*cont.*)
  democratization and, 5, 42–43, 78, 83–84,
    86, 112, 118, 264, 268
  elections and, 84, 216, 231
  petition signing and, 95, 109
  political campaign work and, 84
  political efficacy and, 139, 194, 197, 266
  political party–development work and,
    18, 84, 91, 93, 267
  in Russia, 5, 18, 21, 41, 67, 78, 83, 86,
    93, 106, 109–12, 117–18, 122, 126,
    135, 139, 230–31, 264–66, 268–69
elites. *See also* elite-constraining political
    participation; elite-enabling political
    participation
  in authoritarian regimes, 15–16
  democratic institutions and, 8, 15, 17,
    21, 63
  preservation of political power by,
    15–16
  resources of, 18, 42
  in Russia, 60, 63, 66–67, 78, 86, 106, 194
Equal Rights and Lawfulness (Russian civil
    society organization), 164

Family Welfare Groups (PKK; Indonesia),
    167–69, 180
Federation Council (Russian parliament's
    upper house), 56, 60–61
Federation of Independent Trade Unions of
    Russia (FNPR), 156–57
Fish, M. Steven, 5, 54, 198
Freedom House scores
  for civil liberties, 9–10, 58, 67–68, 274
  decline in global freedoms measured
    by, 1
  for Indonesia, 9–10, 67–68, 270, 274
  for political rights, 9–10, 58, 67–68, 270
  for Russia, 9–10, 58, 67, 270
  for the Soviet Union, 58

Gazprom, 62
Ghana, 270
Gibson, James L., 88
glasnost' (political opening in the Soviet
    Union), 45, 58, 164
Golkar Party (Indonesia)
  East Java protests (2001) and, 68
  elections for parliament (1971) and, 49
  elections for parliament (1997) and, 52
  elections for parliament (1999) and, 57

elections for parliament (2004) and, 248
elections for parliament (2009) and, 74
elections for president (1999) and, 57,
    255
elections for president (2009) and, 74
"functional groups" model and, 49–50
New Order era hegemony of, 50–51, 81,
    85, 121, 223–24
origins of, 49, 71
public goods provision by, 190
Suharto and, 49, 56, 121, 223
Gorbachev, Mikhail, 45–47
gotong-royong (mutual aid groups in
    Indonesia), 169–70, 178, 187, 189
guided democracy
  Putin and, 61
  Sukarno and, 3, 48–49
Gus Dur. *See* Wahid, Abdurrahman

Habibie, B.J., 56–57, 255
Hale, Henry, 26n6, 89, 120
House of Representatives (DPR;
    Indonesian lower house of parliament)
  elections (1997) for, 52
  elections (1999) for, 57, 216, 225, 255
  elections (2004) for, 72, 216, 248
  elections (2009) for, 74, 187, 216,
    222–23
  executive-legislative balance and,
    69–71
  Indonesian election laws and, 121–22
  New Order-era elections to, 50
  People's Consultative Assembly (MPR)
    and, 70
  political trust in, 142, 144, 146, 238–39,
    241, 246–48, 261
  Wahid corruption investigations by,
    68–69
Howard, Marc, 161
Huntington, Samuel, 1, 8, 198, 225–26

India, 9–10, 155
Indonesia. *See also* Medan (Indonesia);
    New Order; Surabaya (Indonesia)
  Aceh conflict in, 72–73
  age demographics in, 138
  anti-pornography law proposal (2006)
    in, 74–75
  armed forces in, 50–51, 69, 71
  Asian Financial Crisis (1997–98) and,
    53, 56

attitudes toward elections in, 196,
199–200, 212, 216–17, 221–24,
230–31, 254–57, 261, 263, 266, 273
authoritarian legacy in, 6, 40, 173–74,
176, 199
boycotts in, 100
case selection criteria and, 25
charitable giving in, 177, 180–81, 183,
185, 192, 265–66
Chinese ethnic community in, 70
Christians in, 30, 165, 274
civil liberties in, 40, 57, 67, 69–70,
72–74, 271, 274
civil society engagement in, 19, 21, 108,
113, 124, 127–28, 130–40, 147–48,
150–51, 154–57, 164–81, 183, 185–92,
194, 203–4, 212, 215, 240–41, 265–67,
269, 273
colonial era in, 4–5, 40, 47–48
constitutional amendments (1999–2002)
in, 67, 69–70
constitution (1945) of, 67
contacting of public officials in, 85,
96–102, 107–9, 115–16, 127–29,
132–33, 135–37, 142, 172, 203–4,
215, 238
contentious political behavior in, 41, 51,
74–76, 96–102, 106–8, 112–13, 117,
122, 127–29, 132–33, 135–37, 139,
147, 151, 172–73, 192, 203, 212–14,
238, 241, 262, 266–67
corruption in, 4–5, 68–69, 270–72
decentralization reforms in, 70–73, 254,
271–73
democratization in, 2–6, 10–11, 21,
24–25, 28, 40–42, 67–78, 85, 96, 100,
102, 113, 118, 121, 151, 171, 191,
207, 225–26, 254, 261–64, 267–74,
278
as "deviant case" of democratization,
2–3, 11, 22, 264, 269, 278
direct presidential elections established
(2002) in, 70, 255–56
direct regional elections established
(2001) in, 70, 256–57
educational attainment levels in, 4, 13,
19, 113n24, 134, 138, 163, 185
election laws in, 121–22
elections for parliament (1955) in, 48
elections for parliament (1971) in, 49
elections for parliament (1997) in, 52

elections for parliament (1999) in, 57,
216, 225, 255
elections for parliament (2009) in, 74,
187, 216, 222–23
elections for parliament (2014) in, 216
elections for president (1968) in, 49
elections for president (1998) in, 52, 56
elections for president (1999) in, 57,
255
elections for president (2004) in, 3, 72,
217, 225–26, 248
elections for president (2009) in, 74, 216
elections for president (2014) in, 216–17
electoral clientelism in, 115–16, 272–74
elite-constraining political participation
in, 5, 17–20, 41, 44, 68–69, 74–78,
86–87, 96–98, 103, 108–9, 112–18,
122–23, 126, 131, 135, 138–39, 147,
150, 177, 188, 191–92, 194, 212,
215–16, 230–31, 247, 261, 264–65,
267, 269
executive-legislative balance in, 69–71,
73, 77
Freedom House scores for, 9–10, 67–68,
270, 274
gender demographics in, 138
geography of, 25
independence from Dutch rule and, 3,
5, 48
International Monetary Fund (IMF) loan
(1997) to, 53
interviews from, 27, 30–33, 37–39, 103,
106–8, 113–14, 134, 164–69, 171–73,
175–78, 181, 183, 186–87, 189, 201,
207–8, 213–15, 219, 222–24, 233,
235–39, 241, 257, 272–73
judiciary in, 70, 72–73
keterbukaan (political openness)
campaign (1990s) in, 51, 67, 171
labor laws in, 75
labor unions in, 51, 75, 156
mass killings (1965) in, 3, 49
middle class' absence from, 12
Muslim-majority status of, 4, 6, 22, 96,
270, 278
natural resource endowment in, 4–5
neighborhood associations in, 167–68,
170, 172, 177, 189, 240, 273
Papua conflict in, 74
petition signing in, 97–100, 108n22,
187, 203, 213

Indonesia (*cont.*)
  political campaign rally attendance in,
    96–99, 108, 113–14
  political campaign work in, 96–99, 102,
    108, 113–14, 127
  political efficacy levels in, 20–21, 124–25,
    127, 130–31, 133, 136–40, 142, 144,
    146–47, 192, 194–99, 201–9, 212–17,
    221–26, 230–32, 266–67, 269
  political party–development work in,
    19–20, 71–72, 96–99, 101–2, 108,
    112–15, 117, 121–22, 132–37, 144,
    147, 177, 180, 183, 194, 203, 212–13,
    238, 262, 267
  political party membership levels in, 72,
    77, 114, 156
  political trust levels in, 20–21, 125,
    127–28, 130–31, 138–40, 144,
    146–47, 192, 232–33, 235, 237–42,
    245–49, 253–57, 261–62, 266–67, 269
  price controls in, 13
  protests (1974 and 1978) in, 171
  protests (1996) in, 52
  protests (1998) in, 3, 56, 171, 214
  protests (1999) in, 255
  protests (2000–2001) in, 68–69
  protests (2006) in, 74–75
  religious minorities in, 74, 165, 274
  religious organizations in, 156–57,
    164–67, 171–72, 175, 180, 185–86,
    265, 269–70, 273 (See also *specific
    organizations*)
  religious service attendance levels in, 269
  sociability levels in, 148, 159–60, 164,
    169, 173, 194
  social networks in, 176, 189, 191–92, 265
  socioeconomic development in, 2–4, 13,
    19, 22, 28, 123, 181, 184, 278
  students and student organizations in,
    75, 106–7, 112–13, 170–73, 187–88,
    213
  voter turnout in, 199, 221, 266
Indonesian Democratic Party (PDI). *See
  also* Indonesian Democratic Party of
  Struggle (PDI-P)
  elections for parliament (1997) and, 52
  origins of, 50, 71
  political party–development work by,
    121
  political restrictions and repression
    against, 50, 121

  protests at headquarters (1996) of, 52
  Sukarnoputri's leadership of, 52
Indonesian Democratic Party of Struggle
  (PDI-P), 255
  in East Java, 115, 183
  elections for parliament (1999) and, 57,
    225, 255
  elections for parliament (2004) and, 72,
    248
  elections for parliament (2009) and, 74
  elections for president (1999) and, 57,
    255
  elections for president (2009) and, 74
  political party–development work by,
    121, 183
  Sukarnoputri's leadership of, 57
Indonesian Nationalist Party (PNI), 48
Inglehart, Ronald, 149, 233
Islamic Students Association (HMI), 171

Jokowi (Joko Widodo), 274
Justice Party (PK; Indonesia), 71–72

Kalla, Jusuf, 74
Kaplan, Cynthia, 47
Katznelson, Ira, 11
Kazan (Russia)
  attitudes toward elections in, 219–20,
    231
  case selection criteria and, 25, 29
  civil society engagement in, 178
  contacting public officials in, 104, 108,
    210–12
  contentious politics in, 111
  elections in, 226–28, 230
  income inequality in, 162
  interviews from, 26–27, 30–31, 35, 39,
    103–4, 106, 111, 161–62, 164, 178,
    188, 208–12, 219–20, 224, 226–28,
    230, 237, 242, 258
  Muslims in, 29, 35, 39
  Orthodox Christians in, 35, 39
  petition signing in, 106
  political campaign work in, 105
  political efficacy levels in, 208–12,
    219–20, 224, 226–28, 230
  political party–development work and,
    188
  political trust levels in, 237, 242–44, 258
  Russian cultural movement activists in,
    164, 211–12

sociability levels in, 161–62
student organizations in, 164
as Tatarstan's regional capital, 29
Yabloko Party in, 211
Keio University Research Survey of
Political Society, 26, 202–3, 216, 218
kelurahan (city government unit in
Indonesia), 30, 241
keterbukaan (Indonesian campaign for
political openness, 1990s), 51, 67, 171
Khasbulatov, Ruslan, 55
Khloponin, Aleksandr, 228–29, 259n5
Khodorkovsky, Mikhail, 276
Khofifah (gubernatorial candidate in East
Java), 222
Kim, Jae-on, 83, 111
Komsomol (Soviet Communist youth
organization), 46, 164, 174
KPK. *See* Corruption Eradication
Commission (Indonesia)
Krasnoyarsk (Russia)
attitudes toward elections in, 219–21,
224, 231
case selection criteria and, 25, 29
charitable giving in, 182
civil society engagement in, 180–82
contacting public officials in, 104–5,
108–11, 210–11
elections in, 226, 228–30
interviews from, 27, 31, 36, 39, 103–6,
109–11, 161–62, 180–81, 188,
208–12, 219–21, 224, 226, 228–30,
237, 242, 258–59
Orthodox Christians in, 36, 39
petition signing in, 106
political efficacy levels in, 208–12,
219–21, 224, 226, 228–30
political party–development work and,
188
political trust levels in, 237, 242–44,
258–59
as regional capital, 29
sociability levels in, 161–62
United Russia Party in, 210
Krasnoyarsk Krai (Russian regional
government)
gubernatorial elections in, 226, 228–31,
259n5
Krasnoyarsk as capital of, 29
Liberal Democratic Party in, 115,
210–11

political party–development work and,
184
political party membership numbers
from, 115
Putin's intervention in, 229
Kuznetsov, Lev, 259n5

labor unions
civil society engagement and, 60, 153,
156–58, 160
in Indonesia, 51, 75, 156
in Russia, 54–55, 60, 156–58, 160
Lane, Robert, 196, 200
Law on Legislative Elections (Indonesia,
2008), 73
Law on Regional Autonomy (Indonesia,
2004), 72
Lebed, Aleksandr, 228–29
legitimacy, 20, 234, 262–63
Liberal Democratic Party of Russia (LDPR)
in Krasnoyarsk Krai, 115, 210–11
party development work and, 188
public receptions held by, 210–11
Lipset, Seymour Martin, 11–12
Lubis, Ramli, 272

Madura Island (Indonesia), 222
Makarkin, Aleksei, 260
marga (Batak ethnic kinship groups),
168–69, 215
Masyumi Party (Indonesia), 48, 186n21
McFaul, Michael, 198
Medan (Indonesia)
attitudes toward elections in, 219,
222–24, 231
Batak ethnic group in, 30, 38–39,
168–69, 173n16, 177–78
case selection criteria and, 25, 29–30
civil society engagement in, 167–69, 175,
177–78, 186–87, 189
contacting public officials in, 107–8
electoral clientelism in, 273
ethnic and religious diversity of, 38,
165n7
interviews from, 27, 30–31, 33, 38,
103, 106–8, 113–14, 165n7, 167–69,
173n16, 175, 177–78, 186–87, 189,
208, 213–15, 219, 222–24, 237–38,
241, 272–73
mayoral corruption scandal (2008) in,
272–73

Medan (Indonesia) (cont.)
  neighborhood organizations in, 168
  political campaign work in, 113–14
  political efficacy levels in, 208, 213–15,
    219, 222–24, 231
  political trust levels in, 237–38, 240–41
  as regional capital, 30
  religious organizations in, 167, 177–78,
    186–87, 189
Medvedev, Dmitrii, 58, 65, 225, 237
Megawati Sukarnoputri. See Sukarnoputri,
    Megawati
Memorial (Russian human rights
    organization), 179–81
Michigan Election Studies, 200–201
Minnikhanov, Rustem, 227, 259n5
monocracy, 8
Movement of Muslim Students of
    Indonesia (PMII), 171–72, 187, 214
MPR. See People's Consultative Assembly
    (Indonesia)
Muhammadiyah (Islamic organization in
    Indonesia)
  Central Java and, 167n9
  leadership training and, 186
  Masyumi Party and, 187n21
  membership numbers in, 166
  National Mandate Party (PAN) and, 57,
    71, 186, 189
  sharia law proposal opposed by, 71
  social service programs and, 166
  volunteer work at, 180
Mujani, Saiful, 96, 98

Naberezhnyi Chelny City Center for
    Children's Creative Works, 190
Nahdlatul Ulama (NU; Islamic
    organization in Indonesia)
  in East Java, 166–67, 185, 190
  leadership training and, 185–86
  membership numbers in, 166
  National Awakening Party (PKB) and,
    57, 71, 186, 189
  parliamentary elections (1955) and, 48
  sharia law proposal opposed by, 71
  social service programs and, 166, 190
  United Development Party (PPP) and,
    186n21
  volunteer work at, 180
National Awakening Party (PKB;
    Indonesia)

East Java and, 115, 186
  elections for parliament (1999) and, 57,
    225, 255
  elections for president (1999) and, 57,
    255
  establishment of, 72
  Nahdlatul Ulama and, 57, 71, 186, 189
  Wahid as leader of, 57, 186, 255
National Mandate Party (PAN;
    Indonesia)
  elections for parliament (1999) and, 57
  elections for president (1999) and, 255
  Muhammadiyah and, 57, 71, 186, 189
  origins of, 71
  public goods provision by, 190
  Rais as leader of, 57, 186, 255
Navalny, Aleksei, 276
neighborhood associations (RT/RW;
    Indonesia)
  activities organized by, 168, 170
  civic skills development and, 187
  electoral clientelism and, 273
  gotong-royong activities and, 170, 187,
    189
  high rates of participation in, 177
  New Order era and, 167–69
  political trust in, 240
Nelson, Joan, 16, 79
New Order (Indonesia)
  armed forces' role in, 50–51
  authoritarian nature of regime in, 3, 6,
    49–52, 254
  civil society organizations in, 167–69,
    174–75
  collapse of, 41, 186
  contacting of public officials in, 85
  elections' limitations in, 81, 84–85, 199,
    216, 256
  Family Welfare Groups (PKK) in,
    167–68
  Freedom House scores in, 67
  Golkar Party hegemony during, 50–51,
    81, 85, 121, 223–24
  keterbukaan (Indonesian campaign for
    political openness, 1990s) and, 51,
    67, 171
  limited social pluralism under, 7, 191–92
  mass killings (1965) in, 3, 49
  media restrictions in, 51–52
  neighborhood associations (RT/RW) in,
    167–69

political participation mobilized in, 6,
  80–82, 120–21, 178, 199
political parties in, 49–52, 71, 121
political repression and coercion under,
  6–7, 49, 52
protests (1974 and 1978), 171
protests (1998) leading to downfall of, 3,
  56, 171, 198, 214
public opinion data from, 96
student organizations in, 170–71
New Russia Barometer (NRB) survey,
  218–19
Nie, Norman, 83, 107–8, 126
Nigeria, 1, 9–10, 88, 269
non-voting political participation. *See
  under* political participation
NTV (Russian television station), 62

Orthodox Christianity, 5, 175, 270

Papua (province of Indonesia), 74
party development work. *See* political
  party–development work
Pateman, Carole, 197
PDI. *See* Indonesian Democratic Party
  (PDI)
PDI-P. *See* Indonesian Democratic Party of
  Struggle (PDI-P)
pengajian (Muslim prayer groups in
  Indonesia), 165, 167, 185–87, 273
People's Consultative Assembly (MPR;
  Indonesian parliament)
  appointed members of, 255
  constitutional reforms (1999–2002) and,
    69–70
  direct presidential elections approved
    (2002) by, 70, 256
  elections for president (1998) and, 52,
    56
  elections for president (1999) and, 57,
    255
  House of Representatives deputies as
    members of, 70
  New Order-era elections for president
    by, 50
  sharia law proposal rejected by, 71
  Wahid corruption investigations and, 68
  Wahid removed as president by, 69,
    225–26
People's Democratic Party (Partai Rakyat
  Demokratik, PRD), 171

perestroika (liberalization policies in the
  Soviet Union), 45, 47, 105
petition signing
  in authoritarian regimes, 80, 85
  civic skills and, 187
  as elite-enabling political participation,
    95, 109
  in Indonesia, 97–100, 108n22, 187, 203,
    213
  political efficacy and, 85, 203, 213
  political trust and, 244
  in Russia, 94–95, 102, 104, 106, 109,
    111, 203, 244
Pikalevo (Russia), 110
PKB. *See* National Awakening Party (PKB,
  Indonesia)
PMII. *See* Movement of Muslim Students
  of Indonesia (PMII)
Poland, 55, 60, 122
political campaign work. *See also* political
  party–development work
  age as factor influencing, 127
  civil society engagement's impact on,
    127
  education level and, 127, 129
  elite-constraining forms of, 18, 83–84,
    114
  elite-enabling forms of, 84
  gender and, 127
  in Indonesia, 96–99, 102, 108, 113–14,
    127
  interview data regarding, 103
  lower socioeconomic classes and, 113
  political efficacy and, 127
  in Russia, 89–92, 104–5, 127
  Russians' attitudes toward, 105–6
political efficacy
  authoritarian legacies and, 199–200
  in authoritarian regimes, 197
  civil society participation and, 21, 130,
    136, 139, 149, 203–4, 212
  contacting public officials and, 104–6,
    122, 127, 133, 141–42, 194, 197,
    203–4, 208–12, 215, 266
  contentious politics and, 127–28, 133,
    145–46, 194, 198–99, 203, 212–14,
    266
  definition of, 20, 196
  democratization and, 19–20, 194–200,
    205, 231–32, 265, 267, 269
  education levels' impact on, 126

political efficacy (*cont.*)
  elections and, 20, 28, 194–200, 209,
    212, 216–32, 266
  elite-constraining political participation
    and, 2, 19–20, 128, 131, 194, 196–97,
    212, 215–16, 231, 265–67
  elite-enabling political behavior and,
    139, 194, 197, 266
  external *versus* internal dimensions of,
    196, 200–201, 208
  in Indonesia, 20–21, 124–25, 127,
    130–31, 133, 136–40, 142, 144,
    146–47, 192, 194–99, 201–9, 212–17,
    221–26, 230–32, 266–67, 269
  measures of, 124–25, 138, 200–208
  political campaign work and, 127
  political participation and, 21, 24, 28,
    118, 125, 127–31, 137, 139–40, 147,
    194–202, 205–7, 215, 231–32, 238,
    265–67
  political party–development work and,
    128, 133, 136–37, 143–44, 194, 203,
    209, 212–13
  political trust and, 130, 139
  protests and, 85, 195, 198–99, 212–15
  in Russia, 20–21, 124, 127, 130–31,
    133, 136–41, 143, 145, 147, 192,
    194–99, 201–12, 216–21, 224–31,
    266–67, 269
  in the Soviet Union, 204–5, 209
  subjective competence and, 196, 200
  voter turnout and, 199
political liberalization. *See*
  democratization
political participation. *See also specific*
    participatory acts
  activities excluded from category of, 80
  in advanced democracies, 16, 79
  age as factor influencing, 125–27, 129,
    138
  in authoritarian regimes, 16
  authoritarian regimes' legacies and, 21,
    119–22
  boycotts and, 47, 63, 94–95, 100
  civic skills and, 185–87, 215
  civil society engagement and, 2, 18–21,
    24, 118, 125, 127–31, 135–37,
    139–40, 147–53, 172, 176, 191,
    238, 265, 267
  constraints on, 119–23
  "covert" forms of, 111

education levels' impact on levels of,
    123, 125–26, 134
elite-constraining forms of, 2, 5, 11,
    16–20, 41–44, 63, 66–69, 74–78, 82–
    84, 86–87, 96–98, 103, 106, 108–9,
    111–19, 122–23, 126, 128, 130–39,
    147–51, 176–77, 188, 191–92, 194,
    196–97, 212, 215–16, 230–31, 247,
    261, 264–69, 277–78
elite-enabling forms of, 2, 5, 18, 21, 41,
    67, 78–79, 83–84, 86, 91, 93, 95, 106,
    109–12, 117–18, 122, 126, 135, 139,
    194, 197, 216, 230–31, 264–69
gender as a factor influencing, 125–27,
    129, 134
income levels' impact on, 123
Indonesians' patterns of, 2, 79, 96–99,
    101–3, 106–8, 117–22, 126–47
interview data and, 103
isolated *versus* repeated forms of, 104–6,
    113, 116
measurements of, 87–90
media commentaries and, 83
"mobilized" forms of, 6, 80–82, 94,
    119–22, 158, 178, 199
Nelson's definition of, 16, 79
non-voting dimensions of, 16
political campaign contributions and,
    18
political efficacy and, 21, 24, 28, 118,
    125, 127–31, 137, 139–40, 147,
    194–202, 205–7, 215, 231–32, 238,
    265–67
political trust and, 2, 19–21, 24, 28, 118,
    125, 128–31, 139–40, 147, 232, 234,
    237, 241, 244–45, 247, 261, 265, 267
Russians' patterns of, 2, 79, 88, 90–93,
    101–2, 104–5, 117–20, 122, 126–47
social networks' role in mobilizing, 189,
    265
in the Soviet Union, 6, 80–82, 94,
    119–20, 122, 158, 199
time required for, 16
political party–development work
  age as a factor influencing, 143–44
  civic skills development and, 188
  civil society engagement's impact on, 19,
    128, 132–34, 136–37, 143–44
  dues payments and, 183–84
  education levels' impact on, 106, 129,
    132, 134, 144

elite-constraining forms of, 18–20, 43,
83–84, 86, 96, 98, 114, 117, 128, 177,
267, 277
elite-enabling forms of, 18, 84, 91, 93,
267
gender as a factor influencing, 132, 134,
143–44
in Indonesia, 19–20, 71–72, 96–99,
101–2, 108, 112–15, 117, 121–22,
132–37, 144, 147, 177, 180, 183, 194,
203, 212–13, 238, 262, 267
interview data regarding, 103
political efficacy and, 128, 133, 136–37,
143–44, 194, 203, 209, 212–13
political trust and, 127, 143–44, 238,
262
in Russia, 59, 64, 67, 76, 89–93, 101–2,
105–6, 115, 119–20, 122, 132–33,
135–37, 139, 143, 177, 180, 184, 188,
191–92, 194, 203, 238, 267
Russians' attitudes toward, 105–6
political trust
civil society engagement and, 21, 130,
240–41
contacting public officials and, 127–28,
139, 141–42
contentious politics and, 127–28, 139,
145–46, 238, 240, 262
definition of, 233
democracy and, 233–34
democratization and, 19–20, 28,
232–36, 261–62, 265–67, 269
education levels' impact on, 126
in elections, 241, 255–62
elite-constraining political participation
and, 2, 19–20, 247, 261, 265, 267
evaluations of individuals' political
performance and, 235–36, 239–40,
243, 245, 248, 253, 261
evaluations of political leaders affected
by, 232
global averages in, 246–47
in Indonesia, 20–21, 125, 127–28,
130–31, 138–40, 144, 146–47, 192,
232–33, 235, 237–42, 245–49, 253–57,
261–62, 266–67, 269
measures of, 125, 236
political efficacy and, 130, 139
in political institutions, 20–21, 139,
141–46, 232, 236–50, 252–53, 261,
266–67

political participation and, 2, 19–21, 24,
28, 118, 125, 128–31, 139–40, 147,
232, 234, 237, 241, 244–45, 247, 261,
265, 267
in political parties, 239–40, 246, 249–50
regime-incumbent distinctions and,
234–37
in Russia, 20–21, 125, 127–28, 130–31,
138–40, 143, 145, 147, 192, 232–33,
235, 237–38, 242–47, 249–54,
257–62, 266–67, 269
in the Soviet Union, 249
in specific politicians, 20, 128, 139,
141–46, 232, 236–39, 242–45, 248,
250–51, 253–54, 257–62, 266–67
polyarchy, 7
PPIM. *See* Center for the Study of Islam
and Society
PPP. *See* United Development Party (PPP)
Prabowo. *See* Subianto, Prabowo
Prosperous Justice Party (PKS; Indonesia),
115, 180, 190
protests. *See also* contentious politics
Arab Spring (2011) and, 277
elite-constraining nature of, 20, 79, 86
in Indonesia (1974 and 1978), 171
in Indonesia (1996), 52
in Indonesia (1998), 3, 56, 171, 198, 214
in Indonesia (1999), 255
in Indonesia (2000–2001), 68–69
in Indonesia (2006), 74–75
Indonesians' attitudes toward, 203,
214–15
Indonesian students and, 75, 106–7,
112–13, 172–73
in New Order Indonesia, 51
political efficacy and, 85, 195, 198–99,
212–15
in Russia (2001), 62
in Russia (2005), 66, 105
in Russia (2008), 66
in Russia (2009), 110
in Russia (2011–12), 65–66, 224,
275–76
Russians' attitudes toward, 105, 203
in the Soviet Union (1990), 47, 198
Public Chamber (Russia), 182–83
Pussy Riot (artist collective in Russia), 276
Putin, Vladimir
administrative resources of, 64–65
annual call-in show of, 110, 275

Putin, Vladimir (*cont.*)
  anti-LGBT legislation and, 66, 276
  Beslan school massacre (2004) and, 63,
    257
  centralization reforms (2000s) of,
    61–62
  civil liberties restricted under, 20, 58, 61,
    65, 86, 267, 276
  elections for governors canceled (2004)
    by, 15, 42, 63, 227, 258–61
  elections for president (2000) and, 42,
    225
  elections for president (2004) and, 42,
    58, 63, 225
  elections for president (2012) and, 65,
    275–76
  "guided democracy" and, 61
  Krasnoyarsk Krai elections (2003) and,
    229
  media restricted under, 15, 62, 66, 276
  Pikalevo protests and, 110
  political freedoms restricted under, 15,
    17, 20, 58, 61, 66, 76, 86, 122,
    253–55, 257–62, 266–68, 276
  political trust in, 236–37, 242–43,
    253–55, 257–62, 266–67
  popularity of, 86, 253, 267
  presidential ascension (2000) of, 61, 76
  as prime minister (1999–2000), 61
  as prime minister (2008–12), 65, 110
  protests (2011–12) and, 275–76
  social contact established by, 260
  United Russia Party and, 210
Putnam, Robert, 149
PWS. *See* Association of Residents of the
  Surabaya Strenkali

Rais, Amien, 57, 186, 255
Regional Representatives Council (DPD;
  Indonesia), 70
Roeder, Philip, 81, 111
Rose, Richard, 161
RT/RW. *See* neighborhood associations
  (Indonesia)
Russia. *See also* Kazan (Russia);
  Krasnoyarsk (Russia); Soviet Union
  age demographics in, 138
  anti-LGBT legislation in, 66, 276
  attitudes toward elections in, 196–97,
    199, 216–21, 224–25, 227–31,
    254–55, 257–61, 263, 266

authoritarian backsliding in, 2–3, 7,
    10–11, 41, 58, 61–67, 76, 78, 86, 137,
    159, 197, 219, 236, 253–54, 261, 264,
    270, 275–76, 278
  boycotts in, 63, 94–95
  case selection criteria and, 25
  charitable giving in, 177, 182–84, 189,
    266
  civil liberties in, 20, 40, 58, 61, 65, 67,
    76, 86, 158–59, 181–82, 204–5, 267,
    276
  civil society engagement in, 19, 21, 60,
    86, 124, 127–28, 131–40, 147–48,
    151, 154–64, 173, 175–83, 188–92,
    194, 203–4, 265–67, 269
  Communist legacy in, 6–7, 40, 44,
    119–22, 163, 173–75, 184, 199, 270
  constitutional crisis (1993) in, 55, 58,
    60, 242, 251
  constitution (1993) of, 55–56, 59–60,
    251
  contacting of public officials in, 89,
    92–93, 101–2, 104–11, 117, 120,
    122, 127–29, 132–36, 139, 141, 192,
    194, 197, 203–4, 208–12, 230, 238,
    266–67
  contentious politics in, 67, 76, 93–95,
    101–2, 104–5, 107, 111, 127, 132–33,
    135–37, 145, 194, 203, 238, 275, 278
  corruption in, 4–5, 271
  democratization in, 2–7, 10–11, 21,
    24–25, 28, 40–42, 54, 58–63, 76, 78,
    85, 93, 102, 118, 151, 164, 175–76,
    191–92, 205, 207, 225–26, 229, 243,
    251, 253–54, 261–64, 268–70, 274–78
  as "deviant case" of democratization,
    2–3, 11, 22, 264, 269, 278
  economic crisis (1998) in, 61
  educational attainment levels in, 4, 13,
    138, 163, 185
  election fraud in, 65, 224, 275
  elections for governors canceled (2004)
    in, 15, 42, 63, 227, 254, 257–62
  elections for parliament (1993) in, 59,
    205, 216, 251
  elections for parliament (1995) in, 59,
    90–91, 216, 251–52
  elections for parliament (1999) in, 57,
    216, 225, 255
  elections for parliament (2003) in, 62,
    90–91, 251–52

elections for parliament (2007) in, 65
elections for parliament (2011) in, 65, 275
elections for president (1991) in, 53–54, 199, 205, 216, 225
elections for president (1996) in, 59–60, 90–91, 225–26, 228
elections for president (2000) in, 42, 90–92, 225–26
elections for president (2004) in, 42, 58, 63, 225–26
elections for president (2008) in, 65, 225–26
elections for president (2012) in, 65, 225–26, 275–76
elite-constraining political participation in, 44, 63, 66–67, 106, 117, 119, 128, 131, 215, 230, 265, 267, 276
elite-enabling political participation in, 5, 18, 21, 41, 67, 78, 83, 86, 93, 106, 109–12, 117–18, 122, 126, 135, 139, 230–31, 264–66, 268–69
elites in, 60, 63, 66–67, 78, 86, 106, 194
Freedom House scores for, 9–10, 58, 67, 270
gender demographics in, 138
geography of, 22, 25
income inequality in, 162
interviews from, 26–27, 30–32, 35–36, 39, 103–6, 109–11, 160–64, 170, 173–76, 178–81, 188, 198, 201, 207–12, 219–21, 224, 226–30, 233, 235–38, 242, 258–60
judicial system in, 243–44
labor unions in, 54–55, 60, 156–58, 160
media restrictions in, 15, 62, 66, 262, 276
middle class's absence from, 12–13
Muslims in, 29, 35, 39, 163
NGO registration laws in, 65, 181–82, 276
oil and gas resources in, 4–5, 22, 278
oligarchs in, 13
Orthodox Christianity in, 175, 270
petition signing in, 94–95, 102, 104, 106, 109, 111, 203, 244
political campaign contributions in, 90
political campaign rally attendance in, 90–91
political campaign work in, 89–92, 104–5, 127

political efficacy levels in, 20–21, 124, 127, 130–31, 133, 136–41, 143, 145, 147, 192, 194–99, 201–12, 216–21, 224–31, 266–67, 269
political freedoms restricted in, 15, 17, 20, 58, 61, 66–67, 86, 122, 253–55, 257–62, 266–68, 276
political party–development work in, 59, 64, 67, 76, 89–93, 101–2, 105–6, 115, 119–20, 122, 132–33, 135–37, 139, 143, 177, 180, 184, 188, 191–92, 194, 203, 238, 267
political party membership levels in, 72, 77, 114, 156
political trust levels in, 20–21, 125, 127–28, 130–31, 138–40, 143, 145, 147, 192, 232–33, 235, 237–38, 242–47, 249–54, 257–62, 266–67, 269
privatization and market reform in, 13
protests (2001) in, 62
protests (2005) in, 66, 105
protests (2008) in, 66
protests (2009) in, 110
protests (2011–12) in, 65–66, 224, 275–76
religious organizations in, 156–57, 162–63, 175, 179, 269–70
religious service attendance levels in, 163, 269
sociability levels in, 148, 159–62, 173, 190–92
social networks in, 176, 189–90, 192
socioeconomic development in, 2, 4, 13, 22, 28, 123, 181, 184, 278
student organizations in, 163–64
violence against ethnic minorities in, 66
voter turnout in, 199, 221, 266
Russian Election Study (RES)
civil society engagement measured by, 124, 127, 132–33
contacting measured by, 89, 92–93, 101, 127, 132–33, 141
contentious politics measured by, 94, 101, 127, 132–33, 145
political campaign work measured by, 89–91, 93, 127, 143
political efficacy measured by, 124, 127–28, 138, 204–7, 217–18
political participation measured by, 87–91, 100, 102, 123, 127–30, 141, 143, 145

Russian Election Study (RES) (*cont.*)
  political party–development work
    measured by, 89, 101, 132–33, 143
  political trust measured by, 125, 127,
    236, 249–53
  predicted probability data
    from, 131–37
Rustow, Dankwart, 11
Rutskoi, Aleksandr, 55
Ryzhkov, Nikolai, 54

SBY. *See* Yudhoyono, Susilo Bambang
Schlozman, Kay
  civic skills defined by, 185
  civic voluntarism model and, 147,
    150–51, 177, 189
  on measures of political efficacy, 200
  on resources for political participation,
    177
Serikat Pekerja Seluruh Indonesia (SPSI;
  labor union), 51
serikat tolong-menolong (STM; mutual aid
  groups), 168
Shaimiev, Mintimer, 227, 243, 259n5
sociability levels. *See also* social networks
  civil society engagement and, 147, 153,
    173
  in Indonesia, 148, 159–60, 164, 169,
    173, 194
  in Russia, 148, 159–62, 173, 190–92
  in the Soviet Union, 162
  Tocqueville on, 153
  World Values Survey data on, 159–60
social capital, 153–54
social networks. *See also* sociability levels
  civil society engagement and, 19, 113,
    151, 154, 172–73, 176, 190–92
  education's impact on developing, 170,
    172–73
  elite-constraining political behavior and,
    147
  in Indonesia, 176, 189, 191–92, 265
  political participation fostered by, 189,
    265
  in Russia, 176, 189–90, 192
Soekarwo (gubernatorial candidate in East
  Java), 222
Soldiers' Mothers. *See* Union of the
  Committees of Soldiers' Mothers of
  Russia
Solidarity movement (Poland), 55, 60

Soviet Union
  Afghanistan War veterans in, 110
  associational life in, 89, 158–59, 164,
    170, 174–75
  atheism doctrine in, 44, 163, 174–75, 270
  authoritarian nature of regime in, 44–45,
    254
  collapse (1991) of, 3, 41, 47, 54–55,
    158–59, 163–64, 174, 198
  command economy in, 12–13
  Communist Party's political monopoly
    in, 3, 44–45, 47, 60, 89, 121, 204,
    249, 251
  contacting public officials in, 81, 85,
    88–89, 93, 109–10, 120
  coup attempt (1991) in, 54, 84
  democratization in, 45–46
  elections for Congress of People's
    Deputies (1989) in, 46, 89, 216, 218
  elections for local soviets (1987) in,
    45–46
  elections for regional parliaments (1990)
    in, 53, 89, 251
  elections' limitations in, 44, 81, 84, 89,
    199, 216, 227
  Freedom House scores for, 58
  glasnost' (political opening) in, 45, 58,
    164
  "informal" *(neformaly)* groups in, 46–47
  perestroika (economic liberalization) in,
    45, 47, 105
  political efficacy in, 204–5, 209
  political participation mobilized in, 6,
    80–82, 94, 119–20, 122, 158, 199
  political repression and coercion in, 6–7,
    45
  political trust in, 249
  protests (1990) in, 47, 198
  "public organizations" in, 89
  sociability levels in, 162
  Union Treaty and, 53–54
Stalin, Josef, 45
State Duma (Russian parliament lower
  house)
  constitutional crisis (1993) and, 58, 60,
    242, 251
  constitution (1993) and, 56
  elections (1995) for, 59, 90–91, 216,
    251–52
  elections (1999) for, 90
  elections (2003) for, 62, 90–91

elections (2011) for, 65, 275
executive-legislative balance and, 62–63
political trust in, 242, 246–47, 249–50,
    261
Putin's control over, 61–62, 253
single-member districts in, 56n3, 63
Stoner-Weiss, Kathryn, 184
Strenkali riverbank community
    (Surabaya), 179, 181, 187–88. *See
    also* Association of Residents of the
    Surabaya Strenkali
students in Indonesia
    anti-New Order demonstrations (1998)
        and, 171–72
    civic skills and, 187–88
    as main force for contentious politics in
        Indonesia, 75, 106–7, 112–13, 172–73
    Muslim student organizations and,
        171–72
    New Order era and, 170–71
    People's Democratic Party and, 171
    political efficacy and, 213
subbotnik (neighborhood clean-up groups
    in the Soviet Union), 81, 170
Subianto, Prabowo, 262, 274
subjective competence (Almond and
    Verba), 196, 200
Suharto
    armed forces and, 50–51
    coup and mass killings (1965) under,
        3, 49
    elections for president (1968) and, 49
    elections for president (1998) and, 52,
        56
    Golkar Party and, 49, 56, 121, 223
    International Monetary Fund (IMF)
        and, 53
    Islamic leaders and, 51, 56
    keterbukaan (political openness)
        campaign and, 51, 67
    limited social pluralism under, 7
    New Order regime and, 3, 6–7, 49–52,
        71, 85, 167, 169, 174, 178, 254
    political repression under, 6–7, 49–50,
        52
    protests leading to downfall (1998) of, 3,
        56, 171, 198, 214
    student opposition to, 51, 56
Sukarno
    ascension to presidency by, 48
    authoritarianism of, 49–50

Communist Party of Indonesia (PKI)
    and, 49
    coup (1965) against, 3, 49
    "guided democracy" and, 3, 48–49
    Indonesian Nationalist Party (PNI) and, 48
Sukarnoputri, Megawati
    Chinese New Year established as holiday
        by, 70
    Corruption Eradication Commission
        and, 271
    decentralization reforms and, 71
    elections for parliament (1997) and, 52
    elections for president (1998) and, 52
    elections for president (1999) and, 57, 255
    elections for president (2004) and, 72,
        225–26, 248
    elections for president (2009) and, 74
    Indonesian Democratic Party (PDI) and,
        52
    Indonesian Democratic Party of Struggle
        (PDI-P) and, 57
    political trust in, 238–40, 257, 262
    presidential ascension (2001) of, 69, 225
Supreme Soviet (Soviet Russia's regional
    parliament), 53, 55
Surabaya (Indonesia)
    attitudes toward elections in, 219,
        222–24, 231
    case selection criteria and, 25, 29–30
    civil society engagement in, 166–69,
        171–72, 175, 178–79, 181, 185,
        187–89
    contacting public officials in, 107–8, 215
    contentious politics in, 213
    East Java gubernatorial elections (2008)
        and, 222–23, 231
    electoral clientelism in, 273
    interviews from, 27, 30–31, 33, 37, 39,
        103, 106–8, 113–14, 166–68, 171–72,
        175, 178, 181, 213–15, 219, 222–24,
        237–39, 273
    neighborhood organizations in, 168
    political campaign work in, 113–14
    political efficacy levels in, 213–15, 219,
        222–24, 231
    political trust levels in, 237–41
    as regional capital, 29
    religious organizations in, 166–67, 172,
        185
    Strenkali riverbank community in, 179,
        181, 187–88

Survey of Soviet Values (SSV)
  contacting of public officials measured
    by, 93, 101, 109
  political efficacy measured in, 204–5,
    218–19
  political participation measured through,
    87–88, 100

Tarrow, Sidney, 23–24
Tatarstan region (Russia)
  civil society organizations and, 164
  Communist Party of Russia in, 105,
    114–15
  gubernatorial elections in, 226–28, 230,
    259n5
  Kazan as capital of, 29
  political party–development work in,
    184
  Shamiev as governor of, 227
  United Russia Party in, 190
Tocqueville, Alexis de, 24, 147–49, 153–54
Tolokonsky, Viktor, 259n5
Tudjman, Franjo, 62
Tunisia, 277

Union of the Committees of Soldiers'
    Mothers of Russia, 179–81
Union Treaty (Soviet Union), 53–54
United Development Party (PPP; Indonesia)
  elections for parliament (1997) and, 52
  elections for parliament (1999) and, 57
  Islam and, 49
  Nahdlatul Ulama and, 186n21
  origins of, 50, 71
  political party–development work by,
    121
  political restrictions and repression
    against, 51, 121
United Russia Party
  administrative resources of, 64–65, 184
  elections for parliament (2003) and, 62
  elections for parliament (2007) and, 65
  elections for parliament (2011) and, 65
  hegemony of, 63–64, 191, 224
  in Krasnoyarsk, 210
  party-development work and, 91, 115,
    184, 188, 191
  political trust and, 243
  public receptions of, 210
  social service provision by, 190
Uss, Aleksandr, 228

Verba, Sidney
  on civic culture, 233
  civic skills defined by, 185
  civic voluntarism model and, 147,
    150–51, 177, 189
  on "high-pressure" *versus* "low-
    pressure" political participation, 83
  on measures of political efficacy, 200
  on particularized *versus* social
    contacting, 107–8, 111
  on resources for political participation,
    177
  on subjective competence, 196, 200
  on variables influencing political
    participation, 126
Voice and Equality (Verba, Schlozman,
    Brady), 147, 150, 200
voting. *See* elections

Wahid, Abdurrahman ("Gus Dur")
  Chinese religious legislation and, 70
  corruption charges against, 68–69
  election to presidency (1999) of, 57, 225,
    255
  National Awakening Party (PKB) and,
    57, 186, 255
  political trust in, 239–40
  protests against and for (2000–2001),
    68–69
  removal from presidency (2001) of, 69,
    225–26, 256
Wolfowitz, Paul, 51
World Values Survey (WVS)
  civil society engagement measured in,
    154–59, 163
  contentious political participation
    measured in, 93–95, 99–100
  political participation measured through,
    87–88
  political party membership levels
    measured in, 114, 156
  political trust measured in, 236,
    245–53
  religious service attendance in, 269
  sociability measured by, 159–60

Yabloko Party (Russia), 211
Yashin, Il'ya, 105
Yeltsin, Boris
  Congress of People's Deputies election
    (1989) and, 46

constitutional crisis (1993) and, 55, 58, 60, 242, 251
coup plot (1991) thwarted by, 54, 84
elections for parliament (1993) and, 59
financial crisis (1998) and, 61
political freedoms under, 58
political party affiliation shunned by, 120
political trust in, 242–43, 250–51, 253
popularity ratings of, 59, 243, 260
resignation of, 61, 91n9
Russian parliament's relations with, 55, 60–61
Russian presidential elections (1991) and, 53–54, 199, 205, 225
Russian presidential elections (1996) and, 59–60, 225
Russian Supreme Soviet elections (1990) and, 53

Yogyakarta (Indonesia), 27, 115, 190
Young Pioneers (Soviet Union scouting organization), 188
Youth Oath (Indonesia, 1928), 48
Yudhoyono, Susilo Bambang ("SBY")
  Corruption Eradication Commission and, 271
  elections for president (2004) and, 72, 226, 248
  elections for president (2009) and, 74
  labor laws controversy and, 75
  political trust in, 237–40, 253–54, 257, 262
  popularity of, 257

zakat (Islamic tradition of almsgiving), 185
Zubov, Valerii, 228
Zyuganov, Gennady, 60